DIE PARKETT-REIHE MIT GEGENWARTSKÜNSTLERN / THE PARKETT SERIES WITH CONTEMPORARY ARTISTS

Book Series with contemporary artists in English and German, published three times a year. Each volume is created in collaboration with artists, who contribute an original work specially made for the readers of Parkett. The works are reproduced in the regular edition and available in a limited and signed Special Edition.

Buchreihe mit Gegenwartskünstlern in deutscher und englischer Sprache, erscheint dreimal im Jahr. Jeder Band entsteht mit Künstlern oder Künstlerinnen, die eigens für die Leser von Parkett einen Originalbeitrag gestalten. Diese Werke sind in der gesamten Auflage abgebildet und zusätzlich in einer limitierten und signierten Vorzugsausgabe erhältlich.

PARKETT NR. 56 ENTSTEHT IN COLLABORATION MIT • **VANESSA BEECROFT, ELLSWORTH KELLY, JORGE PARDO** • WILL BE COLLABORATING ON PARKETT NO. 56

JAHRESABONNEMENT (DREI NUMMERN) / ANNUAL SUBSCRIPTION (THREE ISSUES) SFR. 108.– (SCHWEIZ), DM 130,– (BRD), SFR. 118.– (ÜBRIGES EUROPA), US$ 80 (USA AND CANADA ONLY)

Zürichsee Druckereien AG (Stäfa) Satz, Litho, Druck/Copy, Printing, Color Separations

PARKETT-VERLAG AG, ZÜRICH, JUNI 1999 **PRINTED IN SWITZERLAND** **ISBN 3-907582-05-5** **ISSN 0256-0917**

Special thanks to Michael Jenkins, Brent Sikkema Gallery, New York.

HEFTRÜCKEN / SPINE NO. 55–57: LOUISE BOURGEOIS
ODE A MA MERE, 1995, one of a series of 9 drypoint etchings, sheet: 12 x 12" / aus einer Serie von 9 Kaltnadelradierungen, Blattformat: 30,4 x 30,4 cm.

Cover, front page / Umschlag vorn: ANDREAS SLOMINSKI, OHNE TITEL, 1994/95, leicht beschnitten / slightly cropped.

Flap / Klappe: EDWARD RUSCHA, BRAVE MAN'S PORCH, 1996, acrylic on canvas / Acryl auf Leinwand (PHOTO: ANTHONY D'OFFAY GALLERY, LONDON).

Inside cover page & flap / Umschlagklappe innen: SAM TAYLOR-WOOD: SOLILOQUY V, 1998, c-print.

Back cover / Rückseite: SAM TAYLOR-WOOD, NOLI ME TANGERE, 1998, two-screen projection with sound / Projektion auf zwei Leinwänden mit Ton. (BOTH PHOTOS: ATTILIO MARANZANO)

Page /Seite 1: ANDREAS SLOMINSKI, OHNE TITEL, 1990, Pappe, Papier, Gewebe / cardboard, paper, fabric. (PHOTO: PETER SANDER, HAMBURG)

PARKETT **Zürich New York Frankfurt**

Bice Curiger Chefredaktorin/Editor-in-Chief; **Jacqueline Burckhardt** Redaktorin/Senior Editor; **Louise Neri** Redaktorin USA/Senior Editor US; **Susanne Schmidt** Textredaktion und Produktion/Editing and Production; **Trix Wetter · Hanna Koller** Graphik/Design; **Catherine Schelbert** Englisches Lektorat/Editorial Assistant for English; **Claudia Meneghini Nevzadi** Korrektorat/Proof Reading

Beatrice Fässler Vorzugsausgaben/Special Editions; **Beatrice Aschmann** Buchvertrieb, Inserate/Distribution, Advertising; **Conradin Bernoulli** Abonnemente/Subscriptions; **Bettina Hubby** Redaktionsassistenz, Vorzugsausgaben und Marketing USA/Assistant Editor, Editions and Marketing US; **Monika Condrea** Abonnemente USA/Subscriptions US; **Elizabeth Horowitz & Matthew Israel,** Praktikanten USA/Interns US; **Adrian Koerfer** Deutsche Verlagsvertretung/German Representative

Jacqueline Burckhardt – Bice Curiger – Dieter von Graffenried Herausgeber/Parkett Board; **Jacqueline Burckhardt – Bice Curiger – Dieter von Graffenried – Walter Keller – Peter Blum** Gründer/Founders

Dieter von Graffenried Verleger/Publisher

www.parkettart.com

PARKETT-VERLAG AG, QUELLENSTRASSE 27, CH-8031 ZURICH, TEL. 41-1-271 81 40, FAX 41-1-272 43 01
PARKETT, NEW YORK, 155 AV. OF THE AMERICAS, N.Y. 10013, PHONE (212) 673-2660, FAX (212) 271-0704
PARKETT-VERLAG AG, TANNENWALDALLEE 17, D-61348 BAD HOMBURG, FAX 06172-937 444

EDITORIAL Vor einem Jahrzehnt hat Parkett bereits eine Ausgabe Edward Ruscha gewidmet. Es freut uns sehr, heute viele neue, in der Zwischenzeit entstandene Werke in Bild und Texten vorzustellen und ihn zugleich zwei ganz unterschiedlichen jüngeren Künstlern, Einzelgängern auch, gegenüberstellen zu können. Gibt es Verbindendes zwischen Edward Ruscha, Sam Taylor-Wood und Andreas Slominski? So unterschiedlich das Feld ist, in welchem sich die drei Künstler bewegen, gemeinsam ist ihnen eine Freiheit und Sicherheit im Einsatz ihrer Mittel und das Interesse am überraschenden Bild mit nachhaltig wirkendem geistigem Sog.

Man möchte am liebsten bloss Bilder zitieren, ohne sie weiter zu interpretieren: das Füttern des Knaben auf dem Titelblatt und die «Fallen» (Slominski), die Viecher, die nach Salz lechzen (Ruscha), und Taylor-Woods «Fünf revolutionäre Sekunden». Es scheint klar, dass hier ein Stück weit das Geistige mit dem Instinktiven konfrontiert wird. Auch finden wir bei allen drei Künstlern so etwas wie Auslegeordnungen, die Werke sind derart aufgebaut, dass sie den Blick in ganz kalkulierte Bahnen weisen. Wirksam wird dabei «die Macht, Aufmerksamkeit zu lenken», wie Boris Groys es in seinen Reflexionen über «SlominSki» ausdrückt, als «die absolute Macht» des Künstlers (S. 106). Während Ruscha durch die Schrift so viel Inhalt ins Bild holt, dass selbst die abweisendste Felswand davon nicht unaffiziert bleibt, trägt das Eintauchen in einen vielleicht hysterischen Moment in Taylor-Woods Photos dieselbe Unerbittlichkeit in sich, die auch Slominskis Fallen mit ihrer schrecklichen Zielgerichtetheit ins Zentrum rücken. Bei allen drei Künstlern tun die Werke gerne «so, als ob»: Da zeigt uns Sam Taylor-Wood grossformatige Photobilder mit Predellaszenen wie alte Altarbilder, während Andreas Slominskis «Fallen» eigentliche Funktionsgegenstände sind, die wie Skulpturen der Arte Povera aussehen. Und Edward Ruschas Gemälde blähen sich neuerdings den Betrachtern entgegen, als wären es fröhliche Segel oder animierte Sprechblasen.

Auch das «Insert» von Kara Walker spielt das Spiel der Vorspiegelung. Ihre Welt der biedermeierlichen Scherenschnitte ist voller Abgründe, die dem ewig wiederkehrenden Verdrängten erst recht Tür und Tor öffnen.

EDITORIAL Parkett already published an issue a decade ago with the collaboration of Edward Ruscha. It now gives us great pleasure to present many of the new works in word and picture, made in the intervening time, and to juxtapose them with two very different, younger artists. Is there common ground among such highly independent, idiosyncratic artists as Edward Ruscha, Sam Taylor-Wood, and Andreas Slominski? As different as their fields of activity and endeavor are, all three share a freedom and confidence in the use of their chosen artistic means as well as an interest in the surprising image whose magnetic attraction exerts an enduring mental impact.

One would simply like to cite pictures without subjecting them to interpretation: the boy being fed on the cover and the "traps" (Slominski), the critters that crave salt (Ruscha), and the lasting impression of five revolutionary seconds (Taylor-Wood). It is obvious that, to a certain extent, the mind is here confronted with instinct. In addition, all three artists have a way of establishing an order, a layout of sorts, as a basis for structuring their works to direct our gaze in unmistakably premeditated trajectories. They exercise "the absolute power to direct another person's attention," as Boris Groys remarks in his reflections on "SlominSki" (p. 102). While Ruscha's lettering shifts so much content into the space of the picture that even the most uninviting cliff cannot remain unaffected, the immersion in what might be a moment of hysteria in Taylor-Wood's photographs communicates the same implacability that issues from the terrible and single-minded intent of Slominski's traps. The works of all three artists often act "as if": Sam Taylor-Wood shows us large-format photographed images with predella scenes like the paintings on a medieval altarpiece, while Andreas Slominski's actually operative "traps" resemble the sculpture of arte povera. And Edward Ruscha's paintings have taken to billowing toward the viewer like cheerfully uninhibited sails or animated cartoon bubbles.

Kara Walker's "Insert" also toys with pretence. Her world of silhouettage and watercolors, with a Biedermeier touch, opens wide the fathomless depths of eternally repressed emotion.

Bice Curiger

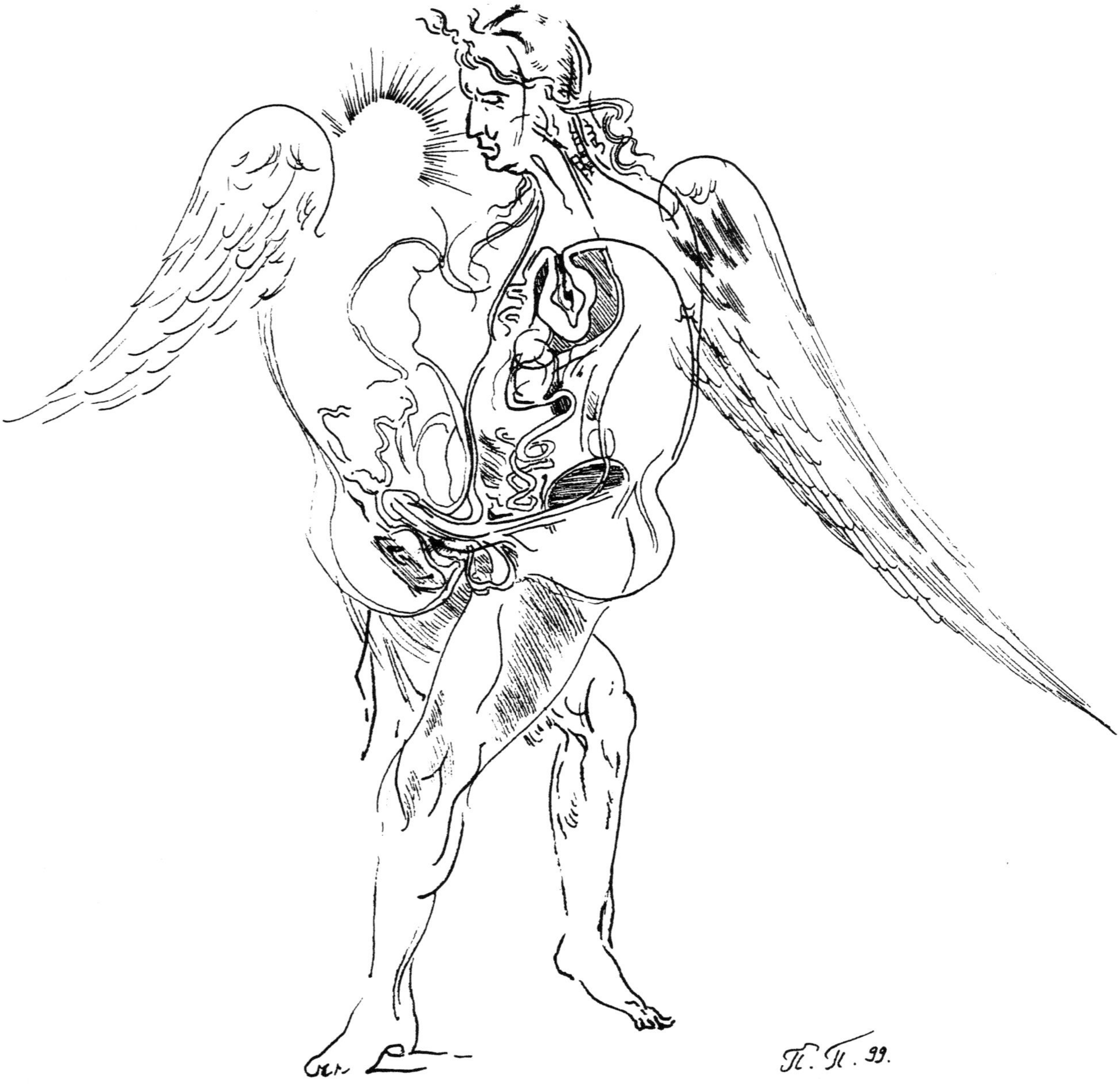

PAWEL PEPPERSTEIN, OHNE TITEL, 1999 / UNTITLED.

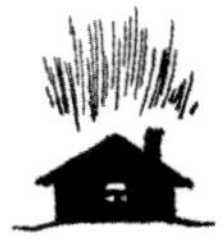

Die Vignetten hat Pawel Pepperstein speziell für diesen Artikel gezeichnet.

BORIS GROYS

PAWEL PEPPERSTEIN: DER KÜNSTLER ALS SUBKULTUR

In der letzten Zeit ist es um die russische Kunst im Westen still geworden. Nach der ersten Perestroika-bedingten Euphorie hat man schnell bemerkt, dass die russische Politik und Ökonomie nicht viel versprechend aussehen. Daraus zog man die falsche Schlussfolgerung, dass auch die neue russische Kunst nicht viel verspreche. Die Entwicklung der Kunst ist aber niemals bloss ein Abbild des allgemeinen sozialökonomischen Erfolgs. Oft wird gerade die Niederlage – oder zumindest die schwere Lage – eines Landes für seine Kunst förderlich und inspirierend. Pawel Pepperstein, dessen Ausstellung «Binokel und Monokel» vor kurzem im Kunsthaus Zug gezeigt wurde, ist der interessanteste Repräsentant einer neuen russischen Künstlergeneration nach Kabakov. Und in seiner Kunst reagiert er vor allem auf die Lage, in der sich die russische Kultur heute befindet.

Der Titel der Ausstellung in Zug verweist auf den Titel des gleichnamigen Buches von Pepperstein, das kürzlich im Verlag Suhrkamp erschienen ist. Dieses Buch bildet aber seinerseits nur einen Teil des Romans *Mythogene Liebe der Kasten,* in dem der Zweite Weltkrieg mythologisiert wird und der ein *work in progress* bleibt. Dabei ist die Korrelation zwischen Bildern und Texten das beherrschende Thema der ganzen künstlerischen Praxis der Gruppe «Medizinische Hermeneutik», deren Mitbegründer Pawel Pepperstein ist und mit deren Namen er die meisten seiner Texte und künstlerischen Arbeiten unterschreibt. Das Verständnis der einzelnen Arbeiten von Pepperstein wird also von der Bekanntschaft mit dem ganzen Diskurs und der ganzen sehr komplizierten Gruppenmythologie der «Medizinischen Hermeneutik» abhängig gemacht. Bemüht man sich um ein solches Verständnis, muss man feststellen, dass der Diskurs der «Medizinischen Hermeneutik» einen wiederum auf weitere Texte und Bilder verweist.

Dieses unendliche Spiel mit Verweisen stellt die eigentliche Strategie der Gruppe dar. In einem seiner Texte schreibt Pepperstein, dass sich die Seele aller Dinge ausserhalb dieser Dinge befindet, wie bei einem Helden aus dem alten russischen Märchen namens Kaschtschej, dessen Lebenskraft in einem Ei aufbewahrt wird, das ausserhalb des Körpers von Kaschtschej versteckt bleibt. Um Kaschtschej zu treffen und zu töten muss man also nicht nach Kaschtschej selbst, sondern nach diesem Ei suchen – wobei eine solche Suche eigentlich immer weiter weg von Kaschtschej führt. So liegt der Sinn eines jeden Bildes oder Textes nicht in ihm, sondern ausserhalb. Und die Hermeneutik, die nach diesem Ei des Sinnes sucht, heisst eben «Medizinische Hermeneutik», weil sie nie zu einem Abschluss kommen kann und Kaschtschej dadurch für alle Ewigkeit am Leben lässt. In dieser Figur der hermeneutischen Schonung wird der aus dem Westen kommende poststrukturalistisch-dekonstruktivistische Ansatz so unüberwindbar mit einem alten russischen Märchen vermengt, dass der Leser die Ironie dieser Vermengung zwar spüren, aber ihrer bestechenden Logik kaum widerstehen kann. Und eine solche Vermengung ist paradigmatisch für die ganze Produktion der «Medizinischen Hermeneutik», die sich durch Bilder,

---

BORIS GROYS ist Professor für Philosophie an der Staatlichen Hochschule für Gestaltung in Karlsruhe.

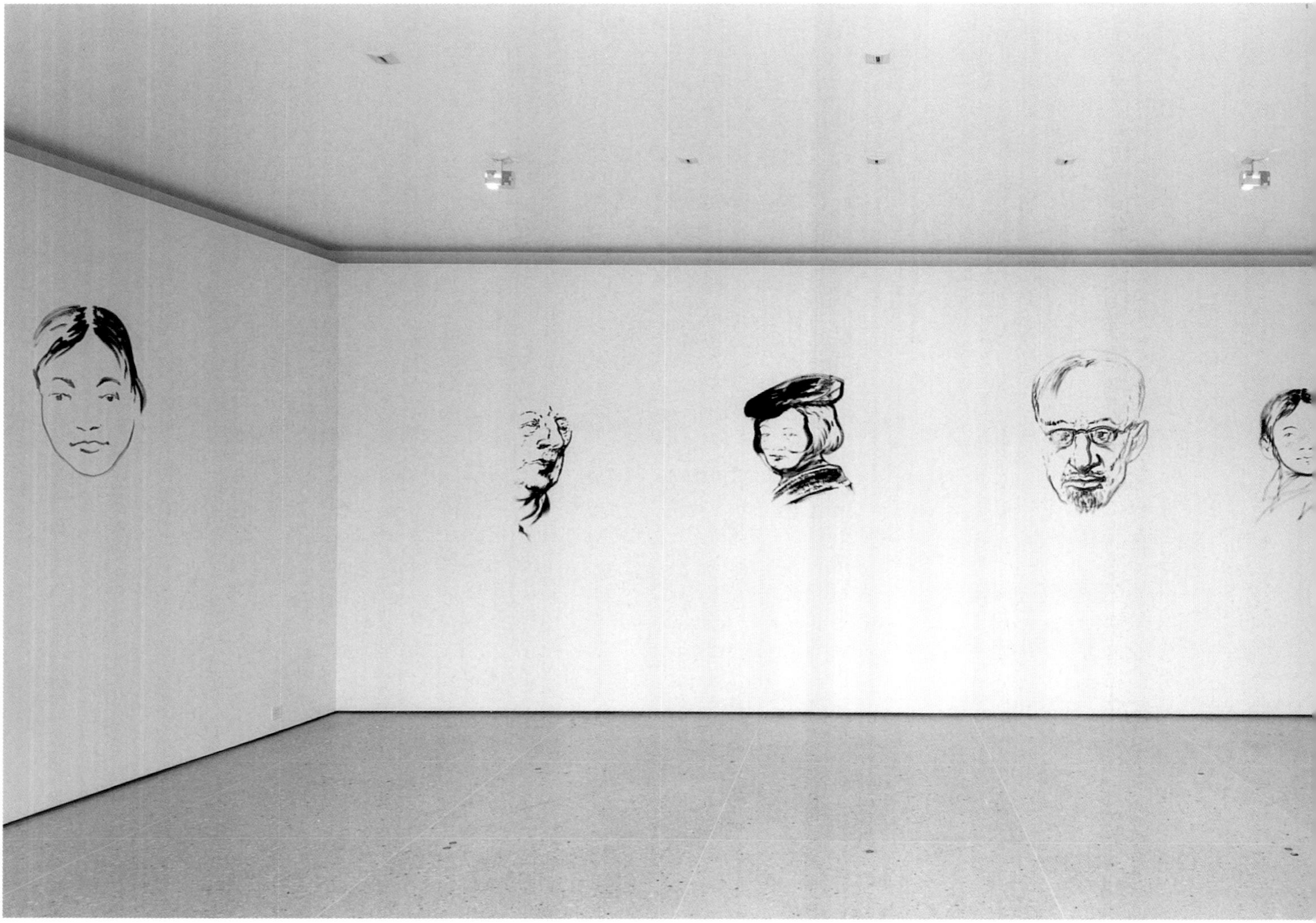

Installationen, Photographien genauso manifestiert wie durch narrative und diskursive Texte.

Die Gruppe «Medizinische Hermeneutik» hat sich am Anfang der 80er Jahre formiert, als der sowjetische Kommunismus untergegangen ist, die russische Gesellschaft sich geöffnet hat und die inoffizielle russische Kultur, zu der die noch sehr jungen Mitglieder der Gruppe ursprünglich gehört hatten, gerade begann, ebenfalls aus ihrer gewohnten gesellschaftlichen Isolation herauszutreten. In dieser Situation der neuen Offenheit, die viele andere russische Künstler damals fasziniert und verführt hat, haben die Mitglieder der «Medizinischen Hermeneutik» umgekehrt versucht, sich erneut sprachlich von der Aussenwelt zu isolieren. Das Ziel hiess, Differenzen zu markieren, im Meer des öffentlichen Geredes nicht unterzugehen, eine sprachliche Distanz zu bewahren, die allein eine analytische, kritische Position zulässt. Nach der Öffnung des Landes wurde Russland von der westlichen kommerziellen Massenkultur in kürzester Zeit überschwemmt. Wie auch viele andere Künstler auf der Welt wurden die russischen Künstler dadurch vor die Frage gestellt, wie sie mit dieser allgegenwärtigen Massenkultur umgehen sollten. Einige predigten eine vollständige Abschottung und Rückbesinnung auf die vermeintlichen nationalen Traditionen, die aber letztendlich nur durch staatliche Kontrolle und Repression, das heisst durch die Rückkehr zur politischen Isolation, hätten abgesichert werden können. Andere fingen

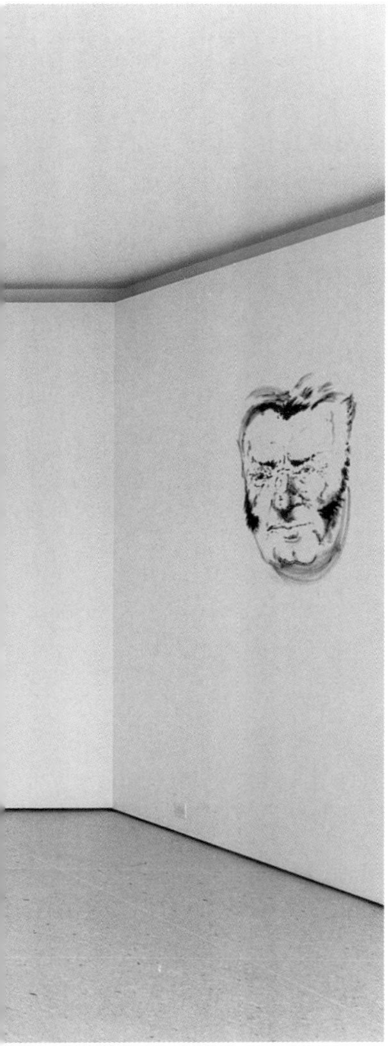

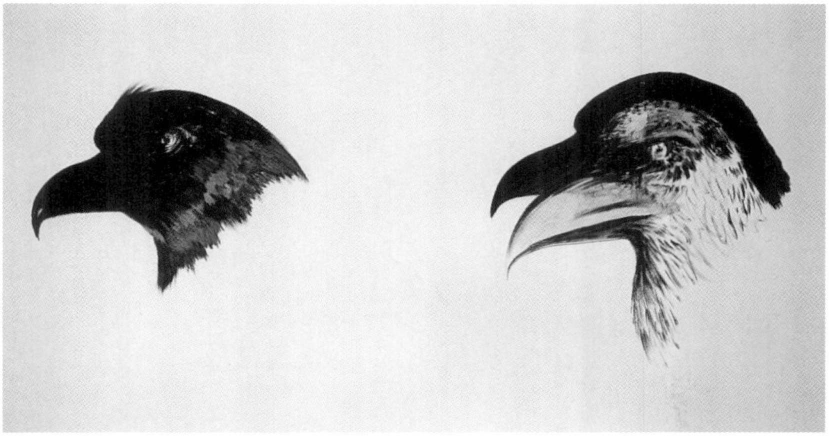

Ausstellung «Inspection 'Medical Hermeneutics' (Sergej Anufrijew, Wladimir Fjodorow, Pawel Pepperstein), Binokel und Monokel, Leben und Werke» im Kunsthaus Zug, 20. September – 8. November 1998: PAWEL PEPPERSTEIN, RAUM DER GESICHTER; RAUM DER VÖGEL / Exhibition views, Kunsthaus Zug, Switzerland: PAVEL PEPPERSTEIN, ROOM OF FACES; ROOM OF BIRDS. (PHOTOS: GUIDO BASELGIA & KUNSTHAUS ZUG)

an Bilder und Mythen der westlichen Massenkultur zu zitieren um einen anderen Umgang mit ihnen zu demonstrieren – eine Strategie, die inzwischen allgemein bekannt ist und ihren Witz dadurch teilweise verloren hat. Die Originalität der künstlerischen Strategie von Pepperstein besteht darin, nicht bloss die äusseren Formen, das heisst Bilder und Texte der Massenkultur zu zitieren, sondern vielmehr ihre inneren Mechanismen und Verfahren.

Jede erfolgreiche Massenkultur entwickelt sich nämlich, wie wir wissen, aus einer relativ kleinen Subkultur, die ihre eigenen Verhaltensmuster, Geschmackskriterien und Riten besitzt. Solche Subkulturen bleiben oft längere Zeit – oder sogar für immer – in sich selbst geschlossen, wie das bei vielen religiösen Sekten nach wie vor der Fall ist. Nur ab und zu beginnen diese Subkulturen gesellschaftlich zu expandieren um zu einer allgemein zugänglichen Massenkultur zu werden. Das künstlerische Programm von Pepperstein und der Gruppe «Medizinische Hermeneutik» besteht im Grunde darin, eine solche Subkultur künstlich zu entwerfen – und zwar im Zustand vor der Explosion, wo sie noch in sich geschlossen und exklusiv ist.

Schon das Funktionieren als Gruppe mit einem ungewöhnlichen Namen erinnert an die Gepflogenheiten der Popkultur von den Beatles bis zu Prodigy. Es handelt sich um die Erfindung einer fiktiven Autorschaft, eines fiktiven Namens, dem die künstlerischen Aktivitäten der einzelnen Mitglieder der

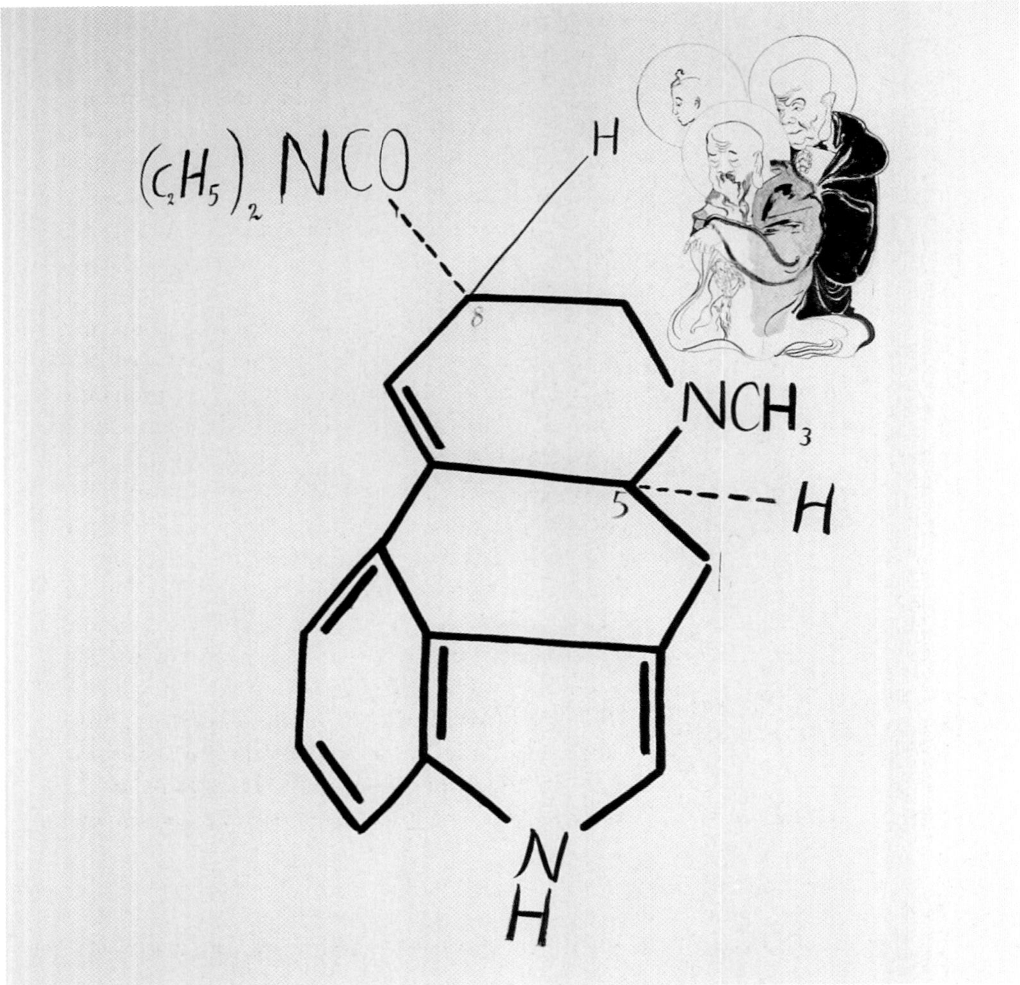

PAWEL PEPPERSTEIN, RAUM DER FORMELN, Kunsthaus Zug 1998 /
PAWEL PEPPERSTEIN, ROOM OF FORMULAS.

Gruppe zugeschrieben werden. Eine solche «weiche», flexible Autorschaft erlaubt der Gruppe neue Adepten anzuwerben, aber auch ihre Identität zu bewahren, wenn einige Mitglieder der Gruppe von ihr abspringen. Beides ist übrigens auch in der Geschichte der «Medizinischen Hermeneutik» vorgekommen. Ihre eigentümliche Sprache aus Termini, Verweisen und Benennungen, die oft nur Eingeweihten zugänglich sind, blieb dabei erstaunlich stabil. Eine künstlerische Praxis, die sich eines solchen festen Sprach- und Bildcodes bedient, funktioniert aber gerade für die Aussenstehenden in der Regel überzeugend und effektiv. So sehen die schwarzweissen Zeichnungen, mit denen Pepperstein die Wände des Zuger Kunsthauses bedeckt hat, auf den ersten Blick durchaus esoterisch aus. Aber gerade aus diesem Grund schaffen diese Räume eine erstaunlich dichte, mystisch geladene Atmosphäre, deren Intensität den Besucher sofort in Beschlag nimmt. All die Darstellungen der Vögel, Gesichter, Heiligen, Landschaften oder chemischen Formeln, die man auf den Wänden sieht, folgen einer strengen, der Konzeptkunst entstammenden und zugleich betont eleganten Ästhetik, die jeglichen visuellen Kitsch dezidiert ausschliesst und dem Besucher den Eindruck vermittelt mit den faszinierenden Überresten einer hohen, uralten, magischen Zivilisation

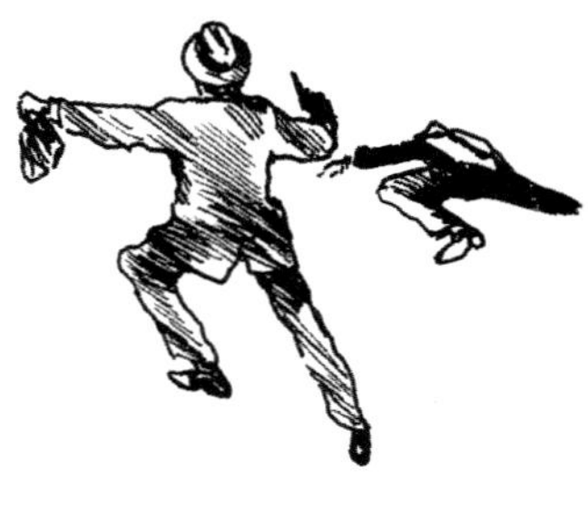

konfrontiert zu sein. Nun handelt es sich dabei aber eigentlich um die Technik der Graffitis, die in allen heutigen Grossstädten zu finden sind und ebenfalls geheimnisvoll aussehen. Hier können wir also die eigentümliche Kombination beobachten von Verfahren der Popkultur und einer Bildsprache, die allerdings keine massenkulturelle Bildsprache ist. Während Keith Haring eine schon existierende und wieder erkennbare Graffiti-Sprache in die Kunsträume gebracht und damit entschärft hat, erfindet Pepperstein vielmehr eine eigene Bildsprache, die wie eine subkulturelle Graffiti-Sprache aussieht und dadurch eine gewisse Gefährlichkeit oder zumindest ein Geheimnis suggeriert.

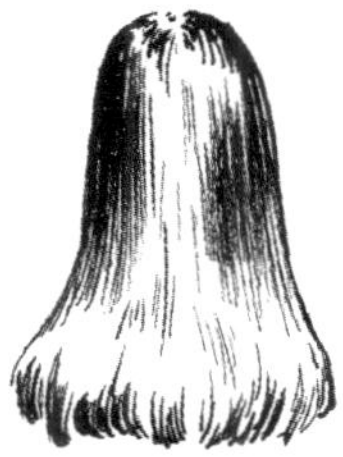

Nun kann die ganze untergegangene Sowjetunion als eine solche geschlossene, gewalttätige und zugleich rhetorisch verfeinerte Subkultur interpretiert werden, die ständig bereit war in eine universelle kommunistische Massenkultur zu expandieren. Dabei fungierte die sowjetische Kommunistische Partei zugleich als fiktiver Autor, dem alle – von Lenin und Stalin bis zu den einzelnen sowjetischen Bürgern – ihre persönlichen Leistungen genauso zugeschrieben haben, wie Pepperstein seine eigenen Arbeiten der «Medizinischen Hermeneutik» zuschreibt. Aber auch innerhalb der russischen inoffiziellen Kultur der 70er Jahre war die Praxis einer solchen fiktiven Autorschaft weit verbreitet: Man kann sich an die fiktiven Autoren erinnern, im Namen derer Kabakov seine Arbeiten gemacht hat, sowie auch auf die Gruppe «Kollektive Aktionen», geleitet von Andrej Monastyrskij, an deren Praxis Pepperstein in vielerlei Hinsicht anknüpft. Hier wird der Versuch unternommen, die russische, sowjetische Kultur unter den neuen medialen Bedingungen als eine Art Pop-Subkultur zu retten, die ihre Identität durch sprachliche Konventionen statt durch politische Repressionen verteidigt.

Freilich bleibt dieser Versuch nur simulativ und spielerisch, weil die realen massenkulturellen Mechanismen der Kommerzialisierung dabei fehlen. Aber für Pepperstein ist nicht sosehr die Durchsetzbarkeit einer Subkultur wichtig als vielmehr die reine Möglichkeit privat oder in einem kleinen Kreis eine neue Subkultur zu erfinden. Auf die Frage, ob eine private Sprache möglich wäre – und nicht nur eine Aussage in einer immer schon existierenden Sprache –, gibt Wittgenstein bekanntlich eine negative Antwort. Aber die Geschichte der Sekten, Religionen, Ideologien und Parteien sagt dagegen: Ja, es ist möglich. Der einzelne Mensch kann eine Subkultur erfinden, die keine bestimmten räumlichen und zeitlichen Grenzen hat, wenn er sich zu einer fiktiven Autorschaft bekennt, zu der sich die anderen unter Umständen auch bekennen können, wie Gott, Kommunismus oder eben «Medizinische Hermeneutik». Unter den Bedingungen der heutigen Massenkultur kann eine nationale oder regionale Kultur nur dann überleben, wenn sie sich als eine solche Pop-Subkultur redefiniert. Und das Gleiche gilt wahrscheinlich auch für jeden Einzelnen von uns.

RAUM DER BÄLLE, Kunsthaus Zug 1998 / ROOM WITH BALLS.

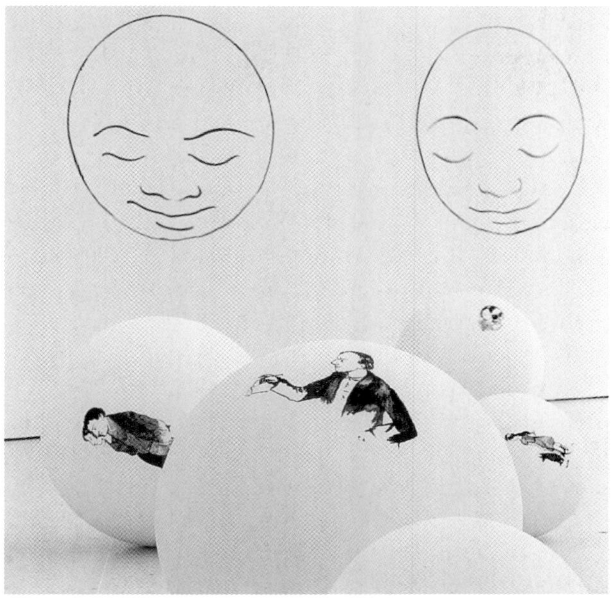

PAWEL PEPPERSTEIN, MÄDCHEN MIT WIRBELSTURM KÄMPFEND, 1998, Lithographie, 39,5 x 35,5 cm.

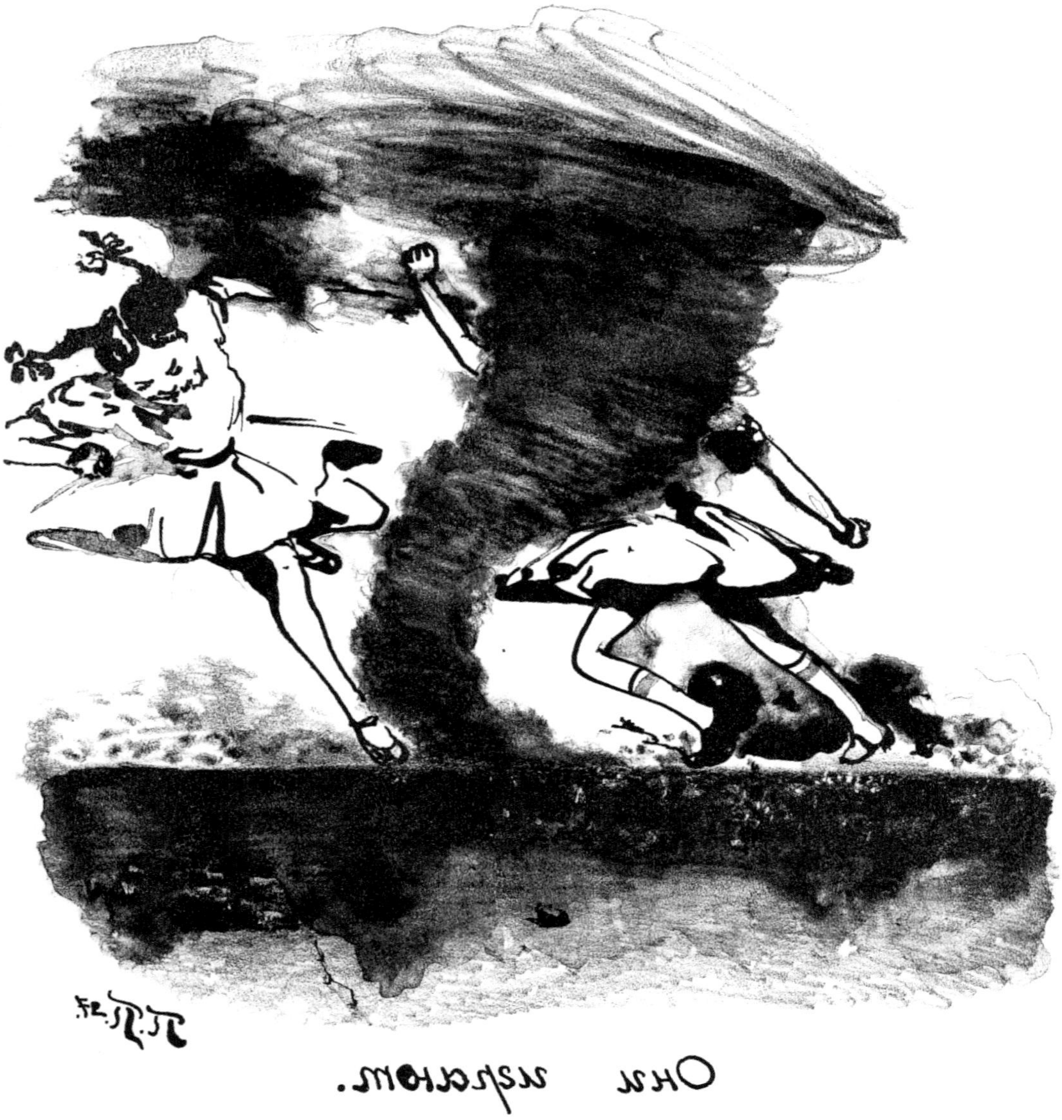

PAVEL PEPPERSTEIN, GIRLS FIGHTING WITH TORNADO, lithograph, 15½ x 14".

Pavel Pepperstein drew the vignettes pictured here especially for this article.

PAWEL PEPPERSTEIN, RAUM DER PRIESTER, Kunsthaus Zug 1998 /
PAVEL PEPPERSTEIN, ROOM OF PRIESTS. (PHOTOS: GUIDO BASELGIA & KUNSTHAUS ZUG)

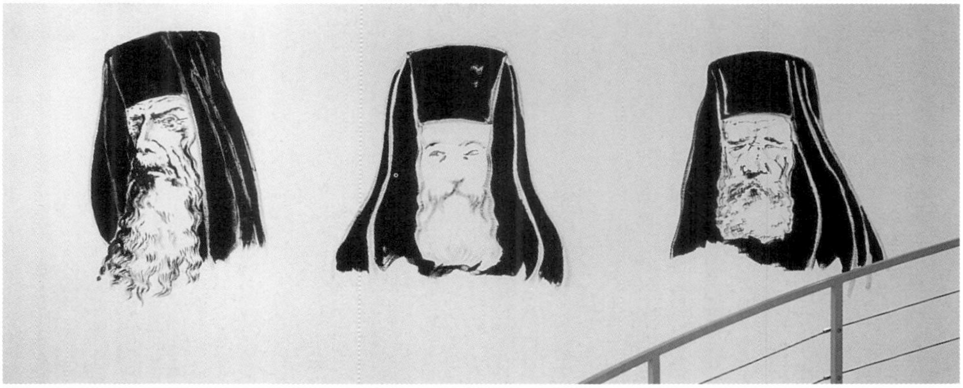

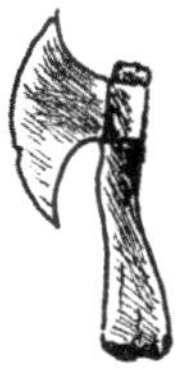

BORIS GROYS

PAVEL PEPPERSTEIN: THE ARTIST AS A SUBCULTURE

The clamor raised about Russian art in the West has subsided. After the initial euphoria in the wake of perestroika, it soon became obvious that Russian politics and the economy did not hold much promise. This led to the false conclusion that Russian art did not hold much promise either. However, the development of the arts is never merely a reflection of general social and economic success. Frequently, in fact, the situation of a country defeated, or at least in dire straits, actually fosters and inspires artistic achievements. Pavel Pepperstein, whose exhibition "Binokel und Monokel" was recently shown in the Kunsthaus in Zug, is the most interesting representative of a new generation of Russian artists following Kabakov. His oeuvre responds primarily to the state of Russian art today.

The title of the exhibition in Zug echoes Pepperstein's book of the same name, published by Suhrkamp Verlag in 1998. This book is in turn part of the novel *Mythogene Liebe der Kasten/Mythogenous Love of Castes*, which mythologizes the Second World War, and will remain a work in progress. The correlation between pictures and words is the dominant theme in the artistic practice of the group co-founded by Pavel Pepperstein, Medical Hermeneutics, which is also the name he uses to sign most of his writings and art works. An understanding of Pepperstein's individual works is thus intimately bound up with a knowledge of the discourse and the highly complex group mythology propagated by Medical Hermeneutics. However, on attempting to acquire such knowledge, we find that Medical Hermeneutics refers us to other words and pictures.

This endless chain of referral proves to be the strategy of the group. In one of his texts, Pepperstein writes that the soul of all things lies outside the things themselves, as in an ancient Russian fairy tale, in which the life force of the hero, Kaschtschej, is preserved in an egg that is concealed somewhere

BORIS GROYS is professor of philosophy at the Staatliche Hochschule für Gestaltung in Karlsruhe, Germany.

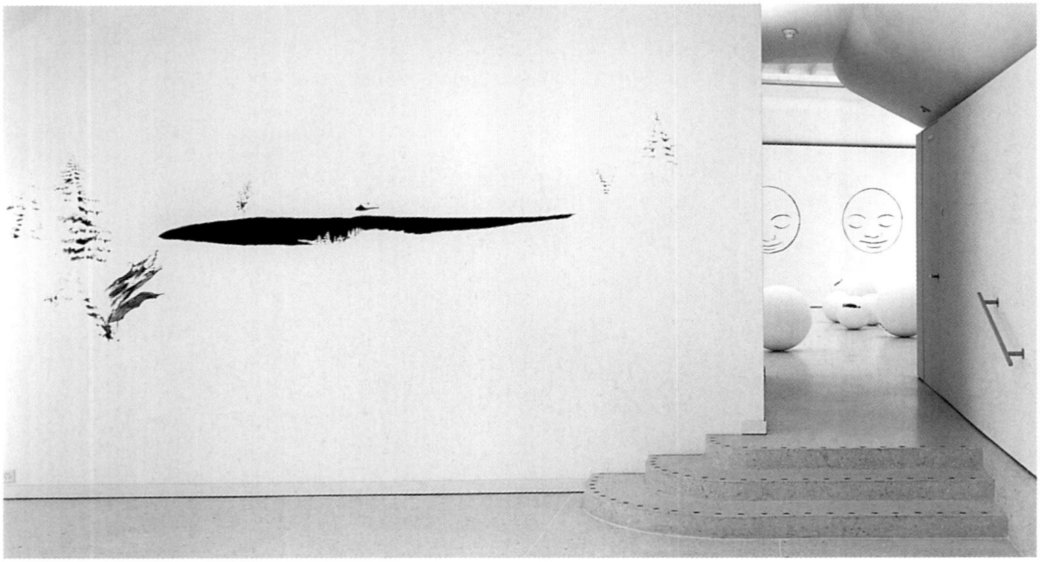

Kunsthaus Zug 1998:
Blick vom RAUM DER SEEN in den RAUM DER BÄLLE /
View from the ROOM OF LAKES into the ROOM WITH BALLS.

outside of his body. In order to find and kill Kaschtschej, one must find the egg, but the search for the egg always leads farther and farther away from Kaschtschej himself. Correspondingly, the meaning of a picture or a text is not found within but somewhere outside. And the hermeneutics that try to track down this semantic egg are called Medical Hermeneutics because they can never come to a conclusion and have to let Kaschtschej live forever after. In this figure of hermeneutic mercy, the poststructuralist-deconstructive thrust of western thought is so insurmountably compounded with an old Russian fairy tale that readers note the irony of the combination but can hardly resist its compelling logic. Such combinations are paradigmatic for the entire production of Medical Hermeneutics, from pictures, installations and photographs to narrative and discursive writings.

The group Medical Hermeneutics joined forces in the early eighties when Soviet communism was on its way out, Russian society was opening up, and unofficial Russian culture, to which the then very young members of the group originally belonged, was just beginning to emerge from its longstanding social isolation. In this situation of unprecedented openness, which fascinated and seduced so many other Russian artists, the members of Medical Hermeneutics took a different tack of renewed isolation from the outside world through language. Their goal was to mark difference, to avoid being immersed in the mire of public talk, and to maintain linguistic distance as the only means of assuming an analytical, critical position. The moment Russia opened up, the country was inundated with commercial mass culture from the West. Russian artists, like others all over the world, were faced with the question of how to deal with this omnipresent mass culture. Some preached complete separation and a return to spurious national traditions, but this would ultimately have meant a return to state control and repression, i. e., a return to political isolation. Others began to adopt the images and myths of western mass culture in order to throw a different light on them—a strategy now so familiar that it has lost some of its punch. The originality of Pepperstein's strategy derives from the fact that not only external forms of mass culture, i. e., pictures and words, are cited but more importantly their inner mechanisms and agendas.

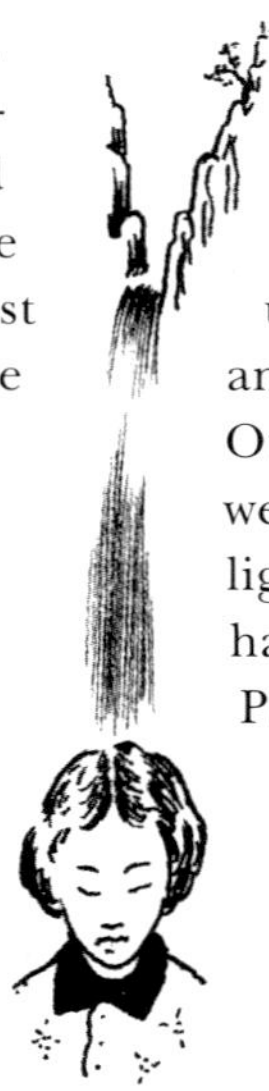

PAWEL PEPPERSTEIN, Wandzeichnung im RAUM DER FLÜSSE, KUNSTHAUS ZUG 1998 /
PAVEL PEPPERSTEIN, wall drawing in the ROOM OF RIVERS.

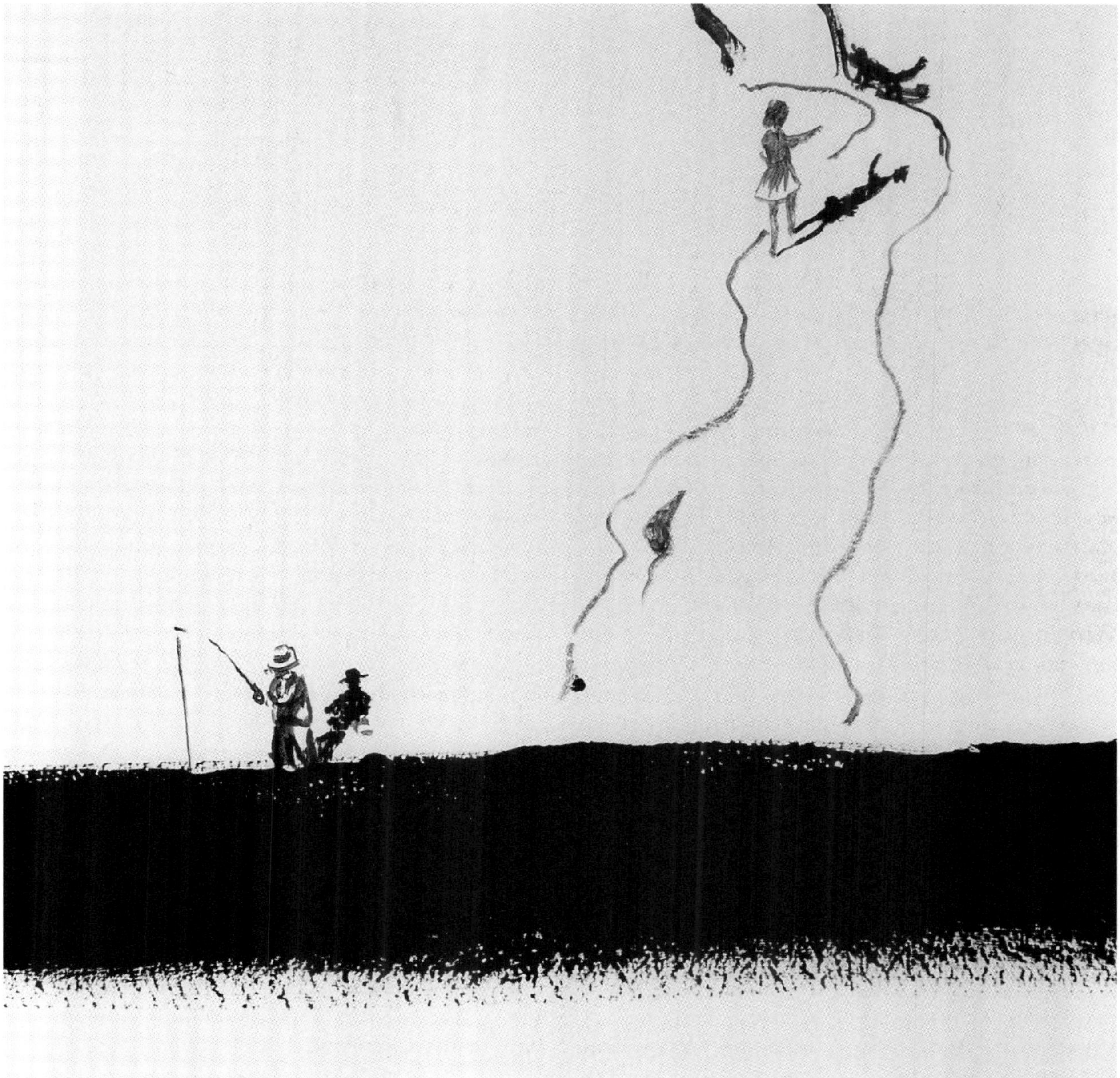

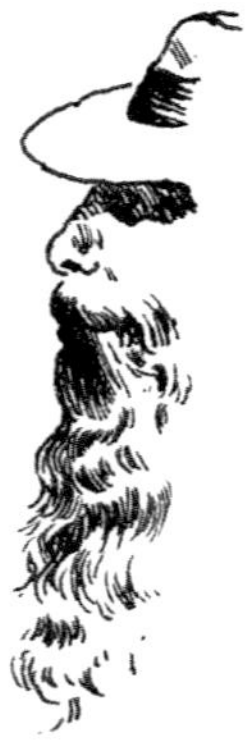

As we know, mass culture springs from relatively small subcultures with their own patterns of behavior, their own criteria of taste, and their own rituals. These subcultures lead a self-contained existence, often for a very long time—sometimes even forever, as in the case of certain religious sects. Occasionally, however, a subculture will begin to spread, to cross social boundaries and finally annex the mainstream. The artistic agenda of Pepperstein and Medical Hermeneutics basically consists of artificially creating a subculture that looks as if it were just about to explode the boundaries of its self-contained and exclusive seclusion.

The way the group functions is insinuated in the unusual choice of name, recalling the mores of pop culture from the Beatles to Prodigy. It is the invention of a fictional authorship, a fictional name to which the activities of the individual members are ascribed. This "soft" and flexible approach to authorship allows the group to recruit new adepts and to preserve its identity when other members of the group drop out. Nonetheless, Medical Hermeneutics' curious vocabulary of terms, references, and designations, whose meaning is often known only to initiates, has remained surprisingly stable. An artistic practice that resorts to such a clearly defined linguistic and pictorial code is, interestingly enough, especially convincing and effective to outsiders. The black-and-white drawings with which Pepperstein covered the walls of the Kunsthaus in Zug look positively esoteric at first sight. Which is precisely why these rooms generate such an astonishingly compact, mystically charged atmosphere whose intensity instantly captivates the viewers. All the representations of birds, faces, saints, landscapes, or chemical formulas follow a strict aesthetic, drawn from Conceptual Art and yet of an explicit elegance that rules out the least indication of visual kitsch and gives viewers the impression of being confronted with the fascinating findings of an ancient, highly advanced, occult civilization. In his "wall art," Pepperstein uses the technique of the graffiti, which are found in all the great cities today and also speak a mysterious, coded language. Here we can observe that curious blend of a device borrowed from popular culture with a pictorial idiom that is anything but popular. Keith Haring moved an existing and recognizable graffiti language into the space of art but Pepperstein has invented a pictorial language of his own that resembles the subcultural language of graffiti and thus suggests a certain danger or at least a certain mystery.

The entire former Soviet Union might be interpreted as a self-contained, violent and yet rhetorically refined subculture, instantly and ceaselessly prepared to expand into a universal communist mass culture. The Soviet Communist Party thereby functioned as the fictional author to whom the members of the group—from Lenin and Stalin to the individual Soviet citizen—attributed their personal achievements, just as Pepperstein attributes his works to Medical Hermeneutics. This practice also had a wide following in Russia's unofficial culture of the seventies. Think of the fictional authors in whose name Kabakov produced his work or the group "Collective Actions," headed up by Andrej Monastyrskij, with whom Pepperstein has much in common. Here the attempt is made, within the parameters of the new media conditions, to rescue Russian Soviet culture as a kind of pop subculture that defends its identity through linguistic convention rather than political repression.

The attempt must necessarily remain simulative and playful because the commercialization of real mass culture is missing but the implementation of a subculture is not as important to Pepperstein as the pure potential of inventing a new one for himself or in the context of a small circle. As we know, Wittgenstein didn't acknowledge the possibility of a private language. But historically established sects, religions, ideologies, and parties have claimed and proved that a private language is possible. An individual can invent a subculture that has no specific boundaries in time and space if s/he espouses a fictional authorship that might also be espoused by others—God, communism, or Medical Hermeneutics. Given the conditions of mass culture today, a national or regional culture can only survive by becoming a pop subculture. The same thing probably also applies to each and everyone of us.

(Translation: Catherine Schelbert)

Mitternächtliche Weltweisheit im Privatkanal

RUDOLF SCHMITZ

Beim mitternächtlichen Surfen durch deutsche Fernsehkanäle kann es passieren, dass man an einem Stück Unbegreiflichkeit hängen bleibt. Es widerspricht allem, was soeben über den Schirm ging, raste und flackerte. Als sei der Computer abgestürzt und in einem Tableau erstarrt, das sich nicht von der Stelle rührt. Da sieht man in jeweils fester Kameraposition eine Person, die über ein skurriles Thema redet – ob der Mensch ein zölibatäres System sei, was aus der Entdeckung der Spiegelneuronen in der Hirnforschung zu folgern sei, welche Weltsicht die Braunbären haben, mit welchem Tier der Schriftsteller Heiner Müller verglichen werden könne. Bisweilen stellt eine Stimme aus dem Off suggestive, assoziativ sprudelnde Fragen. Besondere Nervenkraft kosten jene Momente, in denen dann noch eine Simultanübersetzerin sowohl die ungeduldigen Fragen als auch die bereitwilligen Antworten referiert. Gelegentlich kommt die Blue Box zum Einsatz – irgendwelche entfernt zum Thema gehörenden Bilder werden als Hintergrund eingeblendet. Wenn sich das Frage-und-Antwort-Spiel oder der Monolog seinem rhetorischen Höhepunkt nähert, werden nicht selten eben gehörte Kernsätze eingeblendet, in seltsam altertümlicher Typographie, mit farblichen Höhungen oder gymnastischen Verläufen von Buchstaben und Wörtern.

Im Zeitalter des Medien-Hype wirkt das alles wie eine Rückkehr des Leierkastenmanns, der Moritaten vorträgt. Oder wie eine Reminiszenz an die barocke Emblematik, mit *pictura, inscriptio* und *subscriptio* – also die Mehrfachkodierung von Weltweisheit.

Jene anachronistisch wirkenden Sendungen heissen «Prime Time» oder «10 vor 11», werden aber entgegen dem programmatischen Titel inzwischen weit nach Mitternacht auf den Privatsendern RTL und SAT 1 ausgestrahlt.[1)] Es sind Produktionen des Regisseurs und Produzenten Alexander Kluge, der von der föderalen Mediengesetzgebung profitiert um seine als «Quotenkiller» beschimpften Kassiber zu platzieren. Die Gesetzgebung sieht vor, dass Privatsender mit einem Marktanteil von zehn und mehr Prozent einen gewissen Prozentsatz ihrer Sendezeit anderen Anbietern überlassen müssen um so zumindest einen Keim von Meinungsvielfalt und unabhängiger Berichterstattung zu pflanzen.

Da Alexander Kluge aber auch Magazine wie «Spiegel-TV» und «Stern-TV» produziert, die ausgezeichnete Einschaltquoten vorweisen, kann er die mächtigen Privatsender auch zur Ausstrahlung seiner kauzigen Moritaten zwingen. Er wird deshalb von erzürnten Programmdirektoren gern als «elektronischer Wegelagerer» bezeichnet, eine Wortwahl, die ebenfalls bestätigt, dass vor allem das vermeintlich Anachronistische seiner kurzen mitternächtlichen Sendungen das Blut der Programmgestalter in Wallung bringt.

Allerdings könnte man ohne weiteres der Auffassung sein, dass Alexander Kluge den Primat des Bildes zugunsten des gesprochenen Wortes brechen will. Das Abfilmen von Experten jeglicher Couleur

RUDOLF SCHMITZ, Kritiker und Journalist, lebt in Frankfurt am Main.

von einem festen Kamerastandpunkt – mit gelegentlichen Zooms auf das Gesicht der Protagonisten – behauptet schliesslich nichts anderes, als dass es immer noch darauf ankomme, Leute vor die Kamera zu holen, die «etwas zu sagen» haben. Dann nämlich – so die implizite These dieser Sendeform – werde unser Unterhaltungsbedürfnis voll und ganz erfüllt, so dass wir kein anderes Bild bräuchten als dasjenige eines Gegenübers, des latenten Dialogpartners. Und Alexander Kluge gelingt es fast jedes Mal, Spezialisten zu finden, die aus ihrem Sachgebiet sprechen und zugleich vorführen, dass sie zu faszinierenden Folgerungen kommen, die uns alle angehen. Im besten Fall führt das dazu, dass wir einen Film im eigenen Kopf kreieren und uns selbst als Produzenten erleben.

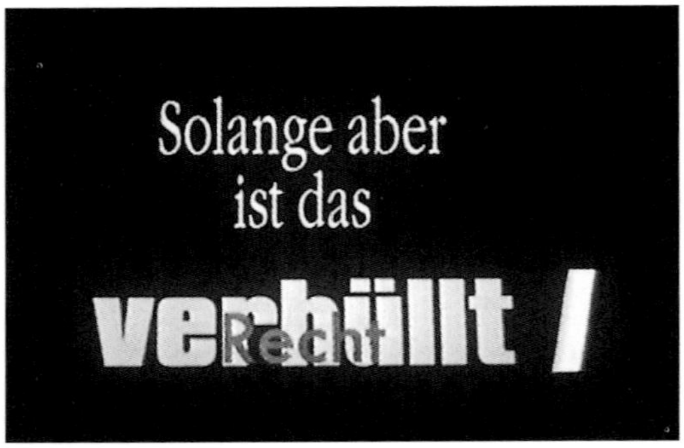

Wenn ein Professor der Hirnforschung vor dem Klettergerüst eines Spielplatzes stehend darüber sinniert, ob nicht tatsächlich ein bestimmter Grad an Nichtkommunizierbarkeit zwischen Individuen seine organische Metapher darin finde, dass auch die Hirnhälften des Menschen anatomisch asymmetrisch seien, also die Projektion aufeinander nicht erlaubten und darüber hinaus diese Ahnung des zölibatären Status in Marcel Duchamps GROSSEM GLAS veranschaulicht sieht, so erlebt man in suggestiver Weise, was Kleist die «Verfertigung der Gedanken beim Reden» nannte. Währenddessen werden Details des GROSSEN GLASES eingeblendet, die in der Folge dem Klettergerüst des Kinderspielplatzes eine ungeahnte semantische Dimension verleihen. Alexander Kluge benutzt Bilder als assoziatives oder

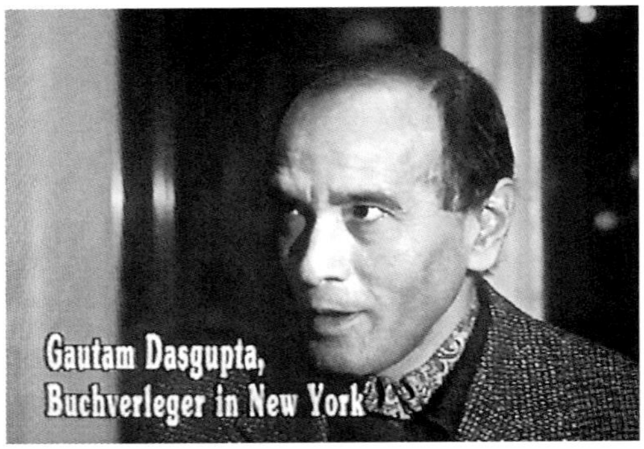

gegenläufiges Material. Das Konfektionsverhältnis, das im Fernsehen Bilder und Worte miteinander verschweisst und zum tausendmal erlebten Einerlei veröden lässt, wird zerlegt. Bilder und Sprache gewinnen ihren autonomen Materialstatus zurück. Der passgenaue Schnitt, die ölige Montage, die unsere Fernsehkultur in Entropie überführen, erscheinen so als fragwürdige Äusserungen von Pseudoprofessionalität.

Mit der Assoziation von Laterna magica, aber auch der Einblendung von Merksätzen – «Es gibt keine Objektivität jenseits des Begehrens» – erinnert Alexander Kluge an die Frühzeit des Mediums, an den Stumm- und den sowjetischen Avantgarde-Film der Revolutionszeit und damit an emanzipatorische Hoffnungen. Der Eindruck von formal «rückwärtsgewandter» Sprache dieser Sendungen ist natürlich auch ein Kontextphänomen. Innerhalb des täglichen Fernseh-Einerleis signalisieren diese «Amateurfilme»

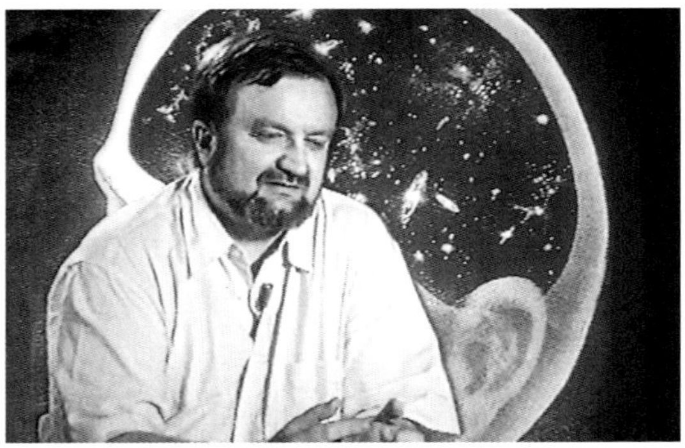

eine grundsätzlich andere Zeitlichkeit, eine differente Wahrnehmungsoption, eine konträre Auffassung der Rolle des Mediums. Es wäre interessant zu untersuchen, ob nicht sämtlichen Sendungen eine umfassende Theorie der Informationsgesellschaft zugrunde liegt. Wenn ein Gespräch mit einer Proust-Expertin unter dem Titel «Begehren, das die Welt regiert – Clinton, Starr, Ovid und Marcel Proust» eingeführt wird, so zeichnet sich der Bogen ab, den Alexander Kluge spannt. Es geht in anthropologischer Perspektive um ein Imaginäres, das immer schon bedient wurde und bedient werden will und sich mit Techniken der Darstellung verbindet, die – in langer Sicht – verblüffend ähnlich sind.

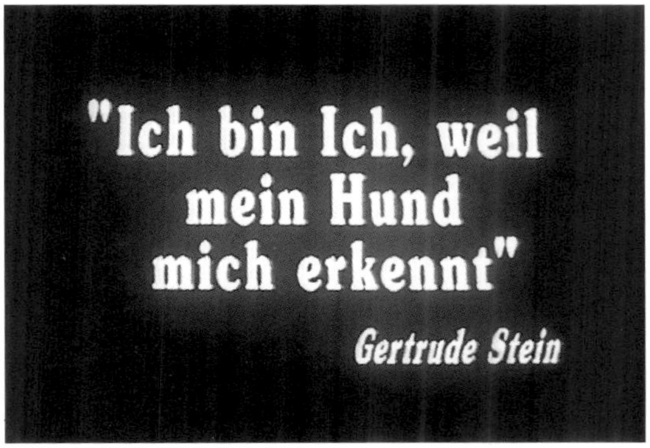

Der erwähnte Filmbeitrag erörtert das Problem, ob Proust den Starr-Report hätte schreiben können oder ob nicht die moralische Anklägerei sich demjenigen verbietet, der hinter jedem Text ein Begehren erkennt. Wäre also die Mehrzahl der Amerikaner, die sich fragen, «Warum will Starr das Obszöne entlarven?», den skeptischen Proustianern zuzurechnen? Dass die literarischen Verfahrensweisen von Marcel Proust oder Heiner Müller bezüglich ihrer Relevanz zur Analyse politischer Öffentlichkeit interessieren, hat mit Kluges ungewöhnlichem Projekt zu tun, die Sphäre der Ästhetik als Paradigma menschlicher Orientierungsleistung ernst zu nehmen. Die unwillkürliche Erinnerung, wie sie im Zentrum von Prousts Methode einer Vergegenwärtigung von Lebenszeit steht, und die Explosion der Erinnerung, die Heiner Müllers Methode charakterisiert, den Toten der Geschichte Stimme zu verleihen, sind zwei Seiten derselben Medaille. In einem Gespräch mit Heiner Müllers New Yorker Verleger wird die erstaunliche Wirkung dieses Schriftstellers darin verortet, dass dieser der erste digitale Schriftsteller gewesen sei. Gemeint ist damit Heiner Müllers antirealistische Haltung, seine Fähigkeit eine Fülle von literarischen Anleihen zu machen und die Wahrheit des Fragments gegen jede Vorstellung von Echtzeit zu verteidigen.

Sosehr Alexander Kluges Mitternachtsmagazine mit der Vorstellung von Weltweisheit kokettieren, sosehr signalisieren sie – genau wie Proust – die Position des «Unreliable Narrators», des unzuverlässigen Erzählers. Damit aber vertrauen sie der Kompetenz des Adressaten. Müllers New Yorker Verleger behauptet, dass ihn sein Schriftstellerfreund stets an einen «knuddeligen Hund» erinnert habe, und verweist dabei auf Gertrud Steins Diktum «Ich bin ich, weil mein kleiner Hund mich kennt». Ziemlich ähnlich verhält es sich mit Alexander Kluges Magazinen. Auch sie, und vielleicht nur noch sie, erinnern die Fernsehkonsumenten daran, dass sie «vorhanden» sind.

Oft enden die Filme damit, dass der Abspann einsetzt, während die Stimmen der Sprechenden noch zu hören sind um schliesslich weggeblendet zu werden. Die Assoziationen, die Diskurse des Imaginären gehen niemals zu Ende. Sie führen ein heimliches, untergründiges Leben. Das relativiert jeweils das gerade erlebte Magazin, aber es aktualisiert die Erkenntnis, dass Buch, Film, Bild niemals zu Ende gebracht sind. Es ist ein Hinweis auf das Nebeneinander konkurrierender Sphären, die nur zum Zwecke ideologischer Formierung und Beschwichtigung als abgeschlossene vorgeführt werden.

Unlängst stellte Alexander Kluge einen jungen Kolumnisten und Mitbegründer der neuen Filmzeitschrift *Revolver* vor. In dessen Kolumne «Wilde Erdbeeren» geht es um die magischen Momente des Kinos. Das Motto des jungen Kritikers ist ebenso verblüffend wie nachvollziehbar: «Jeder Film», so sagt er, «sollte einmal den Horizont zeigen.»

1) Im zweiten Programm des Schweizer Fernsehens DRS wird die Sendung unter dem Titel «BekanntMachung!» ausgestrahlt.

Universal Wisdom at the Bewitching Hour on Private TV

RUDOLF SCHMITZ

While channel-hopping on German television at midnight, you can find yourself stopped short by a slice of incomprehensibility. It contradicts everything that just rambled, raced, or flickered across the screen, as if the computer had crashed and frozen in a motionless tableau. You see a person in front of a still camera, talking about some off-beat topic—whether humanity is a celibate system; what can be concluded from the discovery of mirror neurons in neurological research; the worldview of the grizzly bear; which animal the writer Heiner Müller might be compared to. Occasionally a voice off-camera poses suggestive, associative, burbling questions. It gets particularly nerve-wracking when an interpreter starts translating the impatient questions as well as the obliging answers. Once in a while, the blue box comes into play—pictures projected in the background that are remotely associated with the subject. When the question-and-answer game or the monologue seems to be coming to a climax, key sentences that have just been heard might be intercut on screen in an oddly old-fashioned typography with color highlights or gymnastic sequences of letters and words.

In an age of media hype, the whole thing conjures up images of an organ grinder cranking out street ballads or Baroque emblematic art with *pictura, inscriptio,* and *subscriptio*—that is, multi-encoded universal wisdom.

RUDOLF SCHMITZ is a freelance critic and journalist who lives in Frankfurt am Main, Germany.

These anachronistic shows are called "Prime Time" or "Ten to Eleven," but in contrast to their programmatic titles, they're aired long after midnight these days on the private channels RTL and SAT 1. They are the productions of director and producer Alexander Kluge, who has found a slot for his stiffs, cursed by the establishment as "ratings killers," thanks to federal laws requiring private channels with a market slice of ten or more percent to make a certain portion of their time available to other pro-

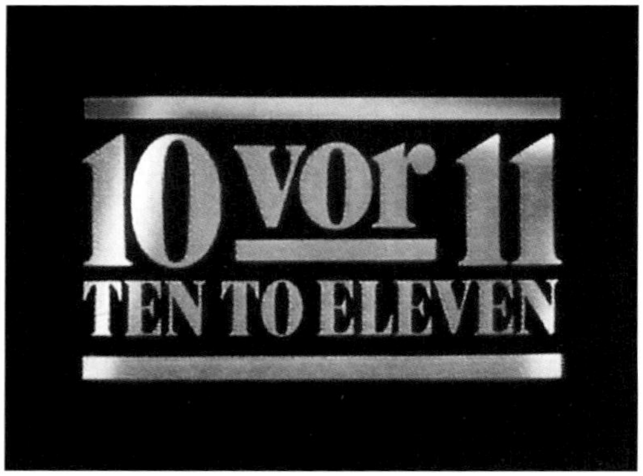

viders to preserve at least a semblance of opinion plurality and independent reportage.

However, since Alexander Kluge also produces programs like Spiegel-TV and Stern-TV, which have excellent ratings, he can force the powerful private channels to air his little oddball ditties. Enraged program directors have been known to call him an "electronic bandit," a choice of epithet that testifies to the

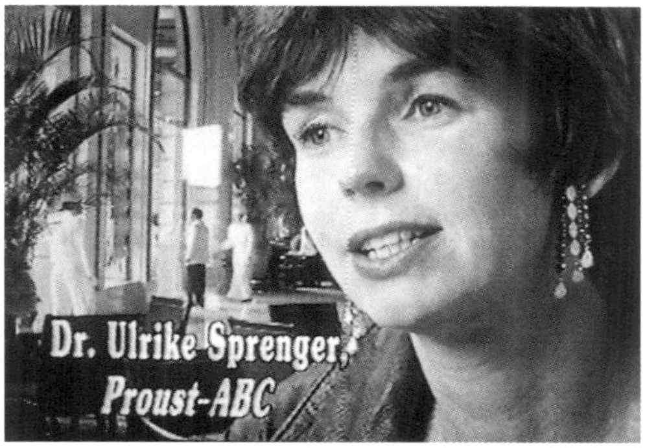

hostility aroused by the supposed anachronistic thrust of his brief midnight forays.

One could, of course, assume that Kluge wants to undermine the primacy of the image for the sake of the spoken word. Training a still camera on experts of every conceivable ilk—occasionally zooming in on the protagonist's face—merely indicates that it still makes sense to get people in front of the camera who have "something to say," because then—this form of presentation implies—our need for entertainment will be truly and completely gratified, so that we need no other image beyond that of the person opposite, the latent partner in dialogue. And Alexander Kluge almost always manages to ferret out specialists who speak as experts in their field and yet still succeed in demonstrating that their fascinating conclusions affect us all. At best, we end up creating a film in our heads and becoming our own producers.

When a professor of neurology standing in front of a jungle gym wonders whether a certain degree of noncommunication among individuals actually does find an organic metaphor in the fact that the two halves of the human brain are anatomically asymmetrical, i.e., that they cannot be projected on top of each other, and compares this indication of a celibate status to Marcel Duchamp's LARGE GLASS, we are witness to the suggestive act of what Heinrich von Kleist calls the production of thoughts in the process of speaking.[1)] In the meantime, details of the LARGE GLASS are intercut that invest the playground equipment with an unimagined semantic dimension. Alexander Kluge deploys pictures to associative or dissociative effect. The television convention of fusing pictures and images until they are mired in a monotony aired a thousand times over is deconstructed. The autonomous material status of pictures and

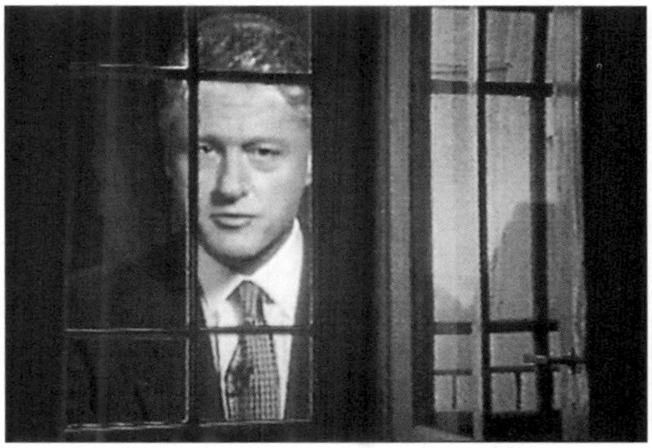

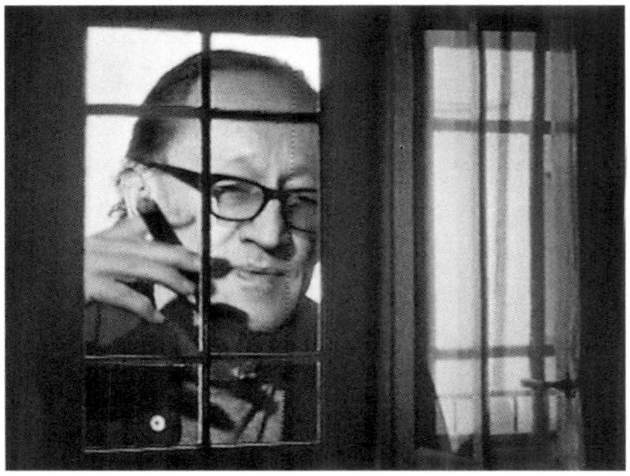

words has been reclaimed. The seamless cuts and the oily montage that plunge our television culture into entropy thus appear as questionable embodiments of pseudo-professionalism.

The association of the *laterna magica* or the device of fading in key sentences—"There is no objectivity beyond desire."—harks back to the early days of the medium, to silent, avant-garde Russian films and thus to emancipatory aspirations. The impression of a formally "backward looking" idiom conveyed by these programs is naturally also a matter of context. Within the nonstop tedium of television, these "amateur films" signal a radically different temporality, a different perceptual option, a contrary approach to

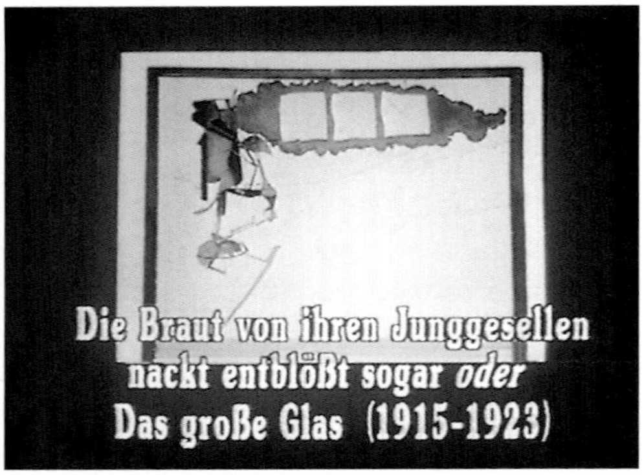

the role of the medium. It would be interesting to examine whether or not these shows are based on an all-embracing theory of our information society. When a talk with a woman specialist on Proust is called "Desire that rules the world—Clinton, Starr, Ovid, and Marcel Proust," we begin to understand Alexander Kluge's trajectory. From an anthropological perspective, the imaginary, the eternal tool now and forever, merges with techniques of presentation, which prove to be astonishingly similar in the long run.

The above-mentioned film contribution explores whether Proust could have written the Starr report or whether moral accusation is denied anyone who sees desire in every text. Does that turn all those Americans who ask themselves "Why does Starr want to expose obscenity?" into skeptical Proustians? The fact that the literary methods of Marcel Proust or Heiner Müller are examined as relevant to the analysis of public politics is related to Alexander Kluge's unusual agenda of taking the sphere of aesthetics seriously as a paradigm for human orientation. The unwitting recollection, which lies at the heart of Proust's method of dealing with time lived, and the explosion of recollection, which characterizes Heiner Müller's method of lending voice to history's dead are two sides of the same coin. In a conversation with Heiner Müller's New York publisher, this writer's astonishing impact is examined in terms of the notion that he was the first playwright of the digital era. What is meant is Müller's antirealistic attitude, his facility for trading in a wealth of literary shares and defending the truth of the fragment against any notion of real time.

Alexander Kluge's midnight shows flirt with the idea of universal wisdom just as much as they signal—like Proust—the position of the "unreliable narrator." But that means they also trust the recipient. Müller's New York publisher underscores the fact that his writer friend reminded him of a "cuddly dog" by quoting Gertrude Stein: "I am I because my dog recognizes me." The case is much the same in Alexander Kluge's shows. They, and possibly only they, still remind television consumers that they are "present." The films often end with the credits starting up while the voices of the speakers are still heard, only fading out later. The associations, the discourses on the imaginary, never end. They lead a subrosa underground life, which relativizes the respective show but updates the insight that the book, the film, the picture never come to an end. It is an indication

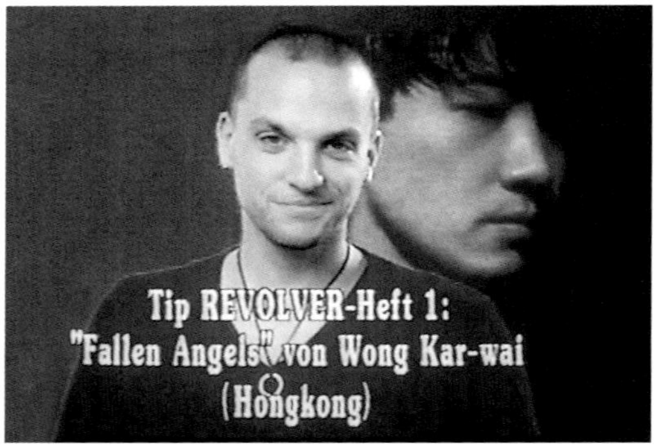

of the synchronous competing spheres, presented as closed only for purposes of ideological formation and appeasement.

Recently Alexander Kluge introduced a young journalist and co-founder of the new film magazine *Revolver*. In his column "Wild Strawberries," the film buff redefines the magic moments of cinema. His motto is as astonishing as it is discerning. "Every film," he says, "should once show the horizon."

(Translation: Catherine Schelbert)

1) Cf. his famous essay: *Über die allmähliche Verfertigung der Gedanken beim Reden* [1805].

COLLABORATIONS

EDWARD RUSCHA
born 1937 in Omaha, Nebraska, lives and works in Los Angeles / geboren 1937 in Omaha, Nebraska, lebt und arbeitet in Los Angeles.

ANDREAS SLOMINSKI
geboren 1959 in Meppen, lebt und arbeitet in Hamburg / born 1959 in Meppen, Germany, lives and works in Hamburg.

SAM TAYLOR-WOOD
born 1967 in London, lives and works in London / geboren 1967 in London, lebt und arbeitet in London.

EDWARD RUSCHA, MIRACLE NO. 61, 1975, zinc oxide and pastel on paper, 22¾ x 28⅝" / WUNDER NR. 61, Zinkweiss und Pastellkreide auf Papier, 57,8 x 72,7 cm.

EDWARD

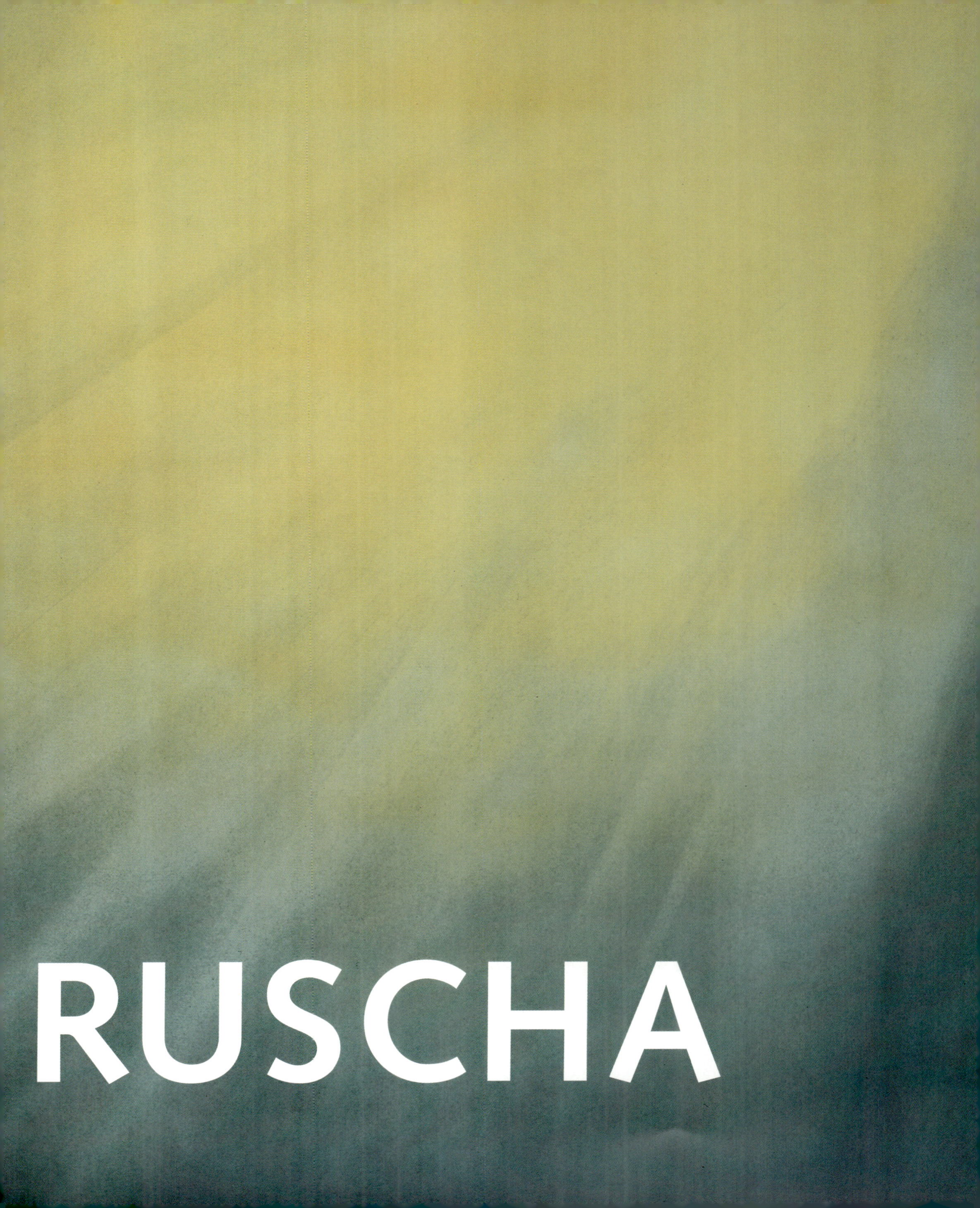

RUSCHA

JEFF PERRONE

Ed Ruscha's Illuminated Manuscripts

I.

I've never been to L.A., and the distance can be thrilling. I have in the past been seduced by the fancy, deracinated sprawl of Joan Didion's *Play It As It Lays*, an L.A. studded with loaded, symbolic signposts and random sadism. I've been pleasurably lulled into submission by the sinuous, ribbony narrative of Robert Altman's *The Long Goodbye*, a movie of windows and water, adapted from Raymond Chandler, avatar of Sunshine Noir, bloated with boasting, tattered glamor. My fantasy L.A. is a dream, a geography, a vista filtered only through books and screen, impossible to uncouple from Hollywood, which to the rest of the world is the "real" L.A., the real America. And I know, from Mike Davis's *City of Quartz*, that fluid boundaries have transformed L.A. into Mexico City Del Norte; and, from Ed Ruscha, that JAPAN IS AMERICA (1991), as Sony becomes Hollywood.

II.

The message traces itself out like miniature skywriting, along a lazily skewed diagonal. We peer up at it, read it as it stretches out to an illusory infinity and an ephemeral ecstasy: QUICK, PASSIONATE, NOISY (1976), a sexual/semantic haiku. The words hover twice, once for each partner. Such is the self-deprecating swagger of our dream combination: sexy and funny. The letters of the text are constructed fonts designed out of sheets of blank paper; a lovely, lightweight elision of the means of self-reference.

III.

The materials of Ruscha's drawings are the basics of modern design. He favors simple, clear, clean layouts, prizing legibility. He prefers elementary production values, such as the knock-out—leaving words white on a colored background—, the text in reverse, punched-out type that burns words on the page, as if in radiant, harsh sunlight, words that appear in the absence of print. When he indulges in a fancier font, it is to give an extra layer of meaning that is fused to the details of style: TULSA (1967) becomes a constructed band of rectilinear and curvilinear, Möbius-strip letters, throwing a shadow across the picture-plane. The precise choice of font conveys the character of the word, impresses a memorability to the sign and transforms nouns into logos, trademarks, products. Style inevitably describes a dating mechanism. Ruscha holds on to a Pop Modernist scheme with roots in the fifties; his insistent clarity of format, which might once have seemed so deadpan, now feels nostalgic, as graphic design in the last decade has become furiously eclectic and chaotic. But it is a longing within limits, for who could get teary-eyed over the bland exoticism of BRONSON TROPICS (1965), with its watered-down geometry sprayed with a fillip of cursive script wiggling up a wall, an anomalously glamorous logo vainly differentiating this architectural banality from all the rest of SOME LOS ANGELES APARTMENTS (1965).

JEFF PERRONE is an artist living in New York City.

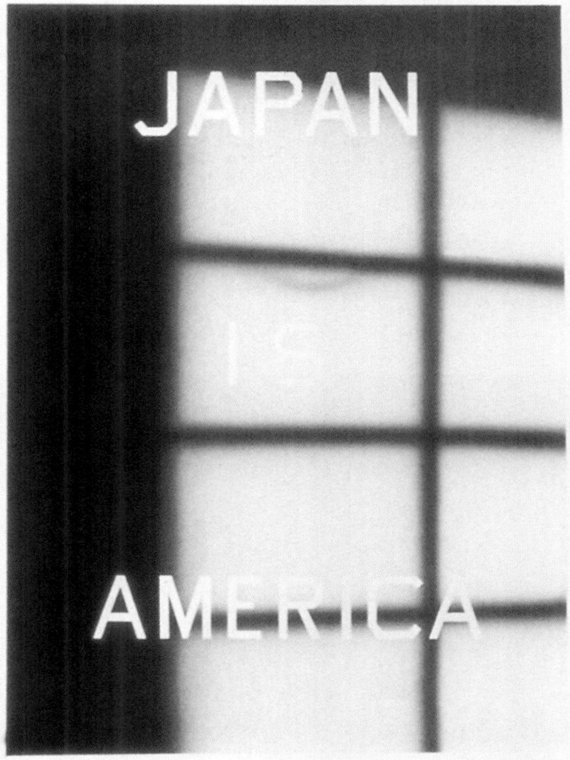

EDWARD RUSCHA, JAPAN IS AMERICA, 1991, acrylic on paper, $40\frac{1}{4}$ x $30\frac{1}{8}$" /
JAPAN IST AMERIKA, Acryl auf Papier, 102,2 x 76,5 cm. (PHOTOS: PAUL RUSCHA)

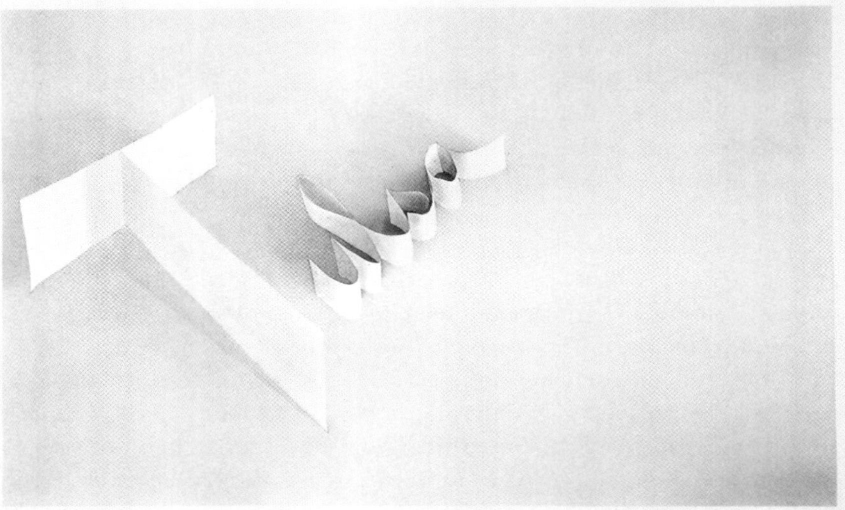

EDWARD RUSCHA, TULSA, 1967, gunpowder on paper, $14\frac{3}{8}$ x $22\frac{3}{4}$" /
Schiesspulver auf Papier, 36,5 x 57,8 cm.

IV.

In the beginning, the word was literally a sign. One of Ruscha's privileged fonts derives from the lop-cornered block-lettering of the iconic sign-of-the-mount, "Hollywood." In HOLLYWOOD STUDY NO. 2 (1968), that sign is the unique conjunction of word and place, a self-defining construction as a stage-set facade precariously supported by exposed struts. Ruscha illuminates this word, this place, by surrounding it with a lurid, garish, unreal sunset backdrop, something out of an early Technicolor movie gone to rot. Or perhaps, it is not something suffocatingly real: a spectacular burst of yellow-orange-red held down by a thick layer of chocolate, a weighted band of dirt, exhaust, and humidity—the visual icon of spoiled beauty, paradise stained and soiled.

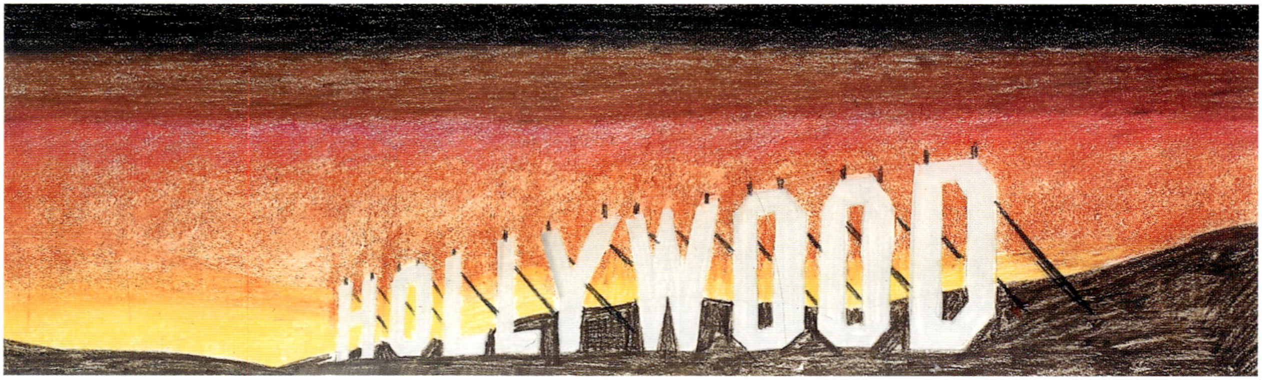

EDWARD RUSCHA, HOLLYWOOD STUDY NO. 2, 1968,
pencil and pastel on paper, $17\frac{1}{2}$ x 44" / HOLLYWOODSTUDIE NR. 2,
Farbstift und Pastellkreide auf Papier, 44,5 x 111,8 cm.

V.

The essence of the art of manuscript illumination resides in the embellishment that creates an environment that goes further than mere signification. The curvy, bulging tacky-serified font of HEAVY INDUSTRY (1962) is imposed upon a sludgy field of toxic waste, bringing to mind those oil pumps engulfed in garbage at the end of Orson Welles' *Touch of Evil.* Yet that same font shows up soft and watery, a series of dewy drops rendering the word POOL (1968). This identification might signal "swimming pool" if it were not made of gunpowder, which suggests a different pool—of blood. Ruscha has the gift for isolating one property of a sign, gently exaggerating it, and generating a sinister narrative: the color red of the "Standard" sign, with a few extra flicks of the brush, breaks out of its designated boundary and sets the gas station afire.

VI.

Several years ago, I stopped laughing out loud in art galleries, because it always turned out, to my surprise, that the work wasn't meant to be funny. I had been caught laughing in church. But I still can't control myself in front of a hilariously shaggy Wegman, and I can't stifle myself before Ruscha's ARTISTS WHO MAKE "PIECES" (1976). This highly polished koan still lays waste to an entire generation of artists who were so concerned with seriousness that they rejected "art" as being frivolous. A beautifully made-by-hand object was taboo, an indulgence in some decadent activity.

EDWARD RUSCHA, ARTISTS WHO DO BOOKS, 1976, pastel on paper, 22¾ x 28⅝ /
KÜNSTLER, DIE BÜCHER MACHEN, Pastellkreide auf Papier, 57,8 x 72,7 cm.

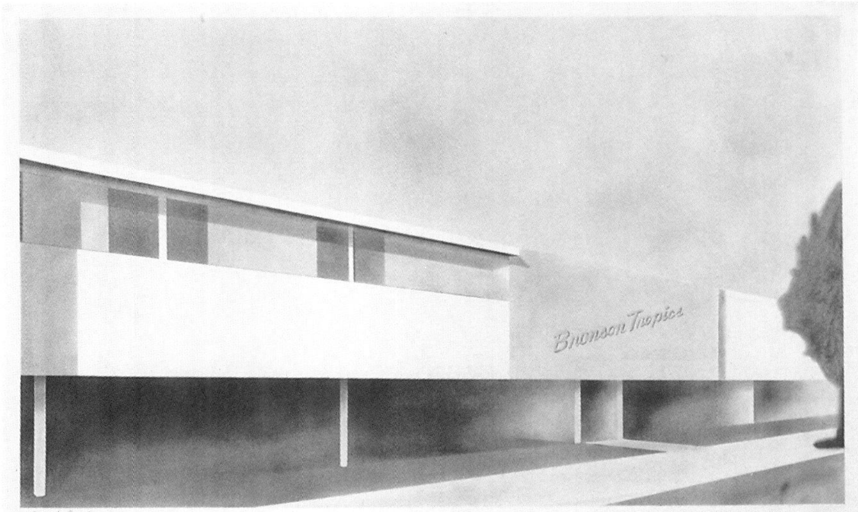

EDWARD RUSCHA, BRONSON TROPICS, 1965, pencil and graphite on paper, 14⅛ x 22½" /
Bleistift und Graphit auf Papier, 35,8 x 57,2 cm. (PHOTOS: PAUL RUSCHA)

VII.

There are no ironic quotation marks around the word "books" in ARTISTS WHO DO BOOKS (1976). And there Ruscha lies, in a star-quality photograph, on a nonchalantly tossed-off bit of slinky satin, covered with an array of his various publications: covered with his codices, the body of the artist with the body of his work. I have never been to Paris, either, but I imagine Ruscha's photodocumentation of L.A.'s palm trees, gasoline stations, apartment buildings, parking lots, and swimming pools to be the American equivalent of Atget's crumbling gardens, mossy statuary, shop windows, and lamp posts. The goal would seem to be the same: to catch on the quick the grain, the temperature, the light of this singular location. There is probably no greater barometer of Ruscha's love of books than his drawings of them. He meticulously recreates NINE SWIMMING POOLS (1972) in a watercolor: the book as a floating illusion, a miniature full of miniature oceans, all contained within their respective rectangles. The folios, slightly ruffled, reveal a splash of blue.

VIII.

Ruscha, mock cleric, teases at the apocalypse in a series titled THE END (1993). Appropriately coded in a Gothic script, this set of depicted film frames, badly scratched, tells us that the movie is over—although Ruscha may be hinting that it is Cinema itself that is finished, and I wouldn't disagree. His ghostly word-play gestures that the screen will go dark, and the lights will go up. And it is this light that is often struggling to break through in Ruscha's work—that magical illumination of enlightenment. It beams from movie projectors; it streams through unseen windows; it shines down from invisible heavens in the MIRACLE drawings (1975). It floods the dark like the search beams of police helicopters hovering over the scene of the crime: our television version of that archetypal L.A. nightmare. In my fantasy L.A., there is always as much shadow as light; enlightenment is always only a possibility, without any assurances. The projected planes of sunlight brightening the lithographic simulations of plywood-planked walls in A WAY OF LIFE (1997) are cautionary: Ruscha crops half of the words "A" and "Life" out of the picture. In another recent drawing, shadow and light—we might as well say good and evil—are reduced to these pessimistic percentages: 90% devil, 10% angel. The Devil holds sway in the book of Ruscha, because, as every fallen Catholic knows, evil is strong, evil is seductive.

IX.

DEVIL, ANGEL (1997): Prankster and priest, a monk with the soul of a stand-up comic.

X.

The "Way" of A WAY OF LIFE, which alludes to art as a calling, recalls the medieval monk's dedication to a dual duty: preserving the austerity and truth of the sacred text, while embellishing it with the abandon of the secular world—a world of humor, color, fantasy, and light. In 1997, Ruscha filled a gallery with a collection of secondhand books, each decorated with an initial, capital "O"—an Omega? An Om? They were displayed to be looked at, not read; but the vowel sound resonated, as if the books were speaking to us. As physical objects, they contained unseen worlds only hinted at by their titles and typographies, and, like all beloved members of our personal libraries, they were simple and portable. The printed page allows you to travel light. Reading Ruscha's WORDS NO. 1 (1985), not left to right, but top to bottom, Chinese-style, you get "Thoughts To Go."

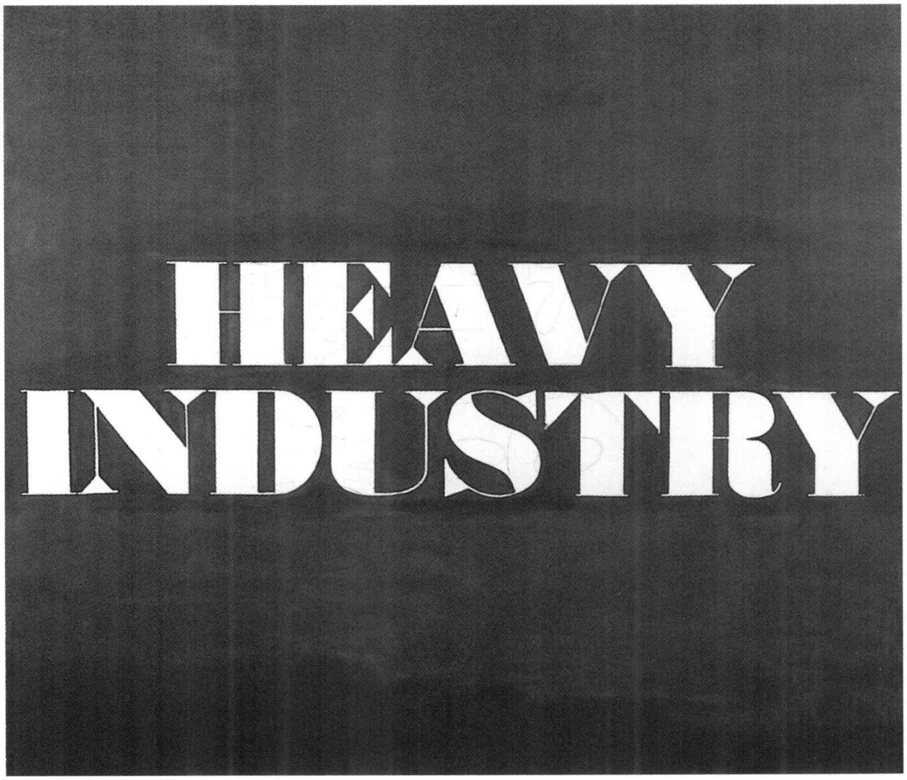

EDWARD RUSCHA, HEAVY INDUSTRY, 1962, oil on canvas, 67 x 71⅝" / SCHWERINDUSTRIE, Öl auf Leinwand, 170,2 x 182 cm.

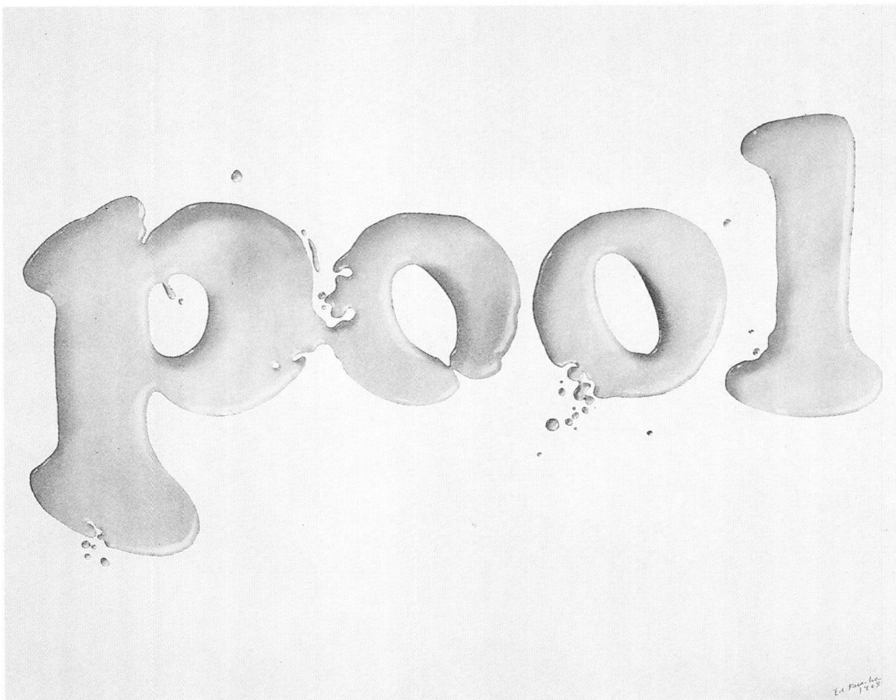

EDWARD RUSCHA, POOL, 1968, gunpowder on paper, 23 x 29" / Schiesspulver auf Papier, 58,4 x 73,7 cm. (PHOTOS: PAUL RUSCHA)

EDWARD RUSCHA, THE END, NO. 2, 1993,
acrylic on paper, 24 x 29 15/16" / ENDE, NR. 2, Acryl auf Papier, 61 x 76 cm.

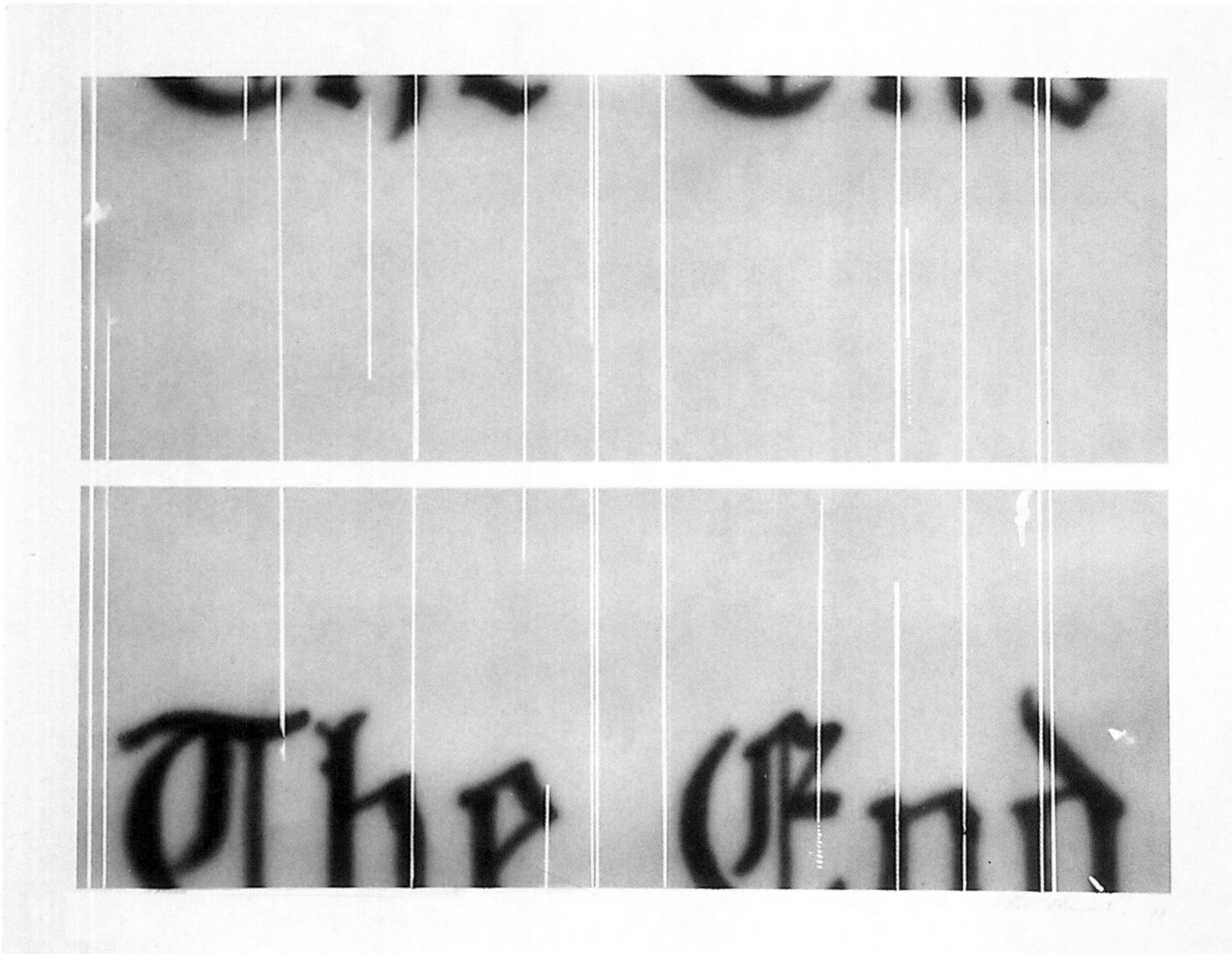

EDWARD RUSCHA, NINE SWIMMING POOLS, 1972, gunpowder and pastel on paper, 23 x 29" /
NEUN SCHWIMMBASSINS, Schiesspulver und Pastellkreide auf Papier, 58,4 x 73,7 cm. (PHOTOS: PAUL RUSCHA)

JEFF PERRONE

Ed Ruschas illuminierte Manuskripte

I.

Ich war noch nie in Los Angeles und die Distanz hat auch ihren Reiz. Einst liess ich mich von der irrwitzigen Entfremdung und Uferlosigkeit von Joan Didions Roman *Spiel dein Spiel (Play It As It Lays)* verführen, einem L.A., das durchsetzt ist mit bedeutungsgeladenen Symbolen und willkürlichem Sadismus. Auch von der verschlungenen Handlung von Robert Altmans *Der lange Abschied (The Long Goodbye)* habe ich mich genüsslich einlullen lassen, einem Film voller Fenster und Wasser – nach dem gleichnamigen Roman von Raymond Chandler, der Ikone des «Sunshine Noir» – und nur so strotzend vor wichtigtuerischer, schmuddliger Grandezza. Das L.A. in meiner Vorstellung ist ein Traum, ein Ort, ein Panorama, das ich allein durch Bücher und Filme aufgesogen habe, es ist untrennbar mit Hollywood verknüpft, das für den Rest der Welt das eigentliche L.A., ja das eigentliche Amerika ist. Aus Mike Davis' Studie *City of Quartz* weiss ich, dass die Durchlässigkeit der Grenzen L.A. in ein Mexico City des Nordens verwandelt hat, und von Ed Ruscha habe ich gelernt: JAPAN IST AMERIKA (1991), so wie Sony zu Hollywood wird.

II.

Entlang einer träge hingeworfenen Diagonale zeichnet sich die Botschaft wie eine Miniaturschrift am Himmel ab. Wir schauen hinauf und lesen sie, während sie scheinbar ins Unendliche und zu ephemerer Ekstase anzuwachsen scheint: QUICK, PASSIONATE, NOISY (Schnell, leidenschaftlich, laut, 1976), ein sexuell-semantisches Haiku. Die Worte vibrieren zweimal, einmal für jeden Partner. So sieht das selbstverachtende Wunschbild unserer Traumpaarung aus: sexy und witzig. Die Buchstaben des Textes sind in einer Kunstschrift, die aus lauter leeren Briefbögen besteht, ein wunderbar schwereloser Verzicht auf Selbstreferenz.

III.

Die Materialien in Ruschas Zeichnungen entsprechen den Grundmaterialien des modernen Grafikdesigns. Er bevorzugt die einfache, klare, saubere Gestaltung und legt Wert auf Lesbarkeit. Er hat eine Vorliebe für elementare Produktionsmittel, etwa die Inversion – die Wörter weiss auf farbigem Hintergrund, der Text in einer wie herausgestanzt wirkenden Schrift, die die Wörter wie auf die Seite gebrannt aussehen lässt, als stünden sie im blendend hellen Sonnenlicht, Wörter, die erscheinen und nichts mit Gedrucktem zu tun haben. Wenn Ruscha sich einmal eine ausgefallenere Schrift erlaubt, so um eine zusätzliche Bedeutungsschicht hinzuzufügen, die unmittelbar mit den Besonderheiten des Schriftstils zusammenhängt: TULSA (1967) wird zu einem konstruierten Band von rechtwinkligen und

JEFF PERRONE ist Künstler und lebt in New York.

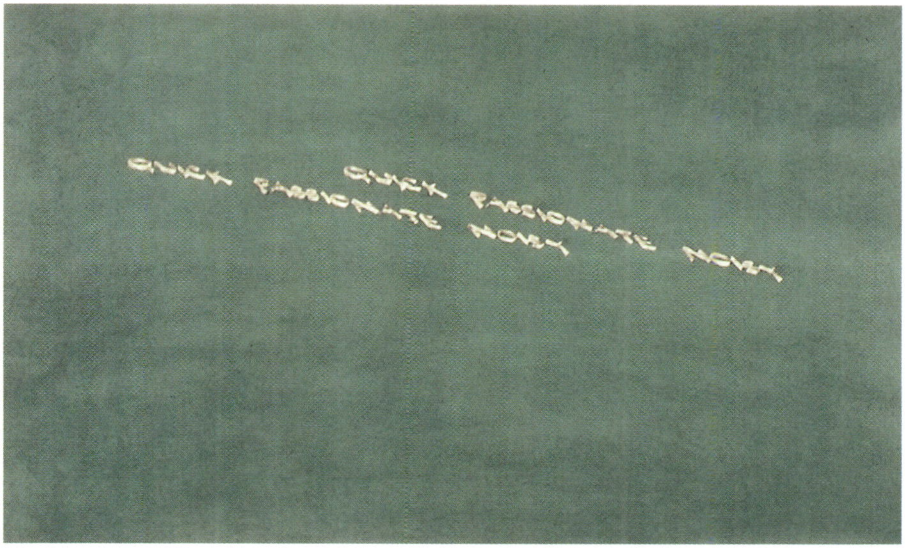

EDWARD RUSCHA, QUICK, PASSIONATE, NOISY, 1976, pastel on paper, 14 1/8 x 22 3/4" / SCHNELL, LEIDENSCHAFTLICH, LAUT, Pastellkreide auf Papier, 35,9 x 57,8 cm.

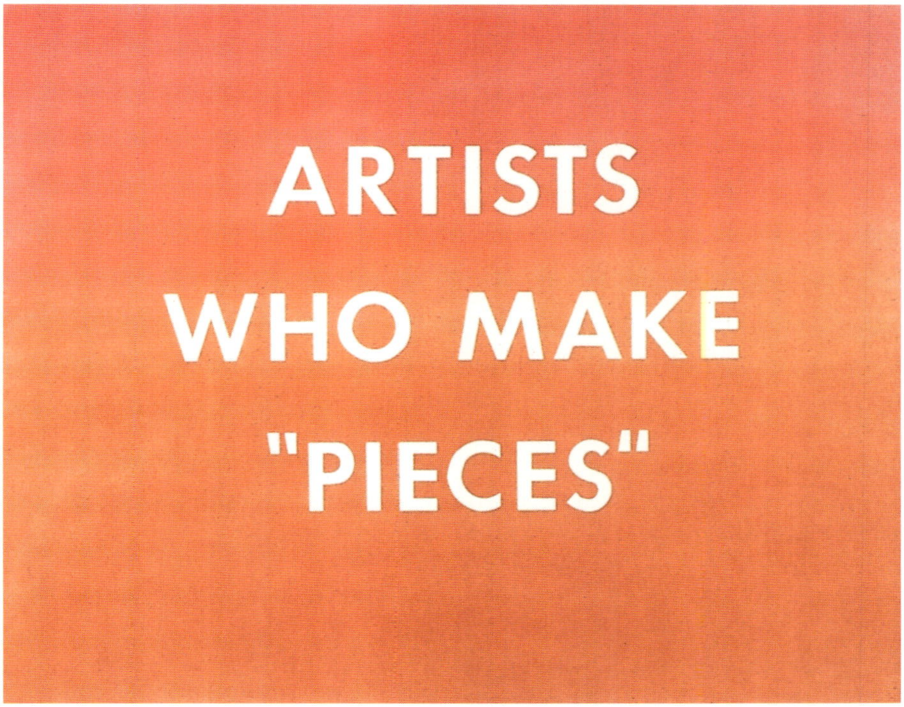

EDWARD RUSCHA, ARTISTS WHO MAKE "PIECES", 1976, pastel on paper, 22 3/4 x 28 15/16" / KÜNSTLER, DIE «WERKE» SCHAFFEN, Pastellkreide auf Papier, 57,8 x 73,5 cm. (PHOTOS: PAUL RUSCHA)

gekrümmten Buchstaben aus lauter Möbius-Schleifen, die ihren Schatten über die Bildfläche werfen. Die Wahl des Schrifttyps verrät den Charakter des Worts, verleiht dem Zeichen seine Besonderheit und verwandelt Substantive in Logos, Markenzeichen, Produkte. Zu jedem Stil gehört unweigerlich eine bestimmte Zeit. Ruscha knüpft an die moderne Pop-Art an, die ihre Wurzeln in den 50er Jahren hat; sein hartnäckiges Festhalten an klaren Formaten, das einst abgegriffen und verstaubt wirken mochte, hat heute einen nostalgischen Touch, weil das Grafikdesign in den letzten zehn Jahren äusserst eklektisch, schwer entzifferbar und chaotisch geworden ist. Die nostalgische Sehnsucht hält sich jedoch in Grenzen, denn wer bekäme schon feuchte Augen vor der kühlen Exotik von BRONSON TROPICS (1965) mit seiner milden Geometrie und der leisen Belebung durch die an einer Wand emporzüngelnden, kursiven Schrift, einem bereits ungewöhnlich glanzvollen Logo, das diese architektonische Banalität stolz abhebt vom Rest der Behausungen in Los Angeles (SOME LOS ANGELES APARTMENTS, 1965).

IV.

Am Anfang war das Wort buchstäblich ein Zeichen. Eine von Ruschas Lieblingsschriften ist vom Hollywood-Schriftzug mit seinen abfallenden Ecken am Hang über Los Angeles abgeleitet. In HOLLYWOOD STUDY NO. 2 (1968) ist dieses Zeichen die einzige Verbindung zwischen Wort und Ort, eine sich selbst entlarvende Konstruktion einer Filmkulisse, notdürftig gestützt durch ein paar sichtbare Stangen. Ruscha illuminiert dieses Wort und damit die Örtlichkeit, indem er es mit einem leuchtend grellen, unwirklichen Sonnenuntergangshintergrund versieht, etwas aus einem frühen, mittlerweile verrotteten Technicolorfilm. Vielleicht ist es auch gar nicht künstlich, sondern nur die exakte Wiedergabe von etwas erstickend Realem: ein spektakulärer Ausbruch von Gelb-Orange-Rot, der von einer dicken Schicht Schokolade, einem lastenden Streifen Schmutz, Abluft und Feuchtigkeit in Schach gehalten wird – ein visuelles Symbol der heruntergekommenen Schönheit, des befleckten, schmuddlig gewordenen Paradieses.

V.

Das Wesentliche in der Kunst der Buchmalerei liegt in der schönen Ergänzung, die eine Umgebung schafft, welche über das bloss Zeichenhafte hinausgeht. Die geschwungene, ausladende Schrift von HEAVY INDUSTRY (Schwerindustrie, 1962) mit ihren schwerfälligen Serifen ist auf eine Landschaft gesetzt, die von giftigen Ablagerungen überzogen ist, und ruft uns jene beinah im Müll erstickenden Ölpumpen am Ende von Orson Welles' *Touch of Evil* (1958) in Erinnerung. Doch dieselbe Schrift löst sich weich und wässerig auf, wenn sie in einer Reihe von tauähnlichen Tropfen das Wort POOL (1968) bildet. Damit könnte Swimmingpool gemeint sein, bestünde die Schrift nicht aus Schiesspulver, was an eine ganz andere Flüssigkeit denken lässt – eine Blutlache. Ruscha hat die besondere Gabe, eine Eigenschaft eines Zeichens herauszufiltern, sie leicht zu übertreiben und damit eine abgründige Geschichte anzudeuten: Die Farbe Rot des «Standard»-Schildes bricht dank wenigen zusätzlichen Pinselstrichen aus ihrem vorgegebenen Feld aus und lässt die Tankstelle in Flammen aufgehen.

VI.

Zwar habe ich schon vor Jahren aufgehört in Galerien lauthals zu lachen, denn zu meiner Überraschung stellte sich jedesmal heraus, dass das jeweilige Kunstwerk überhaupt nicht wit-

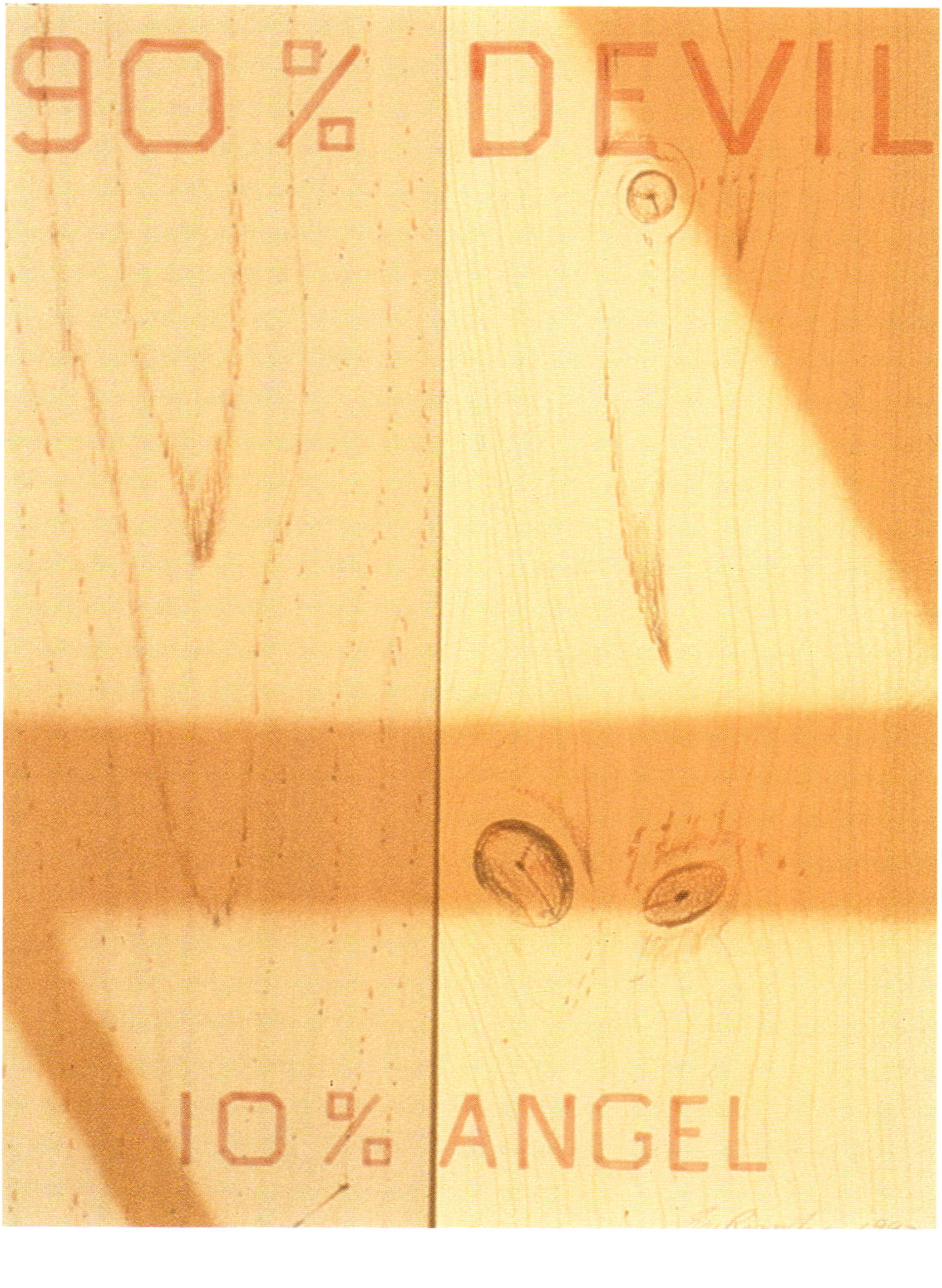

EDWARD RUSCHA, DEVIL, ANGEL, 1997, acrylic and lithograph on paper, 16½ x 12¼" / TEUFEL, ENGEL, Acryl und Lithographie auf Papier, 42 x 31 cm.

zig gemeint war. Ich stand jeweils da, als sei ich in der Kirche beim Lachen ertappt worden. Aber vor einem hoffnungslos zerzausten Wegman kann ich mich nach wie vor nicht beherrschen und auch angesichts Ruschas ARTISTS WHO MAKE "PIECES" (Künstler, die «Werke» schaffen, 1976) kann ich mir das Lachen beim besten Willen nicht verkneifen. Dieses glänzende Paradoxon rechnet mit einer ganzen Generation von Künstlern ab, denen der Ernst ihrer Arbeit so vorrangig war, dass sie «Kunst» als frivol ablehnten.

VII.

In ARTISTS WHO DO BOOKS (Künstler, die Bücher machen, 1976) steht das Wort «Books» nicht in ironischen Anführungszeichen. Ruscha liegt, hingestreckt wie für eine Star-Aufnahme, auf einem nonchalant hingeworfenen Stück edel glänzenden Satins, bedeckt mit einer reichen Auswahl seiner verschiedenen Publikationen: zugedeckt mit seinen Kodices, der Körper des Künstlers unter dem Korpus seines Werks. Ich war auch noch nie in Paris, aber ich denke Ruschas Photodokumentation der Palmen, Tankstellen, Apartmenthäuser, Parkplätze und Swimmingpools von Los Angeles ist die amerikanische Entsprechung zu Atgets verfallenden Gärten, bemoosten Statuen, Schaufenstern und Laternenpfählen. Das Ziel jedenfalls scheint dasselbe zu sein: die Temperatur und das Licht der jeweils einmaligen Örtlichkeit spontan einzufangen. Es gibt wohl kein besseres Barometer für Ruschas Liebe zum Buch als seine Zeichnungen von Büchern. Mit grösster Sorgfalt gibt er das Buch *Nine Swimming Pools* als Aquarell wieder: das Buch als dahintreibende Illusion, eine Miniatur voller kleiner Ozeane, jeder fein säuberlich verstaut in seinem Rechteck. Die leicht aufgeblätterten Seiten enthüllen einen Spritzer Blau.

VIII.

In der Serie mit dem Titel THE END (Das Ende, 1993) macht sich Ruscha als lachender Mönch über die Apokalypse lustig. Natürlich in passender gotischer Schrift verkündet diese Reihe stark zerkratzter Filmbilder das Ende des Films – vielleicht will Ruscha sogar andeuten, dass die Zeit des Kinos überhaupt abgelaufen ist, auch dem würde ich nicht widersprechen. Sein geisterhaftes Wortspiel drückt aus, dass die Leinwand sich verdunkeln wird und die Lichter gleich angehen werden. Es ist dieses Licht, das in Ruschas Arbeiten oft kurz vor dem Durchbruch steht – das magische Aufscheinen des alles aufklärenden Lichts. Es strahlt aus Filmprojektoren; es strömt durch nie gesehene Fenster; in den MIRACLE-Zeichnungen (Wunder, 1975) scheint es herunter von unsichtbaren Himmeln. Es durchdringt die Dunkelheit wie das Flutlicht von Polizeihelikoptern, die über der Szene des Verbrechens kreisen: die TV-Version des archetypischen L.A.-Alptraums. Im Los Angeles meiner Phantasie halten sich Schatten und Licht die Waage; Aufklärung ist immer nur eine Möglichkeit ohne jede Garantie. Die Strahlen des Sonnenlichts, die in A WAY OF LIFE (Eine Lebensweise, 1997) auf die lithographische Simulation einer Bretterwand fallen, sind eine Art Warnung: Ruscha schneidet die Hälfte der Wörter «A» und «Life» aus dem Bild. In einer anderen neueren Zeichnung sind Schatten und Licht – man könnte auch sagen Gut und Böse – zu pessimistischen Prozentzahlen verkürzt: 90% Teufel, 10% Engel. Der Teufel behält die Oberhand in Ruschas Buch, weil das Böse, wie jeder katholische Sünder weiss, stark und verführerisch ist.

IX.

DEVIL, ANGEL (Teufel, Engel, 1997): Fallensteller und Priester in einem, ein Mönch mit der Seele eines Komikers.

X.

Das Wort «Way (Weg)» in A WAY OF LIFE spielt auf die Kunst als Berufung an und erinnert an die Hingabe des mittelalterlichen Mönchs an eine Aufgabe, die zwei Seiten hatte: das Bewahren der Strenge und Wahrheit des heiligen Textes bei gleichzeitiger Verschönerung mit allen Mitteln der säkularen Welt – einer Welt voller Humor, Farbe, Phantasie und Licht. 1997 füllte Ruscha eine Galerie mit einer Sammlung von antiquarischen Büchern, jedes dekoriert mit einer Initiale, einem grossen O. – Ein Omega? Ein Om? Sie wurden ausgestellt um betrachtet, nicht um gelesen zu werden; aber der Vokalton vibrierte im Raum, als ob die Bücher zu uns sprechen wollten. Als physische Objekte enthielten sie unsichtbare Welten, die durch Titel und jeweilige Typographie nur angedeutet wurden, und wie alle Lieblingsbücher in unserer eigenen Bibliothek waren sie einfach und handlich. Die gedruckte Seite wiegt nicht schwer im Gepäck. Liest man Ruschas WORDS NO. 1 (1985) statt von links nach rechts von oben nach unten, nach Art der Chinesen, so erhält man: «Thoughts To Go / Gedanken zum Aufbrechen».

(Übersetzung: Susanne Schmidt)

EDWARD RUSCHA, A WAY OF LIFE, 1997, acrylic and lithograph on paper, 16 x 19¾" / EINE LEBENSWEISE, Acryl und Lithographie auf Papier, 40,6 x 50,2 cm.

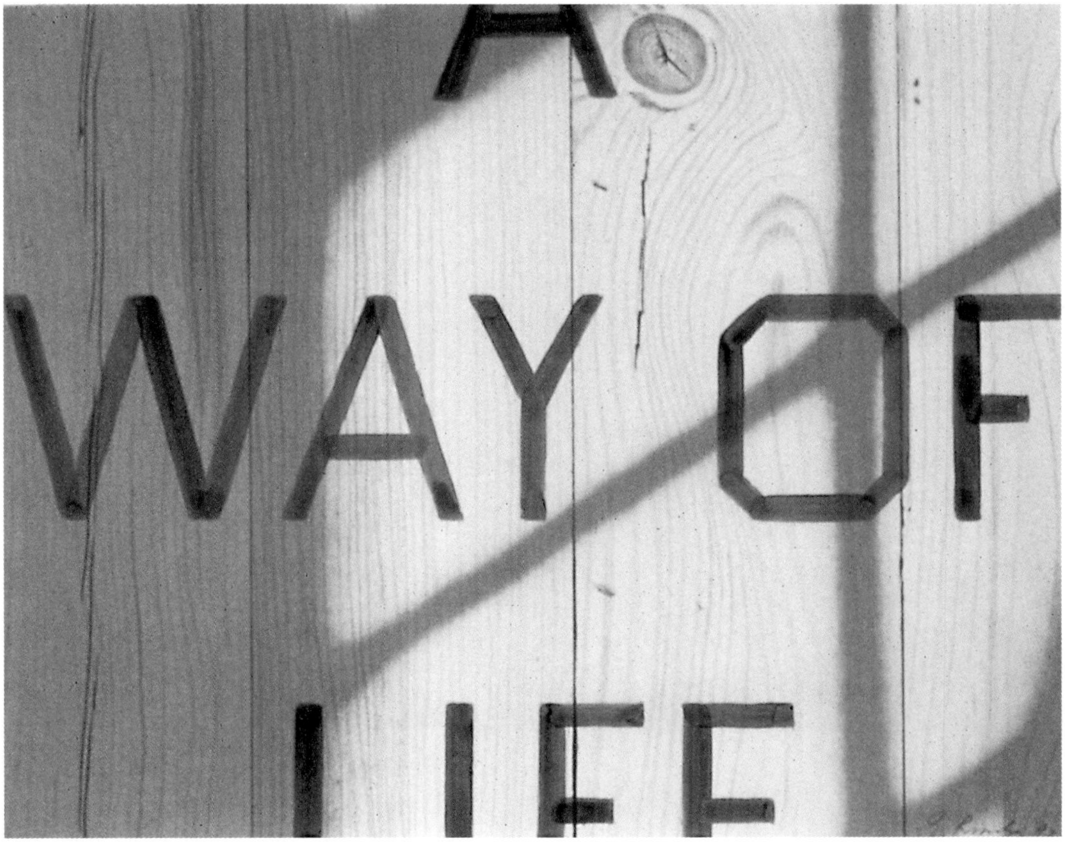

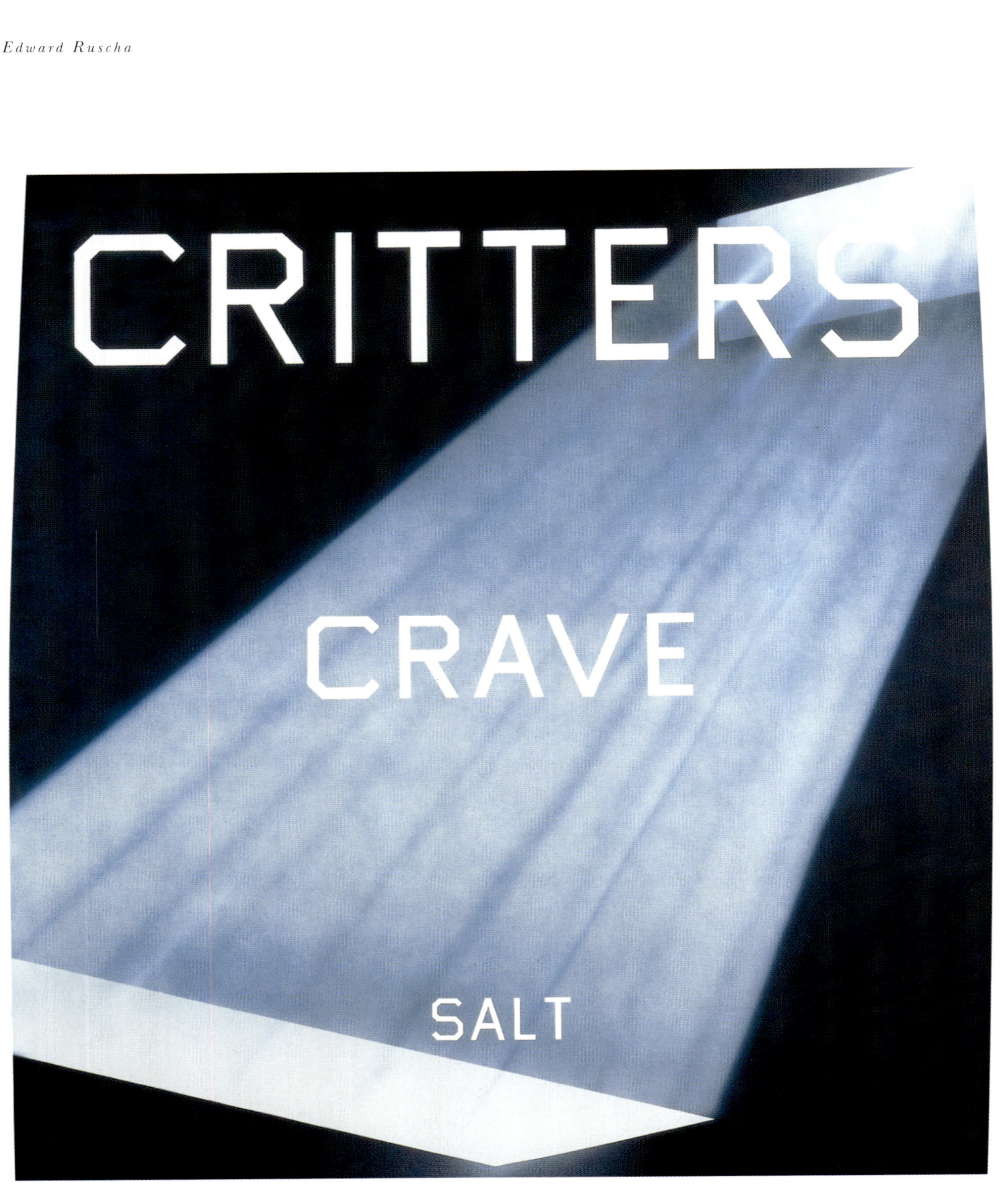

EDWARD RUSCHA, CRITTERS CRAVE SALT, 1997, acrylic on canvas, 76 x 72" / VIECHER LECHZEN NACH SALZ, Acryl auf Leinwand, 193 x 182,9 cm.

Critters Crave Salt

JENNIFER HIGGIE

It swells towards you like a growth in parentheses, a shaped painting of a cell pregnant or gorged with possibilities, the height of a human. Lit with a single ray of dusty moonlight or sunlight, the paint drifts across its surface, transforming the hard angles it describes from an image of claustrophobia into one a little more ambiguous, even hopeful. But hopeful of what? Of release? From the cell, the picture, or from language as something inflexible and limiting?

Three words—CRITTERS CRAVE SALT—shimmer and fade, an hallucination of a phrase ostensibly unconnected to the image it's so intrinsically connected to. Frustrated meaning hovers around them like an unfulfilled hint or code. Look at the painting long enough and its subtle distended surface generates a curious pulsating disorientation—as if you suddenly realize the painting is a little overweight. Like a Malevich, in reproduction the geometry of the shapes in the painting looks flat and poster-like—seen in the flesh the paint is soft, hesitant even, the words decreasing in size and emphasis as they float to the bottom of the picture plane like paper cut-outs tossed from a window.

Like the reverie of someone who just can't get out of the place they've found themselves in, the word CRAVE, positioned at waist height, mirrors the source of all cravings—the stomach, near the heart. A cell—and this is obviously a cell, the window small and high up and impossible to see out of or into—is a space of cravings contained by the unequivocal restriction of either four walls or the four edges of a painting.

Ruscha throws out connections and images that initially look controlled, even cold, and then you realize—none of it makes any sense, in the accepted sense of the word. They're about finding new meanings in things, about seeing something fresh in the dullest or most contained of spaces. You won't ever get it, if getting it is what you want. The language he employs—a kind of taciturn, enigmatic poetry—asks you to position yourself inside the picture, and wander around it until you find your own corner or your own meaning within its established parameters. In this respect, his pictures, despite their restraint, are intensely easy going.

The hard edge of the words echoes the hard edges of the cell. Perhaps both of them are places you'd want to get away from. But the closer you look at the details, the more you can see the cracks in its construction.

It's true that critters crave salt. I had a horse who would wash my sweaty hand with his tongue. We put a large block of salt in his paddock, and he'd stand there licking it for hours, swaying and concentrated with an odd, happy look in his eye. I thought of him when I first saw this painting. It reminded me that, like an animal, you can never know what a painting will do to your imagination.

JENNIFER HIGGIE is Reviews Editor for *Frieze Magazine*. She lives in London.

Viecher lechzen nach Salz

JENNIFER HIGGIE

Es schwillt dir entgegen wie ein unaufdringliches Gewächs, ein Bild in der plastischen Form einer Zelle, die schwanger ist oder einfach ob den in ihr steckenden Möglichkeiten fast aus den Nähten platzt. Es ist so gross wie ein Mensch. Im Licht eines einzigen blassen Mond- oder Sonnenstrahls strömt Farbe über seine Oberfläche und verwandelt das klaustrophobische Bild mit seinen spitzen Winkeln in ein mehrdeutiges, ja hoffnungsvolles Bild. Aber Hoffnung worauf? Auf Erlösung? Erlösung aus der Zelle, dem Bild selbst oder von der Sprache als einer Erstarrung und Einschränkung?

Drei Wörter – CRITTERS CRAVE SALT (Viecher lechzen nach Salz) – glänzen auf und verblassen wieder, die Halluzination eines Satzes, der fürs Erste nicht mit dem Bild zusammenzuhängen scheint, mit dem er seinem Wesen nach jedoch aufs Engste verknüpft ist. Das Rätselhafte ihrer Bedeutung schwingt in ihnen mit wie ein unentschlüsselter Hinweis oder Code. Betrachtet man das Bild lange genug, erzeugt die leicht verformte Oberfläche eine merkwürdige pulsierende Verwirrung – als würde man plötzlich inne, dass das Bild ein bisschen Übergewicht hat. Wie bei einem Malewitsch wirkt die Geometrie der plastischen Formen in der Reproduktion flach wie ein Plakat; im Original dagegen ist die Farbe weich, ja ein Zögern wird spürbar, da die Wörter kleiner werden und an Emphase verlieren, während sie auf der Bildfläche nach unten driften wie aus dem Fenster geworfene Papierschnitzel.

Wie das Traumgespinst von jemandem, der von dem Ort, an den es ihn verschlagen hat, einfach nicht mehr wegkommt, widerspiegelt das Wort CRAVE, auf Taillenhöhe, den Anfang allen Lechzens: den Magen, in unmittelbarer Nähe des Herzens.

Eine Zelle – und darum handelt es sich hier offensichtlich, mit dem schmalen Fenster weit oben, durch das man weder hinein- noch hinaussehen kann – ist ein Ort des Lechzens und Schmachtens, der klar begrenzt ist, entweder von vier Wänden oder von den vier Rändern eines Bildes.

Ruscha wirft Verknüpfungen und Bilder aus, die zunächst kontrolliert, sogar langweilig wirken, bis man realisiert, dass nichts davon Sinn im gängigen Sinn dieses Wortes macht. Es geht darum, in den Dingen neue Bedeutungen zu entdecken, und noch in den langweiligsten und begrenztesten Räumen etwas Frisches und Neues zu sehen. Man wird es nie packen, solange es einem darum geht, etwas zu packen. Die Sprache, die er verwendet – eine Art schweigsamer, rätselhafter Poesie –, verlangt, dass man sich selbst ins Bild hinein versetzt und es umkreist, bis man unter den gegebenen Bedingungen seine eigene Ecke, seinen eigenen Sinn entdeckt hat. In dieser Hinsicht sind seine Bilder trotz ihrer Zurückhaltung ausgesprochen leicht zugänglich.

Die scharfen Kanten der Wörter entsprechen den harten Wänden der Zelle. Vielleicht sind beides Orte, von denen man wegstrebt. Aber je näher man sie im Einzelnen unter die Lupe nimmt, desto eher wird man die Scharten und Risse im Material wahrnehmen.

Im Übrigen ist es wahr, dass Viecher nach Salz lechzen. Ich hatte ein Pferd, das jeweils meine schwitzende Hand mit der Zunge leckte. Wir legten einen grossen Block Salz in seine Koppel und es stand dort und leckte stundenlang, hingebungsvoll und konzentriert, mit einem seltsamen, glücklichen Ausdruck in den Augen. An dieses Pferd musste ich denken, als ich das Bild zum ersten Mal sah. Es erinnerte mich daran, dass man wie bei einem Tier nie weiss, was ein Bild in unserer Phantasie auslösen wird.

(Übersetzung: Susanne Schmidt)

JENNIFER HIGGIE ist Kunstkritikerin und Redaktorin bei *Frieze*. Sie lebt in London.

EDWARD RUSCHA, E. RUSCHA, 1959,
oil on canvas, 43½ x 43½" / Öl auf Leinwand, 110,5 x 110,5 cm.
(PHOTOS: PAUL RUSCHA)

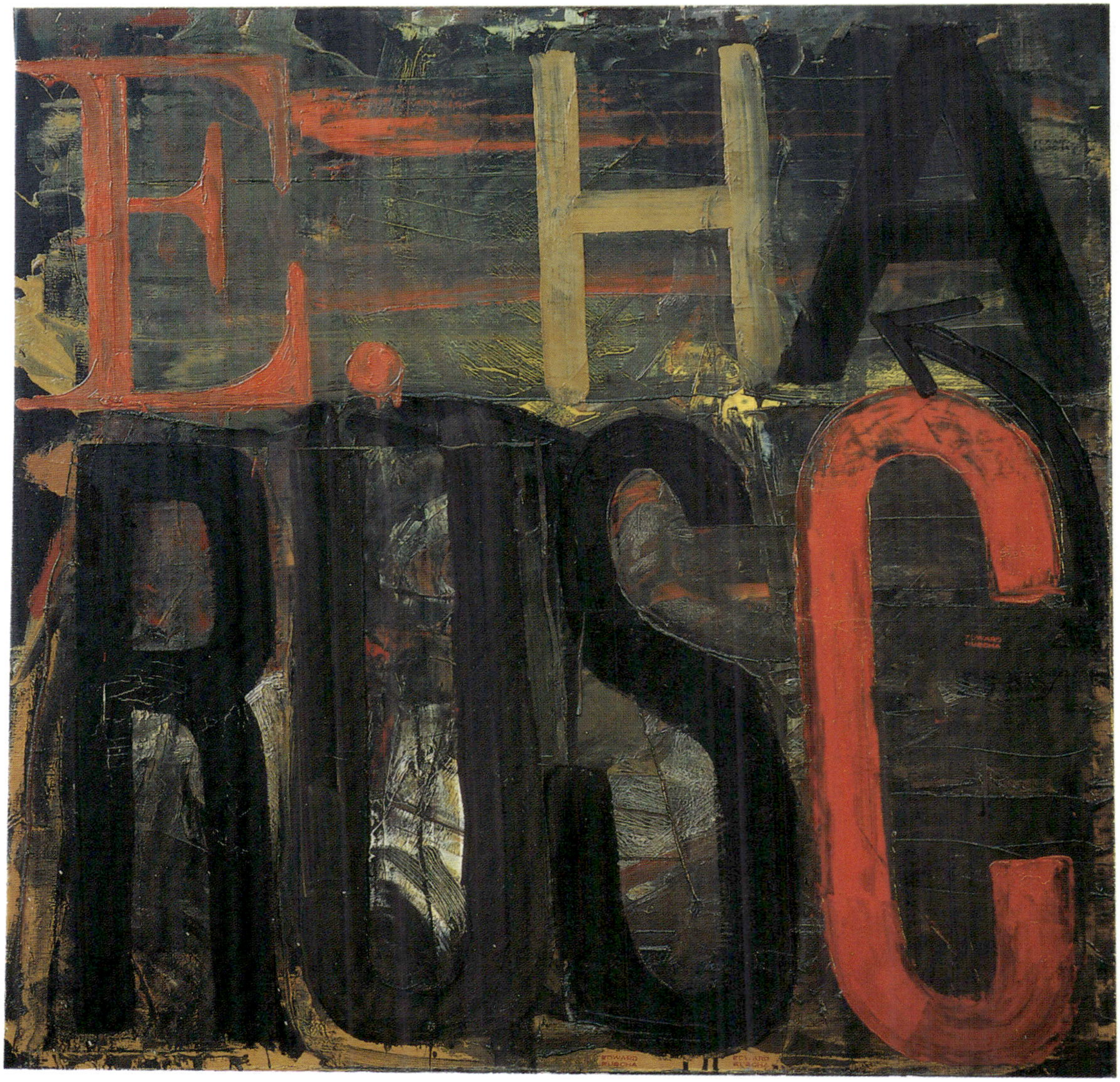

HOWARD SINGERMAN

Ed Ruscha's Modern Language

Ed Ruscha's interest in the place and placing of language was visible from the start, from the red capital E in the upper left-hand corner of his curious 1959 self-portrait; that is where the reader starts as well. The painting, or at least the name on it, moves us from left to right along the bottom half, across the letters R-U-S in black to a red C. A black arrow squeezed between the C and the painting's right edge directs our vision up along the curve of the C, to the letter A and then to H. Reversing those last two letters, spelling Ruscha's name properly, that is something we do at a different moment or if at the same time then perhaps in a different space. Proper nouns, the names of people or places, figure in Ruscha's earliest paintings in a way they no longer do; most of the words Ruscha has used since the mid-sixties are common nouns, even his phrases speak generally. But early on in SWEETWATER and DUBLIN, both from 1960, and BOX SMASHED FLAT (1961) the names of southern towns are carefully rendered in commercial typeface. "Sweetwater" and "Dublin," printed with commas to make clear their geographic designations—the commas call out for a state, for Tennessee and Georgia, respectively—, are rendered in a handsome serif type. The names run like captions beneath paintings, or beneath passages that could stand on their own as paintings: thick, dragged horizontal swathes span the top of SWEETWATER; a hand-painted pop version of an earlier wood and newspaper collage sits at the center of Dublin. Vicksburg is written beneath the flattened hand-painted Sunmaid raisin box that gives BOX SMASHED FLAT its title; it is rendered in a quicker typeface, a three-dimensional shadow style, but its crisp pop illusion is muddied by the paint Ruscha has washed over it.

Perhaps the problem with places like Vicksburg and Sweetwater was that they were too private and too much about somewhere else to sit where Ruscha needed them to sit. Like the paintings they accompanied, the names were too painterly, filled with a "longing inspired... by the places for which they stood." Marcel Proust wrote of place names and their haunting difference in decidedly painterly terms; against the stark, flattened clarity of words, place names offered "a confused picture," an image tinted by the sound, the resonance of the name, drawing from the "brightness or darkness of (its) tone, the color in which it is uniformly painted."[1] Proust's tenebrist color field emerging from the play of light and dark could be stretched to describe Ruscha's own early pictures, the gestural chiaroscuro of E. RUSCHA, the heavily modeled abstract expressionist slabs in SWEETWATER. But E. RUSCHA and SWEETWATER are late in the day; as Yves-Alain Bois writes "By 1960 Abstract Expressionism had become a cliché ... the 'push-pull' had indeed become a slogan."[2] Bois has written on Ruscha's art historical problem on Ruscha's own terms, using the kind of language Ruscha would use to replace the proper noun. Quite consciously, I would imagine, Bois has given Ruscha his formula: From the mid-sixties onwards, Ruscha would use the flat, prosaic language of clichés and slogans to do the work of pictorial organization or, since it is language we are speaking of, of articulation. His push and pull is no longer a

HOWARD SINGERMAN teaches art history at the University of Virginia, and he is author of *Art Subjects: Making Artists in the American University* (Berkeley: University of California Press, 1999).

negotiation between surface design and pictorial depth or between illusion and reality, the old formula for the tautness of the picture plane. Rather it negotiates between language and the time of writing and the space of seeing. And it renders not tautness, the breathing flatness of the modernist picture plane; but blankness, a term that implicates both image and language, both stares and verse.[3)]

A number of theorists have described the division between image and language, the split with which Ruscha plays, and have asserted its necessity for the project of modernist painting. There is, to pick a familiar example, Rosalind Krauss's argument that the ubiquitous modernist grid emblematizes "modern art's will to silence, its hostility to literature, to narrative, to discourse,"[4)] precisely as it forms the basic vocabulary of the "language of vision" or the "grammar of art," to borrow a couple of titles from those books on modern design that educated young artists of Ruscha's generation. Clearly, from the beginning, from the upper left-hand corner of E. RUSCHA, Ruscha has refused the absolute separation that the grid stands for, the pretense of seeing before or beyond language, of vision as innocence or transcendence. He understood early on what modernism's critics have since argued, that language orders and paces the scene of vision and the project of painting. Still, Ruscha is a painter, even, I would argue, a kind of modernist one—and it is language, and the direction and temporality of reading as a discrete activity, that allows him to be one. Language answers the question of composition, a question he takes seriously, unlike most post-abstract expressionist painters, but it answers the question differently. Ruscha, whose design skills are often noted, inverts the lessons of graphic design taught as the grammar of vision. In those books, and in Chouinard's classrooms, it was the foundational, gridded order of vision that determined the place and order of language; words were innocent. In Ruscha's work, it is language that determines and orders—temporally, narratively—the progress of vision. Ruscha didn't paint trademarks for very long; his best known and most effective ones are scenes rather than labels, attached to buildings or set in a landscape, in representational space, however schematic. The problem with the early logo paintings like ANNIE (several paintings in the sixties) or ACTUAL SIZE (1962), which bears the Spam trademark, is that we see them all at once rather than in separate moments or in tension—or rather than either seeing or reading, we only recognize them: the relationship between word and image is given, already designed by some other expert in the language of vision.

Ruscha plays the push and pull of slogans best, I think, in the horizontal paintings of the eighties. Their exaggerated horizontality echoes the directional and temporal extension of language, but their horizontality is also that of vision at its limits: the panorama, as far as the eye can see: the horizon line, the curvature of the earth and the setting sun, over and over again, these are Ruscha's clichés for visual expanse. We read one across the other, narrating lateral distance as temporality, as story and meaning. Distance across the surface, across the time and space of looking, produces the arbitrary, if punctual, randomness of disaster in THREE MURDERS (1981), and the security and seclusion of home in WOLVES, EXPLOSIONS, DISEASE, POISONS—HOME (1980). These stories are schematic, of course, but then, schematically and structurally, all narrative is the traversing of space, the crossing of a frontier we imagine as being temporal. Reading left to right, we read through wolves, disease, and other calamities, ending up at home, at a vanishing point that rests on the side of language and in the space of plot, as narrative outcome or climax. The long form of THERMOMETERS SHOULD LAST FOREVER (1976) leads us somewhere else. The title phrase, hand printed in the same small letters that Ruscha uses in most of the horizontal pictures, is nestled between two low hills in the setting sun, like a cartoon echo perhaps repeated from afar. It reverberates softly from where the sun is setting, from what should be the picture's vanishing point, but reading shifts the space we measure. The print doesn't pull us up to a literal surface against a depicted depth—the task of Cubist script—but changes the vanishing point from the blushing indistinctness of atmospheric perspective to the blankness of meaning, a setting elsewhere.

It is the place of language that structures Ruscha's paintings, rather than any particular phrase, even

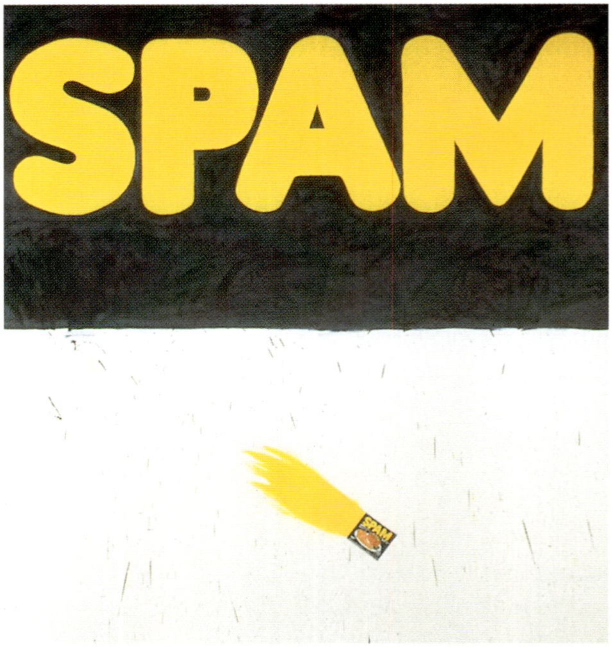

EDWARD RUSCHA, ACTUAL SIZE, 1962, oil on canvas, 72 x 67" / LEBENSGROSS, Öl auf Leinwand, 182,9 x 170,2 cm. (PHOTOS: PAUL RUSCHA)

one as curious as "thermometers should last forever." That is the lesson of the late-eighties silhouette paintings, of a work like DRUGS, HARDWARE, BARBER, VIDEO (1987), with its vertical rank of blank white rectangles, empty shopping center signs. Even in its absence, precisely as absence or displacement, language is Ruscha's figure; it is where we look, but not quite what we look at. Ruscha's writing is a lesion, a blind spot in the picture that constructs the order of vision. It is, to borrow Michael Fried's description of Jackson Pollock's cutouts, "literally where we don't see... a kind of blind spot, a kind of defect in our visual apparatus."[5] This is most curiously the case in those pictures that seem to be only words, simply placards, Ruscha's works on paper of the first half of the seventies. Most are made with powdered pastel, but others are with gunpowder or spinach, onion, lettuce or carrot juice, choices that might not be only idiosyncratic or merely ironic—jokey California conceptualism. His archly and exaggeratedly made surfaces work to secure a continuous visual field, a ground that doesn't disappear under his figures of speech, that isn't made invisible by language—indeed, language, the odd items listed on the gallery wall, is part of what holds the surface together. Against that ground, and from somewhere beneath it, the words in works like THOSE OF US WHO HAVE DOUBLE PARKED (1976) are simply and literally the absence of pigment. They are, again, "literally where we don't see," even if it goes as far as to say that Ruscha's words lie "somewhere within our own eyes." Fried's description might help to recast the problem of these works: The problem of drawing, of figuring, was central to painting after abstract expressionism, as an answer to its clichés. There is, as Frank Stella famously complained, insisting that he did not draw white pinstripes, but painted black paintings, "a distinction between what any artist DOES and what he does NOT do."[6]

Place names have returned quite insistently in Ruscha's most recent works. In the largest of the Metro Plot paintings of 1998, Los Angeles street names march in ranks against an alpine landscape. The word Alvarado in large sans serif type extends nearly the full height of ALVARADO TO DOHENY's right edge; following it as if running east to west, and hanging just off the canvas's top edge above a sharply triangular mountain peak, come the names of the major east-west cross streets of the mid-Wilshire corridor, in regularly decreasing scale: Hoover, Vermont, Western, Rossmore... to La Cienega, Robertson, and Doheny. This is Los Angeles's regularized and motorized landscape, or a curiously and fittingly blank evocation of it, but Ruscha evokes another locale as well: Tomlinson Court Park, a park in Brooklyn, and one of Stella's black paintings of 1959. With the flattening regularity of the type, the obviousness of its repetitions, and the ordered rate of its shrinkage, all rhymed and backstopped by the wall mural image, Ruscha "forces illusionistic space out of the painting at a constant rate"—which is how Stella described what he was after in the black paintings.[7] I could say that allusionistic space is forced out as well, that the paintings are no more about Los Angeles than TOMLINSON COURT PARK is about Bedford-Stuyvesant, but that seems only partly right.

I have come to a place where I could say that Ruscha's paintings are modernist paintings; I've tried to make the case that Ruscha knows and works the lessons and questions of modern painting, and has for a long time. Blankness is, after all, one way to secure a measure of specificity, of autonomy. But in order to state even that, Ruscha's paintings must be non-identical, not quite themselves; in this they are quite unlike Stella's and more like language. Ruscha's paintings need to be about something the way that language is; that is the way they are ordered and timed. And they need to be about somewhere so that they can be pulled from it, emptied out; so we can still feel the hollow. Pictorial illusion and the allusions of place in Ruscha's paintings have always stayed on the surface; beneath them, the hollow echo of language is the space that opens in their stead.

1) Marcel Proust, *Remembrance of Things Past*, vol. 1, trans. C.K. Scott Moncrieff and Terence Kilmartin (New York: Random House, 1981), p. 421. Ruscha's representational images from the mid-sixties—L.A. apartment buildings, birds, bowling balls, pills, etc. are all common nouns, generic and typical—and they are like the mere words Proust contrasts to his moodily colored place names. Words present "a little picture of things, clear and familiar, like pictures hung on the walls of schoolrooms... things chosen as typical of everything else of the same sort."
2) Yves-Alain Bois, *Edward Ruscha: Romance with Liquids, Paintings 1966–1969* (New York: Rizzoli International, in association with Gagosian Gallery, 1993), p. 28.
3) Credit should go to Peter Plagens for raising the issue of Ruscha's blankness, as well as for arguing his serious relationship to modern painting, in "Ed Ruscha, Seriously," in: *The Works of Edward Ruscha* (San Francisco: San Francisco Museum of Modern Art, 1982), pp. 32–40.
4) Rosalind Krauss, *The Originality of the Avant-Garde and Other Modernist Myths* (Cambridge, Mass.: MIT Press, 1986), p. 9.
5) Michael Fried, *Three American Painters* (Cambridge, Mass.: Fogg Art Museum, Harvard University, 1965), p. 17.
6) Frank Stella, in: William S. Rubin, *Frank Stella* (New York: Museum of Modern Art, 1970), p. 18.
7) Ibid., p. 22.

EDWARD RUSCHA, WOLVES, EXPLOSIONS, DISEASE, POISONS—HOME, 1980, oil on canvas, 22 x 80" /
WÖLFE, EXPLOSIONEN, KRANKHEIT, GIFTE – ZUHAUSE, Öl auf Leinwand, 55,9 x 203,2 cm.

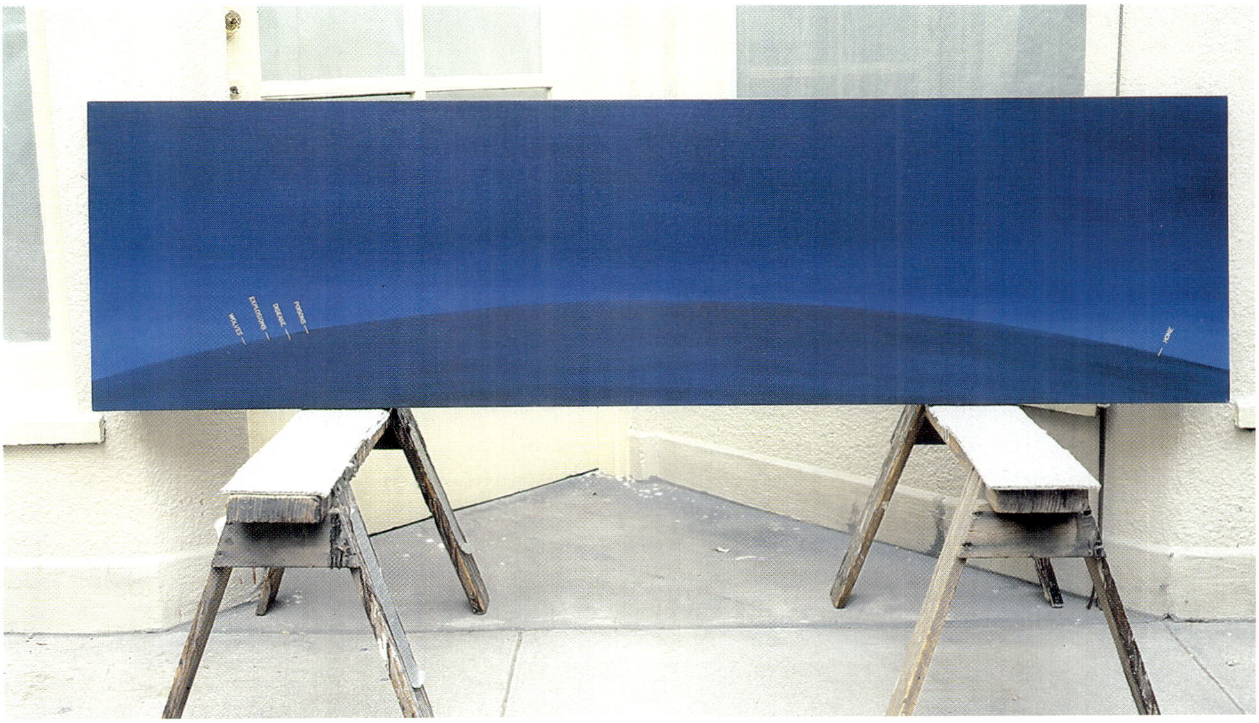

HOWARD SINGERMAN

Die Sprache der Moderne bei Ed Ruscha

Ed Ruschas Interesse für den Stellenwert und die Verwendung der Sprache lag von Anfang an offen zutage, seit dem grossen roten E in der oberen linken Ecke seines merkwürdigen Selbstporträts von 1959; auch beim Lesen beginnt man in dieser Ecke. Das Bild oder wenigstens der Name darauf führt uns von links nach rechts, der unteren Hälfte entlang über die schwarzen Buchstaben R, U, S zu einem roten C. Ein schwarzer Pfeil, der zwischen das C und den rechten Rand des Bildes gedrängt ist, lenkt den Blick entlang dem Bogen des C wieder hinauf zu den Buchstaben A und H. Das Vertauschen dieser beiden Buchstaben und das richtige Buchstabieren von Ruschas Namen ist etwas, was wir zu einem anderen Zeitpunkt tun – oder, falls wir es doch zur gleichen Zeit tun, so an einem anderen Ort. Eigennamen, Namen von Leuten oder Orten, spielen in Ruschas frühen Bildern, anders als heute, eine wichtige Rolle; die meisten Wörter, die Ruscha seit Mitte der 60er Jahre verwendet hat, sind einfache Substantive, auch die Formulierungen sind allgemein gehalten. Aber früher, in SWEETWATER und DUBLIN (beide 1960) oder in BOX SMASHED FLAT (Flach geschlagene Schachtel, 1961), sind die Namen der Orte in den Südstaaten sorgfältig und in einer in der Werbung gängigen Schrift wiedergegeben. «Sweetwater» und «Dublin» – mit nachfolgendem Komma gedruckt um ihre geographische Bedeutung zu unterstreichen (die Kommas schreien förmlich nach der Ergänzung durch den Bundesstaat, Tennessee bzw. Georgia) – sind in einer schönen Schrift mit Serifen gesetzt. Die Namen laufen wie Legenden unter den Bildern oder unter Übergangszonen entlang, die als eigenständige Bilder bestehen könnten: Dichte, langgezogene horizontale Streifen durchqueren den oberen Teil von SWEETWATER; eine von Hand gemalte Popversion einer früheren Holz- und Zeitungscollage befindet sich in der Mitte von DUBLIN. «Vicksburg» steht unter der plattgedrückten, handbemalten Rosinenschachtel, die BOX SMASHED FLAT seinen Namen gab; es ist in einem dynamischeren Schrifttypus wiedergegeben, einem dreidimensionalen, schattierten Stil, dessen frischer, poppiger Eindruck jedoch durch die Farbe gedämpft wird, die Ruscha darüber gewischt hat.

Vielleicht lag das Problem von Orten wie Vicksburg und Sweetwater darin, dass sie zu persönlich waren, zu sehr von einem Anderswo handelten um schön stillzuhalten, wo Ruscha sie haben wollte. Wie die Bilder, die sie begleiteten, waren die Namen zu malerisch, zu sehr erfüllt von einer «Sehnsucht, welche ihnen die Orte eingaben, für die sie standen». Marcel Proust schrieb über Ortsnamen und die ihnen innewohnende Differenz in einer der Malerei entliehenen Sprache: Gegenüber der entschiedenen Deutlichkeit anderer Wörter, lieferten Ortsnamen «ein unbestimmteres Bild, das sich aus ihrem lebhaften oder dumpfen Klang in einer Tönung färbt, in der es dann durchweg gehalten ist...».[1] Man könnte Prousts dämmriges Farbfeld, das aus dem Spiel zwischen Licht und Dunkel hervorgeht, etwas stra-

HOWARD SINGERMAN lehrt Kunstgeschichte an der University of Virginia und ist Autor des Buches *Art Subjects: Making Artists in the American University* (University of California Press, Berkeley 1999).

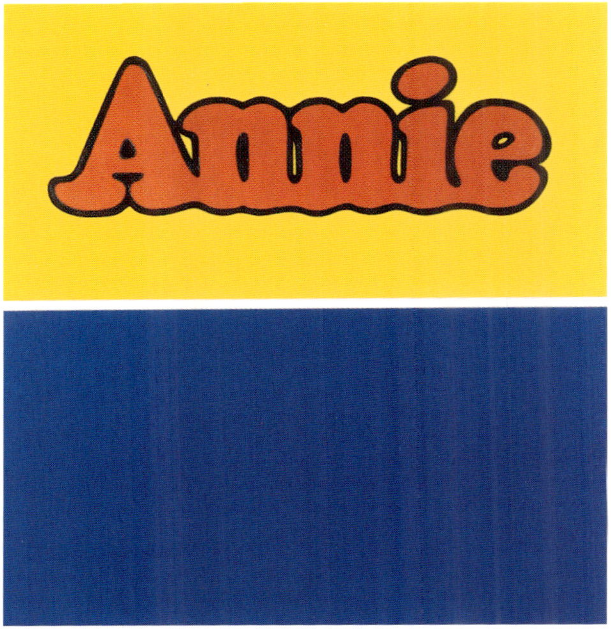

EDWARD RUSCHA, ANNIE, 1962,
oil on canvas, 67 x 72" / Öl auf Leinwand, 170,2 x 182,9 cm.
(PHOTO: PAUL RUSCHA)

pazieren um damit Ruschas eigenes Farbfeld in jenen frühen Bildern zu beschreiben, das gestische Clairobscur von E. RUSCHA, die betont herausgearbeiteten, abstrakt expressionistischen Balken in SWEETWATER. Aber E. RUSCHA und SWEETWATER sind verspätete Nachzügler; wie Yves-Alain Bois in einer der stärksten Interpretationen von Ruschas Werk überhaupt über den Künstler schreibt, «um 1960 war der Abstrakte Expressionismus bereits ein Klischee... ja, das *push-and-pull* war zum Slogan verkommen.»[2] Bois beschrieb Ruschas kunsthistorisches Problem mit denselben Begriffen, in denen der Künstler es dann auch anging, mit genau jener Sprache, die dieser schliesslich an die Stelle der Eigennamen setzte. Ich nehme an, Bois hat Ruscha seine Formel ganz bewusst zugesteckt. Ab Mitte der 60er Jahre wird Ruscha die platte, prosaische Sprache der Klischees und Slogans als Mittel zur Bildorganisation einsetzen oder, da wir von Sprache reden, als Mittel zur Artikulation. Bei seinem *push-and-pull* geht es nicht mehr um die Differenz zwischen Oberflächengestaltung und malerischer Tiefenwirkung, Illusion und Realität beziehungsweise um die alte Formel für die Spannungen der Bildfläche. Es geht vielmehr um die Differenz zwischen der Sprache, der Zeit des Schreibens und dem Raum des Sehens. Und es erzeugt nicht den Eindruck des Gespanntseins oder der atmenden Flachheit der modernen Bildebene, sondern Ausdruckslosigkeit, ein Begriff, der beides einschliesst: Bild und Sprache, Blicke und Dichtung.[3]

Eine Reihe von Theoretikern haben die Differenz von Bild und Sprache beschrieben, die Kluft, mit der Ruscha spielt, und haben deren Bedeutung für die Idee der modernen Malerei betont. Da ist, um ein bekanntes Beispiel zu nennen, Rosalind Krauss' Aussage, dass das sich überall gleichende Grundmuster der Moderne ein Sinnbild sei für die Absicht der modernen Kunst zu schweigen und für ihre Ablehnung von Literatur, Narration und Diskurs,[4] gerade wenn es das Grundvokabular einer «Sprache des Sehens» hervorbringt oder eine «Grammatik der Kunst», um nur einige Titel von Büchern zu nennen, die in der Ausbildung junger Künstler in Ruschas Generation eine Rolle spielten. Ruscha hat eindeutig und von allem Anfang an (seit der oberen linken Ecke von E. RUSCHA) die diesem Muster entsprechende, absolute Ablösung verweigert, dieses so Tun, als ob es ein Sehen vor oder jenseits der Sprache gäbe, ein Sehen in Unschuld oder Transzendenz. Früh hat er verstanden, worüber die Kritiker der Moderne seither gestritten haben, dass es die Sprache ist, die das Gesichtsfeld und die Idee der Malerei strukturiert und ausmisst. Ruscha ist nach wie vor und ganz offensichtlich ein Maler, ich würde sogar sagen eine Art moderner Maler – und es ist die Sprache, die Gerichtetheit und Zeitlichkeit des Lesens als erkennbare Tätigkeit, eine eigene Zeit innerhalb der Bilder, welche ihm erlaubt dies zu sein. Die Sprache beantwortet die Frage der Komposition, eine Frage, die Ruscha, anders als die meisten post-abstrakt-expressionistischen Maler, ernst nimmt, aber die Sprache beantwortet diese Frage auf andere Art. Ruscha, dessen gestalterische Fähigkeiten oft hervorgehoben werden, verkehrt die Lehren der graphischen Gestaltung, wie sie als Grammatik des Sehens verkündet

EDWARD RUSCHA, *ALVARADO TO DOHENY*, 1998, *acrylic on canvas*, 70 x 80" /
ALVARADO BIS DOHENY, *Acryl auf Leinwand*, 177,8 x 274,3 cm. (PHOTO: PAUL RUSCHA)

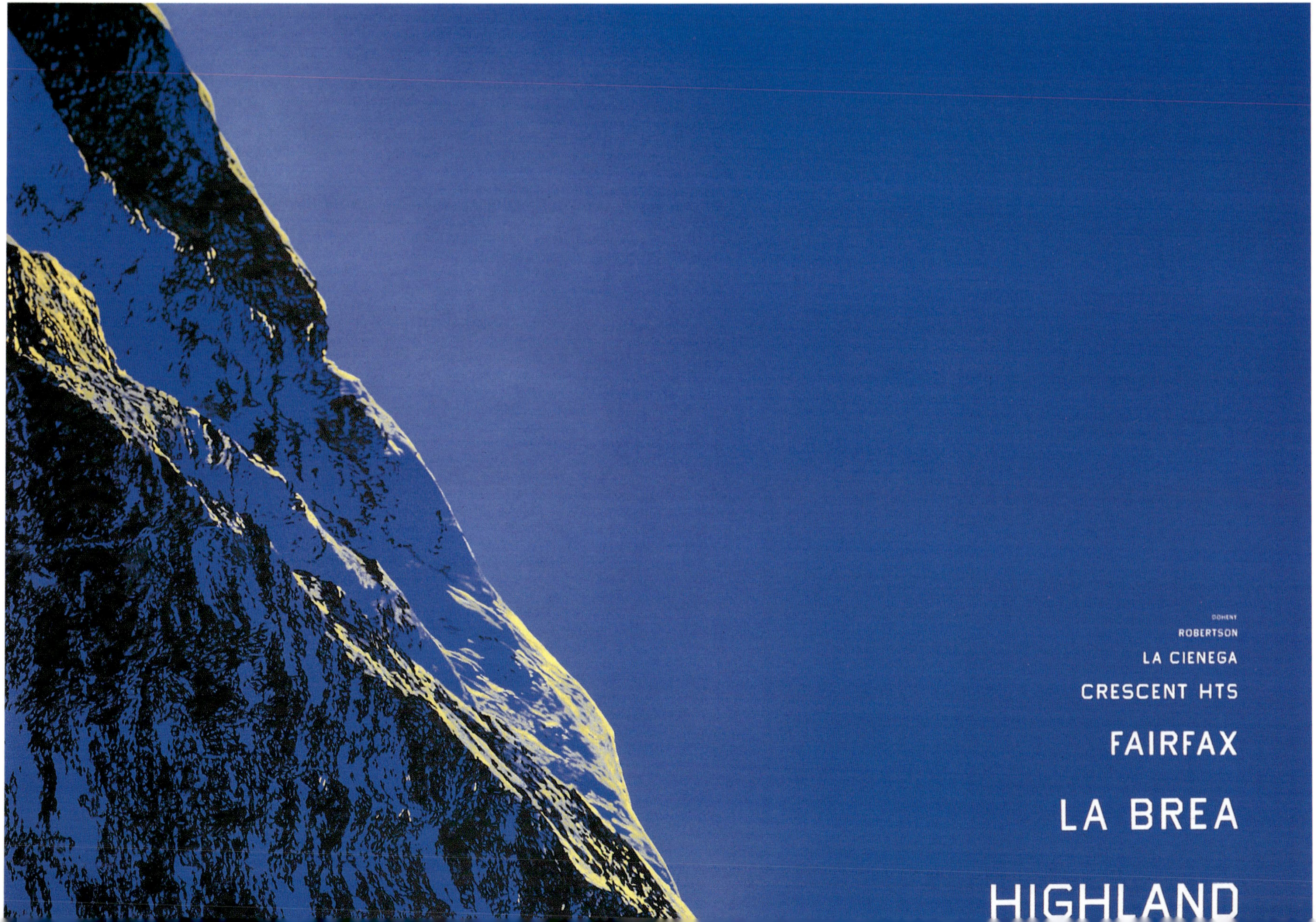

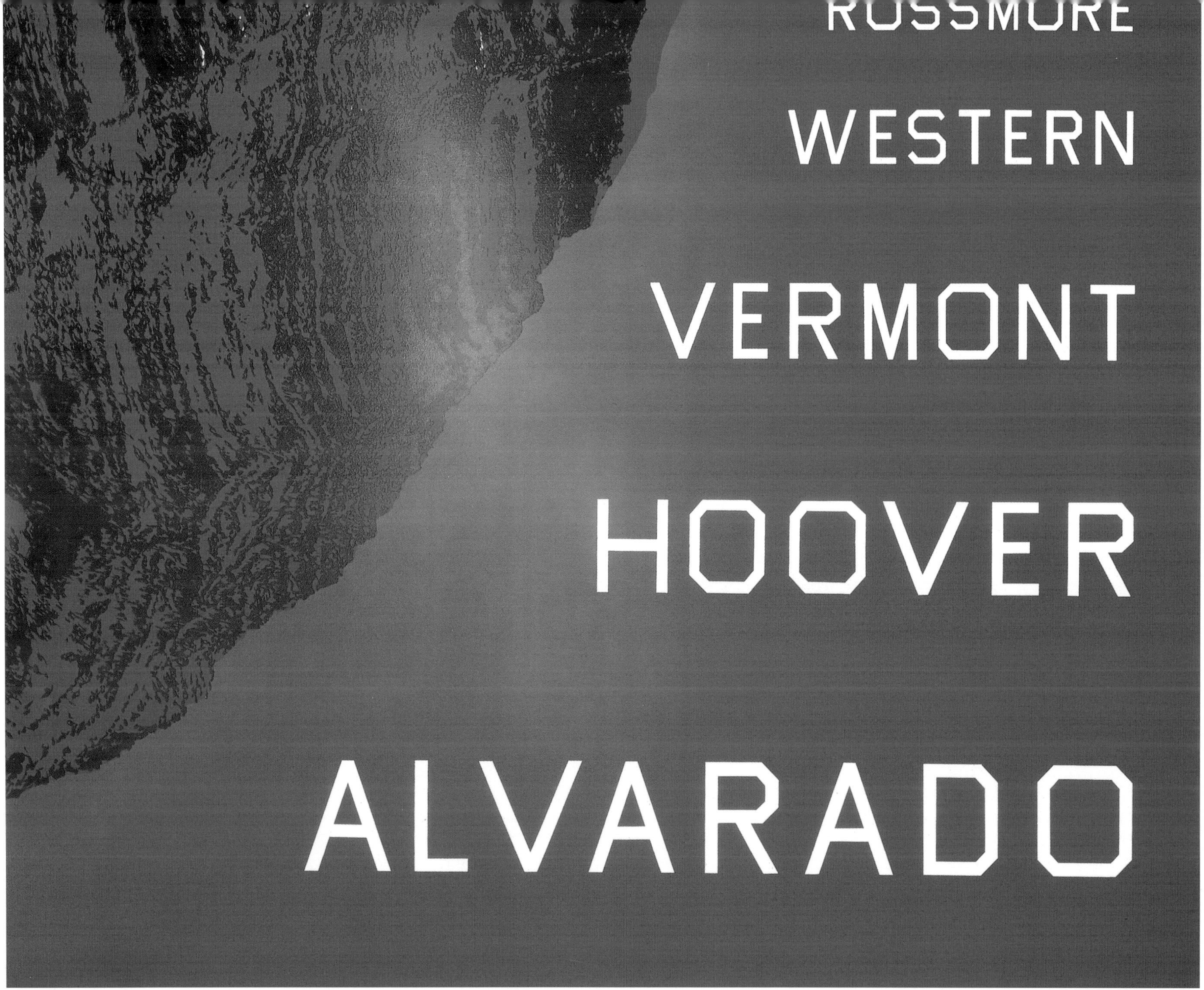
WESTERN
VERMONT
HOOVER
ALVARADO

wurden, in ihr Gegenteil. In jenen Büchern und in Chouinards Klassenzimmern war es die dem Grundraster entsprechende Sehweise, welche Ort und Ordnung der Sprache bestimmte; Wörter waren unschuldig. In Ruschas Werk ist es die Sprache, welche dem Sehen die Richtung weist und ihm eine zeitliche und narrative Ordnung verleiht. Ruscha hat nur für kurze Zeit Markenprodukte gemalt; die besten und wirkungsvollsten glichen dabei eher Szenen als Etiketten, die einem Gebäude oder einer Landschaft, einem, egal wie schematisch, in jedem Fall repräsentativen Ort oder Raum zugeordnet wurden. Die Schwierigkeit mit den frühen Logo-Bildern wie ANNIE (mehrere Bilder aus den 60er Jahren) oder ACTUAL SIZE (1962), welches einen tatsächlichen Markennamen («Spam», ein bekanntes Büchsenfleisch) zeigt, ist, dass wir sie meist alle zusammen sehen, statt einzeln zu verschiedenen Zeitpunkten und in verschiedenen Situationen – oder aber wir sehen und lesen sie weniger, als dass wir sie wiedererkennen: Die Beziehung zwischen Wort und Bild ist vorgegeben, wurde bereits von einem anderen Experten in Sachen Bildsprache festgelegt.

Das Spiel mit der Ambivalenz der Slogans (jenes *push-and-pull*) gelingt Ruscha, glaube ich, am besten in den horizontalen Bildern der 80er Jahre. Ihre übertriebene horizontale Ausdehnung widerspiegelt die richtungweisende und zeitliche Ausdehnung der Sprache, aber diese Dehnung ist auch eine des Sehens, das umfassende Panorama, so weit eben das Auge reicht: die Horizontlinie, die Erdkrümmung, die untergehende Sonne, immer und immer wieder dienen sie Ruscha als Klischee für die Weite des Sehens, des sichtbaren Raums. Wir lesen das eine durch das andere hindurch, entziffern räumliche Entfernung als Zeitlichkeit, verstehen sie als Erzählung und Bedeutung. Die Entfernung auf der Oberfläche, durch Zeit und Raum des Sehens hindurch, erzeugt, wenn auch nur punktuell, die willkürliche Zufälligkeit der Katastrophe in THREE MURDERS (Drei Morde, 1981) und das Geborgene und Private des Zuhause in WOLVES, EXPLOSIONS, DISEASE, POISONS—HOME (Wölfe, Explosionen, Krankheit, Gifte – Zuhause, 1980). Diese Geschichten sind natürlich nur Schemen, aber trotzdem bewegt sich jede Erzählung, schematisch und ihrer Struktur nach, im Raum und überschreitet eine Grenze, die wir uns als zeitliche vorstellen. Wenn wir von links nach rechts lesen, lesen wir von Wölfen, von Krankheit und anderem Unheil und enden beim Zuhause, einem Fluchtpunkt, der neben der Sprache und im Bereich der Handlung liegt, ein erzählerischer End- oder Höhepunkt. Die langgezogene Form von THERMOMETERS SHOULD LAST FOREVER (Thermometer sollten ewig halten, 1976) führt uns woandershin. Der Satz, der dem Bild den Titel gibt – von Hand gedruckt in denselben kleinen Buchstaben, die Ruscha in den meisten dieser horizontalen Bilder verwendet –, schmiegt sich zwischen zwei flache Hügel im Sonnenuntergang, ähnlich dem weit weg widertönenden Echo in einem Cartoon vielleicht. Es widerhallt leise aus dem Sonnenuntergang heraus, von dort, wo eigentlich der Fluchtpunkt des Bildes liegen sollte, aber das Lesen verschiebt den Raum, in dem wir uns bewe-

EDWARD RUSCHA, THERMOMETERS SHOULD LAST FOREVER, 1977, oil on canvas, 22 x 80" / THERMOMETER SOLLTEN EWIG HALTEN, Öl auf Leinwand, 55,9 x 203,2 cm.

EDWARD RUSCHA, DRUGS, HARDWARE, BARBER, VIDEO, 1987,
acrylic on canvas, 72 x 72" /
DROGEN, HARDWARE, BARBIER, VIDEO,
Acryl auf Leinwand, 182,9 x 182,9 cm.
(PHOTO: PAUL RUSCHA)

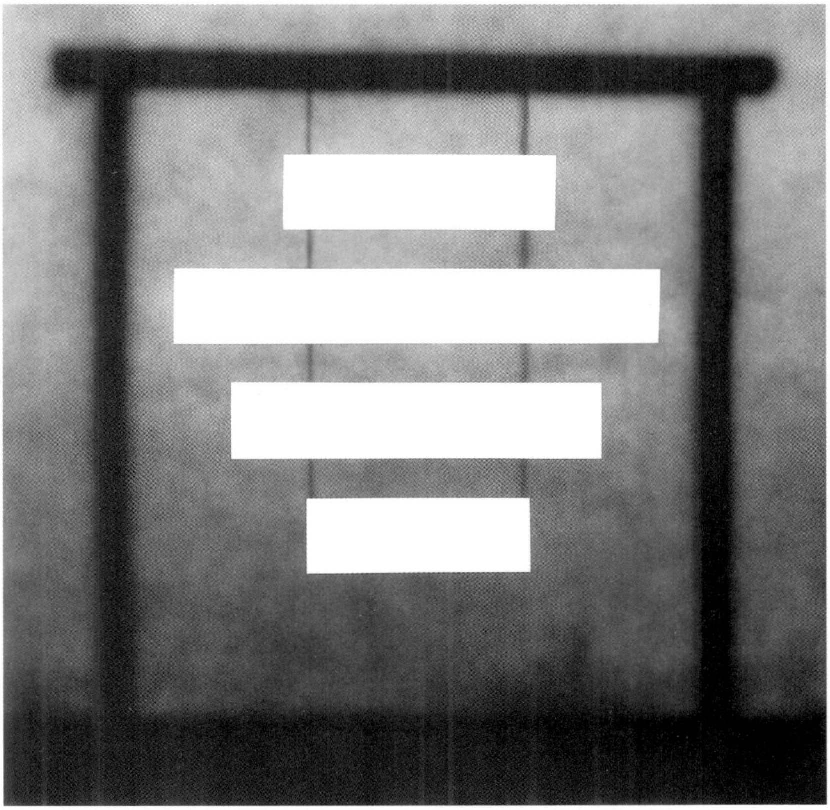

gen. Die gedruckten Lettern versetzen uns nicht auf die buchstäbliche Oberfläche gegenüber der abgebildeten Raumtiefe – was die Aufgabe der Schrift im Kubismus war –, sondern verschieben den Fluchtpunkt auf uns, weg von der rötlichen Unbestimmtheit der atmosphärischen Perspektive auf die blanke Leere der Bedeutung, einen Untergang an einem anderen Ort.

Es ist die Platzierung der Worte, die die Struktur von Ruschas Bildern bestimmt, mehr als irgendein besonderer Ausdruck, und sei er so merkwürdig wie «Thermometers should last forever». Das ist die Lektion, die uns die Silhouetten-Bilder der späten 80er Jahre erteilen, etwa ein Werk wie DRUGS, HARDWARE, BARBER, VIDEO (Drogen, Hardware, Barbier, Video, 1987) mit seiner vertikalen Reihe weisser Rechtecke, leeren Schildern von Einkaufszentren. Selbst wo sie abwesend ist, ja gerade in ihrer Abwesenheit oder ausserhalb des gewohnten Kontextes, setzt Ruscha auf die Sprache; sie ist, worauf sich der Blick richtet, aber nicht wirklich, was wir anschauen. Ruschas Schriftzüge sind Verletzungen oder Schrammen, blinde Flecke im Bild, die ihm seine visuelle Struktur verleihen. Die Sprache ist (um einen Ausdruck von Michael Fried für Jackson Pollocks *cutouts* zu verwenden), «buchstäblich dort, wo wir nicht sehen… eine Art blinder Fleck oder ein Defekt unseres Sehapparates».[5] Das trifft auf merkwürdigste Weise auf all jene Bilder zu, die nur aus Wörtern bestehen, die nichts als gemalte Schilder zu sein scheinen, wie Ruschas Arbeiten auf Papier der ersten Hälfte der 70er Jahre. Die meisten sind in reinem Pastell, manche aber sind mit Schiesspulver oder Spinat, mit Zwiebel-, Lattich- oder Karottensaft gemalt, Materialien, deren Wahl vielleicht mehr als nur eine exzentrische oder ironisch-scherzhafte Spielart kalifornischer Konzeptkunst ist. Seine irritierend und übertrieben ausgearbeiteten Oberflächen sorgen für die Kontinuität des Blickfelds, sie schaffen einen Grund, der hinter den Redewendungen nicht einfach verschwindet, der nicht ausgelöscht wird von der Sprache – die Sprache, diese seltsamen an den Wänden der Galerie aufgelisteten Dinge, ist es zum Teil gerade, was die Oberfläche zusammenhält. Auf diesem Grund und von einem Ort stammend, der dahinter liegt, bestehen die Wörter in Werken wie THOSE OF US WHO HAVE DOUBLE PARKED (Jene unter uns, die in zweiter Reihe geparkt haben) buchstäblich einfach aus der Abwesenheit von Farbpigment. Wiederum sind sie «buchstäblich dort, wo wir nicht sehen», obwohl es hier übertrieben wäre, zu sagen, dass Ruschas Worte «irgendwo in unseren eigenen Augen» lägen. Frieds Beschreibung könnte uns dabei helfen, die Problematik dieser Arbeiten zu verstehen: Das Problem des Zeichnens und Darstellens war für die Malerei nach dem Abstrakten Expressionismus zentral als Reaktion auf dessen Klischees. Es gibt laut Frank Stellas berühmter Klage, als er darauf bestand, dass er nicht weisse Nadelstreifen gezeichnet, sondern schwarze Bilder gemalt habe, «einen Unterschied zwischen dem, was ein Künstler TUT, und dem, was er NICHT tut».[6)]

In Ruschas jüngsten Arbeiten tauchen Ortsbezeichnungen mit einiger Regelmässigkeit wieder auf. Im grössten der Metro-Plot-Bilder von 1998 nehmen Strassennamen von Los Angeles gleich reihenweise Aufstellung vor einer Berglandschaft. Das Wort «Alvarado» in grosser serifenloser Schrift nimmt vertikal fast die ganze Höhe von ALVARADO TO DOHENY's rechtem Bildrand ein; als liefen sie von Osten nach Westen, und vom oberen Leinwandrand über einem spitzen, dreieckigen Berggipfel herunterhängend folgen direkt anschliessend die Namen der wichtigeren Ostwest-Querstrassen durch den Mid-Wilshire-Korridor, und zwar in regelmässig abnehmender Grösse: Hoover, Vermont, Western, Rossmore ... bis zu La Cienega, Robertson und Doheny. Das ist die reglementierte, autogerechte Landschaft von Los Angeles oder zumindest eine merkwürdig exakte, entleerte Wiedergabe davon, aber Ruscha beschwört noch eine ganz andere Örtlichkeit herauf: Tomlinson Court Park, ein Park in Brooklyn, und was noch wichtiger ist, eines von Stellas schwarzen Bildern von 1959. Mit der flach wirkenden Regelmässigkeit der Lettern, der Offensichtlichkeit ihrer wiederholten Aufeinanderfolge und ihrem allmählichen Kleinerwerden, unterstützt durch den Wandbildcharakter des Ganzen, vertreibt Ruscha «systematisch den illusionistischen Raum aus dem Bild». – So beschrieb Stella, worum es ihm in seinen schwarzen Bildern ging.[7)] Man könnte sogar sagen, dass er auch den «allusionistischen» Raum (den Raum der Anspielung, den Referenzraum) aus dem Bild treibt, da die Bilder so wenig von Los Angeles handeln wie TOMLINSON COURT PARK von Bedford-Stuyvesant, aber das scheint nur zum Teil zuzutreffen.

Ich bin an einen Punkt gelangt, wo ich schreiben könnte, dass Ruschas Bilder zur Moderne gehören; ich habe versucht darzulegen, dass Ruscha die Lektion und die Fragen der modernen Malerei gelernt hat und kennt, und das schon seit geraumer Zeit. Die Auslassung ist letztlich ein mögliches Mittel um ein gewisses Mass an Genauigkeit und Autonomie zu bewahren. Aber nur schon um diese Möglichkeit zu erhalten müssen Ruschas Bilder nicht-identisch sein, dürfen nicht ganz sich selbst sein; in dieser Hinsicht sind sie ganz anders als Stellas Bilder und sind näher bei der Sprache. Ruschas Bilder müssen von etwas handeln, wie Sprache von etwas spricht; so ist ihre Struktur und ihre Zeitlichkeit beschaffen. Und sie müssen von einem Ort handeln, damit man sie davon wegziehen, entleeren kann, so dass der Hohlraum spürbar wird. Die malerische Illusion und die geographischen «Allusionen» in Ruschas Bildern bleiben immer der Oberfläche verhaftet; hinter ihnen eröffnet das hohle Echo der Sprache den Raum, um den es wirklich geht.

(Übersetzung: Susanne Schmidt)

1) Marcel Proust, *Auf der Suche nach der verlorenen Zeit*, Bd. 1, übers. v. Eva Rechel-Mertens, Suhrkamp, Frankfurt am Main 1979, S. 513. Ruschas repräsentative Bilder ab Mitte der 60er Jahre – Apartmenthäuser in Los Angeles, Vögel, Bowling-Kugeln, Pillen – entsprechen alle einfachen Substantiven, Gattungen oder Typen, und damit exakt jenen Wörtern, die Proust seinen stimmungsgefärbten Ortsbezeichnungen gegenüberstellt. «Die Wörter führen uns von den Dingen ein kleines, deutliches, landläufiges Bild vor Augen, wie man sie an die Wände eines Schulzimmers hängt, um den Kindern zu zeigen, was eine Hobelbank, ein Vogel, ein Ameisenhaufen ist, und zwar in einer Gestalt, die allen der gleichen Art gleichmässig nahe kommt.» Ebenda, S. 512–513.

2) Yves-Alain Bois, *Edward Ruscha: Romance with Liquids, Paintings 1966–1969, with a Conversation between Edward Hopps and Edward Ruscha*, Rizzoli & Gagosian Gallery, New York 1993, S. 28.

3) An dieser Stelle möchte ich auf Peter Plagens verweisen, der Ruschas «Blankness» zur Sprache gebracht und auch dessen sehr ernsthafte Beziehung zur Malerei der Moderne erörtert hat, vgl. dazu «Ed Ruscha, Seriously», in: *The Works of Edward Ruscha*, San Francisco Museum of Modern Art 1982, S. 32–40.

4) Rosalind Krauss, *Die Originalität der Avantgarde und andere Mythen der Moderne*, Herta Wolf (Hrsg.), übers. v. J. Heininger, Verlag der Kunst, Amsterdam und Dresden 1997.

5) Michael Fried, *Three American Painters,* Fogg Art Museum/Harvard University, Cambridge, Mass., 1965, S. 17.

6) Stella in: William S. Rubin, *Frank Stella*, Museum of Modern Art, New York 1970, S. 18.

7) Ebenda, S. 22.

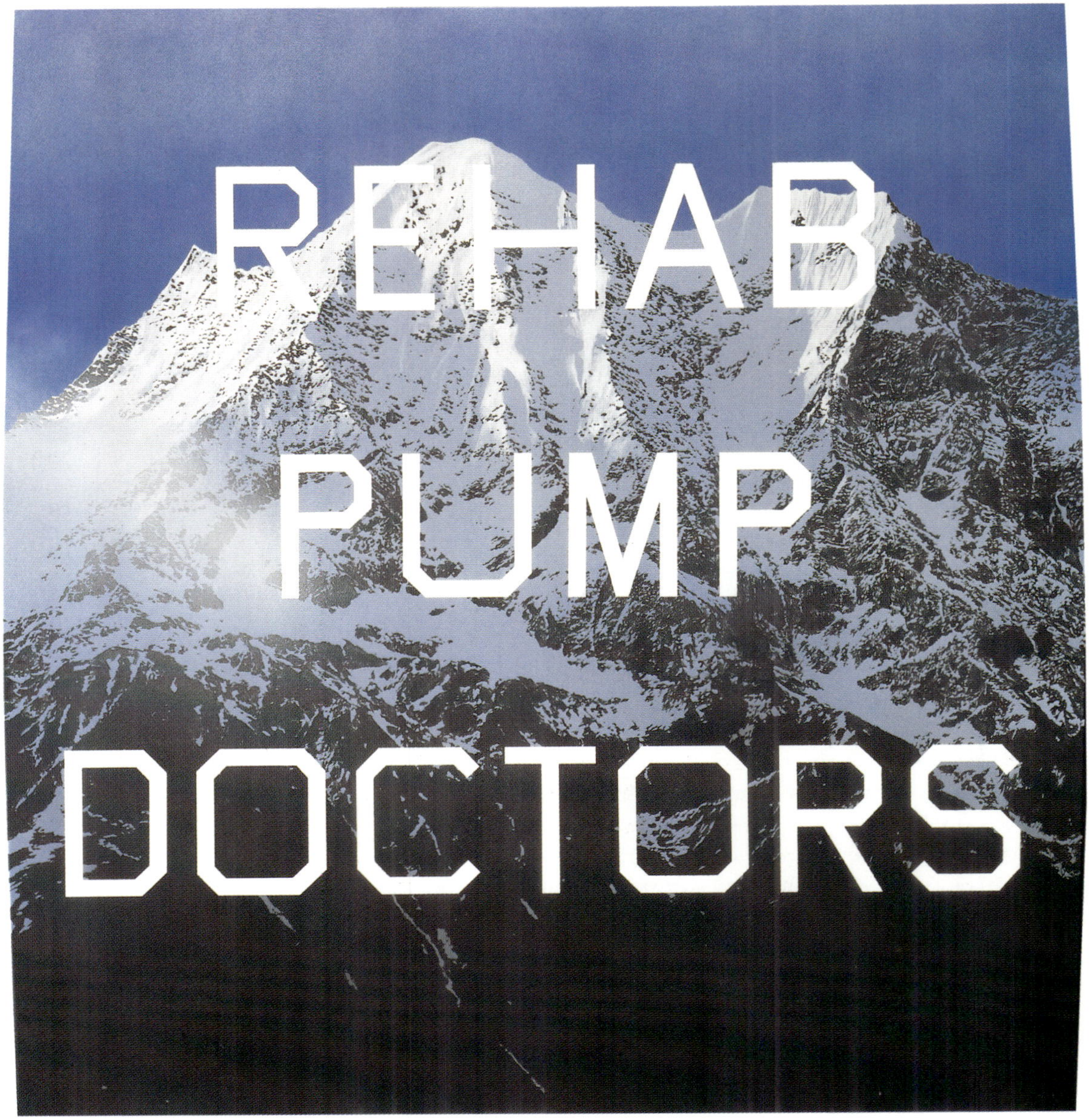

EDWARD RUSCHA, REHAB PUMP DOCTORS, 1998, acrylic on canvas, 76 x 72" /
REHA HERZ-SPEZIALISTEN, Acryl auf Leinwand, 193 x 183 cm. (PHOTO: ANTHONY D'OFFAY GALLERY, LONDON)

KATJA SCHENKER

SCHNEEBLIND

1998 malt Ruscha grossformatige Bergbilder: SWOLLEN TUNE steht in weissen Lettern auf einem schattigen Fels, obwohl es eher still sein müsste in der Abgeschiedenheit. Angeschwollen sind die Bilder. Auf zwei oder vier Seiten wölbt sich das Chassis, als ob die Gesteinsmassen die Bildfläche sprengten. Durch die angedeutete Plastizität wirken sie mächtiger, monumental. Ein Berg ist ein Wahrzeichen und in den meisten Fällen von weit her sichtbar. Ein anderes Bild zeigt einen tief verschneiten Gipfel. Ein steil abfallender Hang wird von der Sonne beschienen. Ich werde geblendet, erblicke Schatten gegenüberliegender Berge und kleiner Erhebungen und am Grat die Verwehungen, Eiszacken, die im Licht transparent leuchten. Der gut sichtbare Berg wird durch das Eis, das unsichtbare, bedeckt.

In der Mitte des Bildes steht mit Grossbuchstaben IS. Die Schrift erscheint auf der Malerei. Sie wurde hinzugefügt – als eine Art Bestätigung. IS sagt, dass etwas existiert. Im Bild sind es die Schriftzeichen, der Berg, die Schatten, Schnee und Eis. Das geschriebene Wort garantiert die Präsenz dessen, was das Bild zwar zeigt, was aber schwer darstellbar beziehungsweise sichtbar ist: wie etwas Verborgenes oder Transparentes. Die Schrift versichert, dass der Berg ist, der Schnee ist, das Eis ist. Die Buchstaben sind nicht zu übersehen: ein gerader Strich und die S-Form, die jedoch nicht rund erscheint, sondern Ecken und Kanten der Felsen imitiert. Beim Buchstabieren höre ich AI ES – ICE ist in IS mitgemeint, verborgen, aber hörbar. Die Schriftzeichen können mehrere Bedeutungen annehmen. Sie sprechen von Existenz, Präsenz und tönen gleichzeitig das Gegenteil an. Denn Eis ist in doppelter Hinsicht ungewiss: als etwas Durchsichtiges, nahezu Unsichtbares und weil es schmilzt. Eis ist vergänglich. Unter der starken Sonneneinstrahlung wird es nicht lange bestehen. Das Dasein von Eis ist gefährdet. Die Existenz, welche die dritte Person Singular von sein, *to be*, garantiert, wird dadurch, dass in denselben Schriftzeichen auch ICE mitklingt und an das Vergängliche, nicht Sichtbare erinnert, verunsichert. Das Wort stellt sich durch seine Mehrdeutigkeit selber in Frage.

Wenn ich genau hinschaue, stelle ich fest, dass die Buchstaben I und S nicht satt dunkelbraun auf das Bild gemalt wurden. Ruscha hat die Farbe transparent aufgetragen. Die Zeichen sind durchsichtig. Durch sie hindurch sehe ich die Berglandschaft, den Schnee. Was die Doppeldeutigkeit des Geschriebenen, aber auch das Bild des zugeschneiten Berges zum Ausdruck bringen: die Gefährdung dessen, was ist, widerfährt den Zeichen. Sie sind als durchscheinende präsent. Die Ambivalenz von Sein und Vergehen, von sichtbar – unsichtbar wird am Wort optisch erfahrbar.

Es geht um das Sehen. Ich bleibe als Betrachterin draussen. Ein dunkler Felsvorsprung versperrt mir den Zugang zum Bild. Aus der Entfernung schaue ich auf die Bergspitze. Kein Mensch hat je diese Landschaft betreten. Es sind keine menschlichen Spuren vorhanden. Ich sehe ein Bild: Kreissegmente in allen Ecken, zwei blaue oben, unten dunkle, dazwischen eine Kreuzform und Farbe, die schräg über die Leinwand rinnt. Ruscha schafft eine fast geometrische Komposition mit dem deutlichen Bezug auf die Malerei. Vor der 2 x 2 Meter grossen Leinwand stehend – Weiss hüllt mich ein. Die Augen verlieren sich in der leeren Mitte, erblinden; die Schrift holt sie an die Bildoberfläche. Ich erfahre die Beziehung von IS – ICE – EYES.

KATJA SCHENKER hat Kunstgeschichte und Komparatistik studiert. Sie schreibt und lebt in Zürich.

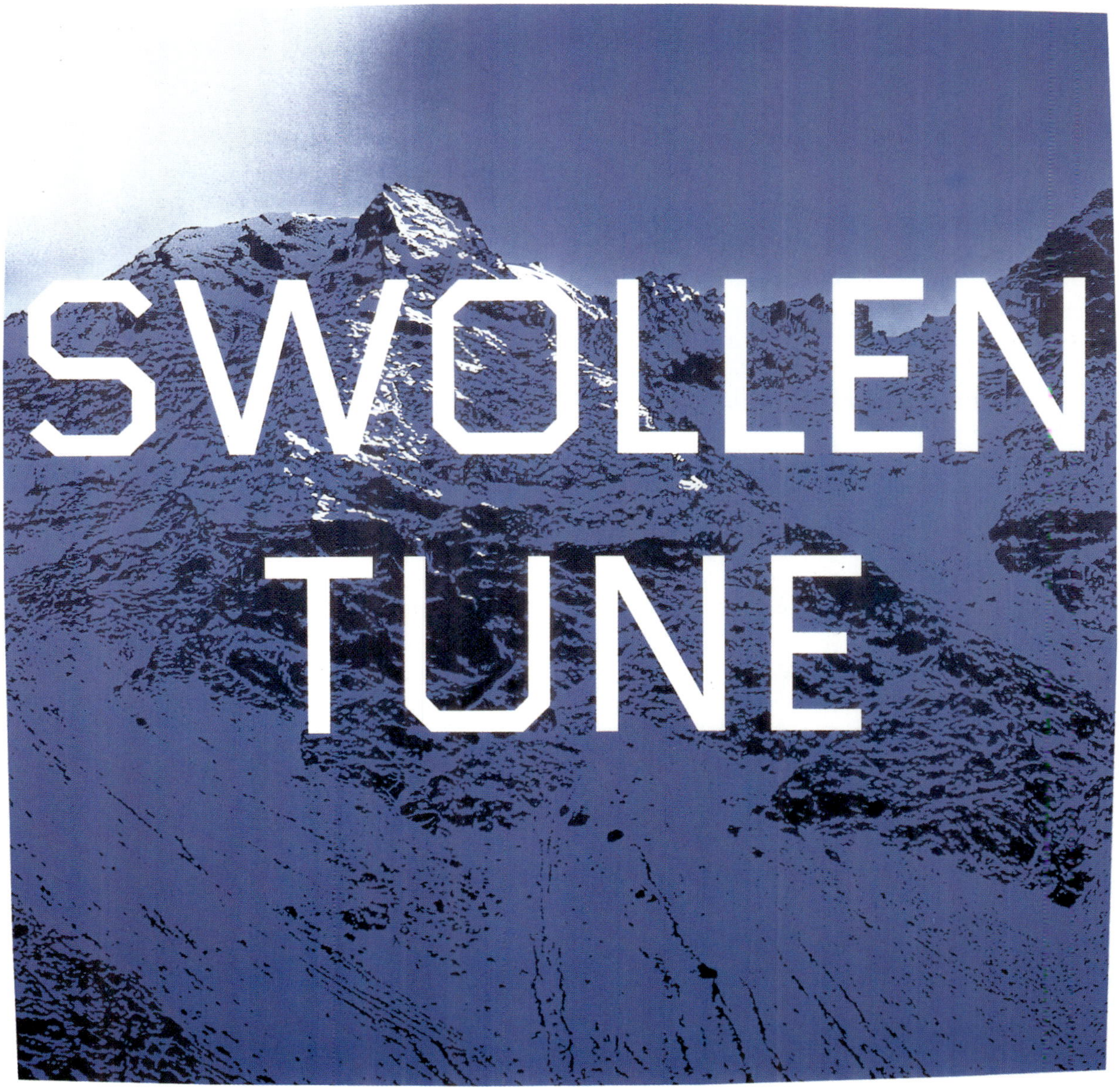

*EDWARD RUSCHA, SWOLLEN TUNE, 1997, acrylic on canvas, 77½ x 77½" /
GESCHWOLLENE MELODIE, Acryl auf Leinwand, 196,9 x 196,9 cm.* (PHOTO: PAUL RUSCHA)

KATJA SCHENKER

WHITE-OUT

In 1998, Ruscha painted large-format mountains: white lettering on a shadowy cliff reads SWOLLEN TUNE although actually it must be silent in the solitude. The pictures swell; the frame spreads as if the masses of stone had exploded the picture plane. The indication of volume makes them mightier, more monumental. A mountain is a landmark and, in most cases, visible from afar. Another painting shows a snow-covered peak. A steeply inclined slope shines in the sunlight. I am blinded. I catch sight of shadows on the mountains opposite, of small rises, snowdrifts on the ridge, and jagged points of ice sparkling transparent in the light. The clearly visible mountain is covered with invisible ice.

In the middle of the picture, two huge letters: I-S. The lettering has been superimposed on the painting. Added—as a kind of confirmation. IS says that something exists: the letters, the mountain, the shadows, the snow, the ice. The written word ensures the presence of what the picture shows, though it is hard to represent, hard to see, like something concealed or transparent. The lettering guarantees that the mountain is, the snow is, the ice is. The letters cannot be ignored: a vertical straight line and an S-shape, not rounded but imitating the jagged angularity of the cliffs. Spelling it out, I hear I-ESS. ICE is incorporated, hidden, but audible in IS. The letters assume several meanings. They bespeak existence and presence and their opposites at once, because ice is uncertain in two respects. It is transparent, almost invisible and it melts. It cannot long endure the powerful rays of the sun. Its existence is endangered. Existence guaranteed by the third person singular of "to be" wavers because ICE reverberates in the same letters, recalling things that are transient and not visible. The word undermines itself through its own ambiguity.

On looking more closely, I realize that the letters I and S have not been painted a saturated dark brown. They are transparent signs. The landscape, the snow, shines through them. The ambiguity of the written word and the picture of the snow-covered mountain reveal that the threat to what is also affects the signs. They are present as translucent beings. The ambivalence of being and passing away, of visible and invisible becomes an optical experience.

It is a question of sight. As a viewer, I remain outside. A darkly protruding boulder blocks my access to the picture. I look at the mountain peaks from a distance. No human being has ever set foot in this landscape. There are no human traces. I see a picture: circular segments in all of the corners, two blue ones at the top and dark ones below, a cruciform shape in between and paint that runs diagonally across the canvas. Ruscha has created an almost geometrical composition with unmistakable reference to painting. Standing in front of the canvas, six and a half feet square, I am immersed in white. My eyes, lost in the central void, become blind; the lettering draws them to the surface. I experience the relationship of IS—ICE—EYES.

(Translation: Catherine Schelbert)

KATJA SCHENKER has studied art history and comparative literature. She writes and lives in Zurich.

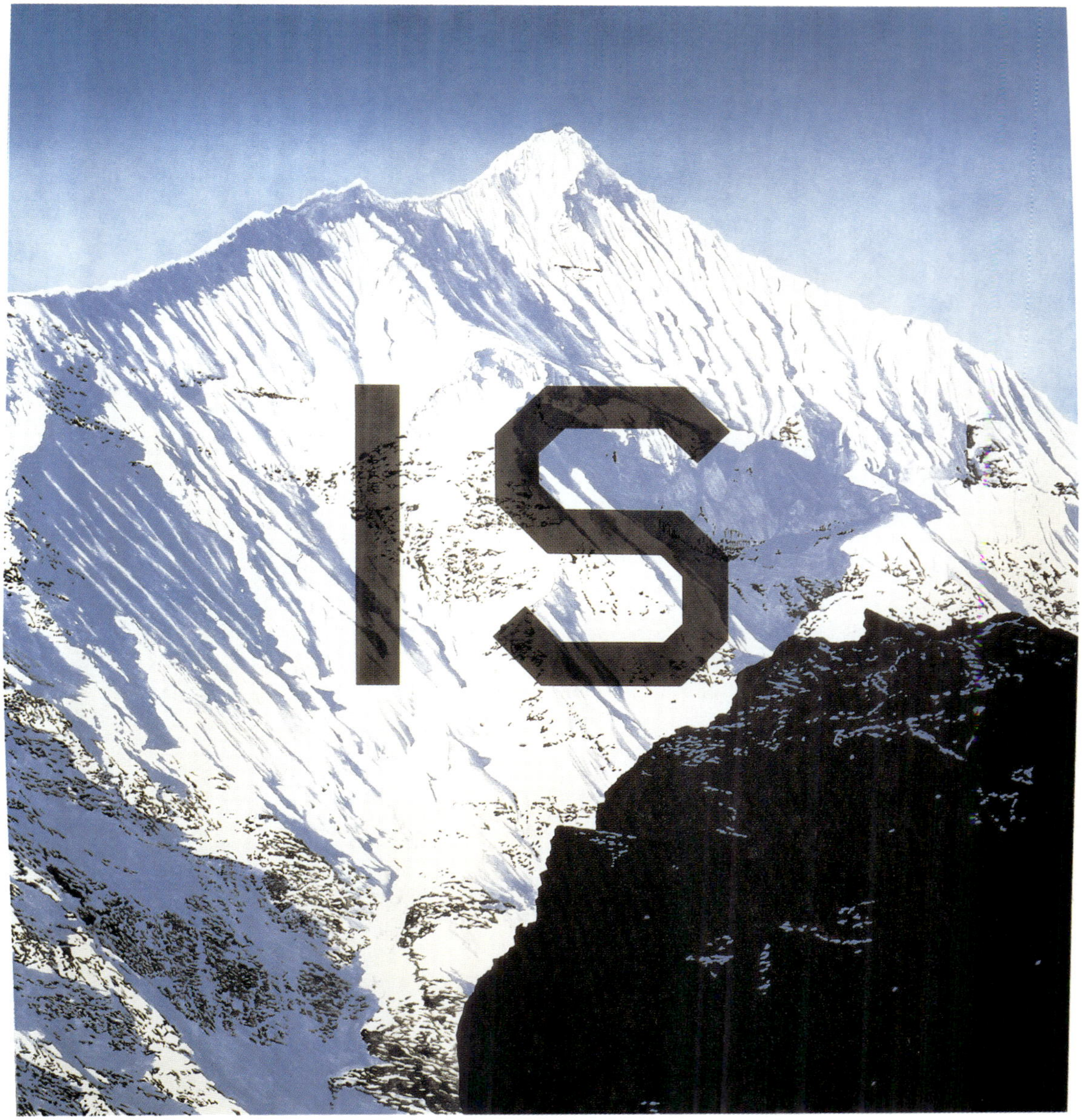

EDWARD RUSCHA, IS, 1998, acrylic on canvas, 76 x 72" /
IST, Acryl auf Leinwand, 193 x 182,9 cm. (PHOTO: PAUL RUSCHA)

JOE SCANLAN

THE BALLAD

DIE BALLADE VON ED RUSCHA

What to say about Ed Ruscha?
I floated that question the other day
While driving north in my Chevrolet
Through the crease of the Hudson Valley.

The morning rain had turned snow by noon,
But now the clouds were making some room
For the final hour of the sun's wan swoon
On the purple cushions of the Catskills.

Bierstadt was here, and Church, and Heade,
Gifford and Kensett and Cole (I believe),
Pinkham Ryder stayed home yet helped sow the seeds
Of a mythic Manifest Destiny.

But now we've been West seven score and ten,
What has become of our schooled brethren
Who make pictures that capture our moments and then
Get confined to the vaults of museums?

When was the spirit of the road trip undone?
Where has the thrill of uncertainty gone?
Why must all things get nailed down at once?
What are we so afraid of?

I pose these questions to Ed Ruscha
'Cause I'm always confused and impressed by the way
His ambitions have never led him astray
From doing the things he loves.

Was wäre zu sagen über Ed Ruscha?
Kürzlich stellte ich mir diese Frage
in meinem Chevrolet auf der Fahrt nach Norden
durch die Senke des Hudson Valley.

Der Morgenregen war gegen Mittag in Schnee übergegangen,
aber nun lichteten sich die Wolken
zu einer letzten Stunde matten Sonnenzaubers
auf den Purpurkissen der Catskill-Höhen.

Bierstadt war hier und Church und Heade,
Gifford und Kensett und Cole (glaube ich),
Pinkham Ryder blieb zuhause und strickte doch mit
an der schicksalhaften Entwicklung Amerikas.

Aber nun, nach 150 Jahren im Westen:
Was ist aus den gewandten Kameraden geworden,
mit ihren Bildern, die unsere Zeit festhalten und dann
in den Kellergewölben von Museen verschwinden?

Wann ist uns das Unterwegssein abhanden gekommen?
Wo ist der Reiz des Wagnisses geblieben?
Warum muss alles gleich festgenagelt werden?
Wovor fürchten wir uns so?

Ich stelle diese Fragen Ed Ruscha,
weil ich davon verwirrt und beeindruckt bin,
wie sein Ehrgeiz ihn nie davon abhielt
zu tun, was er gern tut.

OF ED RUSCHA

He intimates stories that haven't been told,
Through places and words which are yet to unfold,
Like a body removed before it is cold—
The outline left on the pavement.

Er deutet noch nie erzählte Geschichten an
mit Orten und Wörtern, die erst entschlüsselt sein wollen,
als sei ein Toter hastig weggeräumt worden
und nur sein Umriss auf dem Asphalt zurückgeblieben.

Like Roussel detailing a scene before
He tells you what all of the details are for,
Ruscha's works are barely secure,
Like thought balloons, tethered but floating.

Wie bei Roussel, der ins Detail geht, bevor
er ausführt, wozu alles gut ist,
sind Ruschas Werke keine sichere Sache,
wie Gedankenballone – an der Leine, doch schwebend.

"Hollywood, Sunset, Santa Monica, Vine"
Shows intersections painted in simple black lines,
I've never been there but I do realize
As places they're meant to be famous.

«Hollywood, Sunset, Santa Monica, Vine»,
eine Unterteilung aus einfachen schwarzen Linien,
ich war nie dort, aber ich weiss,
diese Orte sollen berühmt sein.

Joan Didion lived nearby and said:
"We tell ourselves stories in order to live."
How's that for a phrase that acts as a sieve!
It captures the essence of things.

Joan Didion lebte in der Nähe und sagte:
«Wir erzählen uns selbst Geschichten um leben zu können.»
Wie wärs, diesen Satz als Sieb zu verwenden!
Er fängt das Wesen der Dinge ein.

Standard Station, Amarillo, Texas,
Staked out in klieg-lit, two-point perspective,
Suggests that a lone patch of I-27
Could be a celebrity site.

Standard Station, Amarillo, Texas,
klar umrissen, grell erleuchtet, in Zweipunkt-Perspektive,
ganz so, als ob ein verlassener Fleck auf der I-27
das Zeug zur Sehenswürdigkeit hätte.

As if the appearance of petroleum and cigs
Could hit like a spotlight swung from a rig,
Emblazing the moment you stretch out your legs
Like an actress on Oscar night.

Als ob der Anblick von Benzin und Glimmstengeln
uns treffen könnte wie ein Scheinwerferstrahl,
den Moment vergoldend, in dem du deine Beine räkelst
wie eine Schauspielerin an der Oscar-Verleihung.

After hours of nothing but you and the wheel,
The station is all that you hope will be real,
Until there, like a vision, it starts to congeal.
That's why he painted it.

Nach Stunden allein mit dir und dem Lenkrad
wird die Tankstelle zur einzigen Hoffnung auf Wirklichkeit,
bis dahin friert sie ein wie eine Vision.
Darum hat er sie gemalt.

JOE SCANLAN lives in New York / lebt in New York.

EDWARD RUSCHA, HOLLYWOOD, SUNSET, SANTA MONICA, VINE, 1998, acrylic on canvas, 70 x 138" / Acryl auf Leinwand, 177,8 x 350,5 cm.

(PHOTO: PAUL RUSCHA)

Painted the lighting opaque and impure,
Celebrated a structure we've all seen before,
And honored a dignity long since ignored,
Even though we still crave it.

Hat das Licht gemalt, opak und schmuddelig,
eine Architektur zelebriert, die wir alle kennen,
und zollt einer Würde Tribut, die längst nichts mehr gilt,
obwohl wir nach wie vor danach lechzen.

Now, how can a picture so resound?
How can it sing of the moments we've known?
Of light coalescing, of liquids aglow?
Of life, of pleasure, of loneliness?

Wie nur kann ein Bild diese Resonanz haben?
Wie kann es Augenblicke besingen, die wir erlebt haben?
Voll schmelzenden Lichts, voll glimmender Flüssigkeiten?
Voll Leben, voll Freude, voll Einsamkeit?

Culled from a landscape of mountains and plains,
Bathed in a city of asphalt and names,
Woven in layers of normalcy and fame,
Until each becomes fused with the other.

Gepflückt aus einer Landschaft mit Bergen und Ebenen,
getaucht in eine Stadt aus Asphalt und Namen,
verwoben in Schichten aus Normalität und Ruhm,
bis jedes mit jedem verbunden ist.

It can be quite cathartic to realize you're then
No longer in charge of the time that you've been,
For Edward has shaken that time through a sieve
And said: I'll keep it for you.

Es kann ganz schön kathartisch sein zu erkennen,
dass man nicht länger Herr der Zeit ist, wie mans mal war,
denn Edward hat jene Zeit durch ein Sieb geschüttelt
und gesagt: Ich bewahr sie für dich auf.

I've been 'cross this country from valley to canyon,
Seen everything I could get my two hands on,
And sure as my guitar and laptop say Scanlan,
Ed Ruscha is an American hero.

Ich bin durch dieses Land gereist von Tal zu Canyon,
habe alles gesehen, worauf ich meine zwei Hände legen konnte,
und so sicher, wie auf meiner Gitarre und meinem Laptop «Scanlan» steht:
Ed Ruscha ist ein amerikanischer Held.

Not due to his cash and his long accolades,
Nor because he owns guns and salutes at parades,
But because he's accepted that all good things fade,
As his grand motivation.

Nicht dank seines Geldes und seinen endlosen Auszeichnungen,
auch nicht, weil er Gewehre hat und bei Paraden salutiert,
sondern weil er die Tatsache, dass alle guten Dinge vergänglich sind,
als ideale Motivation für sein Tun akzeptiert hat.

To picture in fragments the places he's been,
To outline the phrases that lodge in his brain,
To publish the photos he's taken and then
Recirculate them.

Die Orte, an denen er war, ausschnittweise wiederzugeben,
die Wendungen, die in seinem Hirn wohnen, nachzuzeichnen,
die Photos, die er gemacht hat, zu veröffentlichen und
wieder in Umlauf zu bringen.

So when pundits start hawking some new all-time best,
Remember the wisdom Reyner Banham once passed,
That all the possessions Americans grasp,
Are measured by their expendability.

Wenn also die Propheten den neuen Star aller Zeiten ausrufen,
denk an das weise Wort von Reyner Banham,
dass alle Besitztümer, nach denen die Amerikaner greifen,
an ihrem Verbrauchswert gemessen werden.

I'll close with a phrase that sticks in my head,
One I think Ed Ruscha would be pleased to have said,
Some advice Yogi Berra once gave to a friend:
"When you come to a fork in the road, take it."

Zum Schluss noch ein Wort, das mir nicht aus dem Kopf geht,
Ruscha wärs wohl recht, hätte er es gesagt,
ein Rat, den Yogi Berra einst einem Freund gab:
«Wenn du zu einer Abzweigung kommst, folge ihr.»

(Übersetzung: Wilma Parker)

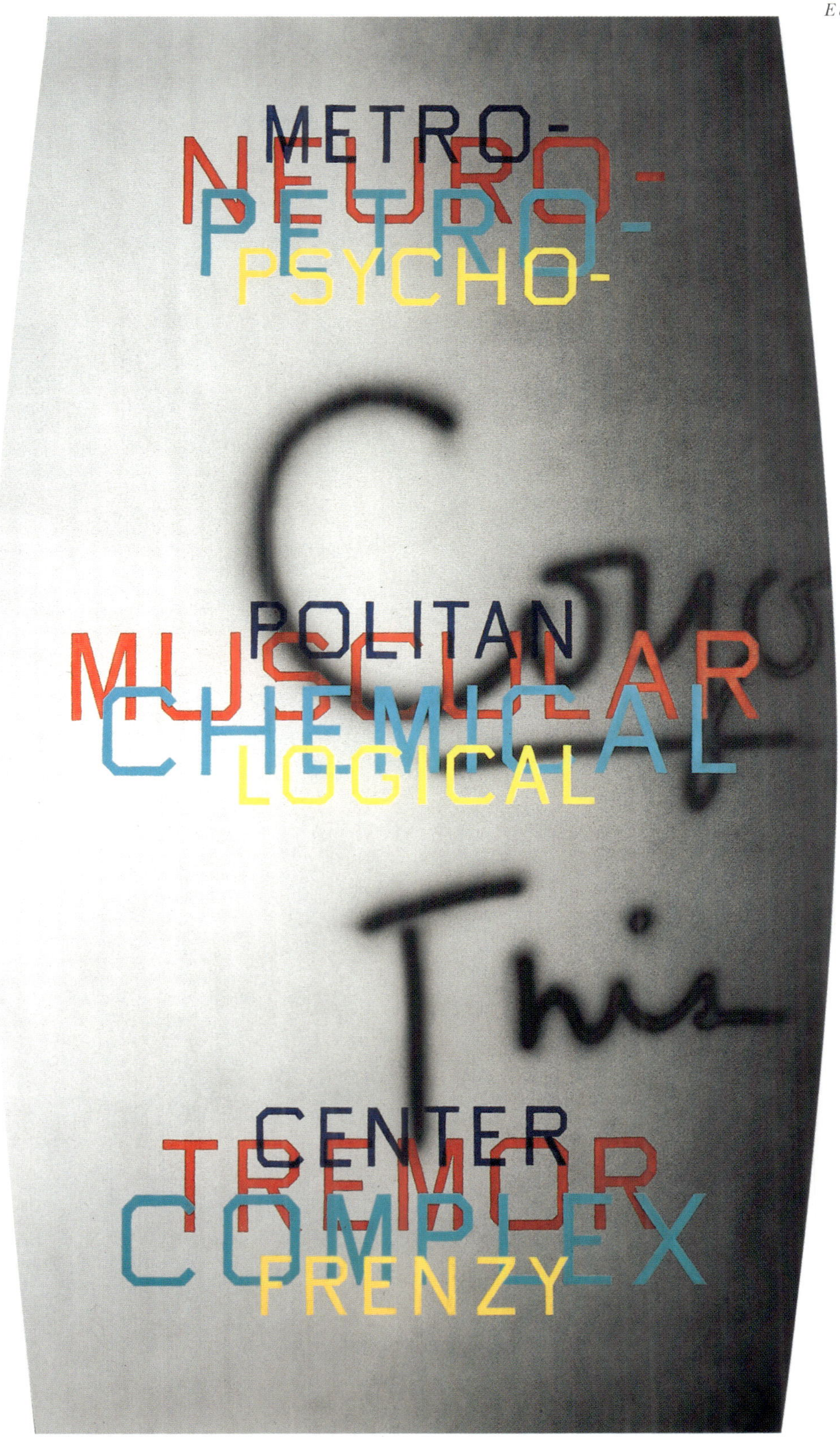

EDWARD RUSCHA, METRO, PETRO, NEURO, PSYCHO, 1998, acrylic on canvas, 79⅞ x 46" / Acryl auf Leinwand, 202,8 x 116,8 cm.

Edition for Parkett EDWARD RUSCHA

VINE/MELROSE, 1999
Two-color lithograph on Rives, 22¼ x 30⅛"
Printed by Hamilton Press, Venice, California
Edition of 60, signed and numbered

Zweifarbige Lithographie auf Rives, 56,5 x 76,5 cm
Druck: Hamilton Press, Venice, California
Auflage: 60, signiert und nummeriert

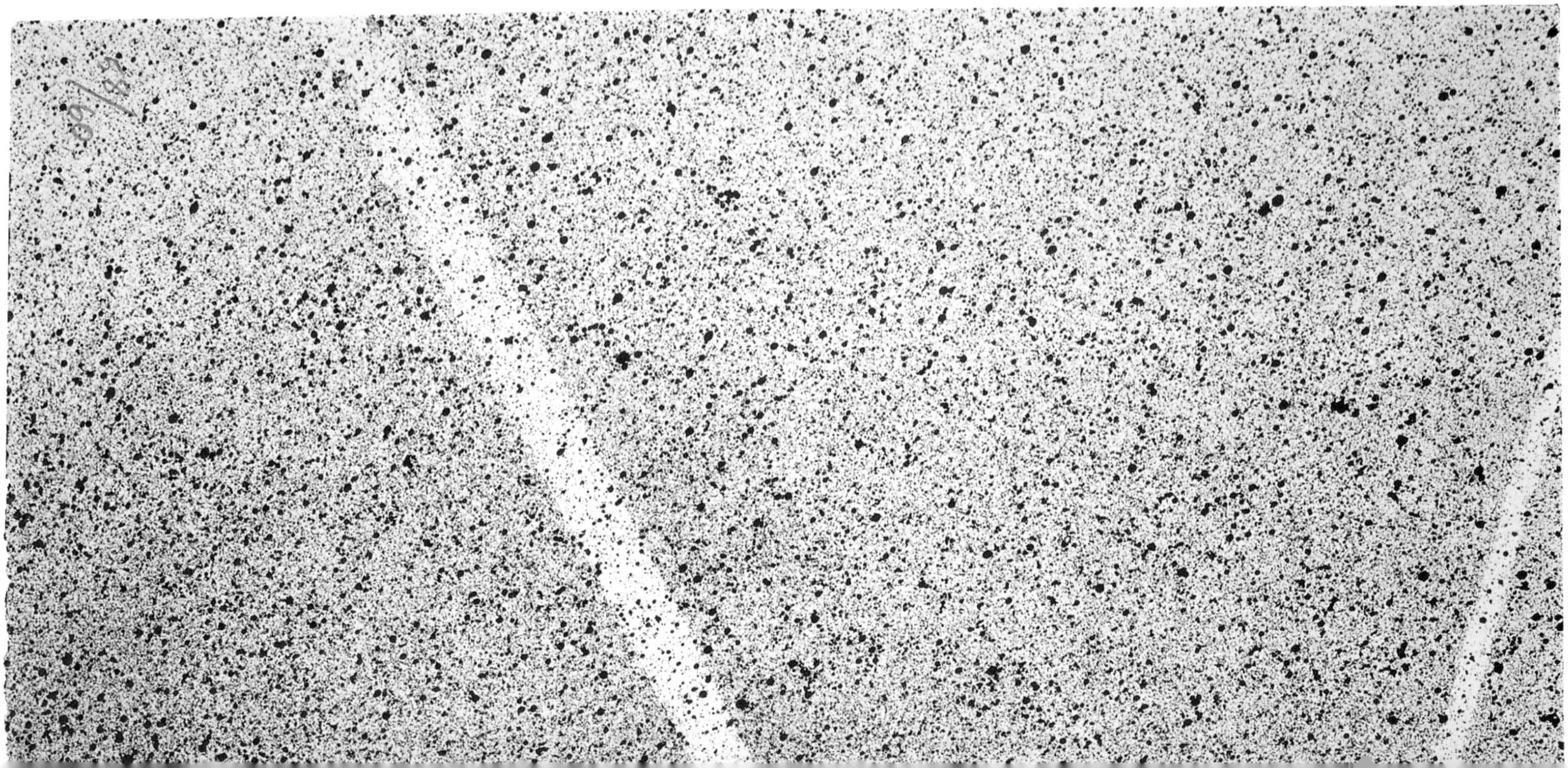

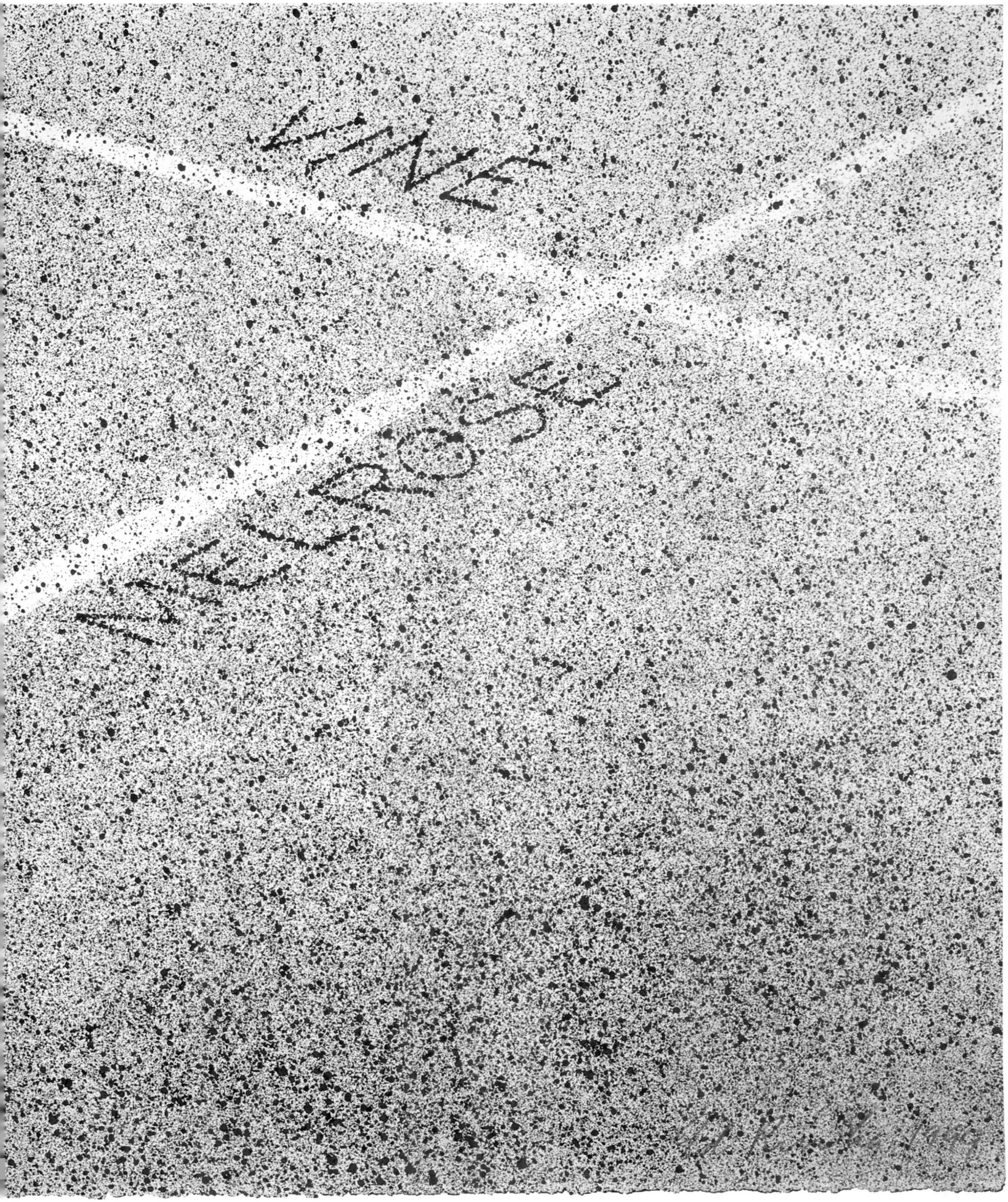

(PHOTO: MANCIA/BODMER, ZÜRICH)

Andreas Slominski

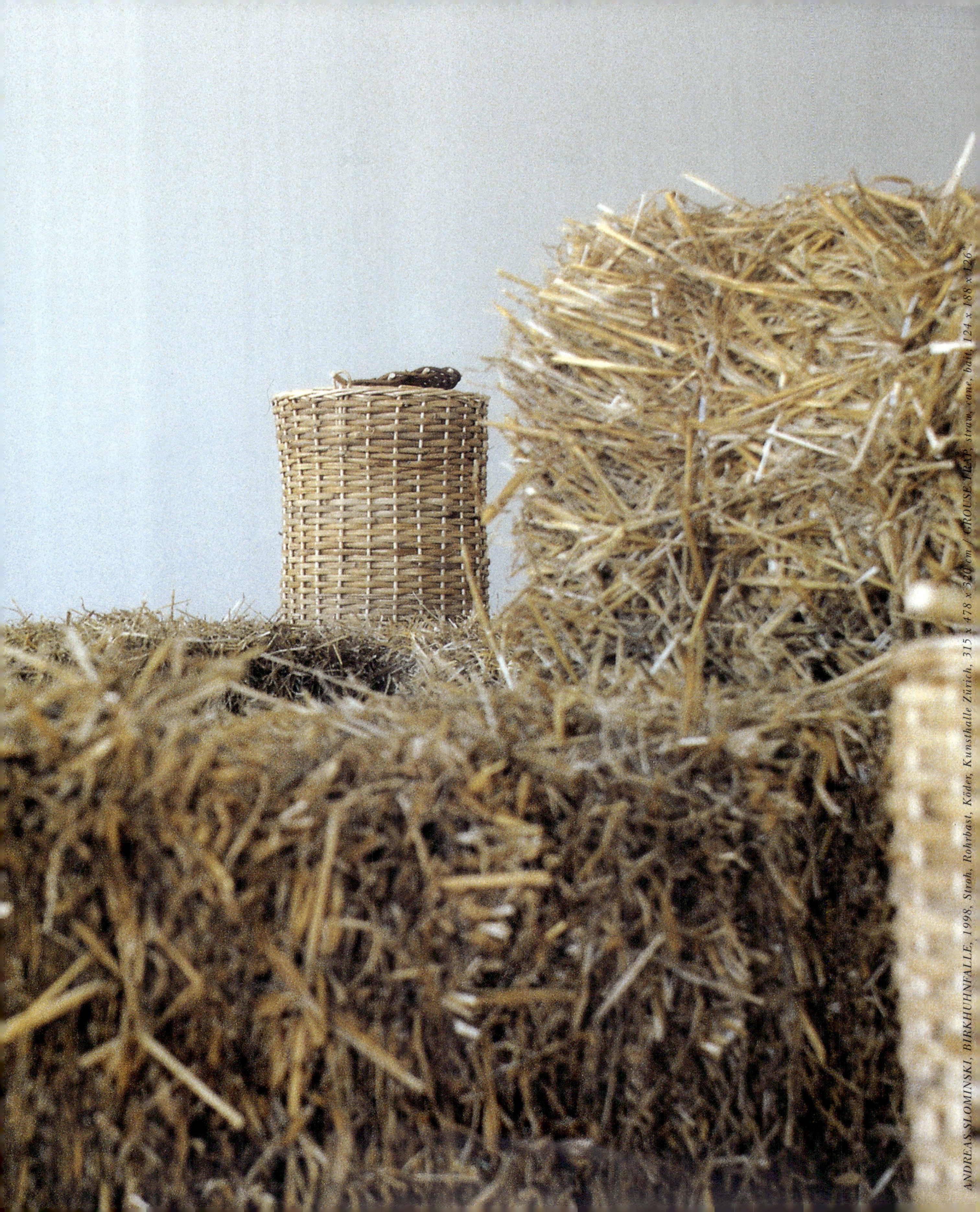

ANDREAS SLOMINSKI, BIRKHUHNFALLE, 1998, Stroh, Rohrbast, Köder, Kunsthalle Zürich, 315 x 478 x 320 cm / GROUSE TRAP, straw, cane, bait, 124 x 188 x 126".

BERLIN DETOURS

NANCY SPECTOR

At the press conference for Andreas Slominski's exhibition of commissioned work at the Deutsche Guggenheim, Berlin, I spoke—as one does in such situations—in very general terms about his art. I described his career-long obsession with trapping—as both a concept with rich metaphorical associations and an age-old profession with intricate rules and strategies of the hunt. Emphasizing his esteem for the craft, I told of Slominski's in-depth knowledge of snares, decoys, baiting systems, and the feeding habits of his prey. At the same time, I pointed out how his fully functioning traps, which are created for the sole purpose of display, problematize the critically sacrosanct model of the readymade. Referring to his trickster persona, I asked rhetorically whether Slominski may be considered an artist who makes traps or a trapper who makes art. There was more information, however, that I chose not to share in this situation, much of which referred, albeit indirectly, to the tainted history of twentieth-century Berlin. This omission was premised less on my avoidance of sensitive subject matter in the headquarters of Deutsche Bank, the museum's corporate sponsors, than on my realization that meaning in Slominski's art reveals itself in waves, one layer at a time. Underneath its ever-present narrative of ensnarement and the occasional slapstick routine, there lies a sharp critical edge, the content of which emerges only in relation to the environment in which it is encountered. The work is site-reliant, not site-specific. Context seeps in slowly, informing and adding fresh connotative dimensions to already thematically resonant art.

Slominski's performative contributions to "Skulptur. Projekte in Münster 1997" demonstrated this permeable aspect of his work. In a priceless example of his fanatical attention to detail, the artist placed a bicycle inner tube around a street lamp, but instead of throwing it over the top—the logical thing to do—he had the lamp excavated from the sidewalk and its electrical wiring disconnected so he could slip it on from the bottom up. In an equally absurd action, Slominski arranged for a giraffe in the Münster zoo to lick a postage stamp, which he then adhered to an envelope and promptly mailed. Beyond their status as exercises in remarkable futility, these gestures commented on the odd nature of this presentation of public art, which invades Münster every ten years, dispersing sculptures, installations, and curious interventions throughout the small, picturesque city. During its opening days, hundreds of curators, collectors, and critics descend on the town with their maps and rented bicycles to sniff out the scattered, and in some cases, very well hidden, art works. The effect has been described by Hans-Ulrich Obrist as a "truffle-pig-syndrome," and the hilarity of this situation was not lost on Slominski. The lone bicycle tire (which was stolen within the first week of its installation and thus not even visible) slyly mocked the art-world tourists on wheels. And the episode at the zoo

NANCY SPECTOR is Curator of Contemporary Art at the Solomon R. Guggenheim Museum, New York. She organized the Andreas Slominski exhibition at the Deutsche Guggenheim, Berlin, February 20–May 9, 1999.

poked fun at the notion of experiencing artworks in their "native" habitat, of observing them in the "wild," so to speak.

That same summer at the Venice Biennale, Slominski exhibited a toy-like windmill—mini-golf scale—but still capable of grinding grain, which made a playful critique of the exhibition environment. A recurring motif in his art, the windmill resonates with cultural meanings specific to Northern Europe—ranging from its idealized agrarian past to the kitsch of its modern garden ornaments. In the high-profile setting of the Biennale's main international exhibition, this colorfully painted windmill sat smack in the middle of the gallery's central walkway, thus turning the vast hall of the Corderie into an amusement park or, at least, a putting range.

Different exhibition contexts have interjected far more sobering undertones into other examples of Slominski's work. For a 1996 installation at Portikus, he filled the gallery with the weathered wings of an old windmill that he found in Achim, which, like unearthed artifacts, were encrusted with dirt and dried moss. During the exhibition, Slominski could, on occasion, be seen in the gallery sawing pieces off these enormous wooden wings and feeding them into an antiquated workshop stove. While he claimed to be doing nothing more than utilizing and burning the available wood in order to heat the building—hence the work's title, HEIZEN—it was difficult to avoid reading something more diabolical into the equation—something more historically specific to Germany's not-so-distant-past.

Similar innuendoes surfaced during Slominski's 1996 installation at the Kunstsammlung Weimar, which featured an assortment of cheerfully colored, miniature windmills. These are "garden variety" mills in that they approach the size of lawn statuary. Some are rendered with exacting craftsmanship and realistic architectural details, while others are more schematically designed and resemble Lego creations. The titles offered an inventory of possible functions for the Lilliputian mills: one could be used to wind thread, another to mix plaster, another to grind poppy seeds, another to press grapes, and so on. In typi-

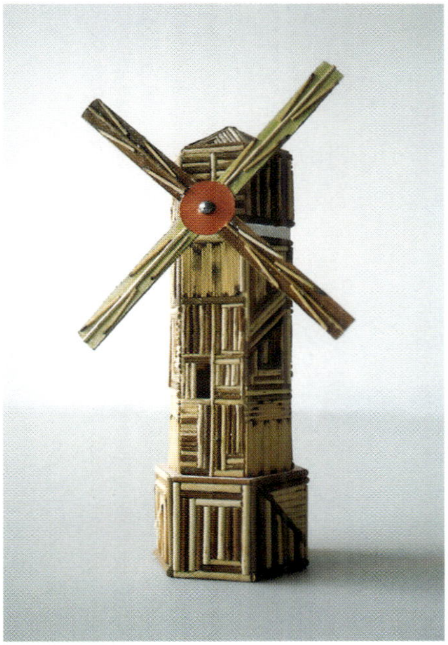

ANDREAS SLOMINSKI, MONDSCHEINMÜHLE, 1996, Holz, Pappe, Metall, ca. 43 x 18 x 10 cm, Kunstmuseum Winterthur / MOONSHINE WINDMILL, wood, cardboard, metal, ca. $16\frac{7}{8}$ x 7 x $3\frac{7}{8}$".

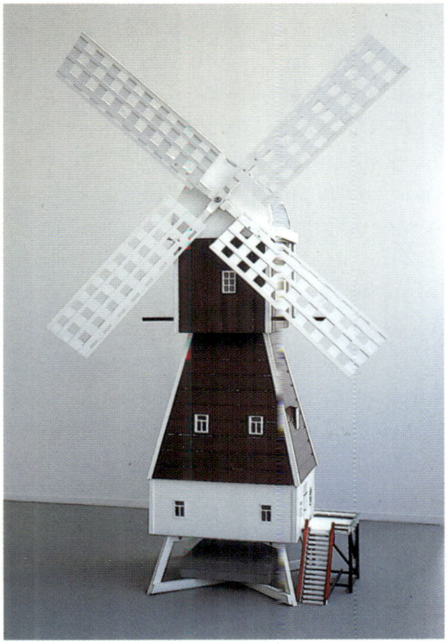

ANDREAS SLOMINSKI, SCHLAFSPIEGELMÜHLE, 1996, verschiedene Materialien, ca. 350 x 150 x 150 cm / MIRROR-OF-SLEEP WINDMILL, mixed media, ca. $137\frac{3}{4}$ x 59 x 59". (PHOTO: ARNO DECLAIR, HAMBURG)

cal Slominski fashion, one could even be used to trap birds. While clearly playful in intent, this gingerbread-world presentation evolved to self-consciously acknowledge the museum's geographical proximity to Buchenwald, the Nazi concentration camp located just outside Weimar, which is now a Holocaust memorial. During the installation process, Slominski discovered a lucky penny—a coin minted in 1943—while rummaging in the dirt on the edge of the camp, which he then placed in a glass vitrine set in the middle of the windmills. By virtue of its date, this lone coin became a symbol for World War II and the atrocities which had taken place nearby. As a coda to the installation, Slominski arranged for the gallery windows to remain open at all times so that the winds blowing from Buchenwald could be registered by the movement of the windmill wings. Like traps, the mills were set to react to changing air currents and, in doing so, they recorded the breeze. A sinister draft permeated the room; one was led to ponder what kind of wind blew through Weimar, once upon a time. This fairy-tale realm transmogrified into something somber and menacing. The pint-size windmills, their wings slowly rotating, stood as silent witnesses to unspeakable crimes.[1)]

The impact of Slominski's installation at the Deutsche Guggenheim, Berlin was strangely similar. What began as a straightforward presentation (if there is such a thing in Slominski's world) of a multi-component bird trapping station, evolved into a powerful architectural metaphor for Cold War Berlin. Conceived as a large, multifarious trapping compound, the work features a two-story, tar-paper covered hut for the trapper, from which he can control the various hinged, double-clap nets spread out all around him. Baited with fake hedges, red berries, water, or birdseed, these trapping devices are attached to the main hut with long cords, which the trapper can yank to trigger their springs, should a bird land in any one of the compartments. A mechanical bird decoy in the upper register of the room lures unsuspecting finches or thrushes into the nets. Animal traps designed specifically for the small predators waiting to feed on the captured birds are strategically arranged to capitalize on this parasitic situation. All is ready for the hunt. Hidden from view in the confines of his hut, cords in hand, the trapper peers into his panoptical trap through small observation slits. We can't see him, but he can see us.

While installing this trapping complex, Slominski reflected on how context often and inadvertently acts upon his work. We were discussing his Weimar installation and how the inclusion of the lucky penny shifted the meaning of the work into unexpected and allusive territories. He commented on the militaristic appearance of the trapper's hut, which looked alternately like a tank or a bunker, and said that it could even refer to the observation towers that once lined the Berlin Wall isolating the G.D.R. sector from the West. The museum's location close to the Bran-

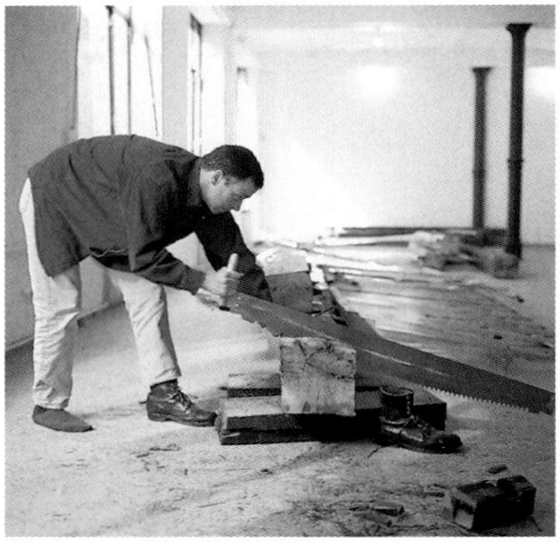

denburg Gate in what was formerly East Berlin, where the four-meter high, concrete and barbed wire Wall had once crossed the city like a scar, further strengthened this reading. The double-clap net traps suddenly assumed ominous proportions in their symbolic association with the Wall's infamous death strip, a 161 kilometer border patrolled by 252 watchtowers, 136 bunkers, glaring search lights, and Alsatian sniffer dogs. That these traps—designed to snare entire flocks of birds in one snap—are made to human scale only underscores the grim correspondences here.[2)]

Once I became aware of these correlations, other aspects of the exhibition took on new and unanticipated shades of meaning, as was the case with Slominski's witty intervention outside the museum on Unter den Linden, one of the city's grandest boulevards. An emblem of urban order, the street's tree-lined central promenade is scrupulously maintained. Each of the 370 trees is numbered, registered, and its growth carefully monitored. Disrupting this image of Teutonic order, Slominski "planted" a

Seite/Page 72:
ANDREAS SLOMINSKI, HEIZEN, 1996,
Mehl eines Windmühlenflügels in den Schuh sägen /
HEATING, dust of a windmill vane
being sawed into a shoe.
(PHOTO: ARNO DECLAIR, HAMBURG)

ANDREAS SLOMINSKI, FUCHSFALLE, 1998,
Holz, Weidengeflecht, Socke mit Lockstoff,
ca. 45 x 120 x 120 cm / FOX TRAP, wood, thatching,
sock with scent lure, ca. 17⅝ x 47¼ x 47¼".

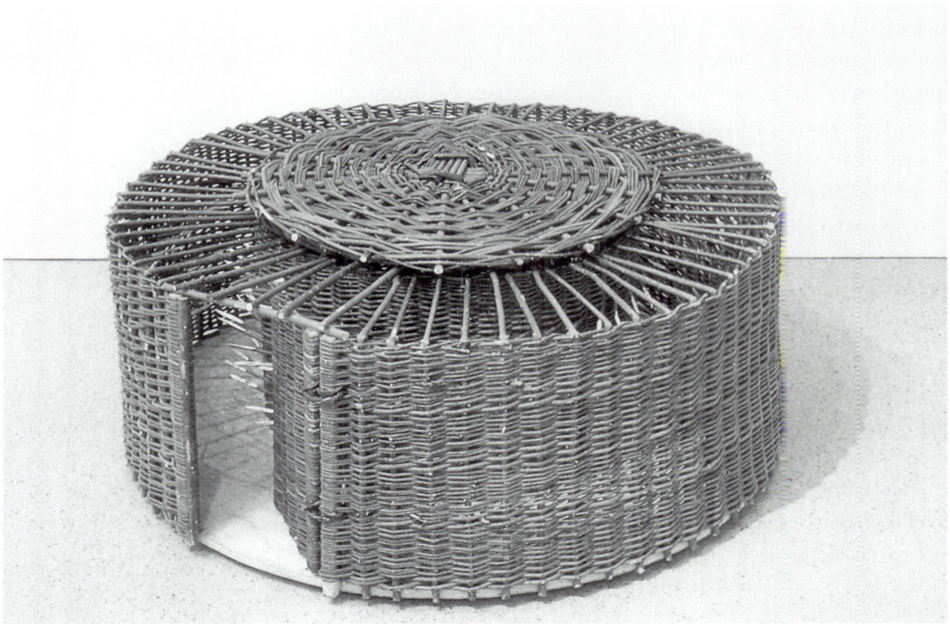

dead tree stump slightly off-center from the uniform arrangement. There it sat, barely noticeable, creating a subtle sense of imbalance, a minor visual disturbance in the surrounding cityscape. Encountering the little stump, one might have thought that a wayward tree, which had dared to grow out of place, had been summarily punished. When the city authorities were alerted to the inexplicable presence of this unruly stump, police barricades were set up around it, transforming Slominski's practical joke into a crime scene.[3)]

The penal references stuck with me, and after the exhibition opened I did a little research on Unter den Linden and its cherished lime trees. They were originally planted in 1648 by the Great Elector Friedrich Wilhelm to flank a riding path that stretched

ANDREAS SLOMINSKI, HEIZEN, 1996, Verfeuern von Windmühlenflügeln, Portikus Frankfurt / HEATING, the burning of windmill vanes. (PHOTO: BARBARA KLEMM)

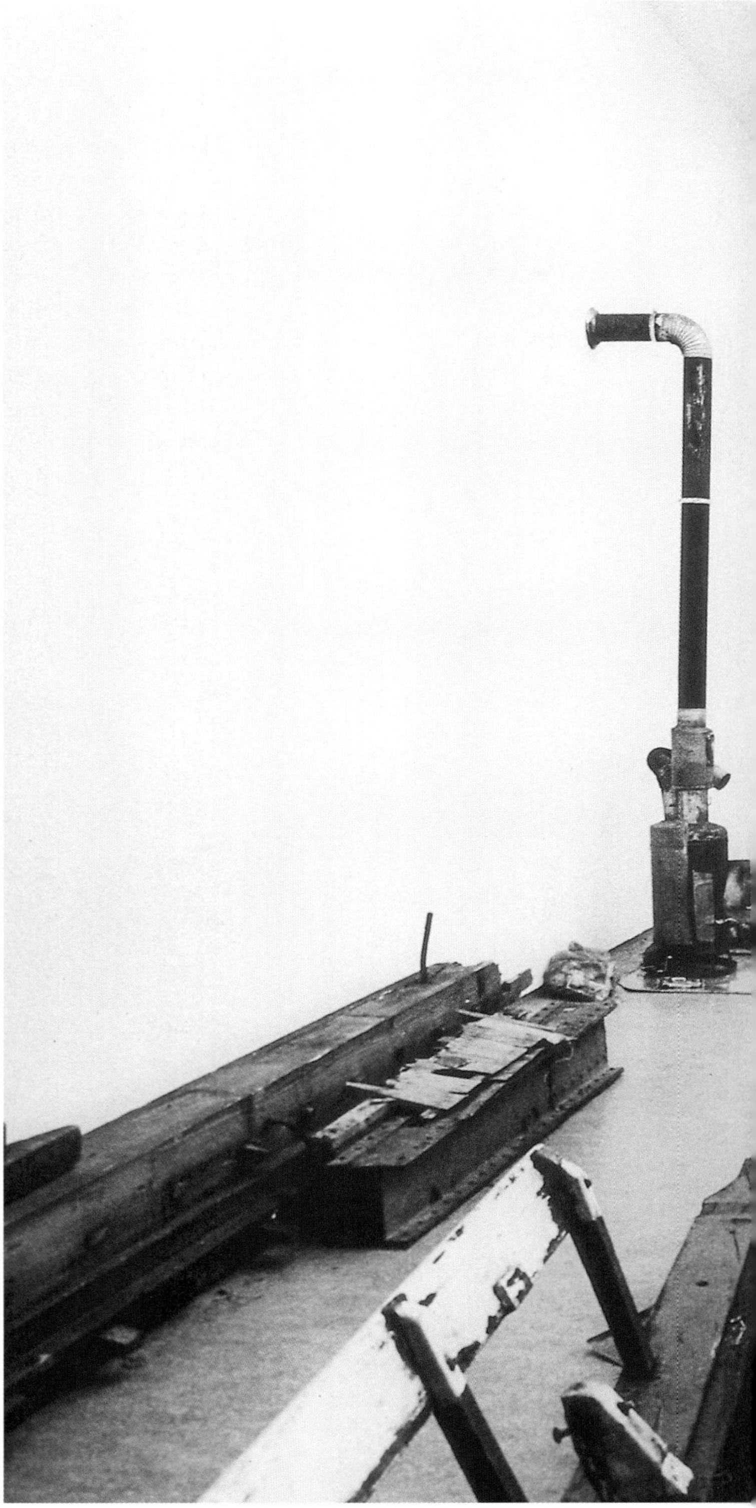

toward Berlin's Grunewald, and he valued them so highly that he threatened to cut off the hands of anyone who harmed them.[4] When Karl Friedrich Schinkel, master architect of nineteenth-century Berlin, established its neo-classical urban plan, he made Unter den Linden a central vector, lining it with embassies, government buildings, financial institutions, a university, and an opera house. The trees, of course, flourished in such a stately environment. During the Third Reich, Hitler had all the trees chopped down in order to carve a wider swath for military parades and wartime maneuvers. Years later the Communists replanted Unter den Linden, adding trees only as far as Pariser Platz, some distance from the Brandenburg Gate, portal to the West. After the Wall was toppled in 1989, a West Berlin horticultural foundation donated enough trees to complete the remaining stretch of the boulevard. In retrospect, the relative health of Unter den Linden's trees serves to measure the shifting episodes of urban harmony and political strife in Berlin. Did Slominski know this peculiar history when he decided to stage an action on the boulevard's promenade, to extend the exhibition into the street, and to play a seemingly innocent trick on uninformed passersby? I suspect so, but if not, context once again rushed in to inform the art, adding depth to an already profound work, and providing new detours in meaning.

1) Portions of this section have been borrowed from Nancy Spector, "Of traps, tricks, and other riddles," in: *Andreas Slominski* (New York: Solomon R. Guggenheim Museum, 1999).
2) Berlin gallerist Barbara Weiss noted that the BIRD TRAPPING COMPOUND resembled the Quadriga statue on top of the Brandenburg Gate in that the arrangement of the nets around the hut looked like the triumphant chariot and horses frozen forever in time and space above the demarcation line of the once divided city.
3) Op. cit.
4) This and the following information on Unter den Linden is borrowed from Andrew Gumbel, *Berlin*, (London: Gadogan Books, 1991), p. 57.

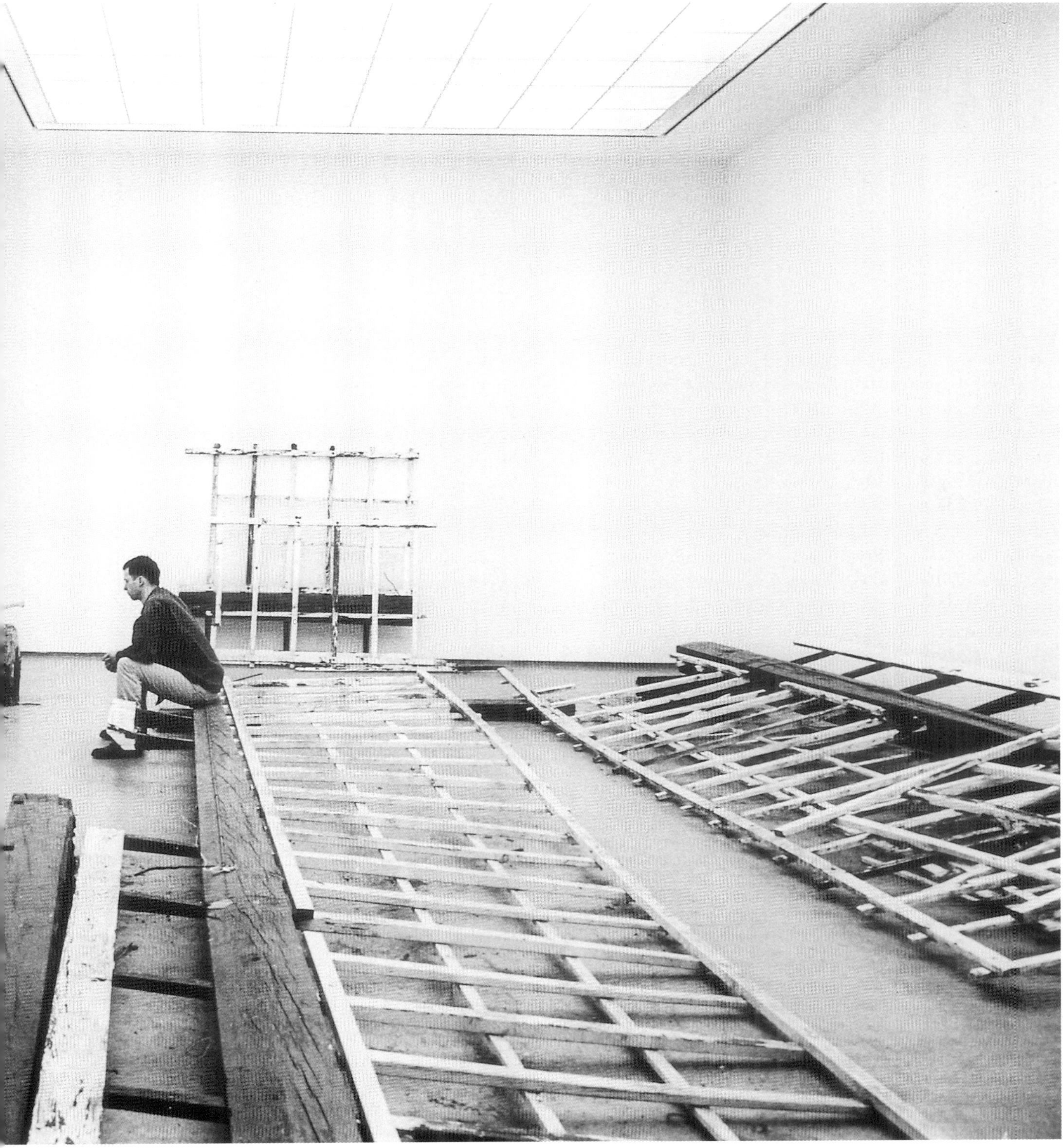

BERLINER UMWEGE

NANCY SPECTOR

Auf der Pressekonferenz zu der von der Deutschen Guggenheim, Berlin, in Auftrag gegebenen Slominski-Ausstellung äusserte ich mich dem Anlass entsprechend nur sehr allgemein zu seiner Kunst. Ich beschrieb seine für das ganze Werk charakteristische Leidenschaft für Fallen – sowohl als Konzept, mit dem sich viele Metaphern verbinden lassen, wie auch als uralten Beruf mit komplizierten Regeln und Jagdstrategien. Ich erwähnte Slominskis Hochachtung für das Handwerkliche und seine fundierten Kenntnisse, was Fallen, Köder, Fangvorrichtungen und Fressgewohnheiten der Beute betrifft. Gleichzeitig wies ich darauf hin, wie seine voll funktionstüchtigen Fallen, die er jedoch einzig und allein für Ausstellungen bauen lässt, das sakrosankte Modell des Ready-made kritisch hinterfragen. In Bezug auf Slominski, den «Trickster», stellte ich die rhetorische Frage, ob man ihn als Künstler sehen sollte, der Fallen macht, oder als Fallensteller, der Kunst macht. Ich hätte noch einiges zu seiner Kunst sagen können, zog es aber unter den gegebenen Umständen vor, diese Dinge, die sich, wenn auch indirekt, auf die problematische Geschichte Berlins im zwanzigsten Jahrhundert bezogen, für mich zu behalten. Ich tat es nicht, weil ich in der Zentrale der Deutschen Bank, dem Sponsor des Museums, das heikle Thema vermeiden wollte, sondern weil mir klar geworden war, dass Slominskis Werk sich in Wellen offenbart und dass dabei eine Schicht nach der andern zutage tritt. Hinter dem narrativen Element des Fangens und den gelegentlichen Slapstick-Nummern verbirgt sich eine messerscharfe, kritische Spitze, die man nur in Bezug auf die Umgebung verstehen kann, in der man sie entdeckt. Die Arbeiten sind ortsabhängig, aber nicht ortsspezifisch. Der Kontext dringt langsam in sie ein, liefert zusätzliche Informationen und verleiht einer bereits themenreichen Kunst neue assoziative Dimensionen.

Die Performances, die Slominski zur Ausstellung «Skulptur. Projekte in Münster 1997» beisteuerte, illustrierten diesen durchlässigen Aspekt seines Werkes. In einem kaum zu überbietenden Beispiel für seine Detailbesessenheit legte der Künstler einen Fahrradmantel um eine Strassenlaterne, doch statt ihn, wie es logisch gewesen wäre, von oben darüber zu streifen, liess er die Laterne per Kran aus dem Boden hieven und die elektrischen Leitungen kappen um ihn von unten anzubringen. In einer ähnlich absurden Aktion liess Slominski eine Giraffe aus dem Zoo von Münster eine Briefmarke ablecken um sie auf einen Umschlag zu kleben, den er dann auch prompt abschickte. Abgesehen von ihrem Status als Übungen in Absurdität waren diese Gesten ein Kommentar zu dieser manchmal sehr merkwürdigen Schau von Kunst im öffentlichen Raum, die alle zehn Jahre über Münster hereinbricht um die kleine malerische Stadt mit Skulpturen, Installationen und seltsamen Aktionen zu überschwemmen. Zur Eröffnung fallen hunderte von Kuratoren, Sammlern und Kritikern ein, bewaffnet mit Lageplänen und geliehenen Fahrrädern um die verstreuten und gelegentlich

NANCY SPECTOR ist Kuratorin für zeitgenössische Kunst am Solomon R. Guggenheim Museum, New York. Sie organisierte die Andreas Slominski-Ausstellung in der Deutschen Guggenheim, Berlin (20. Februar – 9. Mai 1999).

auch gut versteckten Werke aufzuspüren. Hans-Ulrich Obrist hat diesen Effekt als «Trüffelschweinsyndrom» bezeichnet und auch Slominski blieb die Komik der Situation nicht verborgen. Der einsame Fahrradreifen – er wurde gleich in der ersten Woche gestohlen und war deshalb für die Besucher nicht einmal sichtbar – war ein hintergründiger Kommentar zu den Kunsttouristen auf Rädern. Und die Episode im Zoo machte sich über das Konzept lustig Kunstwerke in ihrem «natürlichen» Habitat erfahrbar zu machen, sie sozusagen in freier Natur zu observieren.

Im selben Sommer zeigte Slominski auf der Biennale in Venedig eine wie ein Spielzeug wirkende Windmühle, die – obwohl sie durchaus echt und funktionstüchtig war – ihrer Grösse nach eher in eine Minigolf-Anlage gepasst hätte und das ganze Ambiente ins Lächerliche zog. Bei der Windmühle, einem oft wiederkehrenden Motiv in seinem Werk, klingen viele Momente der nordeuropäischen Kulturlandschaft an, von der idealisierten ländlichen Vergangenheit der Region bis hin zum Kitsch moderner Gartendekoration. In der anspruchsvollen Umgebung des grossen internationalen Ausstellungsraums prangte diese buntbemalte Windmühle mitten im Hauptgang und verwandelte die grosse Halle der Corderie in einen Lunapark oder zumindest einen Minigolfplatz.

Andere Ausstellungskontexte liessen in Slominskis Arbeiten eher ernüchternde, härtere Untertöne mitschwingen. Für eine Installation, die er 1966 im Frankfurter Portikus zeigte, füllte er den Schauraum mit den morschen Flügeln einer alten, in Achim aufgestöberten Windmühle, die, Ausgrabungsobjekten gleich, mit Erde und vertrocknetem Moos überzogen waren. Im Lauf der Ausstellung tauchte Slominski hin und wieder im Museum auf und sägte von den riesigen Holzflügeln Teile ab, mit denen er einen alten Holzofen befeuerte. Er behauptete zwar, nur Brennholz zu machen um den Raum zu heizen –, HEIZEN war der Titel dieser Installation – aber man konnte sich nicht des Gefühls erwehren, dass etwas anderes, Ominöses hereinspielte, das mit der jüngeren deutschen Geschichte zu tun hatte.

Ähnliches suggerierte die 1996 in der Ausstellung «Nach Weimar» installierte Arbeit, die aus einer Gruppe von knallbunten Miniaturwindmühlen bestand. Da sie die Grösse von Gartenskulpturen hatten, fielen sie in die Kategorie Dekoration. Einige waren handwerklich perfekt und wiesen realistische architektonische Details auf, während andere sehr viel schematischer und wie aus Legosteinchen zusammengesetzt wirkten. Die Titel der Arbeiten ergaben eine Liste der möglichen Funktionen dieser Liliputmühlen: Mit einer liessen sich Fäden aufrollen, mit einer anderen Gips mischen, mit einer dritten Mohn mahlen, einer weiteren Trauben keltern und so weiter. Und, typisch Slominski, eine konnte sogar als Vogelfalle benutzt werden. Obwohl die Absicht eindeutig spielerischer Natur war, vermittelte diese Zuckerbäckerwelt doch das unbehagliche Gefühl, dass man sich hier ganz in der Nähe des ehemaligen Konzentrationslagers Buchenwald befand, das jetzt eine Holocaust-Gedenkstätte ist. Als Slominski die Installation aufbaute, fand er in einer Ecke des Lagers einen Glückspfennig aus dem Jahr 1943, den er zwischen den Windmühlen in einer Glasvitrine ausstellte. Die verwaiste Münze wurde aufgrund ihres Datums zu einem Symbol für den Zweiten Weltkrieg und die Greuel des Todeslagers. Slominski vervollständigte die Installation, indem er die Fenster der Galerie öffnen liess, damit die Bewegung der Mühlenflügel den Wind von Buchenwald dokumentieren konnte. Wie Fallen sollten die Mühlen die wechselnden Winde einfangen und die Windstärke anzeigen. Ein unheimlicher Luftstrom erfüllte den Raum und zwang den Besucher darüber nachzudenken, aus welcher Richtung wohl damals in Weimar der Wind wehte. Die Märchenwelt verwandelte sich in etwas Düsteres, Bedrohliches. Die Windmühlenzwerge mit ihren langsam rotierenden Flügeln wurden zu stummen Zeugen der unsäglichen Verbrechen.[1)]

Bei der Installation Slominskis in der Deutschen Guggenheim, Berlin, stellte sich seltsamerweise derselbe Effekt ein. Was als ganz einfache Sache (falls es das in Slominskis Welt überhaupt gibt) begonnen hatte, nämlich als aus verschiedenen Elementen zusammengesetzte Vogelfangstation, wurde zu einer überzeugenden Metapher für das Berlin des Kalten Krieges. Die als grosses, vielseitiges Fallenensemble konzipierte Arbeit enthält auch eine zweistöckige, mit Teerpappe verkleidete Hütte für den Fallensteller, von der aus er die vor ihm ausgebreiteten, mit Scharnieren versehenen Schlagnetze kontrollieren kann. Diese mit falschen Hecken, roten Beeren, Wasserschälchen oder Körnern bestückten Fangvorrichtungen sind durch lange Leinen mit dem Unterstand verbunden, an denen der Fänger nur zu ziehen braucht, um den Mechanismus auszulösen, sobald sich ein Vogel in einen Teil der Falle vorwagt. Eine Vogelattrappe im oberen Teil des Raums lockt ahnungslose Finken oder Drosseln ins Netz. Und auch auf die kleinen Raubtiere, die allenfalls versuchen könnten die Situation auszunutzen und sich über die gefangenen Vögel herzumachen, warten einige speziell dafür entwickelte, geschickt platzierte Fallen. Alles steht bereit. Ausser Sichtweite, versteckt im Innern seiner Hütte, die Leinen in der Hand, beobachtet der Fallensteller seine Fanganlage durch schmale Sehschlitze. Wir sehen ihn nicht, aber er sieht uns.

Beim Aufstellen seiner Fallen dachte Slominski viel darüber nach, wie oft und ganz ohne sein Zutun der Kontext seine Arbeiten beeinflusst hat. Wir sprachen über seine Weimarer Installation und wie der Glückspfennig das Werk auf eine ganz unerwartete Ebene voller Anspielungen verlagert hatte. Zum militärischen Aussehen des Unterstands, der mal einem Panzer, mal einem Bunker glich, bemerkte er, man könnte auch die Wachtürme der Berliner Mauer, die den Ostsektor vom Westen der Stadt getrennt hätten, damit assoziieren. Dass das Museum in der ehemaligen DDR lag und ausserdem ganz in der Nähe des Brandenburger Tors, wo die vier Meter hohe, mit Stacheldraht bestückte Betonmauer die Stadt wie eine Wunde durchschnitten hatte, machte diese Interpretation umso plausibler. Im Zusammenhang mit dem berüchtigten Todesstreifen der Mauer, einer 161 Kilometer langen, mit 252 Wachtürmen, 136 Bunkern, grellen Scheinwerfern und Schäferhunden gesicherten Grenze, nahmen die Schlagnetze plötzlich bedrohliche Proportionen an. Die Tatsache, dass diese Fallen, die einen ganzen Schwarm von Vögeln mit einem Schlag fangen konnten, die Grösse von Menschenfallen hatten, verstärkte die makabren Analogien.[2)]

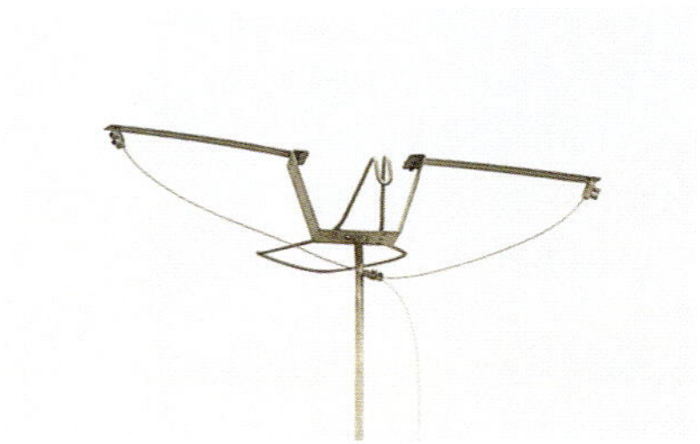

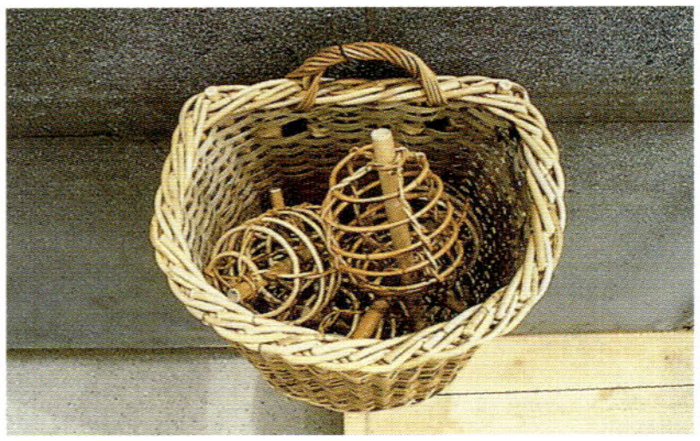

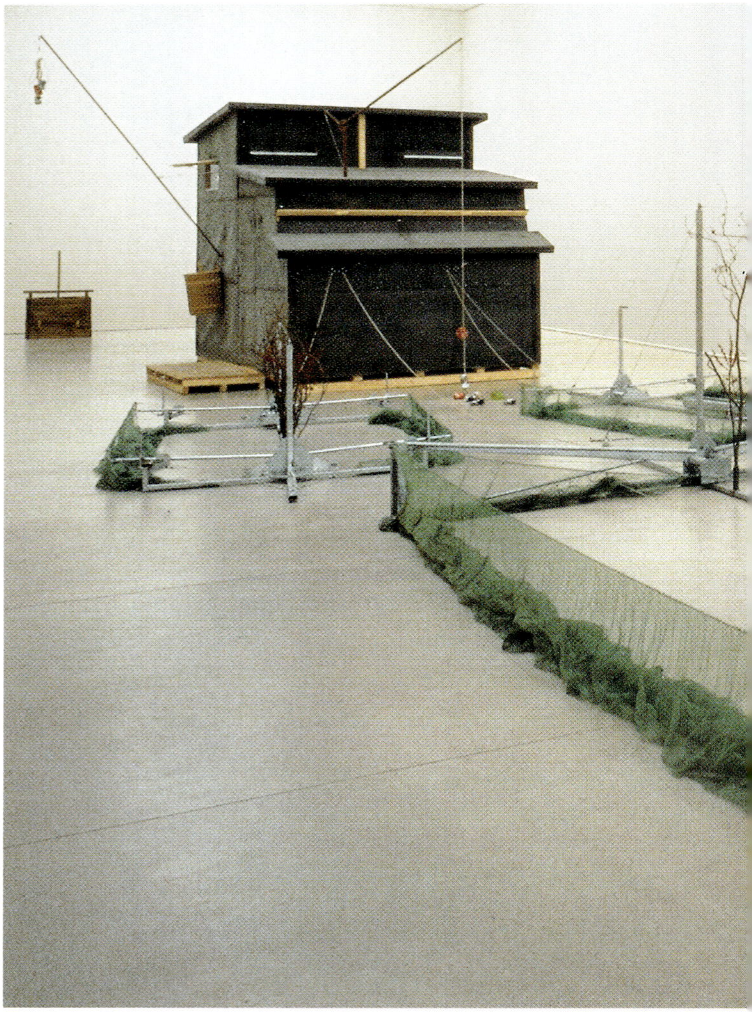

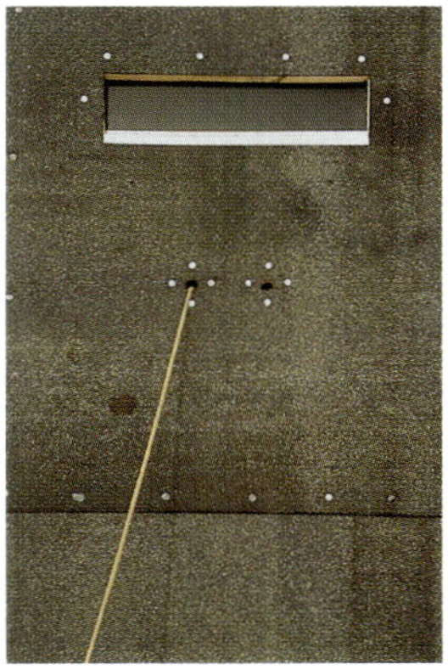

ANDREAS SLOMINSKI, VOGELFANGSTATION, 1998–99, Übersicht und Details, Deutsche Guggenheim, Berlin / BIRD TRAPPING COMPOUND, installation views and details. (PHOTO: MATHIAS SCHORMANN, BERLIN)

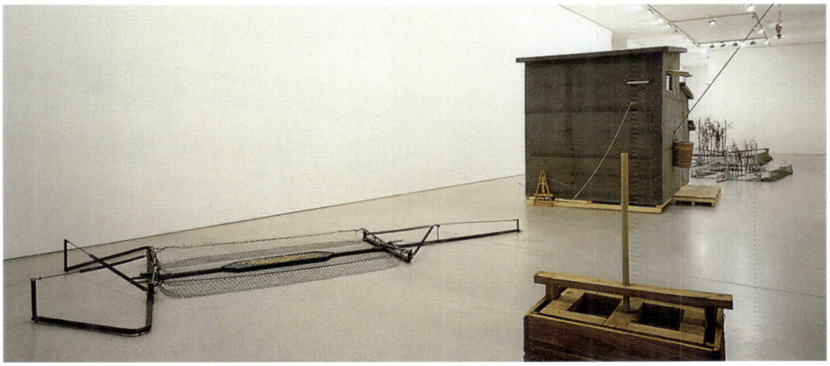

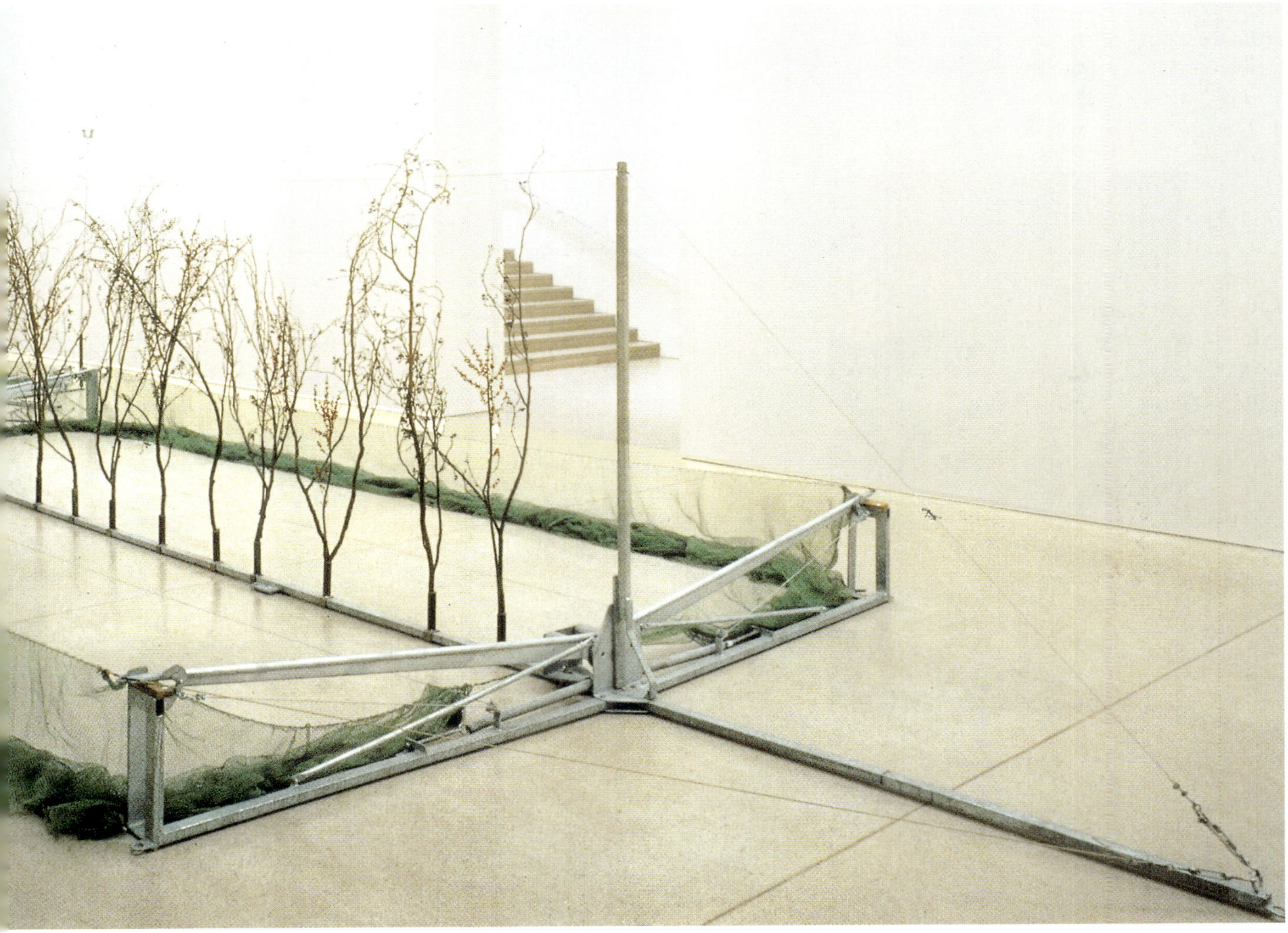

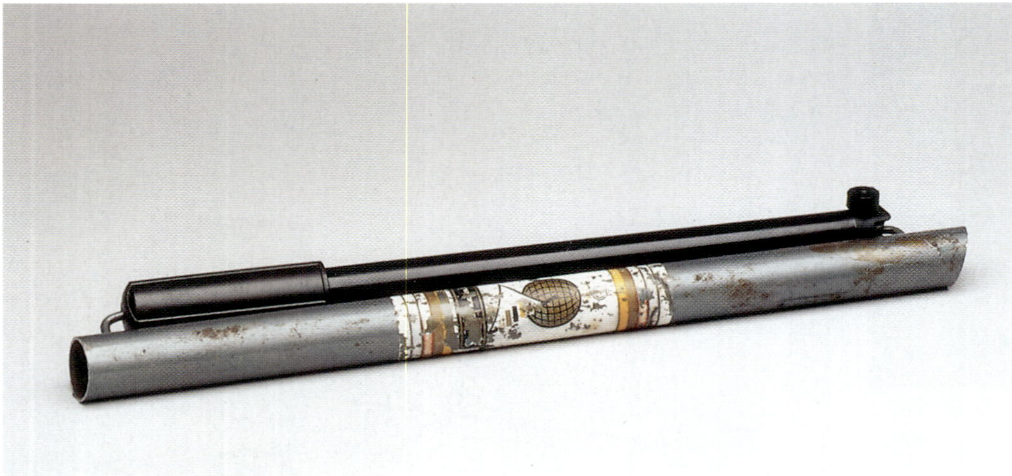

ANDREAS SLOMINSKI, GESTOHLENE LUFTPUMPE, 1998 / STOLEN BICYCLE PUMP, *Deutsche Guggenheim, Berlin.* (PHOTO: EBERLE & EISFELD, BERLIN)

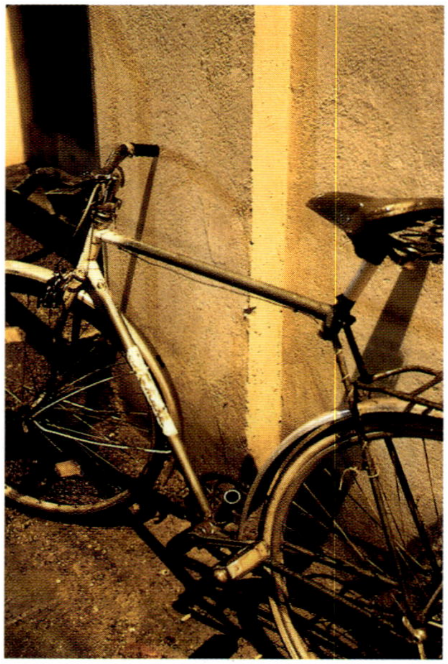

Nachdem mir diese Entsprechungen bewusst geworden waren, erschienen auch andere Aspekte der Ausstellung in einem neuen, unvermuteten Licht, etwa Slominskis witzige Aktion ausserhalb des Museums auf dem berühmten Boulevard Unter den Linden. Als Symbol urbaner Ordentlichkeit wird der von Bäumen gesäumte Grünstreifen sorgfältig gepflegt. Jeder der 370 Bäume ist nummeriert, von der Umweltbehörde registriert und sein Wachstum wird genauestens verfolgt. Diese Manifestation teutonischer Ordnungsliebe wurde von Slominski in Frage gestellt, indem er etwas abseits von der schnurgeraden Allee einen toten Baumstumpf «pflanzte». Und da stand er dann, leicht zu übersehen, aber trotzdem den Eindruck erweckend, dass in dem urbanen Gefüge etwas durcheinander geraten war, eine optische Unregelmässigkeit. Jemand, der über den Stumpf stolperte, mochte ihn für den Überrest eines aus der Reihe getanzten Baums halten, der es gewagt hatte, nicht an der für ihn bestimmten Stelle zu wachsen, und mit dem man deshalb kurzen Prozess gemacht hatte. Als dieser Baumstumpf den Behörden gemeldet wurde, wurden polizeiliche Absperrungen aufgestellt und der Schauplatz von Slominskis Streich verwandelte sich im Nu zum Tatort.[3)]

Die behördliche Massnahme blieb mir im Gedächtnis und nach der Eröffnung der Ausstellung machte ich mich sachkundig, was es mit Unter den Linden und diesen gehegten und gepflegten Bäumen auf sich hatte. Ursprünglich waren sie 1648 von dem Grossen Kurfürsten Friedrich Wilhelm gepflanzt worden und säumten einen Reitweg, der von der Stadt zum Grunewald führte. Der Herrscher hatte sein Herz an sie gehängt und drohte damit, dass er jedem, der sie beschädigte, die Hand abhacken liesse.[4] Als Karl Friedrich Schinkel, der Meisterarchitekt, der im neunzehnten Jahrhundert das Bild der Stadt bestimmte, sein klassizistisches Konzept realisierte, machte er Unter den Linden zu einer der wichtigsten Achsen, an der er Botschaften, Regierungsgebäude, Banken und eine Oper ansiedelte. In einer so prachtvollen Umgebung gediehen natürlich auch die Bäume. Während des Dritten Reichs liess Hitler die Bäume fällen um für seine Militärparaden und Kriegsmanöver mehr Platz zu haben. Jahre später forsteten die Kommunisten dann die Allee Unter den Linden wieder auf, doch nur bis zum Pariser Platz kurz vor dem Brandenburger Tor, dem Tor zum Westen. Als 1989 die Mauer fiel, stellte eine Westberliner Stiftung für Landschaftspflege genügend Bäume zur Verfügung, damit auch dieses letzte Stück wieder bepflanzt werden konnte. Rückblickend kann man am Zustand der Bäume ablesen, wie sich Epochen städtischer Harmonie mit Epochen politischer Unruhe abwechselten. Kannte Slominski diese Geschichte, als er beschloss auf dem Grünstreifen des Boulevards eine Aktion durchzuführen, die Ausstellung auf die Strasse auszudehnen und ahnungslosen Passanten einen auf den ersten Blick harmlosen Streich zu spielen? Ich vermute ja, aber falls ich mich täusche, ist der Kontext wieder einmal der Kunst freudig beigesprungen und hat einem bereits tiefgründigen Werk zusätzlich Tiefe verliehen und uns neue Umwege zu seinem Verständnis erschlossen.

(Übersetzung: Uta Goridis)

1) Teile dieses Absatzes stammen aus Nancy Spectors Katalogbeitrag «Von Fallen, Finten und anderen Rätseln», in: *Andreas Slominski*, Deutsche Guggenheim, Berlin 1999, S. 11.

2) Die Berliner Galeristin Barbara Weiss bemerkte, dass die VOGELFANGSTATION (1998/99) insofern der Quadriga auf dem Brandenburger Tor ähnelte, als die Konstellation der Netze vor der Hütte an jene der ewig reglos in Zeit und Raum verharrenden Pferde vor dem Triumphwagen erinnerte.

3) Op. cit., S. 13.

4) Diese Informationen stammen aus dem Buch von Andrew Gumbel, *Berlin*, Gadogan Books, London 1991, S. 57.

ANDREAS SLOMINSKI, BAUMSTUMPF, 1998, Deutsche Guggenheim, Berlin / TREE STUMP. (PHOTO: EBERLE & EISFELD, BERLIN)

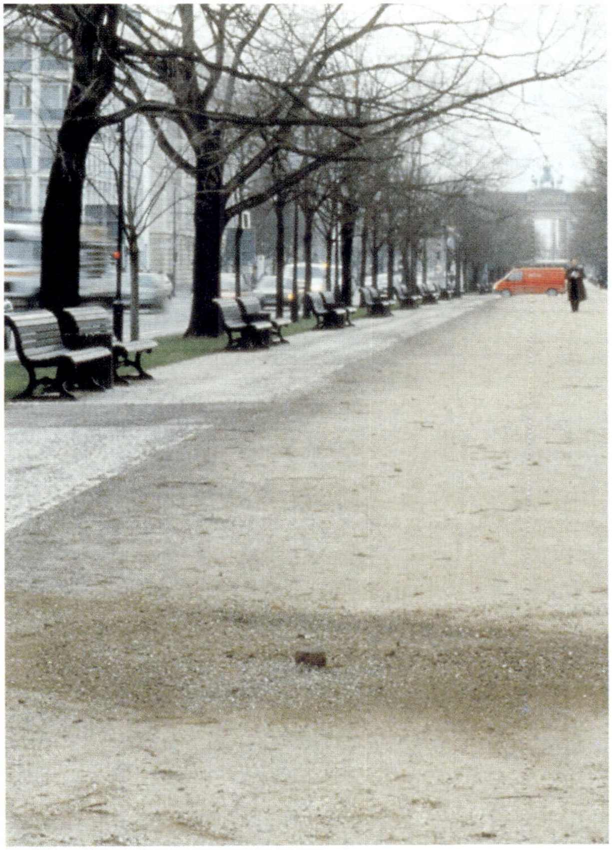

Mäusedome am Rande

PATRICK FREY

So wie auch bei seiner neuesten, bisher grössten Falle, der VOGELFANGSTATION (1998/99), sind bei Andreas Slominski immer wieder Dinge und Materialien in Verbindung zu sehen, über denen ein Hauch von Natursehnsucht zu schweben scheint, gemischt mit einer Prise handwerklicher, oder jedenfalls ländlich-ökologischer Low-Tech-Nostalgie: grüne Netze, Äste und Zweige, graubraune Altholzbretter, verzinktes Eisenblech, Schnüre.

Natürlich trügt der Schein, das Verhältnis zur Natur und zum Naturnahen ist selbst bei der hyperökologisch anmutenden BIRKHUHNFALLE (1998) mit ihren Strohballen und ihren Röhren aus Weidengeflecht ein rein utilitaristisches: Die ländlichen Materialien und der natürliche Look sind ein Mittel zum Zweck, die Ökologie ist im Grunde fallenstellerische Ökonomie. Denn wenn hier etwas nach Natur aussieht oder riecht, dann geht es um eine spezielle Erscheinungsform des Mimetischen. In Anlehnung an einen Ausdruck aus der Fauna könnte man von Mimikry sprechen, allerdings geht es hier um so etwas wie simulierte Mimikry, um eine doppelte Täuschung also, und dieses doppelte Täuschungsmanöver gehört wesentlich zum Fallenhaften der Konzeption, nicht bloss des Künstlers Slominski, sondern jedes realen Fallenerfinders und Fallen(her-)stellers. Um in der natürlichen Umgebung des zu fangenden Tieres nicht aufzufallen müssen viele der Fallen mit Versatzstücken des Naturhaften hergestellt werden. Beim Erfinden, Konzipieren und Fertigen von Fallen geht jeder Fallensteller bereits mit Kunst und Künstlichkeit um, mit künstlichen Materialien und Gestaltung – allerdings auf einer für uns scheinbar simplen und armseligen mimetischen Ebene, denn beim realen Fallenstellen müssen nicht Menschen mimetisch getäuscht, geködert und gelockt werden, sondern Tiere mit ziemlich einfachen «Suchbildern». Zum Beispiel schreckhafte Vögel, die vor dem Klappern farbiger Büchsen unter die Zweige von dekorativ aufgereihten künstlichen Bäumchen – und damit unter das zuklappende Netz – flüchten sollen, oder ein Fuchs, der mehr seiner Nase als dem Auge vertraut und dessen vom betörenden Geruch des Köders übertölpelte Schlauheit nicht ausreicht die hochgradige Künstlichkeit der aus Plastikröhren labyrinthisch montierten FUCHSFALLE (1998) und damit das gefährliche Wesen jeder Falle, ihre Falschheit nämlich, und, darin verborgen, die fallenhafte Ausweglosigkeit zu erkennen.

Bei der VOGELFALLE (1996/97) besteht die Tarnung des Vogelfängers, der die Schnürzüge bedienen muss um eine der vier Fallen auszulösen, aus einem kleinen Unterstand aus Draht und Jutesäcken, der sehr schematisch, aber gerade dadurch auch regressiv-rührend, an die Gestalt eines Pferdes erinnert, ein grosses Kinderspielzeug, das komisch ist und brutal, wenn man sich vorzustellen versucht, ob Vögel beim Anblick dieser Maskerade tatsächlich «denken» würden: «O wie ruhig steht da ein hellbraunes Pferd neben dem Wasserschälchen und den köstlichen Sonnenblumenkernen und Hanfsamen...»; und ob diese hungrigen Vogel-Bewusstseine die Schnürzüge einfach gar *nicht sehen* würden, und auch nicht, dass das Pferd ein viereckiges Jutezelt ohne Beine ist und dass auf dem Pferd

---

PATRICK FREY ist Kabarettist, Kunstkritiker und Verleger. Er lebt in Zürich.

des Anthropozentrums

geschrieben steht, dass die Kaffeebohnen darin aus Nicaragua stammen. Die Frage wäre dann, ob dies also keineswegs nur eine unbeholfene unfreiwillig komische Pferdedarstellung sein könnte, sondern im Gegenteil ein perfektes Kunst-Pferd, eine absolut perfekte Pferde-Simulation für Kohlmeisen und Grünfinken, so vollendet, dass kein Vogel je auf die Idee käme einfach mal kurz um die Pferde-Attrappe herumzufliegen um die Hohlheit des Pferdeleibes zu bemerken und in sein Inneres zu spähen, das leer ist, bis auf die Schnürzüge und eine leere Mineralwasserkiste aus blauem Plastik als Sitz für den Fallensteller.

Bezeichnenderweise gilt das Interesse des Bildhauers Slominski von Anfang an keineswegs der künstlerisch höchst verlockenden Aura einer im Gebrauch befindlichen Falle. Während er bereits ab 1986 in der Regel keine authentischen Fallen mehr als solche ausstellt, sondern diese sammelt und dann für seine Ausstellungen exakt nachbaut, oder nach alten Plänen und Abbildungen rekonstruiert, sind die allerersten seiner Kunst-Fallen von 1984/85 zwar tatsächlich *objets trouvés*, aber auch diese findet er nicht etwa als gebrauchte Fallen im Keller oder im Wald, auratisch aufgeladen vom Drama des Realen, von verzweifelten Befreiungskämpfen, von Blut, Haar, Federn und anderen, im Beuys'schen Sinne «natürlichen» Spuren und Zeichen, sondern als brandneue Fallen auf dem Regal eines Metallwarengeschäftes.

Beim Transfer in die Räume der Kunst interessiert ihn allein die radikal verschärfte Funktionalität, und einen Teil dieser gewissermassen existenziellen Funktionalität der Fallen-Objekte bildet eben ihre ganz spezifische, auf Täuschung ausgerichtete Künst-

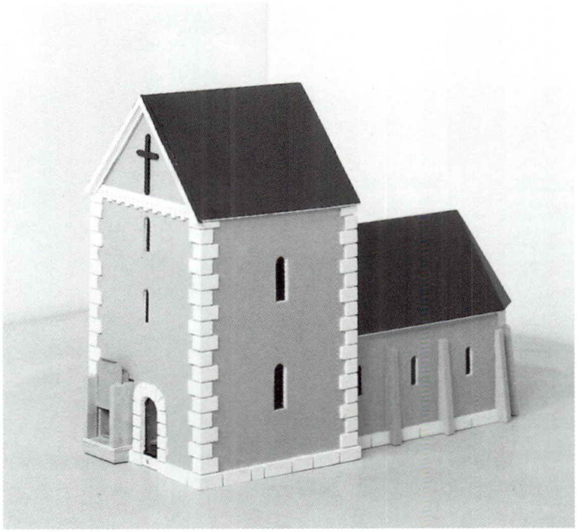

ANDREAS SLOMINSKI, MAUSEFALLE, 1998, Kunstmuseum Winterthur, ca. 42 x 22 x 50 cm / MOUSETRAP, ca. 16½ x 8¹¹⁄₁₆ x 19¹¹⁄₁₆".

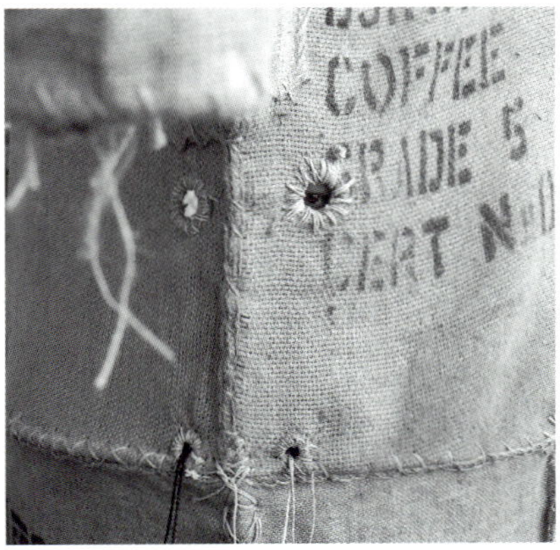

ANDREAS SLOMINSKI, VOGELHERD, 1996–98, Ausschnitt: Pferdehütte / FOWLING FLOOR, detail: horse-shaped shelter. (PHOTO: ALEXANDER TROEHLER, ZÜRICH)

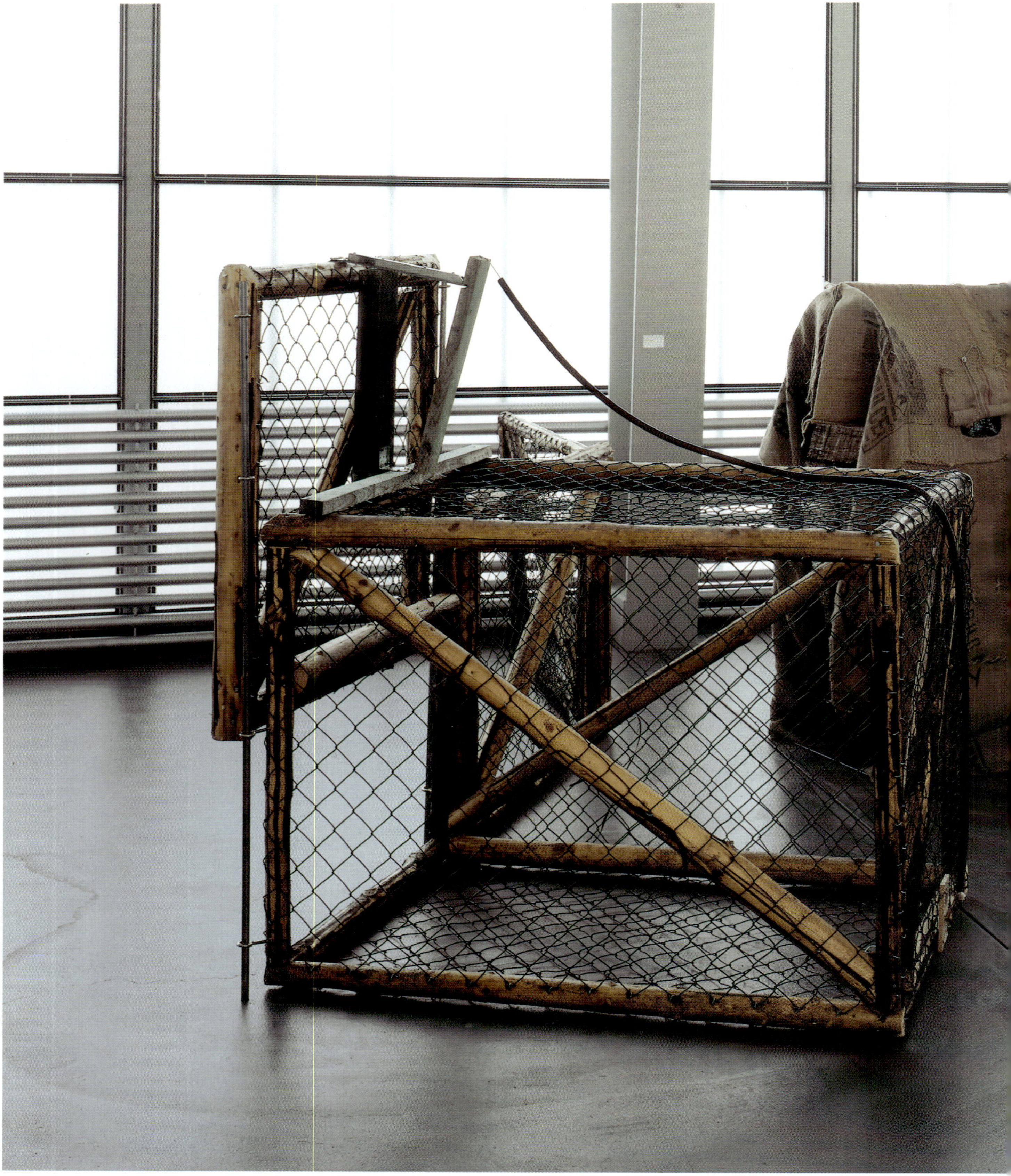

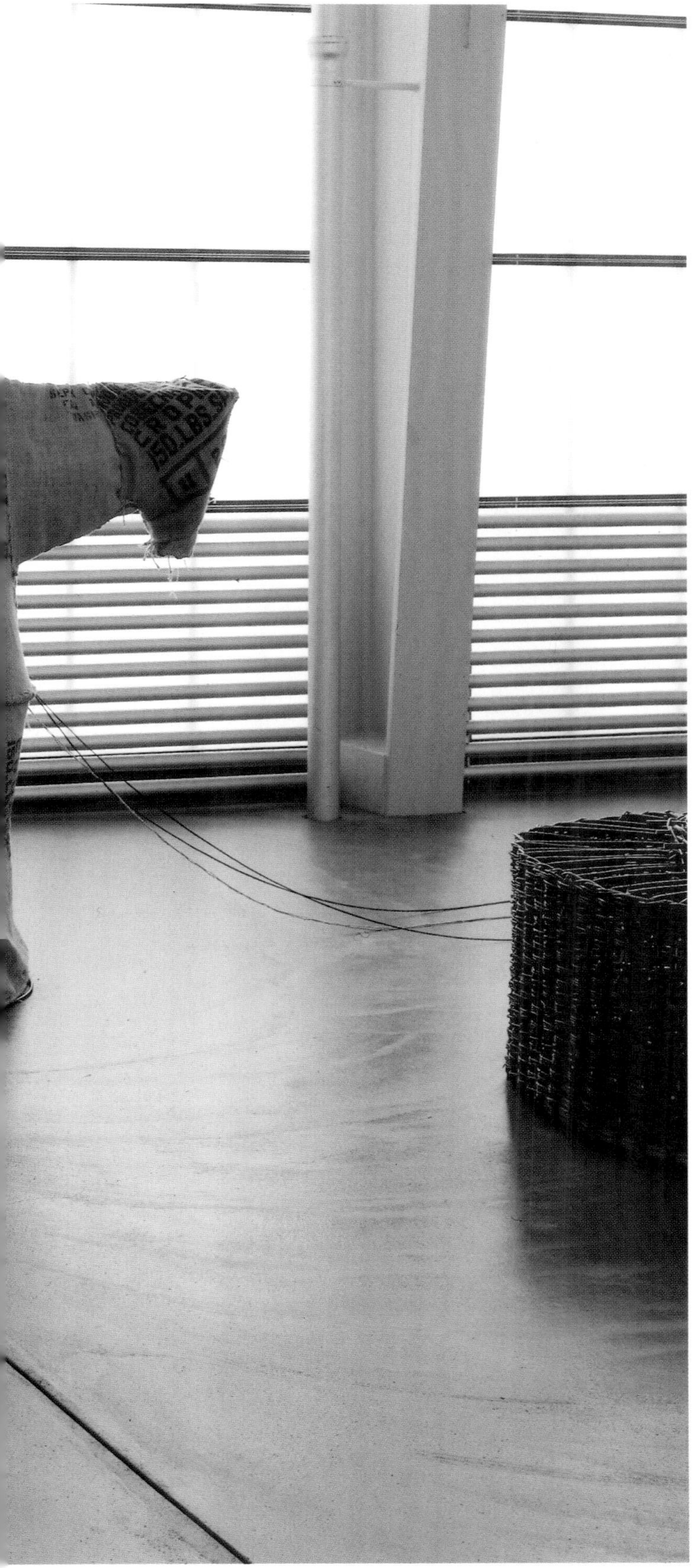

lichkeit. Darin liegt die Virtuosität und die Brisanz des Slominskischen Konzeptes: erkannt zu haben, dass hier, auf einer ebenso paradigmatischen wie fatalen Schnittstelle zwischen Technik und Natur beziehungsweise zwischen Mensch und Tier, eine Klasse von Gegenständen zu finden ist, die bereits vor jedem Zugriff eines Objektkünstlers nicht etwa nur eine kunsthandwerklich reizvolle – diese soll hier nicht interessieren –, sondern eine spezifisch künstlerische Qualität aufweisen.

Mit mimetischen oder apparatischen Mitteln treiben Fallen ein Spiel mit Tricks und Täuschung, dessen mögliche zeichenhafte oder skulpturale Schönheit vom Wesentlichen – der gefährlichen Wahrheit – nie getrennt in Erscheinung tritt, sei es, indem die gestalthafte oder prozessuale Schönheit einer Falle die Gefahr unmittelbar offenbart, oder dass sie das Wesentliche in ihrem Innersten verbirgt, dort, wo der Köder gelegt wird.

Die WÜHLMAUSFALLE (1984/85), eine graziöse Figurine, ist die Gestalt gewordene Mäusephobie, die Schreckhaftigkeit selbst auf vier wie hysterisch gespreizten Beinen aus Stahldraht, die beim Zuschnappen elegant und effizient, begleitet von einem hässlichen metallischen Klang, die zarten Nackenwirbel der Mäusekörperchen zertrümmern werden.

Skulptural oder gleichsam architektonisch von grossem Reiz ist auch die FALLE von 1984/85, eine auf flachem achteckigem Holzsockel errichtete freitragende Kuppel aus Eisendraht, deren – seitlich und im Scheitelpunkt des Kuppelbaus – ästhetisch perfekt angebrachte Eingänge natürlich keine Mauselöcher, sondern in Wahrheit fiese Drahttrichter sind, durch die es kein Entkommen aus dem Mäusedom mehr gibt.

Im Hintergrund: ANDREAS SLOMINSKI, VOGELHERD, 1996–98 (Ausschnitt: Pferdehütte), Jute, Metall, Kunststoff, Netz, Karton, Schnur, Tränken, Köder, 165 x 965 x 239 cm. Vorne: HUNDEFALLE, 1998, Holz, Metall, Draht, Kunststoff, Köder, 174 x 402 x 167 cm, Ausstellung Kunsthalle Zürich /
In the background: FOWLING FLOOR (detail: horse-shaped shelter), burlap, metal, plastic, net, cardboard, string, water bowls, bait, 65 x 380 x 94". In front: DOG TRAP, wood, metal, wire, plastic, bait, 68½ x 158¼ x 65¾". (PHOTO: ALEXANDER TROEHLER)

Sieht die Hausmaus die unnatürlich zentralsymmetrische Gestalt der kleinen Drahtkuppel oder die sich ungewohnt verengende Perspektive der Eingangstrichter? Wird die Wühlmaus an dem grauen Metallding, das eines Tages unmittelbar vor ihrem Mauseloch steht, die anorektische Grazie der Überspanntheit, die ästhetische Immanenz schreckhaft-hysterischen Zuschnappens bemerken? Oder sogar eine Art von Gefallen daran finden und vor lauter Gefallen die Falle nicht mehr sehen?

Das sind zwar etwas merkwürdige, aber keineswegs unsinnige Fragen, denn genau hier liegt das Paradoxe und Faszinierende am fallenstellerischen Dispositiv: Fallen sind zwar so etwas wie früheste Ingenieurskunst, doch weder der technische Erfindungsreichtum noch die wirkungsästhetischen Manipulationen scheinen wirklich auf Menschen oder gar auf die kleine Zielgruppe der Kunstkonsumenten und -konsumentinnen ausgerichtet zu sein. In dieser Hinsicht sind die Gestaltungskriterien einer Falle auch nicht mit den künstlerischen (Neben-)Absichten zum Beispiel beim Bau einer Brücke zu vergleichen. Die dekorative Grazie der «falschen» Bäumchen bei der VOGELFANGSTATION (1998/99) ist ganz und gar nicht dasselbe wie zum Beispiel die dekorativen allegorischen Gravuren von Blättern und Ranken auf dem Schaft eines Jagdgewehrs.

Auch wenn wir mit anthropozentrischer Arroganz im Innersten immer noch überzeugt sind, dass Tiere kein Wissen um den eigenen Tod und deshalb auch kein Bewusstsein von Kunst haben können, findet im Laufe der Betrachtung der für die Kunst rekonstruierten und funktionierenden «Fallen» von Andreas Slominski eine Offenbarung statt: Alles, was an diesen Dingen künstlerischen Charakter hat, geht uns ursprünglich und eigentlich gar nichts an. Alles Wesentliche an Fallen ist für ihr jeweiliges Beutetier gemacht, insgesamt und in jedem Detail, die anderen Kriterien ihrer Beschaffenheit sind sekundär.

Und so stehen wir beim Anblick der Slominski-Fallen irgendwann im Laufe der Betrachtung plötzlich vor seltsamen, uns sehr fremden Gegenständen, und zwar fremd in künstlerischer Hinsicht. Das wirklich Fremde und Seltsame an ihnen ist ihre immer gespannte, immer gefährlich einladende Schönheit, die nicht wirklich für unser synästhetisches Erfahrungssystem bestimmt zu sein scheint, sondern auf die sensorischen Kriterien von Ratten, Birkhühnern oder roten Wegschnecken (und deren Überlistung) hin konzipiert wurde.

Im Grunde ist es, als stünden wir rituellen Gegenständen, Vorrichtungen oder Installationen eines Stammes gegenüber, von dem uns nicht nur diese Rituale und überhaupt das gesamte Glaubens- und Sinnsystem, sondern nahezu alles fremd und unbekannt wäre, was über Morphologie, Anatomie und etwas Verhalten hinausginge. Vom synästhetischen Erfahrungssystem einer roten häuschenlosen Wegschnecke haben wir absolut keine Ahnung, geschweige denn von ihrem ästhetischen Bewusstsein. Wir kennen zwar ein paar Bilder kopulierender Schnecken und in sensomotorischer Hinsicht wissen wir, dass sie sich auf einer selbstproduzierten Schleimspur fortbewegen. Was sie bei all dem empfinden, wissen wir nicht. Das In-der-Welt-Sein einer roten Wegschnecke ist uns ein vollkommenes Rätsel.

Die FANGRINNE FÜR SCHNECKEN (1998), die Slominski im selben Jahr in der Kunsthalle Zürich installierte, ist auf den ersten Blick eine flache minimalistische Skulptur. Ein vollkommen unauffällig in die Raumecke platziertes, längsrechteckiges Boden-Wand-Stück, aus grünlichen, diskret auf Nauman verweisenden Fiberglasprofilen, die als flache Rampe zu einer Längsrinne hinaufführen. Auf der Rampe ist das Fiberglas stark gekörnt, innen in der Rinne spiegelglatt. Auf der Rampe sollen die roten Wegschnecken vermutlich gut vorankommen um dann in der Rinne, in der sich wahrscheinlich das Regenwasser sammeln wird, die Kontrolle über ihre Schleimspur zu verlieren und derart zu enden. Oder wird die dreissig Zentimeter weite Reise über die rauh gekörnte Rampe vielleicht zur Tortur, unternommen nur wegen des Dufts von Wasser in der lockenden Rinne, eine Foltertour, die nur von ganz wenigen der roten Wegschnecken überhaupt überstanden werden wird, jenen Glücklichen, die dann zur Belohnung ihre letzten Minuten auf der wohltuend glatten, feuchten Oberfläche verbringen dürfen, wobei sie die tief im Glanz lauernde Gefährlichkeit erst erkennen werden, wenn es bereits zu spät sein wird? So, wie es für den menschlichen Betrachter an dieser Stelle der Betrachtung längst zu spät ist,

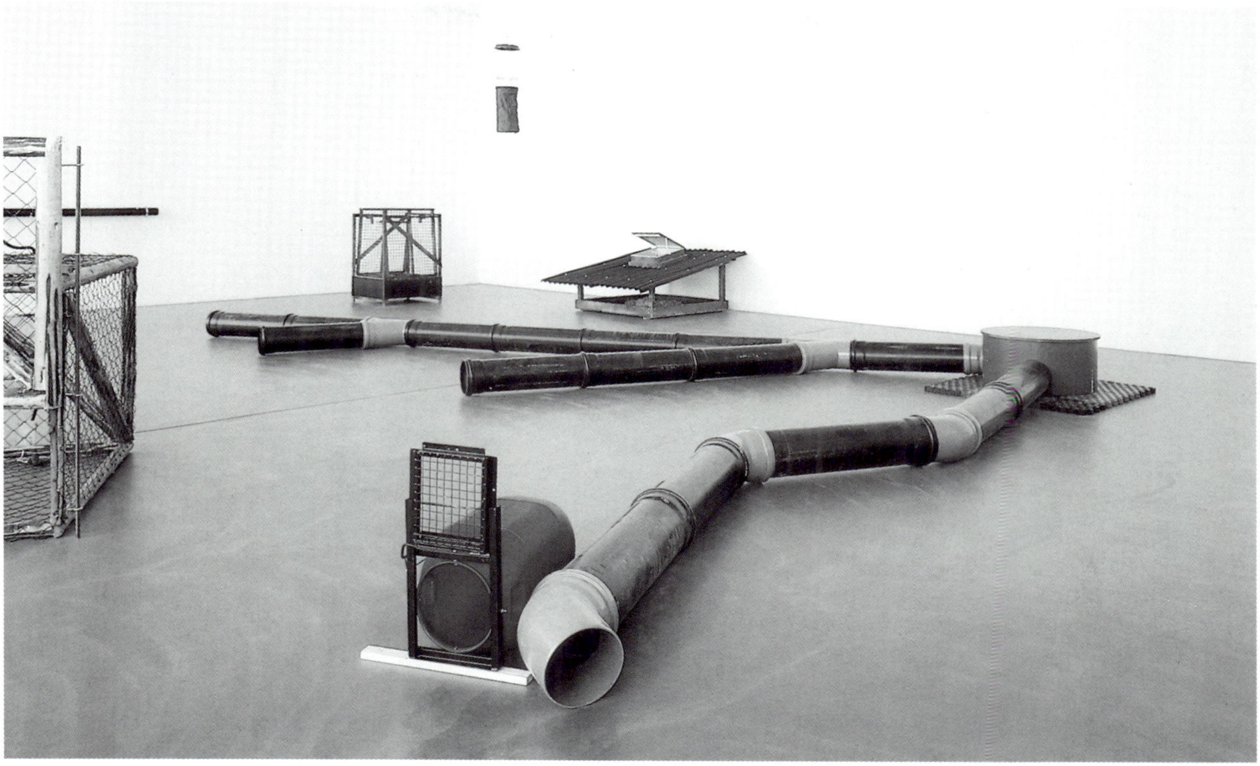

sich verflüchtigende Begrifflichkeiten wie «minimalistisch» oder «auf Nauman verweisend» wieder dingfest und sinnvoll zu machen, was je nach (Kunst-)Psyche oder bildungskapitalistischem Wertesystem des Betrachters zu verstörender Irritation oder grosser Erleichterung führen kann.

Die im reinen Funktionieren versteckte Schönheit von Slominskis Fallen-Skulpturen entfaltet sich erst so richtig beim Erkennen der Komplikation, mit der die reine Funktionalität erst wirklich formbildend, beziehungsweise signifikant wird. Und weil die Wege der Komplikation uns so fremd und geheimnisvoll erscheinen, ist da zugleich so etwas wie eine genuine Art-Brut-Qualität zu finden, etwas Primäres, frei von Naivität, voll Bewusstheit und mitten im Zentrum der Gegenwartskunst.

In den grossen Komplikationen von Slominskis «Fallen» finden wir also einen ganz neuen und

ANDREAS SLOMINSKI, FUCHSFALLE, 1998, Kunststoff, Metall, Spreu, Lockstoff, Köder, Installation in der Kunsthalle Zürich, 71 x 874 x 662 cm (im Vordergrund) / FOX TRAP, plastic, metal, straw, scent lure, bait, 28 x 344 x 260 5/8" (in front).

genuinen Ausdruck jener vom künstlerischen Autoren-Subjekt befreiten Gelassenheit, jener bewusst inszenierten, vollkommenen Absichtslosigkeit, von der die Autoren der modernen Kunst immer wieder träumten und an der sie sich müde vom Ichsein, erschöpft vom autoritären Selbst immer wieder versuchen. Es malt. Oder: Höhere Wesen befahlen. Bei Slominski, dessen Arbeiten uns enthüllen, auf welch hochkomplizierte und zugleich skandalös einfache Art ein Werk mit seinem Adressaten in Bezug gesetzt werden kann, liegt die Brisanz der künstlerischen Absichtslosigkeit in der klaren Absicht des Fallenstellers.

Mouse Domes at the

PATRICK FREY

Like many of his other works, VOGELFANGSTATION (Bird Trapping Station, 1998/99), Andreas Slominski's most recent, largest trap, uses materials that are somehow imbued with a longing for nature mixed with a dash of craft-daft nostalgia, or at the least rural, ecological low-tech kind: green nets, branches and twigs, old planks of gray-brown wood, galvanized metal, cords.

Of course appearances are deceptive. Even in the apparently hyper-ecological BIRKHUHNFALLE (Grouse Trap, 1998), with its bales of straw and wicker-work tubes, the relationship to nature and all things natural is purely utilitarian: The rural materials and the natural look are the means to an end. The trappings of ecology are no more than economy. For whenever anything here reeks of nature, as it were, we are in fact dealing with a special kind of mimesis. To use a term from the animal kingdom one might even describe it as mimicry, albeit a kind of simulated mimicry, that is to say a double deception—and this double deception manoeuver is at the heart of the trap-like quality of the overall concept, not only as conceived by the artist Slominski but also by the real-life deviser, maker, and setter of the trap. To avoid attracting the attention of the prey in its natural surroundings, traps often have to be disguised with natural-looking props. Any trapper inventing, designing, and constructing a trap is already using art and artifice, artificial materials and structures—even if only on a seemingly simple, meagre mimetic level, for real traps are not intended as a mimetic deception to fool human beings, but to bait and to lure animals with their relatively basic "searching images." Timorous birds, for instance, take refuge from clattering colored tin-cans hanging from the branches of decoratively arranged, small, artificial trees only to find a net closing in around them; the fox who trusts his nose more than his eyes and, duped by the alluring scent of the bait, may not be wily enough to recognize the extreme artificiality of the labyrinthine, plastic-tube FUCHSFALLE (Fox Trap, 1998) and by implication the underlying danger of every trap, its falseness and the inherent impossibility of escape from ensnarement.

In VOGELFALLE (Bird Trap, 1996/97), the bird-catcher who has to operate the cords in order to spring one of the four traps is disguised in a small shelter of wire and burlap bags, which is reminiscent—schematically but thus all the more regressively touchingly—of the shape of a horse, a big children's toy which is funny and brutal if you try to imagine whether the bird, seeing this masquerade, would really "think," "Oh how peacefully that light brown horse is standing next to the water dish and the delicious sunflower seeds and hemp seeds...," and whether the hungry bird-minds would simply f a i l t o s e e the cords, and also fail to see that the horse is a four-cornered burlap tent without legs and that there is writing on it saying that it contains coffee beans from Nicaragua. The question would then be whether this is not just some unwittingly amusing, clumsy image of a horse but in fact a perfect art-horse, an absolutely perfect horse-simulation for great tits and green finches, so superb that no bird

PATRICK FREY is a performer, critic, and publisher who lives in Zurich.

Periphery of Peopledom

would ever dream of quickly flying once round it and perhaps spot the hollowness of its horse-body and maybe peer into its insides which are empty apart from the cords and a blue plastic, upturned mineral-water crate for the trapper to sit on.

Interestingly enough, right from the outset Slominski the sculptor was not drawn by the—artistically extremely enticing—aura of a trap in use. While he has generally not exhibited genuine traps as such since 1986—instead he collects traps and then makes exact copies of them for his exhibitions, or reconstructs them according to old plans and pictures—his very first art-traps from 1984/85 were indeed *objets trouvés*, but even these he did not find as used traps in the cellar or in the woods, auratically charged with the drama of reality, redolent of desperate struggles to escape, with "natural" Beuysian traces and signs, with blood, fur, feathers and the like: on the contrary he bought them brand-new off the shelf at the hardware store.

His interest in transposing them into the realms of art is solely the resultant radical intensification of their functionality, and part of this, in some senses existential, functionality of the trap-objects derives from their very specific artifice focusing entirely on deception. This is what lends Slominski's concept its virtuosity and explosive energy: to have recognized that here on the interface between technology and Nature, or between humans and animals—an interface that is as paradigmatic as it is fatal—is a class of objects which, even before any intervention by the object-artist, are not only of interest on a structural, craft level—for that is not the issue here—but which display a specific artistic quality of their own.

By means of mimesis and practical devices, traps play a game with tricks and trickery, with a potential symbolic or sculptural beauty that is always inextricably linked with their very essence—the dangerous truth—whether it be that the gestalt-like or functioning beauty of a trap openly reveals the danger or whether its essence remains hidden deep inside where the bait is set.

The WÜHLMAUSFALLE (Vole Trap, 1984/85), a graceful figurine, is the reification of rodentophobia, a realization of terror on four so-to-speak hysterically extended steel legs which snap together with an ugly metallic clang as they elegantly and efficiently pulverize the tiny creature's cervical vertebra. Another work with considerable sculptural or even architectural appeal is the FALLE (Trap, 1984/85): a self-supporting dome of wire mesh on a flat, octagonal wooden plinth. Of course the aesthetically perfect entrances at the side and at the apex of the dome are not mouse holes but mean wire cones which preclude any hope of escape from the mouse dome.

Does the house mouse see the unnaturally symmetrical shape of the little wire dome or the unusually narrowing perspective of the entrance cones? When the vole sees the gray metal thing directly in front of its hole one day, will it notice its overly taut, anorexic grace, the aesthetic immanence of terror-struck, hysterical snapping shut? Or maybe take a kind of delight in it and for sheer delight not properly see what it has alighted on?

Somewhat odd but by no means meaningless questions, for herein lies the paradoxical nature and fascination of traps and trap-like structures: In a way traps are one of the earliest forms of engineering, yet neither the wealth of technological invention here nor the visually aesthetic manipulations carried out on these traps seem really to be directed towards human beings nor even towards their own small target group of art consumers. In this sense the design criteria of a trap cannot be compared with the artistic (side) effects and intentions involved, for instance, in the construction of a bridge. The decorative grace of the "fake" trees in VOGELFANGSTATION (1998/99) is absolutely not the same as, for instance, the decorative, allegorical engraving of leaves and tendrils on the stock of a huntsman's rifle.

Even if, in our anthropocentric arrogance, we are still convinced in our hearts that animals have no awareness of their own death and can thus also have no awareness of art, when we observe Andreas Slominski's traps—reconstructed and functioning for the sake of art—one thing is revealed to us: Everything artistic about these things originally had nothing to do with us. Everything that matters about the traps is made for the intended prey, from the overall concept down to each last detail. Any other features of their construction are secondary.

And so as we gaze at the Slominski traps, at some point we suddenly see that they are indeed peculiar, very strange objects—strange, that is to say, from an artistic point of view. The really strange, peculiar thing about them is their ever taut, ever perilously enticing beauty which does not really seem to be geared towards our synaesthetic sensibilities but towards the sensory capacities of rats, grouse, or orange slugs (and how to outwit these).

Basically it is as though we were faced with ritual objects, devices and installations belonging to a tribe whose rituals and whose entire sensory and belief systems—in fact practically everything—were foreign and unknown to us, everything, that is, that went beyond morphology, anatomy, and some aspects of behavior. We have not the faintest idea of the synaesthetic sensibilities of a naked orange slug, not to mention its aesthetic awareness. It is true we have seen pictures of copulating slugs and in sensory-motor terms we know that they propel themselves forwards on a trail of mucous that they themselves produce. What they feel about all this is unknown to us. The being-in-the-world of an orange slug is a complete mystery to us.

At first sight the FANGRINNE FÜR SCHNECKEN (Ditch to Trap Slugs, 1998) is a flat Minimalist sculpture: a rectangular wall and floor piece placed inconspicuously in the corner of the room with greenish sections of fiberglass (discreetly reminiscent of Nauman) sloping up to a long ditch. The fiberglass on the ramp is roughly grained while inside the ditch it is slippery smooth. Presumably the slugs would make

good progress up the ramp only to lose control over their own mucous trail in the ditch—where rainwater would no doubt collect—and thus they would die. Or would the twelve-inch journey up the rough, grainy ramp perhaps be sheer torture which the slug only submits itself to because of the scent of the water in the alluring ditch, a tortuous undertaking which only a very few of the slugs would survive at all, those fortunate few who would be rewarded by being able to spend their last minutes on the soothingly smooth, damp surface only to notice too late the danger lurking in its gleaming depths? In just the same way that at this point it is far too late for the human observer to cling to and try to make sense of fleeting notions like "Minimalist" or "reminiscent of Nauman," which—depending on the individual viewer's (art-)psyche and cultural capital value-system—could induce baffling discomfort or considerable relief.

The beauty lurking in the pure functionality of Slominski's traps only becomes fully evident as the viewer recognizes the complexity of the way in which pure functionalism truly determines the form and is significant as such. And because the ways of this complexity seem to us so strange and mysterious, the work takes on a genuine *art brut* quality, something basic yet not naive, self-aware and right at the center of contemporary art.

Thus in the huge complexity of Slominski's traps we find a completely new and genuine expression of that ease untrammelled by artistic author-subject relationships, that consciously staged, total lack of intention which the artists of Modernity have always dreamt of and which they have always taken another run at, tired of their own existence-as-I and exhausted by their own authoritarian Self. It paints. Or: Higher Beings Commanded. In Slominski's works, which reveal the complexity and yet scandalous simplicity with which a work can establish contact with its addressee, it turns out that the explosive energy of his artistic lack of intent stems from the all too clear intent of the trapper. *(Translation: Fiona Elliott)*

ANDREAS SLOMINSKI, FANGRINNE FÜR SCHNECKEN, 1998, Kunststoff, Metall, 10,5 x 411 x 40 cm /
DITCH TO TRAP SLUGS, plastic, metal, 4 1/8 x 161 3/4 x 15 3/4".
(PHOTO: ALEXANDER TROEHLER, ZÜRICH)

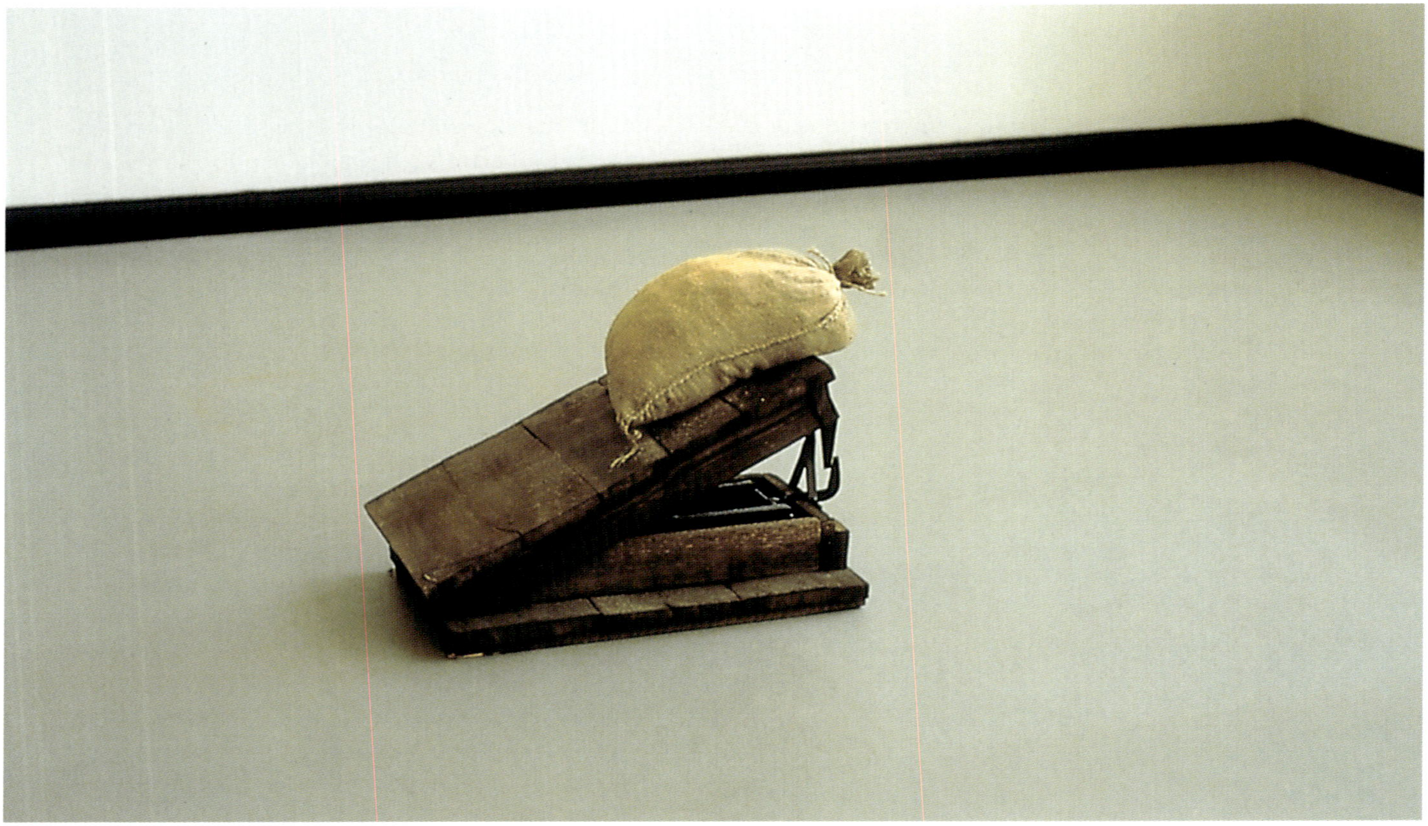

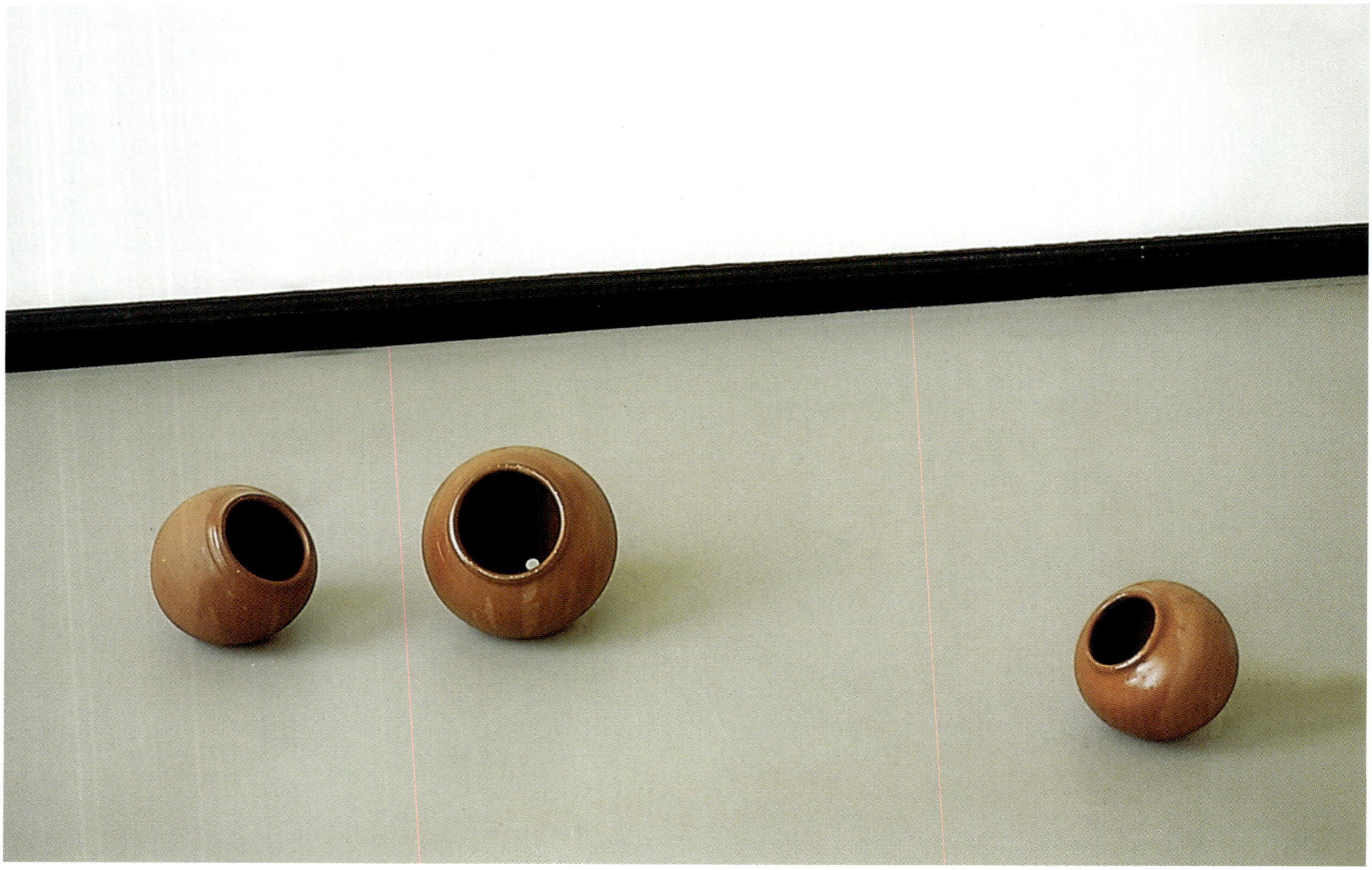

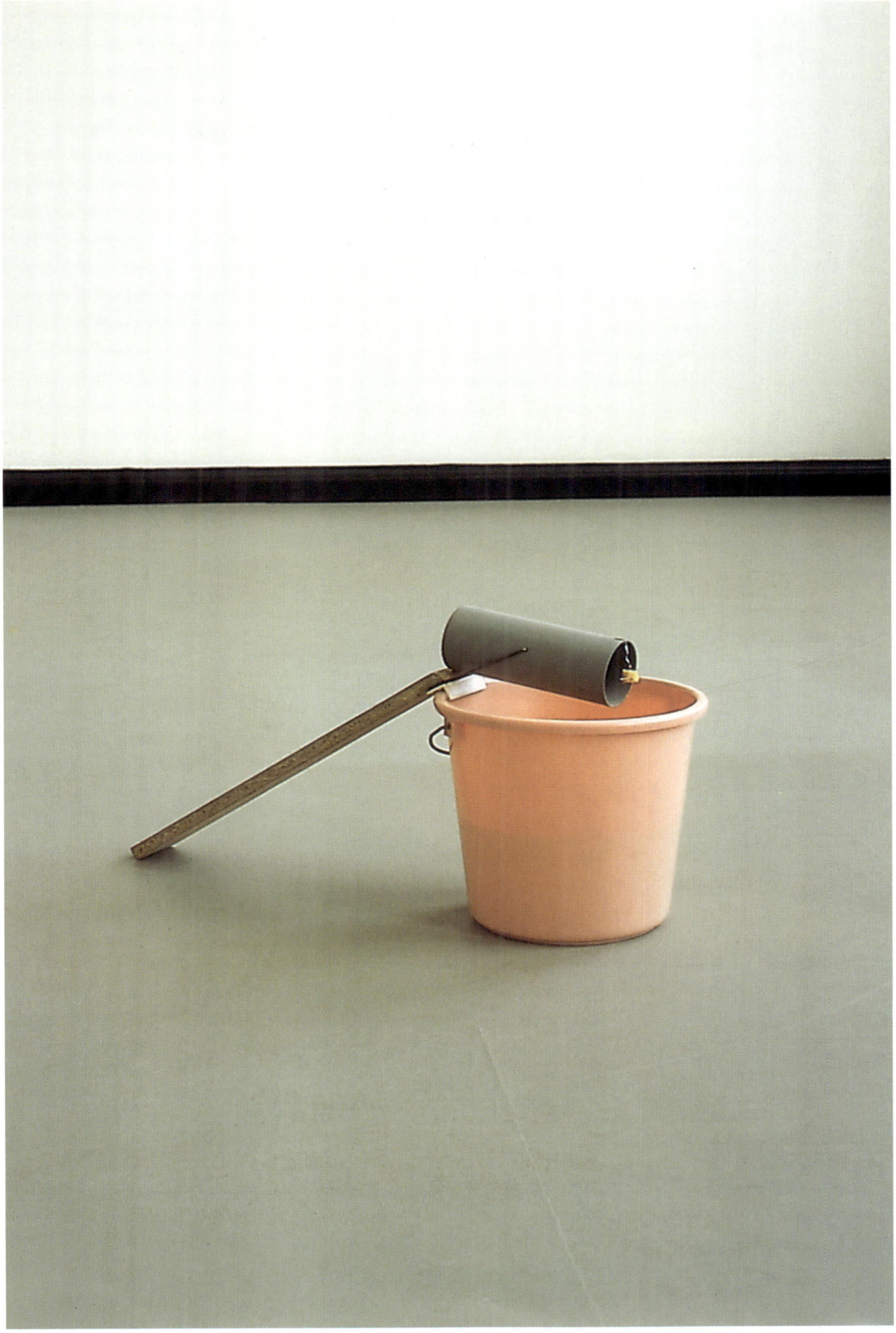

ANDREAS SLOMINSKI, *WÜRGEFALLE FÜR KLEINRAUBZEUG, 1992 (links oben), WOLFSFALLEN, 1993 (unten), und MÄUSEMASSENFANG, 1990 (rechte Seite):*
alle Kunsthalle Hamburg / TRAP TO THROTTLE SMALL VERMIN, 1992 (top), WOLF TRAPS, 1993 (bottom), and MASS MOUSETRAP, 1990 (right-hand page).

JULIAN HEYNEN

Wortlos

Andreas Slominski: Manchmal denke ich, dass beinahe jedes Wort über seine Arbeiten schon eines zu viel sein könnte. Und doch verfällt man immer wieder ins Berichten und ins Erzählen. Wenn der Gegenstand vor einem so wörtlich ist wie hier und wenn der Künstler fast ostentativ zur Seite tritt und schweigt, weckt das die Lust auf Geschichten. Seine Objekte und Taten provozieren offensichtlich die wortgewandte Beschreibung und den poetisch gestimmten Kommentar. Wo die Arbeiten wie ein kunstvoll-lakonischer Rückzug auf ein Terrain anmuten, das erst noch zu entdecken wäre, rüstet sich das Verständnis mit reichem Gerät. Und nicht zuletzt will womöglich auch der Verdacht der Eulenspiegelei mit ausgreifenden Schilderungen der Umstände beruhigt werden.

Es ist auch etwas Richtiges an diesem Hang zu den Worten, an dieser Neigung die Bilder-Gesten des Künstlers in die Sprache hinein auszudehnen. Denn neben der Wörtlichkeit schwingt in jeder Arbeit zugleich eine nur halb verdeckte Ausdruckskraft, die als Sprungbrett über den Sachverhalt hinaus dienen könnte. Die kleinen Staubtuchstapel haben in ihrer Sorgfalt und Frische eine Dichte, die Gedanken über Skulptur ebenso anregt wie fragile Emotionen. Oder sollte es ein Zufall sein, dass die elegant-melancholische Biegung des Halses der Giraffe, die die Briefmarke anleckt, an jene der Strassenleuchte erinnert, um die in derselben Stadt ein Fahrradreifen geraten war? Und woher kommt in einer grossen Ausstellung mit Fallen die plötzliche Gewissheit sich mitten in einem Landschaftsgemälde zu befinden? Noch der banalste Gegenstand, der in den Szenen des Künstlers zum Träger der Handlung wird (etwa der hölzerne Eisstiel im leeren Kaufhausschaufenster), spricht ohne weiteres solch eine vernehmliche Sprache. Noch bevor man etwas über die Umstände seines Auftritts erfährt, hat er schon einen Eindruck hinterlassen. Seine Form hat zusammen mit dem vielleicht nur vagen Wissen über seine Funktion beim Betrachter eine Stimmung erzeugt, die sich zu einem Sinn vorarbeiten könnte. Das Wort, das aus dem Gegenstand zu sprechen scheint, ist aber eben nur eine Andeutung; es ist zu kurz und zu verhalten oder zu fremd um schon als Rede zu gelten. Aber es ist ein Reiz, der überspringt, um durch Erzählung das Wort zum Stück zu ergänzen.

Und dann erst die Umstände hinter den Gegenständen! Bisweilen enthüllt der Künstler sie selbst durch Photos und Filme. Aber auch wenn er es nicht tut, die Geschichten sprechen sich herum – dafür wird er schon irgendwie gesorgt haben. Sind sie einmal in der Welt, kann man sie von den Gegenständen natürlich nicht mehr trennen; sie sind Teil von ihnen. Ja, einmal hat er sie – in der Form eines Gerüchts – sogar in den Mittelpunkt gestellt, als es hiess, irgendwo in der Wand eines leeren Raumes sei (unsichtbar) eine Menschenhand eingemauert. Sollte man also vielleicht das ganze Augenmerk auf die Berichte vom Hintergrund dessen, was man vor Ort

JULIAN HEYNEN ist stellvertretender Direktor der Krefelder Museen Haus Lange, Haus Esters und Kaiser Wilhelm Museum. Er lebt in Krefeld.

vorfindet, richten? Wäre es sinnvoll, den Gegenstand nur zum Anlass zu nehmen und seine Bedeutung in der Prägnanz oder auch der Rätselhaftigkeit der Geschichte aufgehen zu lassen? Hätte der Künstler seine Fallen dann womöglich gar nicht im Sichtbaren, sondern im Vorstellungsraum der Erzählungen über sein Tun aufgestellt? Das wäre immerhin eine Möglichkeit. Er würde so recht gut in seine Zeit passen, indem er nur die Ausgangspunkte setzt, von denen aus sich als eigentliche Arbeit ein mehr oder weniger offener Diskurs oder eine Kette von Aktionen entwickelt. Die Berichte und Geschichten würden dann die Gegenstände nicht überwuchern oder verdrängen, sondern sozusagen erst rechtfertigen.

Oder ist es ganz anders? Vielleicht sind die Erzählungen und Spekulationen nur das Murmeln und Tuscheln, das in der Umgebung entsteht, wenn sich die Sache selbst dermassen auf das Notwendigste zurückzieht. Das Rauschen der Worte wäre dann der Versuch den Schrecken zu besänftigen, den die Sprachlosigkeit der Arbeiten auslöst. Dieses Fehlen von Sprache hat etwas mit der Plötzlichkeit zu tun, mit der sich einem die Gegenstände zu erkennen geben. Das Wesentliche geschieht nämlich in jener ersten Sekunde, in der man den Museumsraum betritt und unerwartet das alte, bepackte Fahrrad sieht. Oder in jenem Bruchteil eines Moments, wenn der unbekannt-unschuldige Gegenstand zu Füssen die Worte Falle und Zuschnappen ins Bewusstsein schickt. Aber etwa auch dann, wenn die unendliche Ruhe des Staubtuchstapels die Teilnahmslosigkeit des Betrachters urplötzlich unterbricht und affektiv

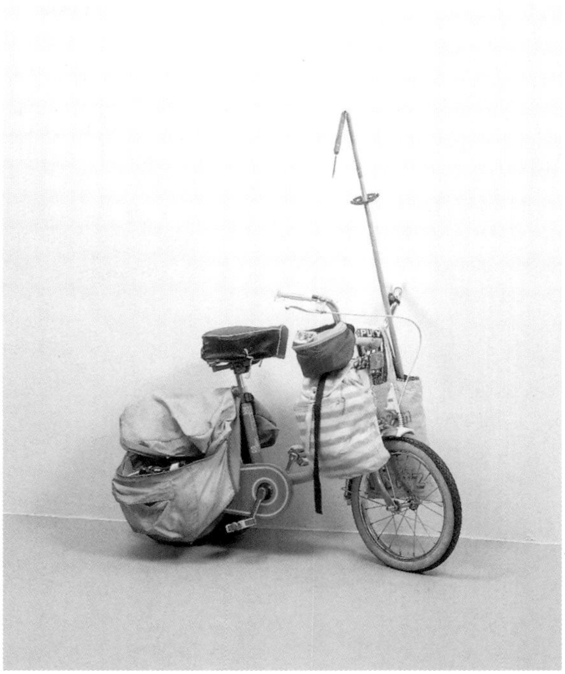

ANDREAS SLOMINSKI, OHNE TITEL, 1996–97, Kinderfahrrad, Flaschenhälse, verschiedene Materialien, 130 x 110 x 50 cm / UNTITLED, children's bicycle, bottle necks, mixed media, 51⅛ x 43¼ x 19¾". (PHOTO: ARNO DECLAIR, HAMBURG)

durchschneidet. Danach mag sich eine Untersuchung anschliessen, die Details blosslegt und das Erlebnis so zu sichern sucht. Sie ist nicht falsch und auch nicht unnütz, aber als Nachbearbeitung wird sie immer hinter dem ersten – und womöglich unwiederholbaren – Moment zurückbleiben. Man denke an ein gelungenes Gedicht, wo zwei oder drei Worte so aneinander geraten, dass etwas Unerhörtes, etwas völlig Unbekanntes eintritt, das man dennoch sofort «versteht». Selbst hier, wo das Material die Sprache ist, fehlen in diesen Augenblicken die Worte, ist reine Chemie am Werk. Die Gegenstände und Aktionen des Künstlers kommen von diesseits der Sprache. Es sind reine Bilder, die es gar nicht darauf anlegen, die Sprache zu erreichen. Ihr Moment ist der Augenaufschlag – stumm, aber dicht und klar. Andreas Slominski: wort-los.

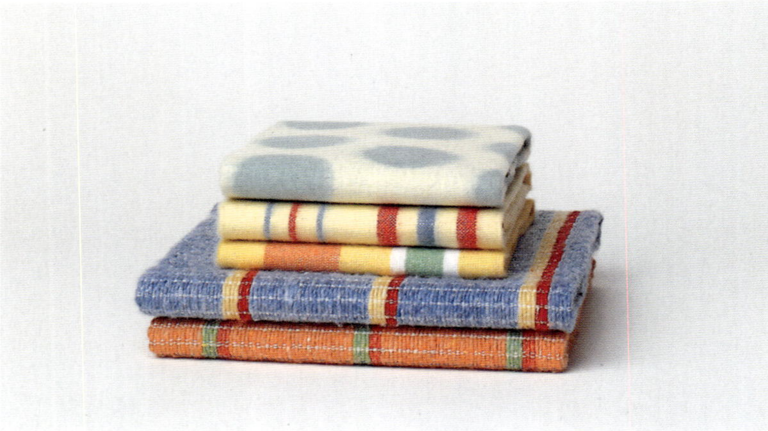

ANDREAS SLOMINSKI, OHNE TITEL, 1988, Stoff, Museum für Moderne Kunst, Frankfurt, 10 x 20 x 19,5 cm / UNTITLED, fabric, 3⅞ x 7⅞ x 7¾".

JULIAN HEYNEN

Wordless

Andreas Slominski: Sometimes I think that practically any word about his work is a word too many. And yet it's hard to resist the temptation to talk about it. When the objects are as literal as these and when the artist fades wordlessly and almost ostentatiously into the woodwork, the desire to tell stories automatically arises. His objects and deeds inevitably provoke eloquent description and poetically attuned commentary. Where the works suggest an artistically laconic retreat to a terrain that has yet to be discovered, the interpreting viewer resorts to an arsenal of elaborate equipment. And in the final analysis, extensive accounts of the circumstances may even serve to allay the suspicion of a certain affinity with Till Eulenspiegel.[1)]

There is also a certain rightness about this predilection for words, this tendency towards a verbal elaboration of the artist's pictorial gestures, because, in addition to being so literal, each of the works makes an imperfectly concealed expressive impact that could serve as a springboard for reflection beyond the givens of these gestures. The little stacks of dust cloths, so fresh and carefully folded, have a density that inspires thoughts as much about fragile emotions as about sculpture. Or is it mere coincidence that the melancholy elegance of the giraffe bending its neck to lick the stamp calls to mind the streetlamp in the same city with a bicycle tire wrapped around it? And in a large exhibition of traps, why are we suddenly so certain that we are in the midst of a landscape painting? Even the most mundane object used as the vehicle of action in the artist's scenes (like the wooden ice-cream stick in the department store window) effortlessly speaks such a distinct language. Even before we learn anything about the circumstances of its appearance, it has already made an impression. Its form possibly combined with only a vague idea of its function is enough to conjure up a mood that could pave the way to meaning. But the word that may seem to emanate

---

JULIAN HEYNEN is assistant director at the Krefelder Kunstmuseen (Haus Lange, Haus Esters, Kaiser Wilhelm Museum). He lives in Krefeld, Germany.

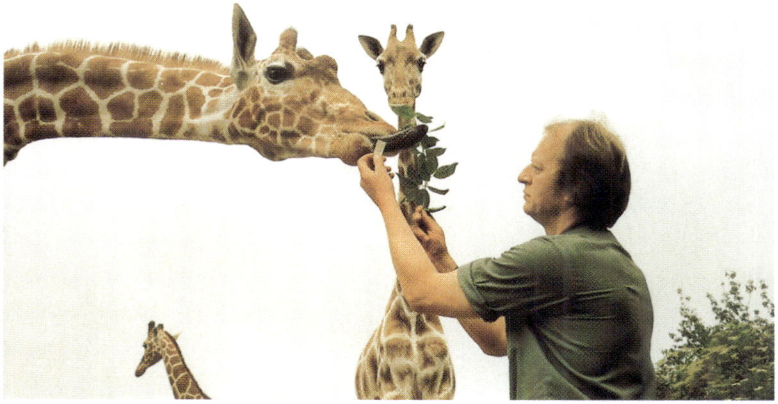

ANDREAS SLOMINSKI, ANFEUCHTEN EINER BRIEFMARKE, 1996, *Aktion am 26. Juni 1996 mit Tierpfleger Ferdinand Heinemann, «Skulptur. Projekte Münster 1997»* / WETTING A STAMP, *action on June 26, 1996 with keeper Ferdinand Heinemann.*

from the object is merely an insinuation; it is too short and too understated or odd to count as speech. But it acts as a stimulus to complement it with narrative.

And then there are the circumstances behind the objects! Sometimes the artist discloses them in photographs and films. But even when he doesn't, he sees to it that the stories get around—one way or another. And having leaked out, they instantly become inseparably intertwined with the objects. In one case, Slominski centerstaged the story itself by circulating the rumor that a human hand had been concealed in the wall of an empty room. Should we perhaps focus our attention entirely on the background of the things we encounter on site? Would it make sense to treat the object only as a catalyst, whose meaning takes shape in the striking clarity or enigmatic mystery of the story? And would the artist then have set up his traps in the space of the imagination created by the reports of what he does, rather than in visible space? That would certainly be a possibility. It would be most appropriate, for then he would simply posit points of departure as trajectories for the actual works, which would develop in the form of a more or less open discourse or a chain of actions. Instead of overwhelming or displacing the objects, these stories and accounts would, in fact, be their justification.

Or is it a giraffe of an entirely different color? Perhaps the stories and speculations are simply the murmur and susurrus that ensues when the thing itself yields only what it must and nothing more. The rush of words would then be the attempt to lessen the shock caused by the speechlessness of the works. The lack of language is related to the suddenness with which the works accost us. The essence of the experience lies in those first seconds when we enter the museum space and unexpectedly come upon the old, twisted bicycle. Or in that split second when the familiar and innocent thing at our feet shoots the words "trap" and "snap shut" into our brains. But also when the eternal tranquillity of the pile of dust cloths abruptly cuts into and affectively cuts through our detachment. Later then, we might join in an investigation that exposes details, and thus seek to fix the experience. That is neither wrong nor useless but, as a posterior act, it will never equal the first—and probably irrevocable—moment. Think of a successful poem in which two or three words meet up with each other in a way that is utterly incredible, utterly unheard of—and instantly makes compelling sense. Even here, where the material consists of language, words fail and pure chemistry is at work. The artist's objects and actions come from this side of language. They are pure images that make no claim to achieving speech. Their moment is the wink of an eye—mute, but intense and clear. Andreas Slominski: word-less. *(Translation: Catherine Schelbert)*

1) Legendary German practical joker, similar to Punch.

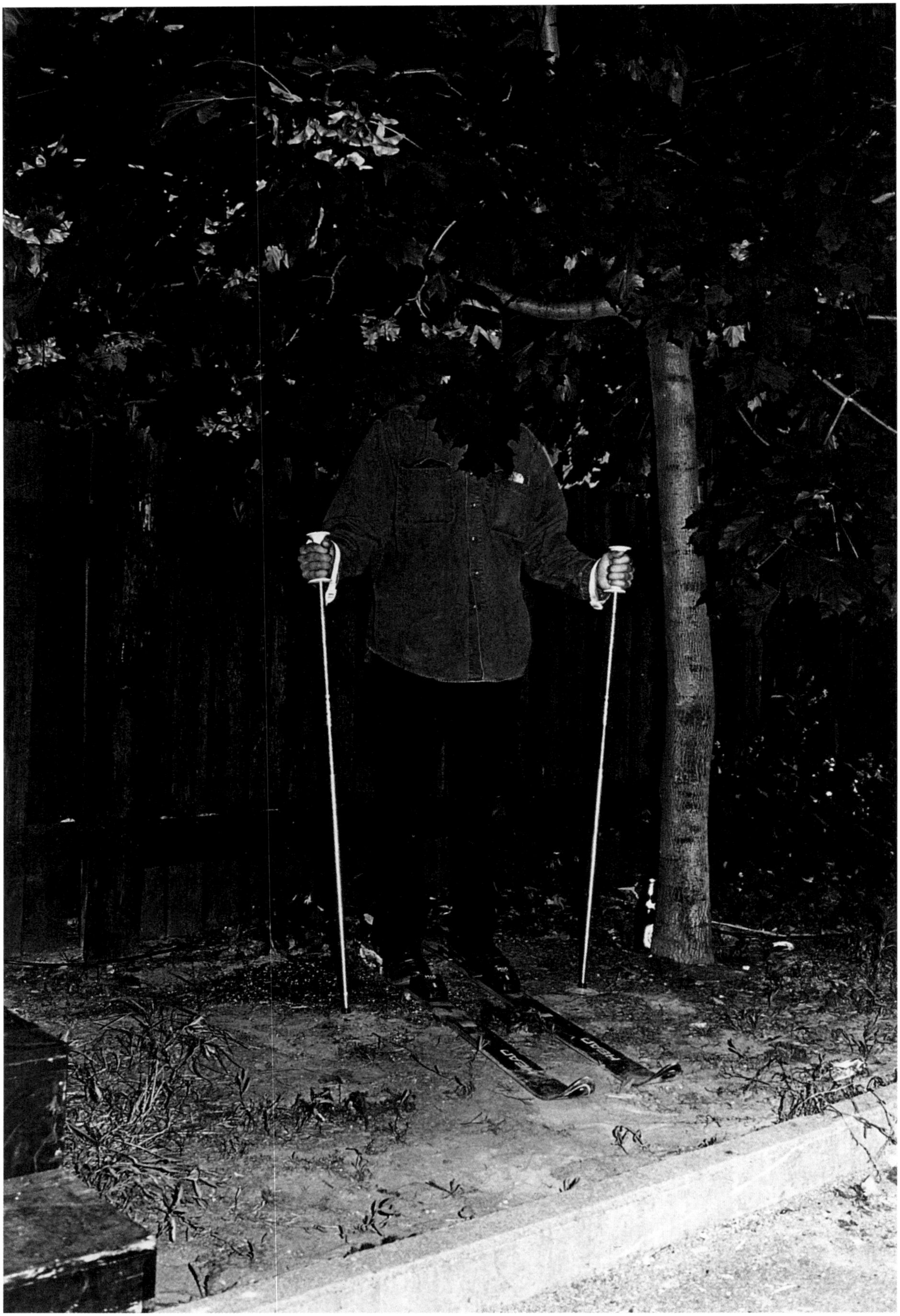

ANDREAS SLOMINSKI, SLOMINSKI, 1996, TAT (Theater am Turm), Frankfurt am Main.

BETTINA FUNCKE & JENS HOFFMANN

"SlominSki"
A Conversation with Boris Groys

Bettina Funcke/Jens Hoffmann: *People going to see "SlominSki" by Andreas Slominski during Phase 2 at the Theater am Turm (TAT) in Frankfurt in 1996 found themselves in the deserted backyard of the theatre with a little flight of steps and a viewing platform, from where the visitor—expecting an artwork—could see industrial tanks lit up on the other side of a fence. The artist himself, all kitted out on this very hot evening with skis and ski-poles, was standing inconspicuously by the platform, half hidden under the branches of a tree. The viewers who had stepped up to the platform in happy anticipation of an art experience gazed all around, and it was only when they went down again that some of them spotted Slominski standing there.*

Is this game with the observer's gaze an attempt by the artist to distance himself from the ambivalence between the everyday or the profane on one side and art on the other, by ironically drawing attention to this dichotomy?

Boris Groys: You can't really distance yourself from the ambivalence because you are invoking it at the same time. It's the same as with a readymade: You put something in a frame—and by association it begins to look like a picture. So this already makes it clear that we are dealing with a picture. What we see in the frame must be a picture, and this picture is a readymade, a "cutting from reality."

The question that Slominski is trying to solve is: How do you create a situation beyond an institution in which you can still denote art as such? I would say that the means he chooses are very traditional. The fact is that you don't need a frame in a museum, you can exhibit anything there. But beyond the museum, Slominski has to signal his presence by putting his signature to the situation. This configuration of frame plus signature or frame plus name is like an "art certificate."

BF/JH: *But if that's the case then artists have to work with the museum in mind in order to be really radical—because otherwise they would automatically have to submit to some conventional form.*

BG: Our experience of art collected in museums has trained our gaze to such an extent that we can readily identify very diverse items as artworks, and I am always intrigued by the question: but how? I wouldn't like to say that working beyond the museum is pointless. It's not pointless, it's always an experiment—not an experiment in the sense of deviation and innovation, but in the sense of identity and continuity. It's an experiment which explores what we can and cannot identify as art in this culture, this epoch, this time, this place.

We are deluding ourselves if we believe that we can always identify art, but don't know what a pos-

---

BETTINA FUNCKE is a writer who lives in New York. She is currently editing a book of collected essays and writings of Boris Groys forthcoming in English. *JENS HOFFMANN* is a curator who lives in Berlin and New York. He was assistant curator at the Solomon R. Guggenheim Museum and coordinated the recent exhibition of Andreas Slominski at the Deutsche Guggenheim, Berlin.

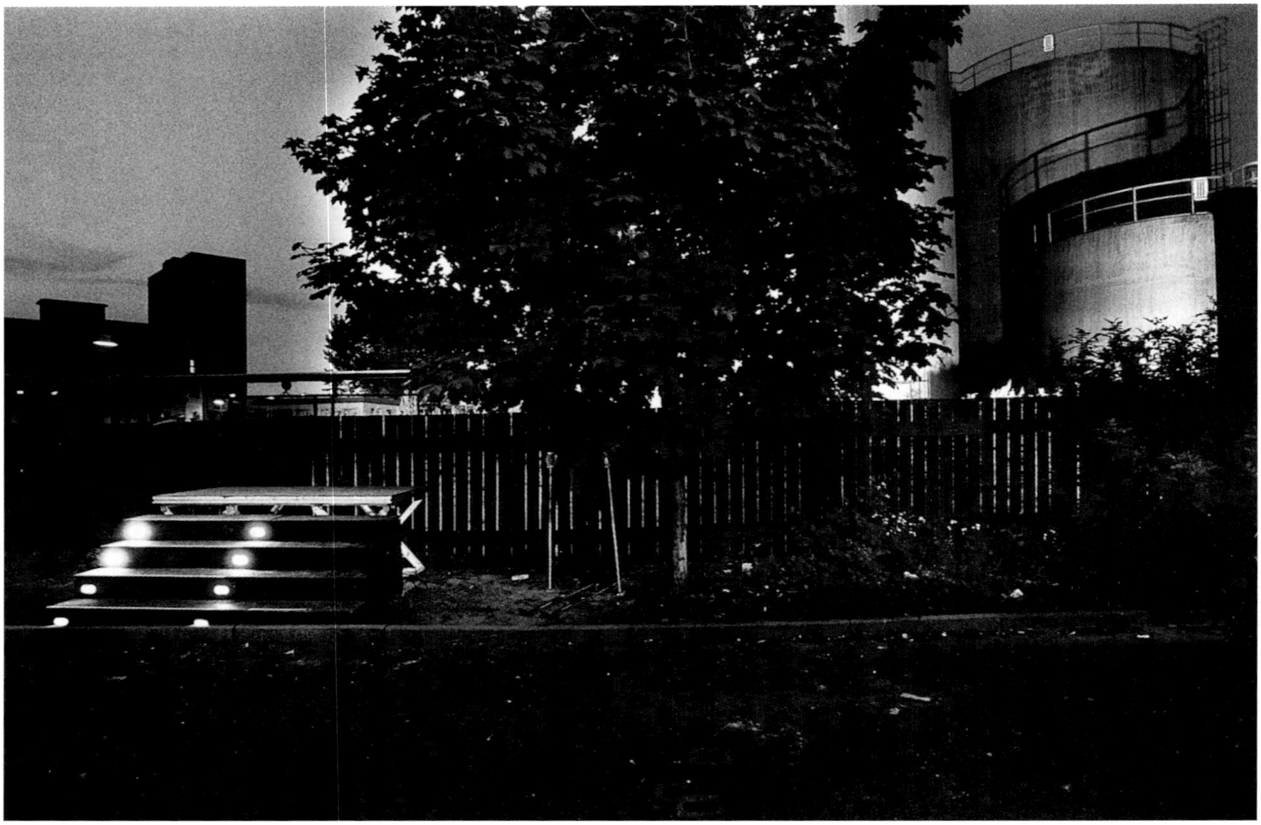

ANDREAS SLOMINSKI, *SLOMINSKI*, 1996, TAT (Theater am Turm), Frankfurt am Main. (PHOTOS: WONGE BERGMANN)

sible deviation looks like. What we really don't know, is what art is supposed to look like. Cultural history also has a part to play in this. It is like the famous question put by Lacan: "What does the woman want?" In exactly the same way, you could also ask: "What does art want of us? What does society want of us?" We don't know. It's not just that we don't know how we should deviate from expectations but we don't even know what those expectations actually look like. That question is itself always open to question. Cultural history is interested primarily in deviations and not in expectations. In order to be revolutionary you first have to find out what the status quo is. The strangest thing about our culture is that we actually don't know. We constantly come up against the question: What is the norm? What is dictated to us by society? What is expected of us? It's an open question. And so, it seems to me that art which distances itself from the constraints of the museum and works more with expectations—that is to say more with the fulfillment of expectations than with deviations from these expectations—is doing something interesting. It is showing us what is expected of us—which is not something we just instinctively know.

BF/JH: *But I don't have the impression that in his other works Andreas Slominski is particularly trying to match up to expectations. For instance, when he exhibits windmill vanes at Portikus and then comes at irregular intervals to saw them up and burn them, surely he is destroying the very things that could have been put in the archive.*

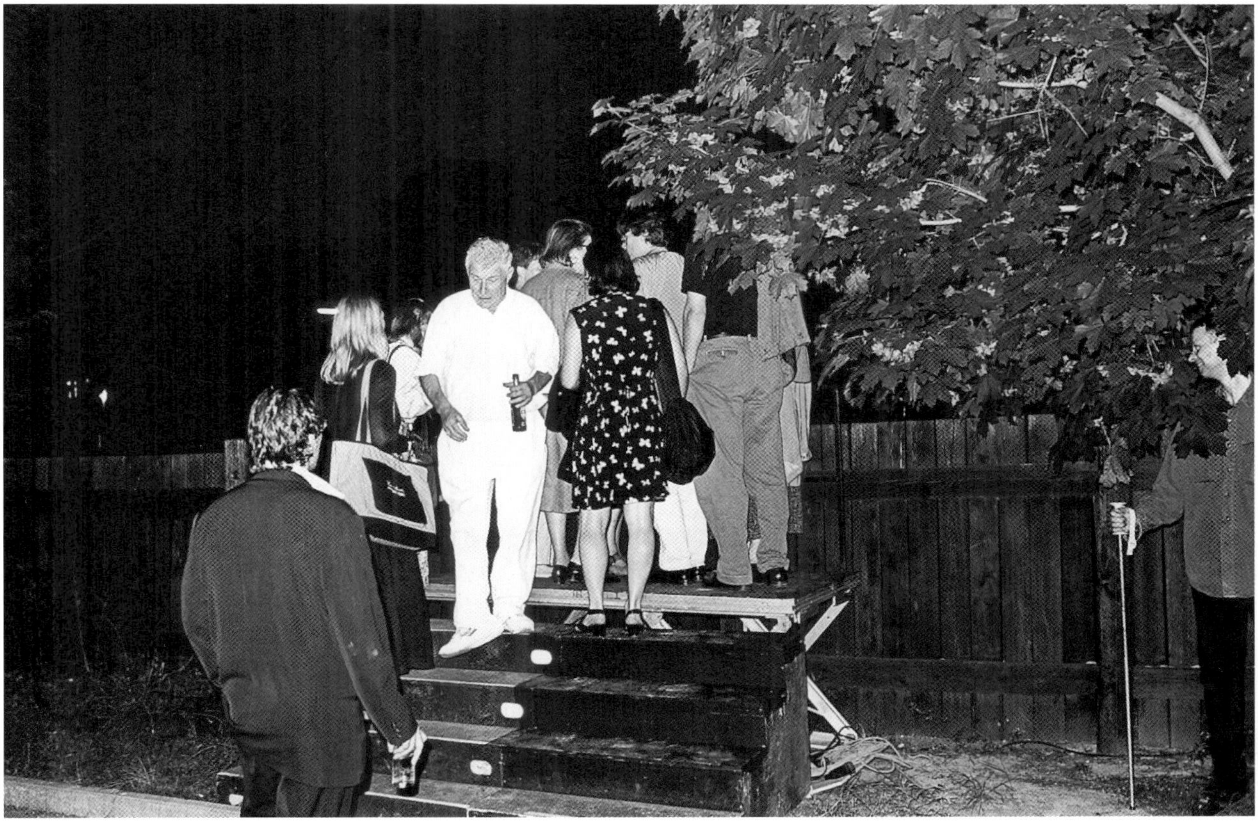

BG: No, no, because he doesn't completely destroy the work, if it is documented in the form of a narrative. Indeed, in our society art functions more and more as a narrative. It was the same in Antiquity. We've got Classical texts by Plato but we've also got stories—for instance there was the man who used to wander through the streets with his lantern, and the one that lived in a barrel, and the one that masturbated in public. These are stories that are just as much a part of philosophy as the philosophical texts that have come down to us. Artists today are doing just the same: One cut off his ear, another one shot himself in the arm. These are stories which fascinate us as stories and are archetypal too. If you do something so that it will be related as a story then you are writing yourself into the narrative archive and you become part of the art archive. I don't think there is any deviation involved there.

Modern art began at a time when the norm was laid down extremely clearly by academic painting. In those days it was immediately noticed if anyone departed from the norm. But nowadays it is hard to say what society expects of art. What does art have to look like to meet current norms? Nobody knows, and if nobody knows, then it is extremely difficult to depart from those norms. It's always a balancing act: fulfilling a norm and departing from it at the same time: No artist can completely reflect this.

BF/JH: *But to get back to Andreas Slominski, we were talking about his windmills. I think that the point about expec-*

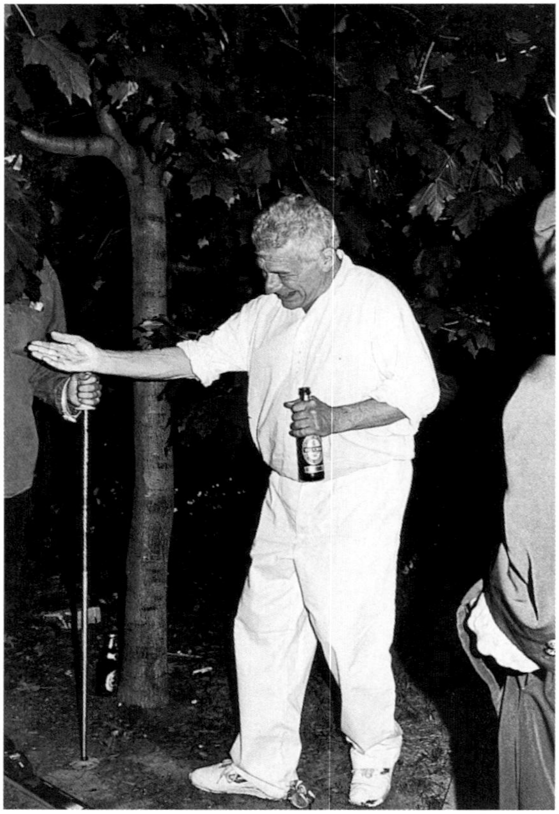

ANDREAS SLOMINSKI, SLOMINSKI, 1996. Im Publikum / In the audience: John Berger. (PHOTO: WONGE BERGMANN)

tations not being fulfilled is rather different. With his windmill vanes, his Action with the golf balls in Krefeld and his bicycle-tire Action in Münster, banal situations are so complicatedly contrived or reconstructed that the ensuing weightiness elevates the everyday into the realm of art, with part of the tension deriving from the fact that in the Action there is always the risk of the desired result not being achieved. The windmill vanes, for example, were transported by truck to Frankfurt from 500 kilometers away in order to be used as firewood to heat Portikus on Sunday mornings—leaving only the windmill stump behind. And countless golf balls had to be hit high over the roof of Haus Esters in Krefeld until one landed precisely on the raised back of a dump truck so that from there it could fly into the gallery through an open window. And the bicycle tire that was placed around a lamp post in Münster was done from below, not above.

BG: Well, the idea of burning windmill vanes reminds me of a comment by Malevich when he said that it would be good to burn all of Rubens's pictures because when it had been done you would have a beautiful memory and would appreciate Rubens again. It's just the same with the windmill vanes: Burning them means drawing attention to the windmills. As long as a windmill is standing there in the landscape you just don't notice it and simply pass it by. But if it's under threat or if it's actually being burnt then suddenly all our attention is concentrated on this thing, and maybe we think: "How beautiful that windmill used to be when it was still there." You remember it in your mind's eye, in your imagination. And so I have the impression that everything that Andreas Slominski does is pointing to something else. That's its real power. Basically the power to direct another person's attention is absolute power. So the strategy is to manipulate me, to manipulate my gaze, and at the same time to avoid being judged by me. He directs my gaze exactly where he wants and at the same time away from himself. He says: "What I am doing is not important, what is important is the windmill." He wants me to look past him. But when I look past him or his work and see something different, then I am entirely in his hands: He can manipulate me however he likes.

So the point is not what an artist's works show, but how they show it, the artistic devices they use. Any real criticism has to be a criticism of the artistic means, a criticism of the manner in which things are shown—and this criticism has to be the focus of an exhibition of the art under discussion. But if a person wants to show a work and also to focus on the formal side of the work, then there has to be a documentation of this as well. The context has to be described as well as how something was made, as is the case in Slominski's documentations. A space has to be created in which the artist's strategies become clear. And I would like to stress that the new art of manipulation is not some kind of new Realism, but that it takes place on a particular level of reflection about manipulation, about how a person's attention may be redirected.

(Translation: Fiona Elliott)

BETTINA FUNCKE & JENS HOFFMANN

SlominSki
Ein Gespräch mit Boris Groys

Bettina Funcke/Jens Hoffmann: *Bei der Arbeit SlominSki von Andreas Slominski im Rahmen des Projektes Phase 2 am Theater am Turm (TAT) in Frankfurt 1996 fanden die Besucher auf einem verlassenen Hinterhof des Theaters eine kleine Treppe mit einer Aussichtsplattform vor, von der aus der kunsterwartende Betrachter über einen Zaun hinweg auf ein städtisches Niemandsland mit erleuchteten Industrietanks blicken konnte. Der Künstler selbst stand an diesem sehr heissen Sommerabend auf Skiern unscheinbar neben der Treppe, halb verdeckt von den Ästen eines Baumes. Die Menschen, die in vorfreudiger Gewissheit eines Kunsterlebnisses auf die Plattform gestiegen waren, liessen ihren Blick suchend umherschweifen um beim Abstieg Slominski vielleicht doch noch zu entdecken.*

Ist dieses Spiel mit dem Blick des Betrachters ein Versuch sich der Ambivalenz von Alltag beziehungsweise dem Profanen auf der einen und Kunst auf der anderen Seite zu entziehen – indem man diese Zwiespältigkeit selbst ironisch vorführt?

Boris Groys: Man entzieht sich nicht wirklich, denn gleichzeitig macht man diese Ambivalenz doch präsent. Es ist immer noch ein Ready-made-Verfahren: Man macht einen Rahmen – und den Rahmen assoziieren wir mit dem Bild. Damit ist schon gezeigt, dass wir es mit einem Bild zu tun haben. Das, was wir in diesem Rahmen sehen, muss ein Bild sein, und dieses Bild ist ein Ready-made, es ist sozusagen ein Ausschnitt aus der Realität.

Die Frage, die Slominski zu lösen versucht, lautet: Wie stellt man ausserhalb des etablierten Museums eine Situation her, in der man die Kunst dennoch markieren kann? Ich würde sagen, dass die Mittel, die er wählt, sehr traditionell sind. Den Rahmen braucht man im Museum zum Beispiel nicht, man kann dort alles ausstellen. Ausserdem gibt er der Situation durch seine Präsenz schon eine Unterschrift, sein Namen ist unter das Werk gesetzt. Diese Konstruktion aus Rahmen und Unterschrift oder Rahmen und Namen ist sozusagen ein Kunstausweis.

BF/JH: *Aber so gesehen müssen die Künstler auf das Museum hinarbeiten um wirklich radikal arbeiten zu können – denn sonst müssen sie sich automatisch einer konventionellen Form unterwerfen.*

BG: Durch den musealen Blick sind wir so trainiert, dass wir sehr unterschiedliche Dinge immer schon als Kunstwerke erkennen können, und für mich ist es immer interessant zu fragen: Wie denn? Ich würde nicht sagen, dass es überflüssig ist, ausserhalb des Museums zu arbeiten. Es ist nicht überflüssig, es ist immer ein Experiment – ein Experiment nicht im Sinne von Abweichung und Innovation, sondern im Sinne von Identität und Erhaltung. Ein Experiment,

BETTINA FUNCKE ist Publizistin und lebt in New York. Zurzeit arbeitet sie an der Herausgabe eines Bandes mit Essays und Schriften von Boris Groys in englischer Sprache; *JENS HOFFMANN* ist Kurator und lebt in Berlin und New York. Er war Assistenzkurator am Solomon R. Guggenheim Museum und Koordinator der diesjährigen Slominski-Ausstellung in der Deutschen Guggenheim, Berlin.

das erforscht, was wir in dieser Kultur, in dieser Epoche, zu dieser Zeit, an diesem Ort als Kunst identifizieren können und was nicht.

Es ist eine Illusion zu glauben, dass wir die Identität der Kunst immer kennen und nur nicht wissen, wie eine mögliche Abweichung aussieht. Was wir eigentlich nicht wissen ist, wie die Identität aussieht. Damit spielt auch die Zeitdiagnostik. Es ist wie mit der berühmten Frage von Lacan: «Was will die Frau?» Genauso kann man fragen: Was will die Kunst von uns? Was will die Gesellschaft von uns? Wir wissen es nicht. Wir wissen nicht nur nicht, wie wir von der Erwartung abweichen sollen, sondern wir wissen auch nicht, wie die Erwartungen eigentlich aussehen. Es bleibt immer eine offene Frage. Die ganze zeitdiagnostische Literatur arbeitet eben damit, mit den Abweichungen und nicht mit den Erwartungen. Um revolutionär zu werden muss man zunächst einmal fragen, was die Ordnung ist. Das Merkwürdigste an unserer Kultur ist, dass wir das eigentlich nicht wissen. Die Frage stellt sich immer neu: Was ist die Norm? Was wird uns von unserer Gesellschaft diktiert? Was wird von uns erwartet? Das ist eine offene Frage. Und so meine ich, dass die Kunst, die sich dem musealen Zwang entzieht und mehr mit den Erwartungen, mit der Erfüllung der Erwartung arbeitet als mit der Abweichung von dieser Erwartung, auch eine interessante Arbeit leistet. Überhaupt ist die Kunst, die den Erwartungen entspricht, eine interessante Kunst. Sie zeigt uns, was von uns erwartet wird. Das wissen wir nicht von selbst.

BF/JH: *Ich habe aber nicht den Eindruck, dass Andreas Slominski mit seinen anderen Arbeiten den Erwartungen entspricht. Wenn er beispielsweise Windmühlenflügel in den Portikus stellt und diese dort in unterschiedlichen Abständen zersägt und verbrennt, vernichtet er ja eigentlich das, was hätte archiviert werden können.*

BG: Ach nein, denn er vernichtet es nicht ganz, wenn es in Form einer Erzählung dokumentiert wird. Die Kunst funktioniert in unserer Gesellschaft überhaupt zunehmend als eine Erzählung. Das war auch in der Antike so. Wir haben aus der Antike Texte von Platon, aber wir haben auch Geschichten – zum Beispiel ist einer mit einer Laterne durch die Strassen gegangen, ein anderer hat in der Tonne gelebt, noch ein anderer hat öffentlich masturbiert. Das sind Geschichten, die genauso zur Philosophie gehören wie die überlieferten philosophischen Texte. Die Künstler von heute tun genau dasselbe: Einer hat sich ein Ohr abgeschnitten, ein anderer hat sich den Arm durchschossen. Das sind Geschichten, die als Geschichten faszinieren und archetypisch sind. Wenn

ANDREAS SLOMINSKI, LATERNE MIT REIFEN, 1996. Linkes Bild: Ausheben der Laterne für das Umlegen des Reifens, «Skulptur. Projekte Münster 1997» / LANTERN WITH TIRE. Left: digging up the lantern to place the tire around it.

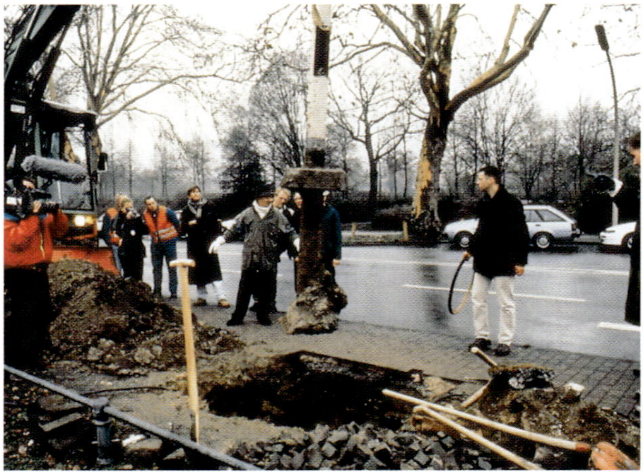

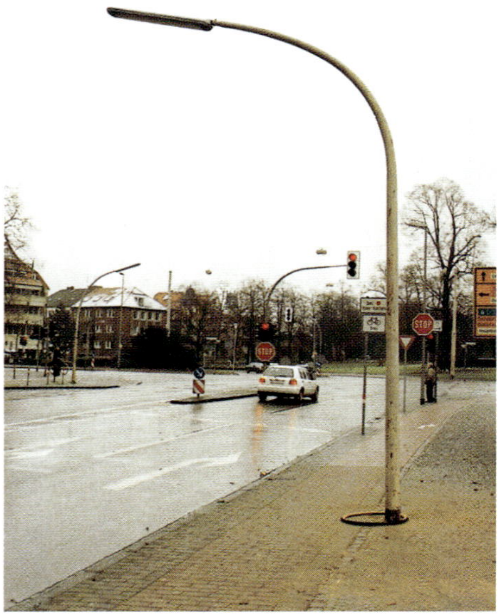

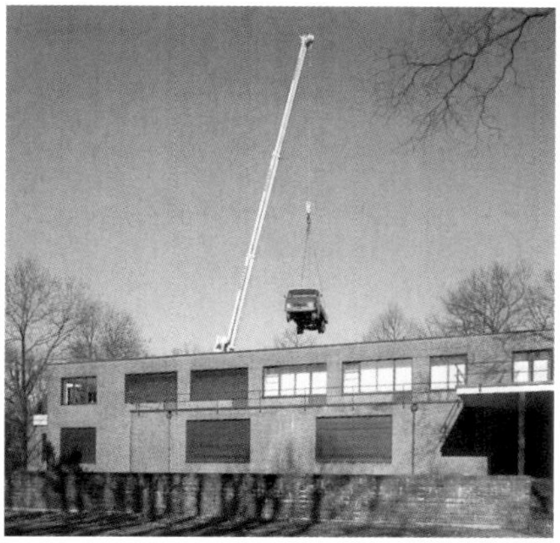

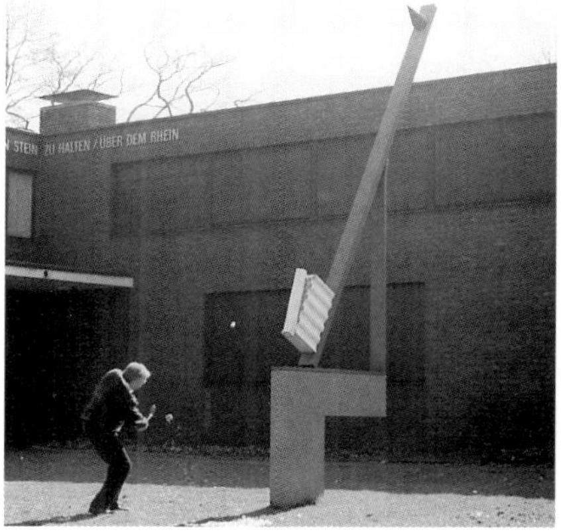

ANDREAS SLOMINSKI, GOLFBALL, 1995, Museum Haus Esters, Krefeld / GOLF BALL.

man etwas tut, damit es als Geschichte erzählt wird, dann schreibt man sich auch in das narrative Archiv ein und wird zu einem Teil des Kunstarchivs. Ich glaube nicht, dass dabei eine Abweichung stattfindet.

Die Entwicklung der modernen Kunst begann zu der Zeit, als die Norm durch die Vorgaben der akademischen Malerei sehr klar war. Und damals war auch sehr klar, worin die Abweichung bestand. Sie wurde sofort bemerkt. Aber in unserer Zeit ist es schwer zu sagen, worin die Erwartung besteht, was die Gesellschaft von der Kunst erwartet. Wie muss eine der Norm entsprechende Kunst aussehen? Niemand weiss es und wenn es niemand weiss, dann ist es sehr schwierig von der Norm abzuweichen. Es ist immer eine Balance, eine Normerfüllung und eine Abweichung zugleich, die vom Künstler auch nicht vollständig reflektiert werden kann.

BF/JH: *Noch einmal zurück zu Andreas Slominski, denn wir haben ja eben über seine Windmühlenflügel gesprochen. Ich denke, der Punkt, an dem er die Erwartung nicht erfüllt, ist ein anderer. Bei den Windmühlenflügeln, bei seiner Aktion mit dem Golfball in Krefeld und auch bei seiner Arbeit mit dem Fahrradreifen in Münster werden die banalen Situationen so kompliziert hergeleitet oder rekonstruiert, dass mit dieser Schwere das Alltägliche zur Kunst aufgewertet wird, wobei das Risiko, dass seine Rekonstruktion nicht zum gewünschten Ergebnis führt, Teil der Spannung ist. Die Windmühlenflügel werden beispielsweise 500 km im Lastwagen nach Frankfurt transportiert um dort im Winter als Heizmaterial jeden Sonntagmorgen im Portikus verbrannt zu werden – ausserdem bleibt eine flügellose Windmühle zurück. In Krefeld mussten zahllose Golfbälle über das Haus Esters geschlagen werden, bis ein Ball die schräg gestellte Lastwagenrampe traf und durchs offene Fenster ins Innere des Museums sprang. Und der Fahrradreifen in Münster wurde von unten um die Strassenlaterne gelegt.*

BG: Wenn zum Beispiel Windmühlenflügel oder zumindest Stücke davon als Brennholz verheizt werden, dann erinnert mich das an die Bemerkung von Malewitsch, es sei gut, alle Bilder von Rubens zu verbrennen, denn wenn man das getan habe, behalte man eine schöne Erinnerung und nehme Rubens wieder wahr. Genauso ist es mit den Windmühlen-

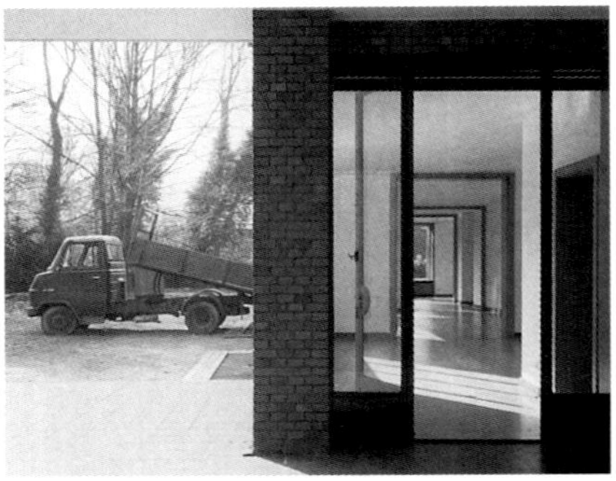
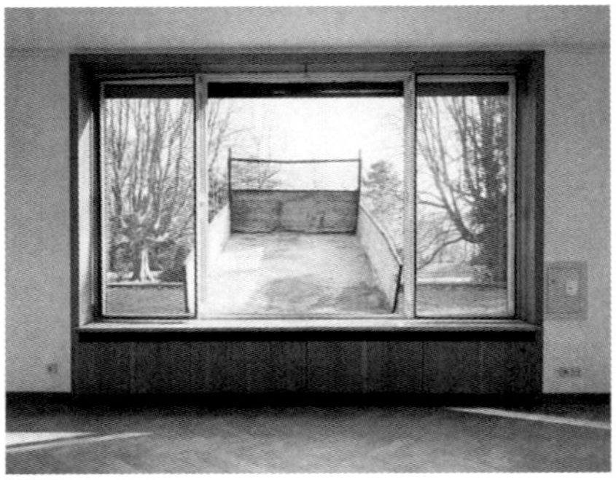
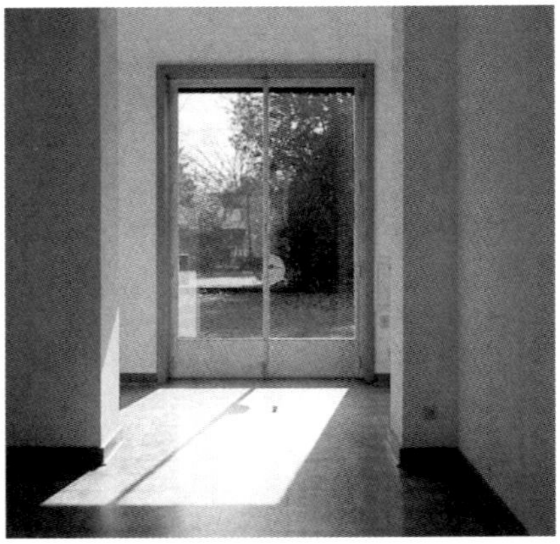

ANDREAS SLOMINSKI, GOLFBALL 1995, Museum Haus Esters, Krefeld / GOLF BALL. (PHOTOS: VOLKER DÖHNE, KREFELD)

flügeln: Sie zu verbrennen bedeutet auf diese Windmühle aufmerksam zu machen. Wenn die Windmühle einfach in der Landschaft steht, bemerkt man sie gar nicht und geht an ihr vorbei. Wird sie aber bedroht oder werden ihre Flügel wie hier angesägt um die Teile in einem kleinen Ofen langsam zu verfeuern, dann denken wir vielleicht: «Wie schön war diese Windmühle, als sie da noch stand.» Man evoziert ihr Bild in der Erinnerung, in der Imagination. Und so habe ich den Eindruck, dass alles, was Andreas Slominski tut, ein Hinweis auf etwas anderes ist. Darin besteht die eigentliche Macht. Die Macht Aufmerksamkeit zu lenken ist im Grunde die absolute Macht. Die Strategie besteht also darin, mich, meinen Blick zu manipulieren und sich gleichzeitig meinem Urteil zu entziehen. Er lenkt meinen Blick, worauf er will und gleichzeitig von sich selbst ab. Er sagt: «Was ich mache, ist nicht wichtig, wichtig ist die Windmühle.» Er will, dass ich ihn übersehe. Indem ich ihn oder sein Werk aber übersehe und etwas anderes sehe, bin ich ihm ausgeliefert: Er kann mich manipulieren, wie er will.

Der Punkt ist also nicht, was die Bilder zeigen, sondern wie sie es zeigen, mit welchen Verfahren. Die eigentliche Kritisierbarkeit des Werkes bezieht sich auf das Verfahren, ist eine Kritik der Art und Weise, wie mir die Dinge gezeigt werden – und diese Kritik muss in einer Ausstellung der eben beschriebenen Kunst thematisiert werden. Wenn man aber eine Arbeit zeigen will, um auch die formale Seite des Verfahrens zu thematisieren, muss eine Dokumentation mit einbezogen werden. Man muss zeigen, in welchem Kontext und wie etwas gemacht wurde, was etwa bei Slominski der Fall wäre. Da muss ein Raum aufgebaut werden, in dem die Strategien des Künstlers klar werden. Ich möchte betonen, dass die Kunst der Manipulation kein neuer Realismus ist, sondern auf einer bestimmten Ebene der Reflexion über Manipulation, über die Lenkung der Aufmerksamkeit stattfindet.

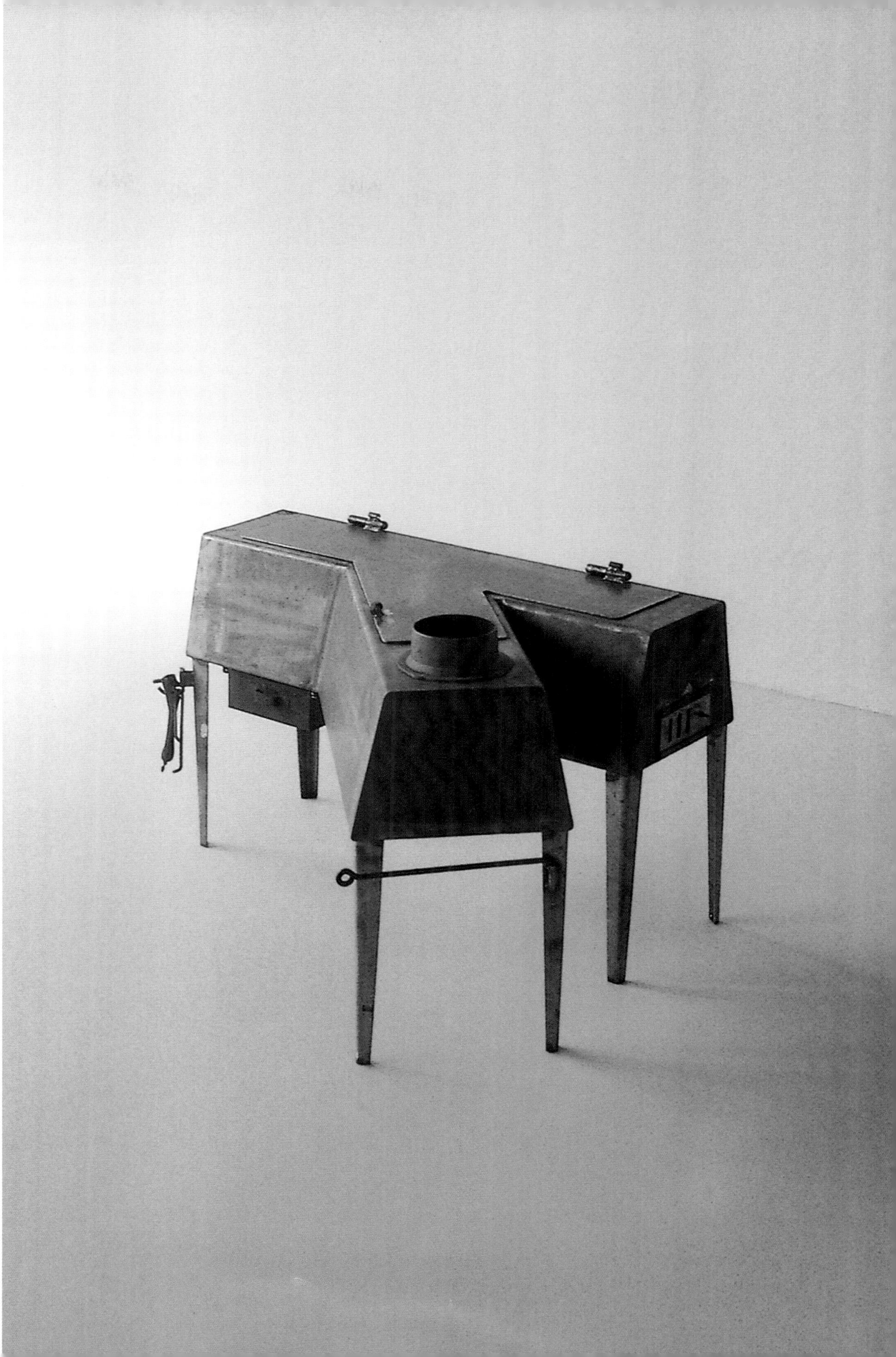

ANDREAS SLOMINSKI, *OFEN ZUM VERFEUERN VON ASTGABELN*, 1997, *ca.* 62 x 91 x 72 cm / *STOVE TO BURN FORKED BRANCHES*, *ca.* 24 3/8 x 35 7/8 x 28 5/16".

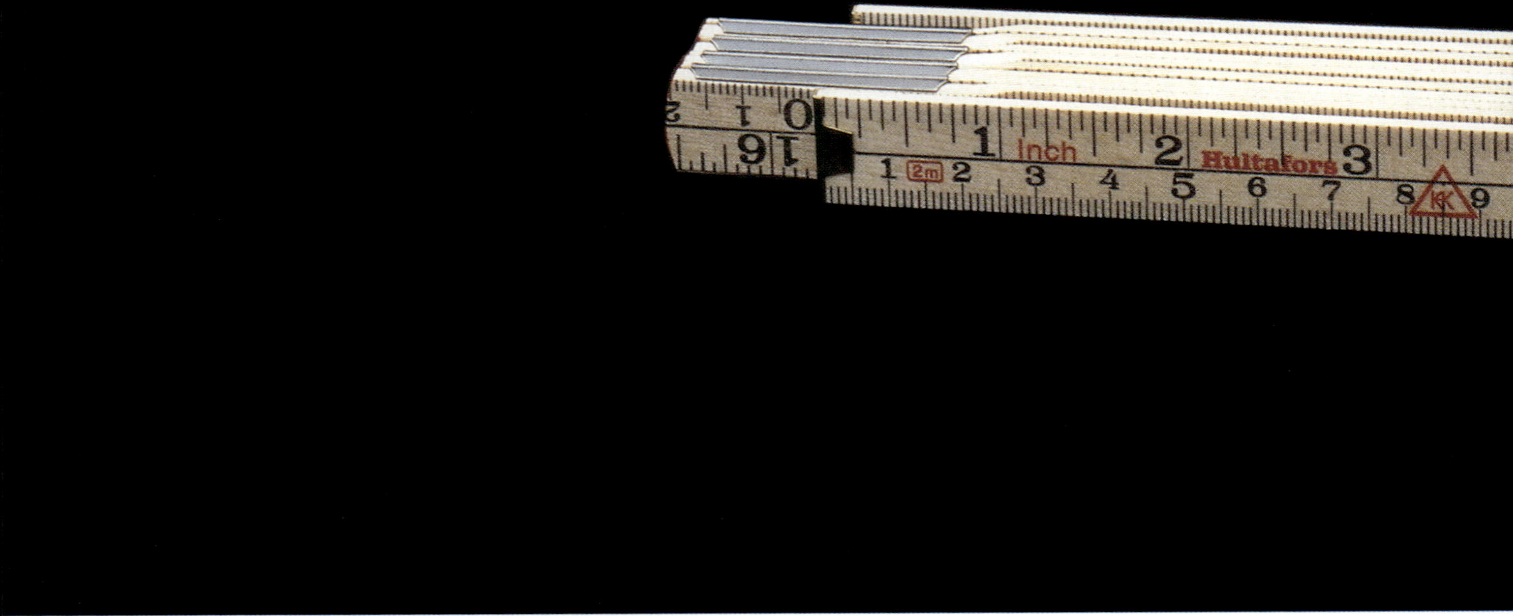

Edition for Parkett ANDREAS SLOMINSKI

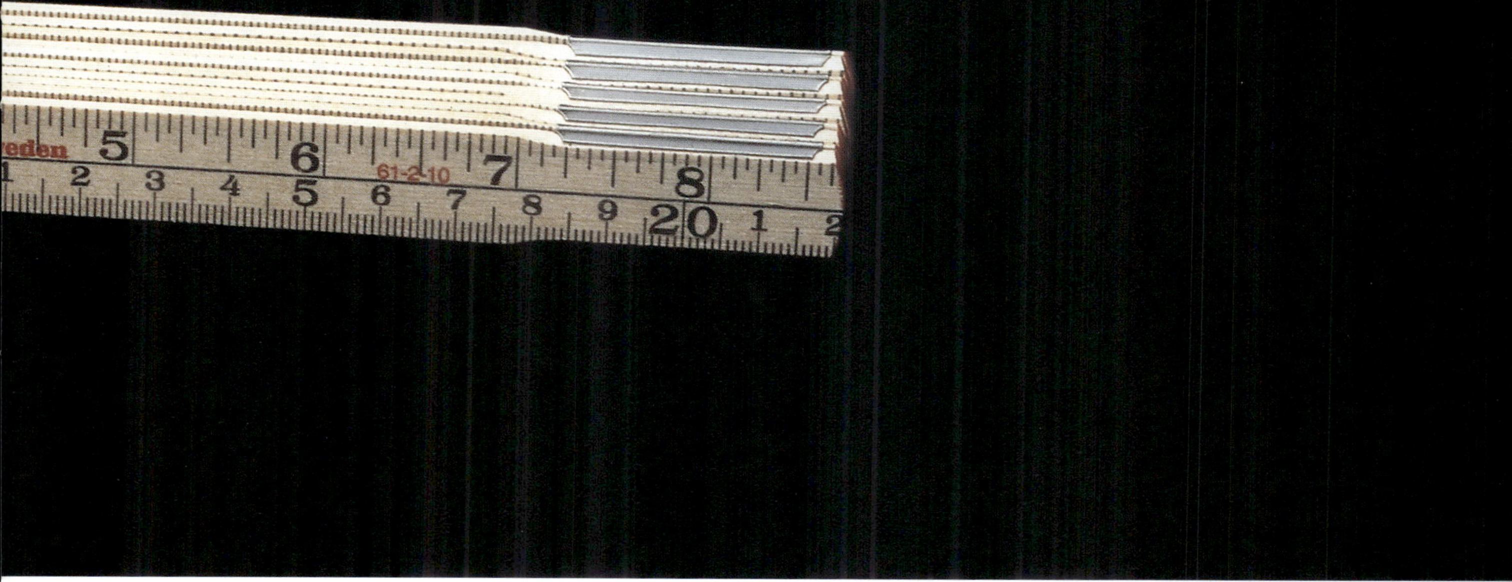

ZOLLSTOCK, 1999
Der Zollstock wird aufgeklappt verschickt.
Länge: 2 Meter
Auflage: 55, mit signiertem und nummeriertem Zertifikat

FOLDING RULE, 1999
The rule will be delivered extended.
Length: 78 11⁄16”
Edition of 55, with a signed and numbered certificate

(PHOTO: MANCIA/BODMER, ZÜRICH)

SAM TAYLOR-WOOD

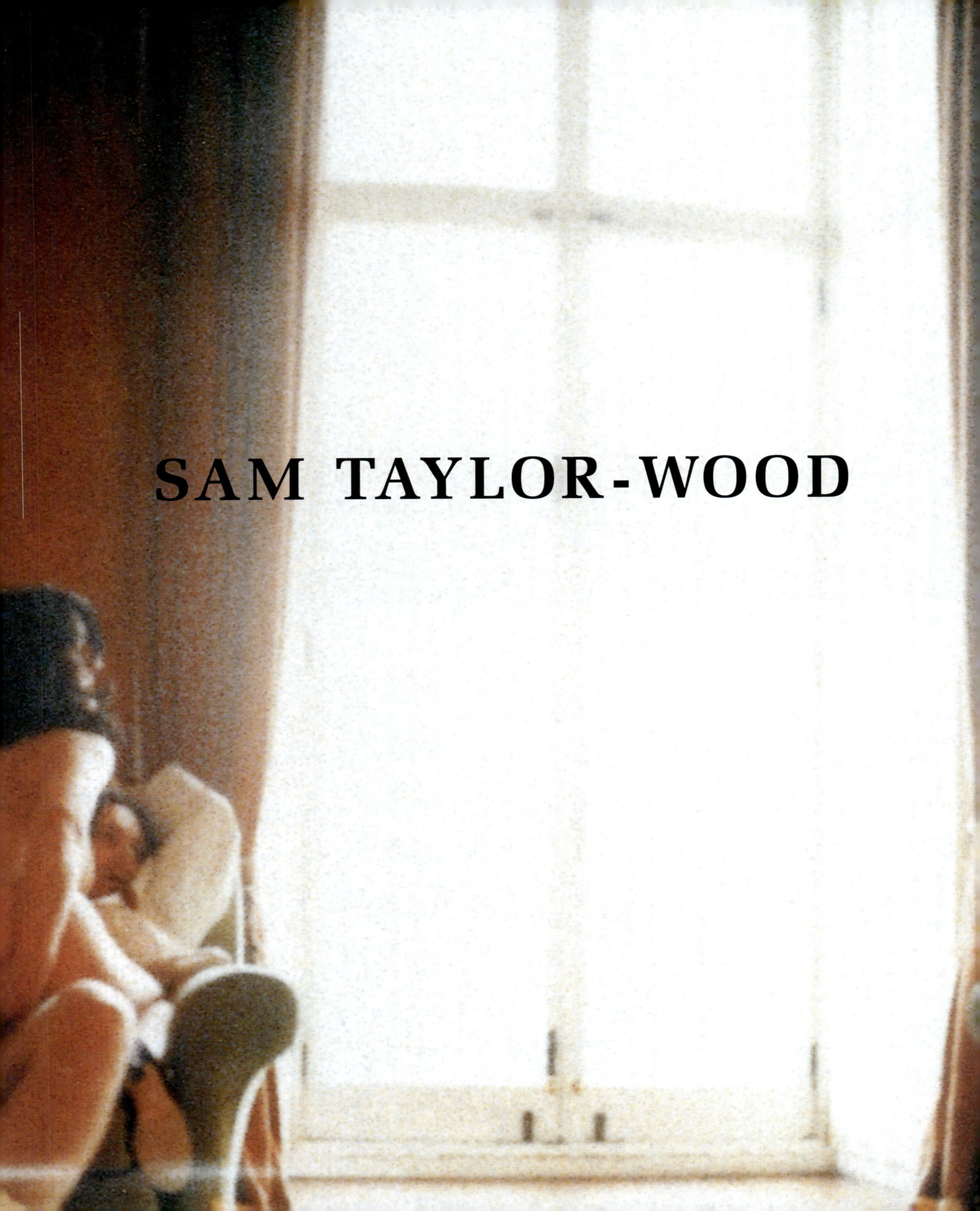

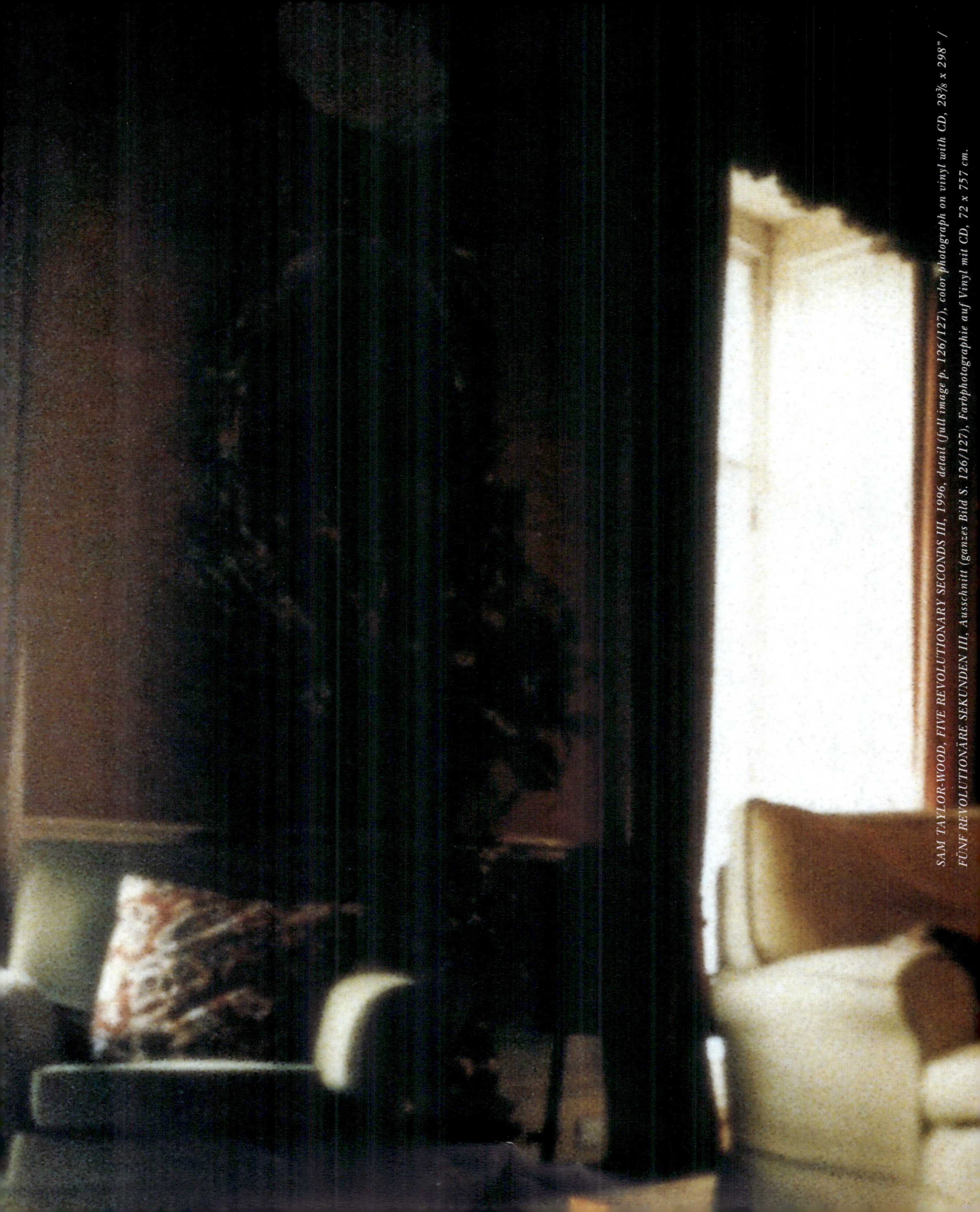

SAM TAYLOR-WOOD, *FIVE REVOLUTIONARY SECONDS III*, 1996, detail (full image p. 126/127), color photograph on vinyl with CD, 28⅞ x 298" / *FÜNF REVOLUTIONÄRE SEKUNDEN III*, Ausschnitt (ganzes Bild S. 126/127), Farbphotographie auf Vinyl mit CD, 72 x 757 cm.

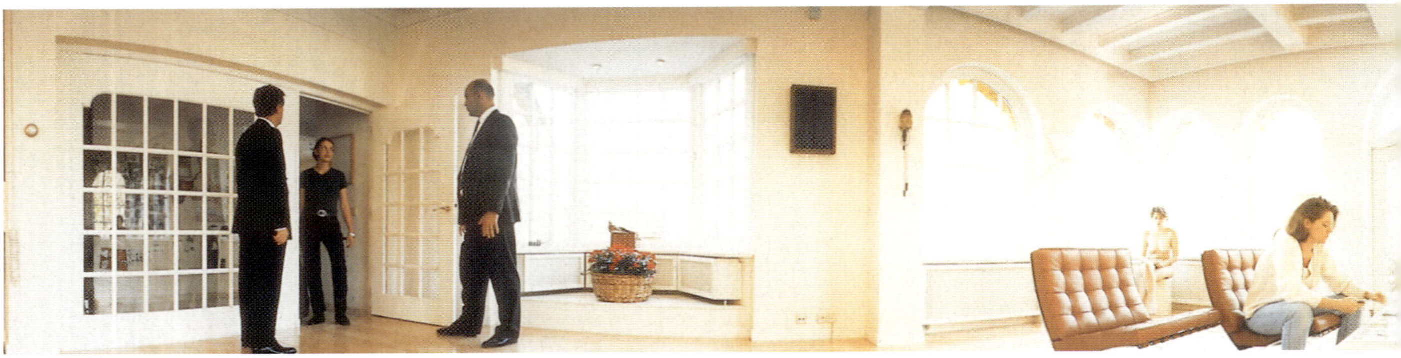

—because a map is precisely that, a connection made visible—
Franco Moretti, *Atlas of the European Novel*

Sustaining the Antagonism
Sam Taylor-Wood's "Five Revolutionary Seconds"

ELISABETH BRONFEN

In a recent film projection entitled HYSTERIA, Sam Taylor-Wood shows us an extreme close up of a woman's contorted face. As her body heaves under the onslaught of powerful emotion, with her head tilting backwards and forwards, the only part of the face we see continually is the opened mouth. Owing to the slow motion as well as the absence of sound, it becomes extremely difficult to distinguish whether she is laughing or crying. As the artist explains, she wanted to amalgamate these two opposed emotional states and blur the difference between them to such a degree that they become the same thing. At the same time the emotional turmoil of the actress was meant to infect the implied spectator who, unable to distance him- or herself from this unnerving expression of an extreme emotional outburst because it defies any unequivocal label, is launched into confusion as well. With the frame by frame dissection of this histrionic display of a momentary loss of self-control, which inevitably draws the viewer into the performance and thus blurs not only the contours of

ELISABETH BRONFEN teaches English Literature at the University of Zurich. One of her most recent publications is a book on hysteria, *The Knotted Subject: Hysteria and its Discontents* (Princeton University Press, 1998).

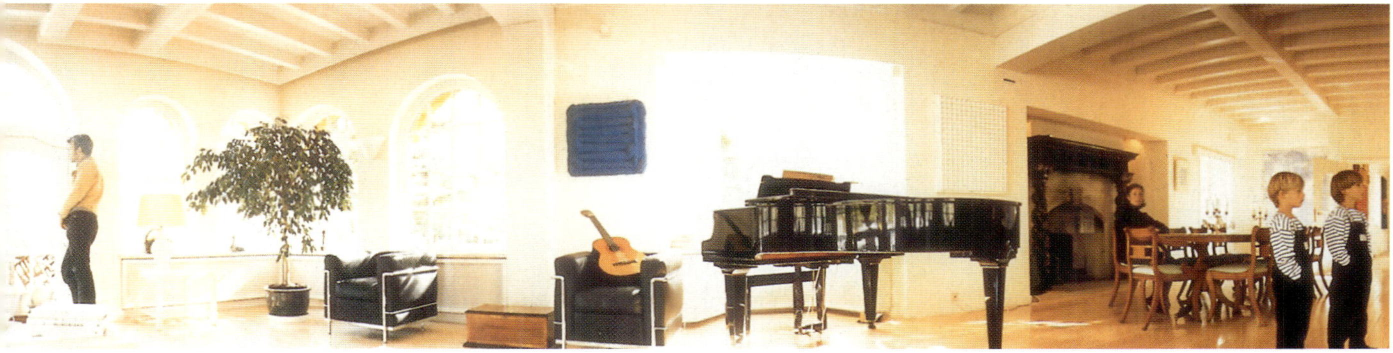

SAM TAYLOR-WOOD, FIVE REVOLUTIONARY SECONDS IV, 1996, color photograph on vinyl with cassette tape, 28⅜ x 298" / FÜNF REVOLUTIONÄRE SEKUNDEN IV, Farbphotographie auf Vinyl mit Videokassette, 72 x 757 cm.

the emotional crisis represented but also the distinction between spectator and spectacle, Sam Taylor-Wood of course pays homage to the iconography of the hysteric attack invented by late nineteenth century psychiatrist Jean-Martin Charcot. Famous both for the public display of his patients' psychosomatic symptoms during his infamous Tuesday Lectures held in the amphitheatre of his clinic, the Salpêtrière, as well as the photographs he produced as part of his effort to map the five phases of the hysteric attack as he saw it, he was the first to exploit the use of visuality for a medical investigation of passionate attitudes.

Given that this elusive and enigmatic psychosomatic disorder, for which no organic lesions can be found, came to serve as the catch-all term for an expression of discontent that defied proper diagnosis, it readily turned into a cultural trope. Its privileged symptoms—a dramatic staging of moments of emotional crisis as well as a bodily enactment of the wandering of fantasy—were seen not only as the expression of unsatisfied desire. Rather, in his revolutionary reinterpretation Sigmund Freud suggested that the hysteric's self-display be seen as a broadcast of complaint about the fragility inhabiting bourgeois notions of happiness and health; an articulation of the discontent underlying any harmonious habitation of the world. The hysteric's provocative staging of emotional excess and incapacitation, he suggested, should be read as an insistence that one confront the vulnerability of the human subject, the anxieties subtending all polished self-fashioning. But, as Freud came to discover so painfully in his own case histories, the most prominent feature of the hysteric subject is a resilient defiance not only of unequivocal classification but also of closure. If, in the course of a hysteric performance of emotional crisis, boundaries become blurred, so too, the intended broadcast of complaint promises to be a never-ending one. The antagonism the hysteric so powerfully, albeit obliquely articulates, pertains to the traumatic knowledge that moves the subject as much as unsatisfied desire does; a fundamental crisis of emotional ease and balance that can never be resolved, only sustained.

Hysteria thus uncannily emerges as a particularly appropriate critical trope for Sam Taylor-Wood's own aesthetic project. Indeed, many of her protagonists recall the passionate attitudes enacted on the Charcotian stage, albeit in postmodern dress. Fully absorbed by their psychic reality—either oblivious to their surroundings or in opposition to those they share an inhabited space with, fighting with each other or cruelly ignoring each other—they all appear to be voicing cultural malaise. As Sam Taylor-Wood explains, "there's a sense right now of people feeling disconnected from the world we live in, of

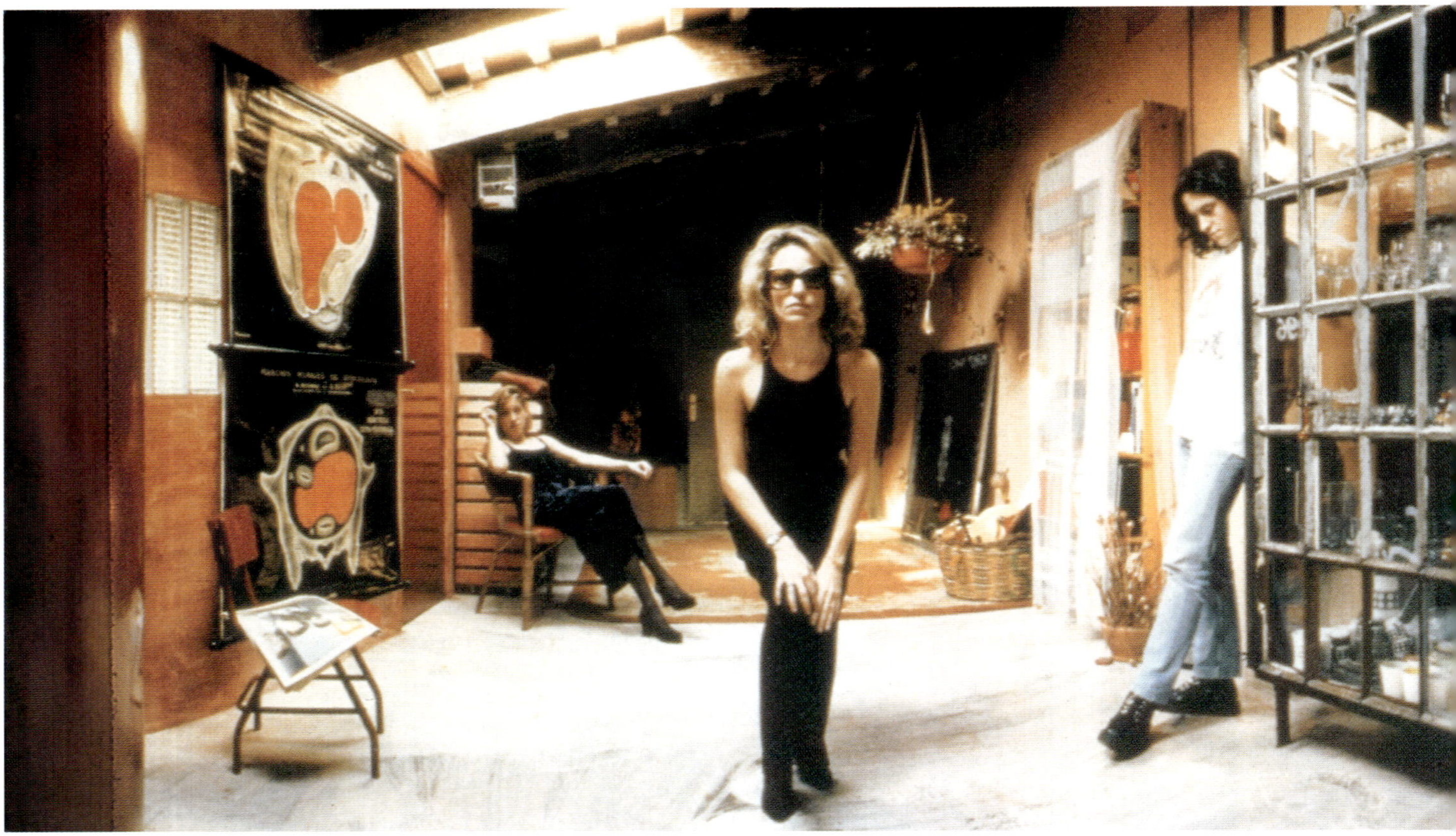

feeling slightly out of harmony with their environment."[1] At the same time she visually maps another insight Freud develops in his early writings on hysteria, namely the fact that even while the psychic apparatus is infected with the anxiety about subjective fallibility and fragility, this traumatic knowledge is delineated from any unconscious or conscious representation by virtue of a gap in the psyche. In other words, even as trauma haunts all the protective fictions we produce so as to be able to inhabit our psychic reality, these narratives point to a fundamental antagonism we have no direct access to. By organizing emotionally confused experiences into a coherent narrative, psychic moments of crisis can once again be integrated into a situation of seeming emotional control and balance. Yet as Slavoj Zizek astutely notes, such assuaging fantasies are not only nothing other than protective fictions in so far as they are "based upon the exclusion of traumatic events and patch up the gaps left by these exclusions." Rather "narrative as such emerges in order to resolve some fundamental antagonism by rearranging its terms into a temporal succession."[2]

In her series entitled FIVE REVOLUTIONARY SECONDS, begun in 1995, Sam Taylor-Wood plays with the double meaning of the word revolution, so as to photographically enact fantasy scenarios that perform the encroachment of repressed antagonisms upon the very representational medium set up to occult this original deadlock. Using a camera invented by the RAF to take aerial shots, she places herself at the center of a space chosen specifically for the appropriateness of its atmosphere. After giving directions to her actors about the passionate attitudes and poses they are to assume, she produces a 360 degrees panoramic shot by panning the room during a five second exposure. As her camera rotates about its axis it registers the different occupants, who, isolated in

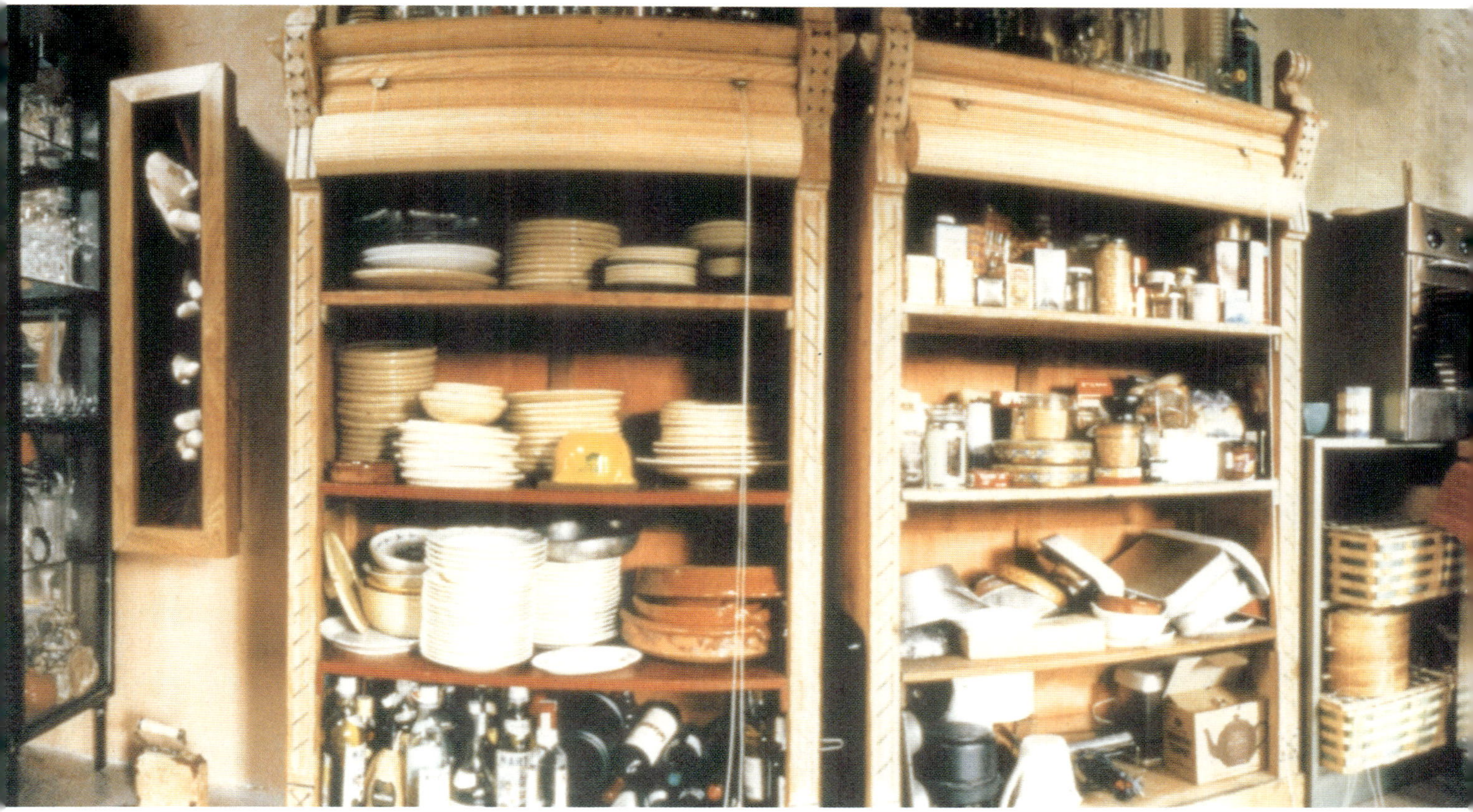

SAM TAYLOR-WOOD, FIVE REVOLUTIONARY SECONDS IX, 1997, left half of image (for other half see next double-spread), color photograph on vinyl with cassette tape, $42^{15}/_{16}$ x $305^{7}/_{8}$" / FÜNF REVOLUTIONÄRE SEKUNDEN IX, linke Bildhälfte (rechte Hälfte siehe nächste Doppelseite), Photographie auf Vinyl mit Videokassette, 109 x 777 cm.

their psychic reality or in an emotionally charged exchange with another person, are oblivious to the other inhabitants of the space they mutually occupy. Her revolutionary motion captures a revolutionary moment, for the scenario she pans is, indeed, an eerie psychic combat zone: In the far left corner of FIVE REVOLUTIONARY SECONDS XIII, for example, a man, wearing nothing but his knickers, stands on the stairway staring at us through the open door. Yet the framing is such that we can not really determine whether this is nothing other than a reflection in a mirror, pointing to a figure whose reference point would be outside the frame on the far right of the picture. As our eye moves further into the depicted scene we find another male figure, dressed in blue, superimposed like a phantom on the tree outside the window, and inside the room, a pair of abandoned shoes. Clearly delineated from and yet also connected to these two confusing apparitions by virtue of the elegant furnishings of the room we find four self-absorbed figures—a man engrossed in reading his book, a young woman lying on the couch looking out at us, dreaming, while a second man leans on the left armrest of the sofa, staring at the reclining body. The final figure is a woman, an empty wine glass in her right hand, staring up at the ceiling. In tandem with the isolation of these figures, we inevitably also note that each pulls our gaze in a different direction—toward something not shown, toward one of the figures in the room, toward an implied day-dream scenario, toward an indicated text, toward a spectral site, and finally toward ourselves as the object of the direct gaze of the barely dressed man. At the same time these opposing principles are sustained as a precarious moment in time, arrested as if at a turning point. For what haunts this scene, together with the spectral figure in the tree outside, is the impending sense that something is about to happen. Yet the

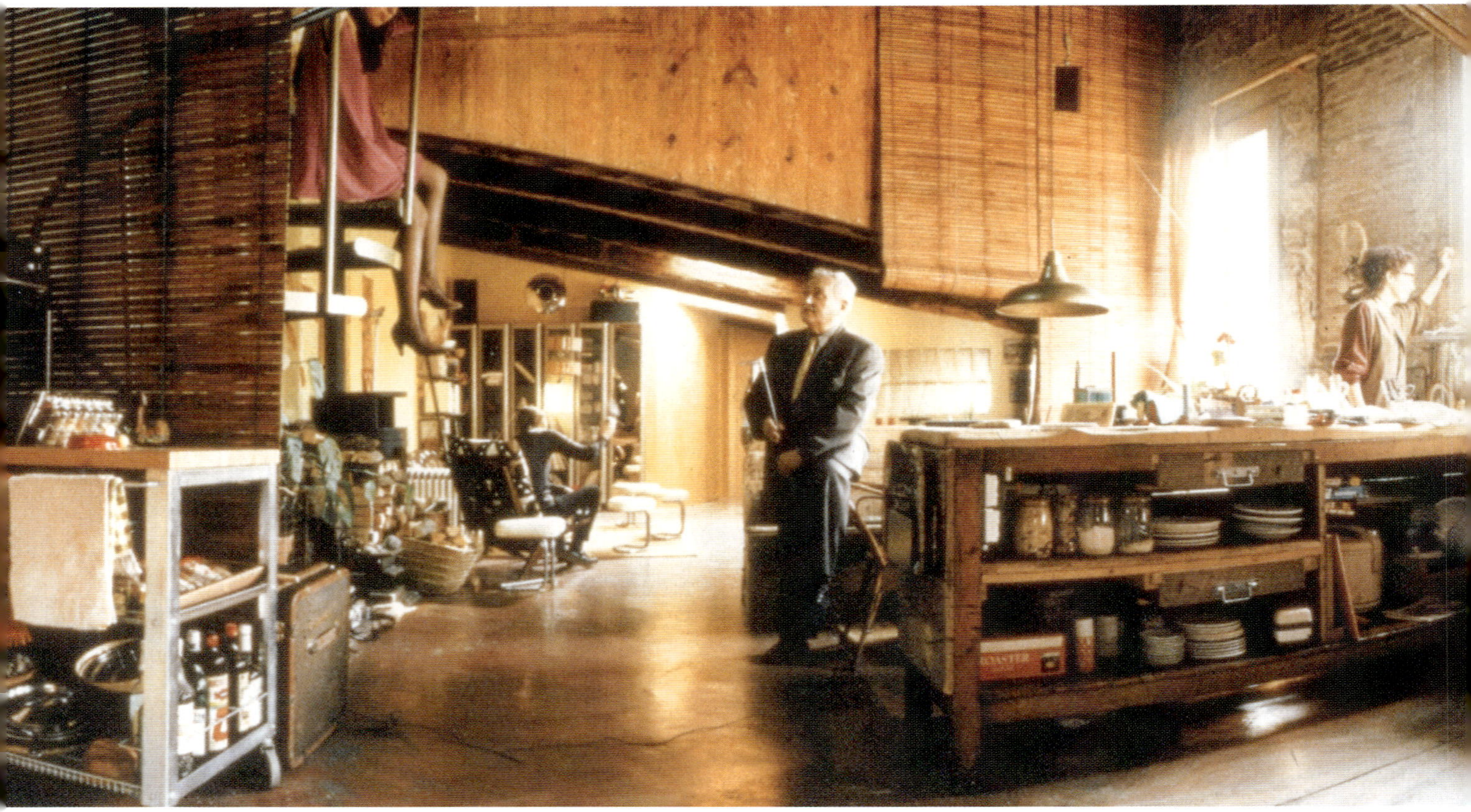

SAM TAYLOR-WOOD, FIVE REVOLUTIONARY SECONDS IX, 1997, right half of image (for other half see preceding page), color photograph on vinyl with cassette tape, 42 15/16 x 305 7/8" / FÜNF REVOLUTIONÄRE SEKUNDEN IX, rechte Bildhälfte (linke Hälfte siehe vorhergehende Doppelseite), Photographie auf Vinyl mit Videokassette, 109 x 777 cm.

antagonism performed by Sam Taylor-Wood's staging of this moment of fragility is such that the seemingly immanent *peripitea* is counteracted by an equally strong premonition that the emotional deadlock displayed cannot be resolved. The figures are forever caught within the intimation of revolution, within what Roland Barthes calls "a risky moment" that promises the closure of a narrative sequence. Anything could happen and nothing will happen—that is the affective message of this overtly dramatic enactment of non-communication.

Another example: In FIVE REVOLUTIONARY SECONDS V we see in the center three men grouped around a table, one sitting on a chair with his back to us, one leaning over the table, apparently menacing the seated figure, and standing slightly behind him, the third man, the onlooker of the debate. The staged argument is refracted in a mirror, which, positioned to the right of the group, gives us a view of the seated man's face though, as he is resting his head on his right arm which is propped up on the table, it is almost entirely covered by his right hand. This scene of strife is counterbalanced by a woman, reclining on a sofa standing left of the table, as though posing for a camera, a spot-light pointed at her face. Further to the left we find a solitary man, sitting on a chair looking out the window, his legs resting on the window sill. Behind him, a second mirror reflects not a body, but the unoccupied chair over which a sweater has been draped casually. To the far left we see the bottom half of a body, hanging from the ceiling. The gender of this figure is as indeterminable as the meaning of this gesture. Suspended between ceiling and floor it functions like a foreign body, both part of the scene and then again not. At the far right a woman dressed in a red gown is fleeing from something or toward something, maybe the half-visible suspended man. We can't really tell. Hers is a blurred

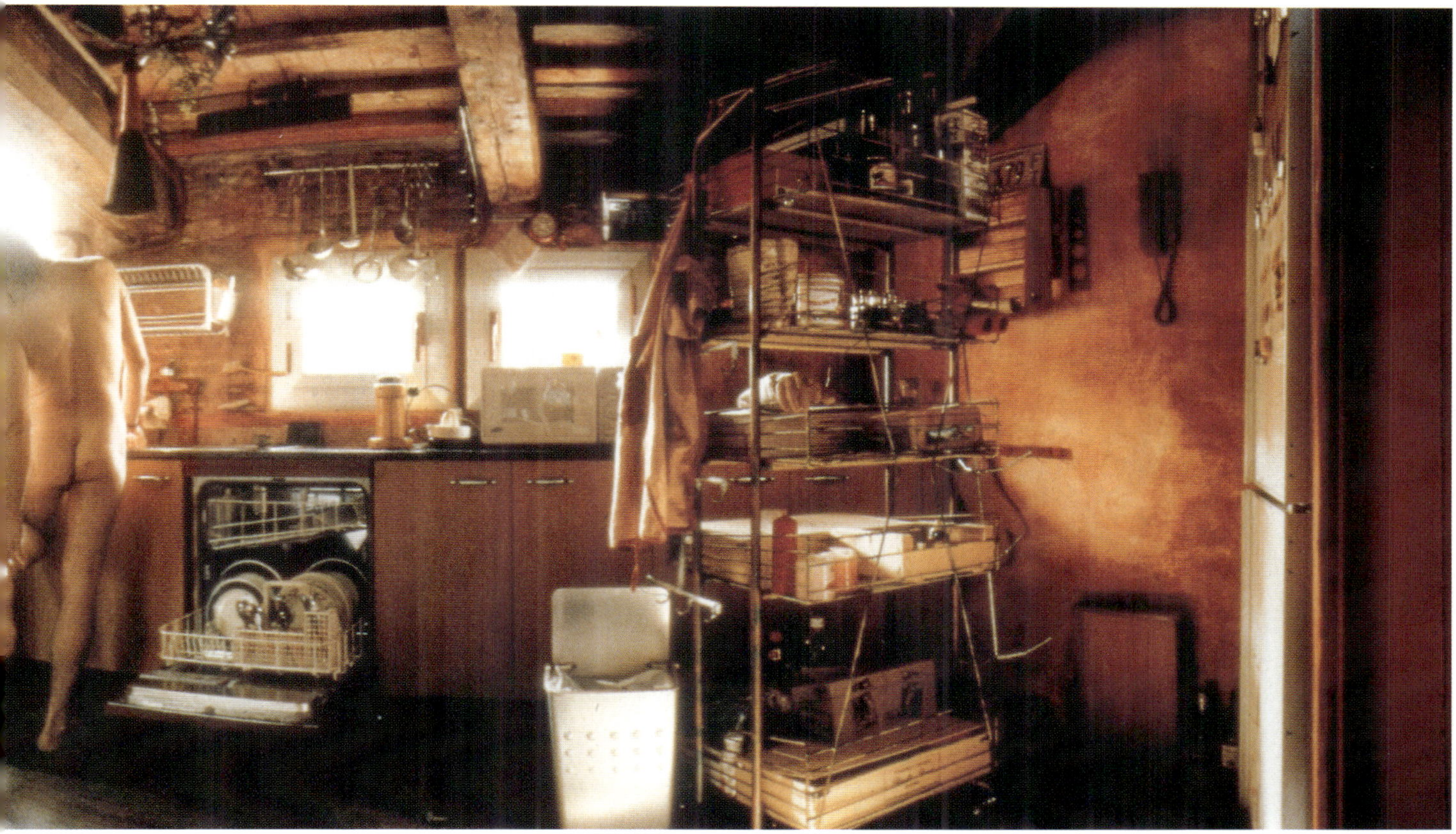

figure, her mobility an antagonistic force counterbalancing the stasis of the others. She, too, functions as an uncanny detail, embodying the turmoil subtending the elegant serene surface of the scene, though her flight is as arrested as the difference which threatens momentarily to disrupt.

As Sam Taylor-Wood explains, her thematic interest in the REVOLUTION series was, from the start, "the idea of decadence, and how people behave within that. And having these dysfunctional social situations in which people don't interact with each other. Each person is isolated within their thoughts, worlds and actions, but held together by this surrounding abundance."[3)] However, as in the classic scene of hysteria, where the performance of psychic anguish has recourse to a mode of expression that mirrors the confusion it seeks to articulate, so too, this artist's mode of representation reflects the antagonistic moments of crisis she displays. Not only the represented situation but the narrative itself is impaired in its coherence. In her interview with Bruce Ferguson Sam Taylor-Wood adds, "But I do see them as dysfunctional narratives. They look like they're beginning to tell a story; you try to make associations between the people and what they're doing but you can't necessarily find a narrative... The scale of them as well—FIVE REVOLUTIONARY SECONDS is twenty-five feet long. So you're looking at the photographs in the same way you might look at a film, because you can't take in the whole image in one go. You're editing what you're looking at, you're flipping between people and giving the story a different structure."[4)]

One could, indeed, call this an aesthetics of hysteria. Not only does Sam Taylor-Wood construct a seamless yet heterogeneous space, in which people are both in close proximity, yet also infinitely distant, because, though in a mutually shared space, they inhabit another site: the scene of their private theater. Her photographic presentation is such that, even as it elicits our desire for narrative, it frustrates our hope for narrative coherence and closure. Instead, like the represented figures caught in solitary reverie, we, too, wander in mind, gazing backwards and forwards within the confines of the depicted scene, only to discover that, even as it opens up a plethora of many possible, even contradictory interpretations, it also makes us aware that any real discovery of the reason for the emotional antagonism displayed, indeed any understanding of the content of the scene, is not accessible to us. Instead the stage for passionate attitudes of others suddenly turns into a mirror, reflecting our own desires, but also our own anxieties. In part because the depicted scenes evoke our own unsatisfiable imaginary activity and ask us to partake in a dialog with our unconscious fantasies, in part because we are forced to participate in the impossible task of resolving the presented moment of emotional crisis into a coherent narrative, we discover our own hermeneutic fallibility. As we oscillate between dreamy participation and self-conscious analysis, what is in fact called forth proves to be the inversion of fantasy: the traumatic knowledge of vulnerability, fragility, implenitude. The revolutionary movement of the camera performs the fact that narrative coherence is a protective fiction covering a gap. This lacuna is not simply mapped as the invisible boundaries between the different, solitary figures. It is also rendered visible at the edges of each panoramic image, where the two parts should meet and yet, where, because the photograph is exhibited as an enormous flat strip, the depicted scene opens out instead beyond the frame, flowing into the space inhabited by the spectator.

The antagonism sustained in all the FIVE REVOLUTIONARY SECONDS thus uncannily undercuts the very notion of panoramic totality Sam Taylor-Wood also veers toward. On the one hand she explains, "I

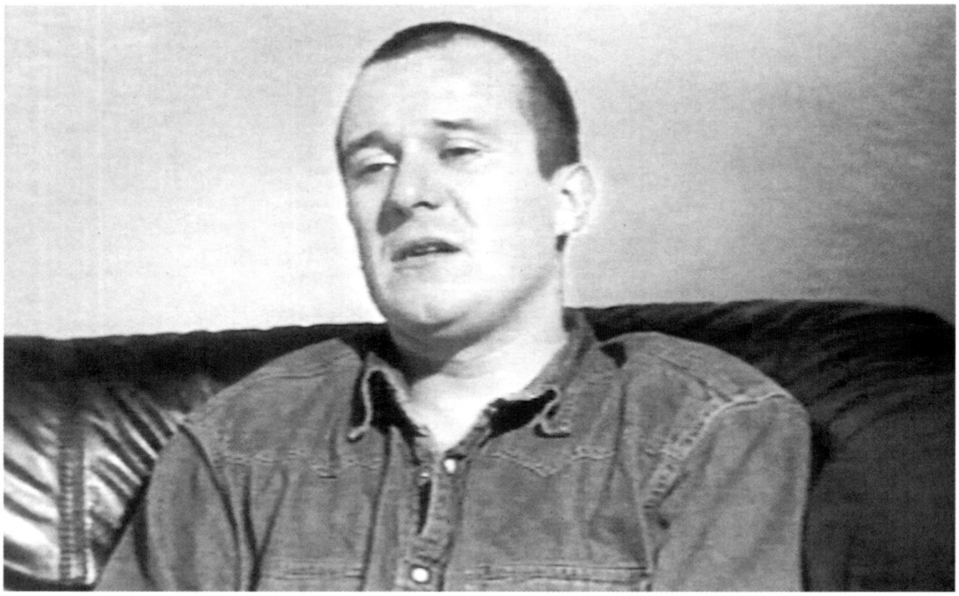

SAM TAYLOR-WOOD, *METHOD IN MADNESS, 1995, 10-minutes projection and sound, dimensions variable /* WAHNSINN MIT METHODE, *10-Minuten-Bildprojektion und Ton, Grösse variabel.*

am trying to gather a complete series of human feelings, even if reflected in more than one person. The same room is the setting for eroticism, rage, pensiveness, creativity, repulsion, anxiety, joy, anguish, pleasure. It is as if I wanted to explain the entire range of the emotional or existential world."[5] And yet this totality can only be rendered in tandem with its opposite rhetorical figure, namely that of dissolution. As she also explains, "I put many characters of FIVE REVOLUTIONARY SECONDS in a situation of unease, through nudity or social status, and then sometimes placing them into a situation of luxury. I have an interest, both personal and social, in ungluing the setting."[6] One can then speak about an aesthetics of hysteria not just because of the correspondence between dysfunctional social setting and a dysfunctional visual narrative which undoes the very scenario it also performs, nor because these images unsettle us in our spectatorial certainty. Rather, visualizing psychic states of excess also emerges as a gesture of self-recognition. Although Sam Taylor-Wood is the onlooker of a scene, enacting the fantasy life of her chosen protagonists, structurally it is her own inner theatre as well. As she explains, "I feel that madness is in everyone. Making art, for me, is balancing myself between my neurosis and my psychosis. I'm only able to keep on an even keel because I'm constantly addressing what my fears and anxieties are."[7]

Her concern with not just keeping the critical boundary between neurosis and psychosis intact but also sustaining the fragility of this boundary, recalls yet another revolutionary turn, namely the one Julia Kristeva describes as the incursion of the semiotic into the symbolic. Our need to ward off archaic psychic material, whose proximity would seriously endanger the balance of the psychic apparatus, is not only located in a realm Kristeva calls the semiotic, so as to signal that though affectively marked it is not symbolically encoded. It finds a counterpoint in poetic language as the medium through which this repressed material returns to break open the balance of symbolic systems—be they psychic or social. Like the borderline schizophrenic, the melancholic and the lover, artists, she argues, have, since antiquity, sought to confront the realm of madness, even while in so doing they refigure it; introducing fissures into the rigidity of symbolic codes though never relinquishing them. In her revolution of photographic language Sam Taylor-Wood borrows not only from this ancient wisdom but also from the other side of the equation, though, perhaps, doing so in a less cathartic manner than intended by the ancient aestheticians. She places us on the threshold as well—sustaining the antagonism.

1) Cited in: "Happening Artist Sam Taylor-Wood," *Interview* (October 1998), p. 72.
2) Slavoj Zizek, *The Plague of Fantasies* (London: Verso, 1997), p. 10–11.
3) Cited in: Bruce Ferguson, "Sam Taylor-Wood," *Bomb* (Fall 1998), p. 48.
4) Ibid., p. 45.
5) Cited in the interview between Germano Celant and Sam Taylor-Wood in: *Sam Taylor-Wood,* exhibition catalogue (Milan: Fondazione Prada, 1998), p. 270.
6) Ibid., p. 210.
7) Cited in: Philip Hoare, "?." *Frank* (November 1998), p. 159.

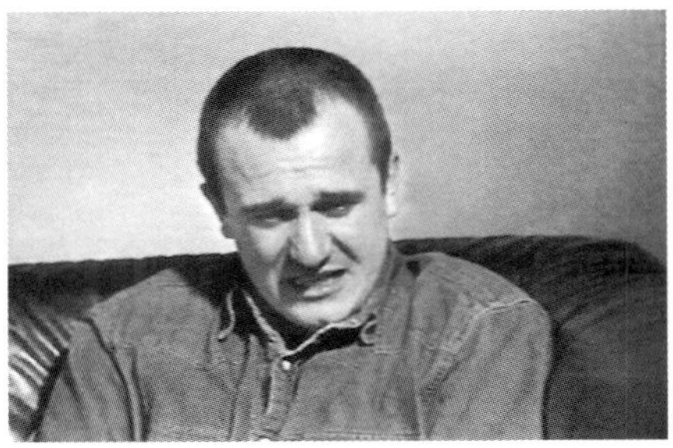

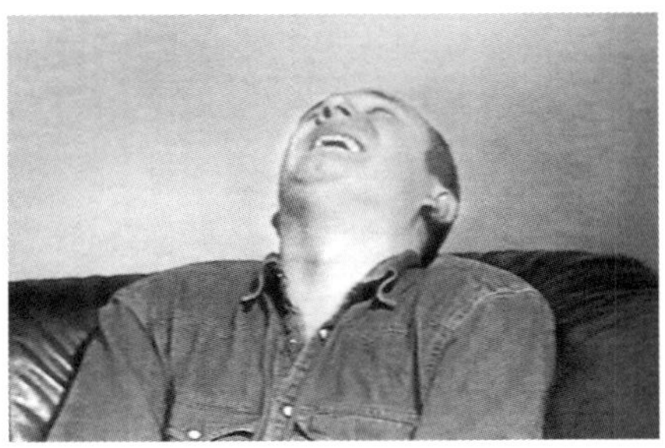

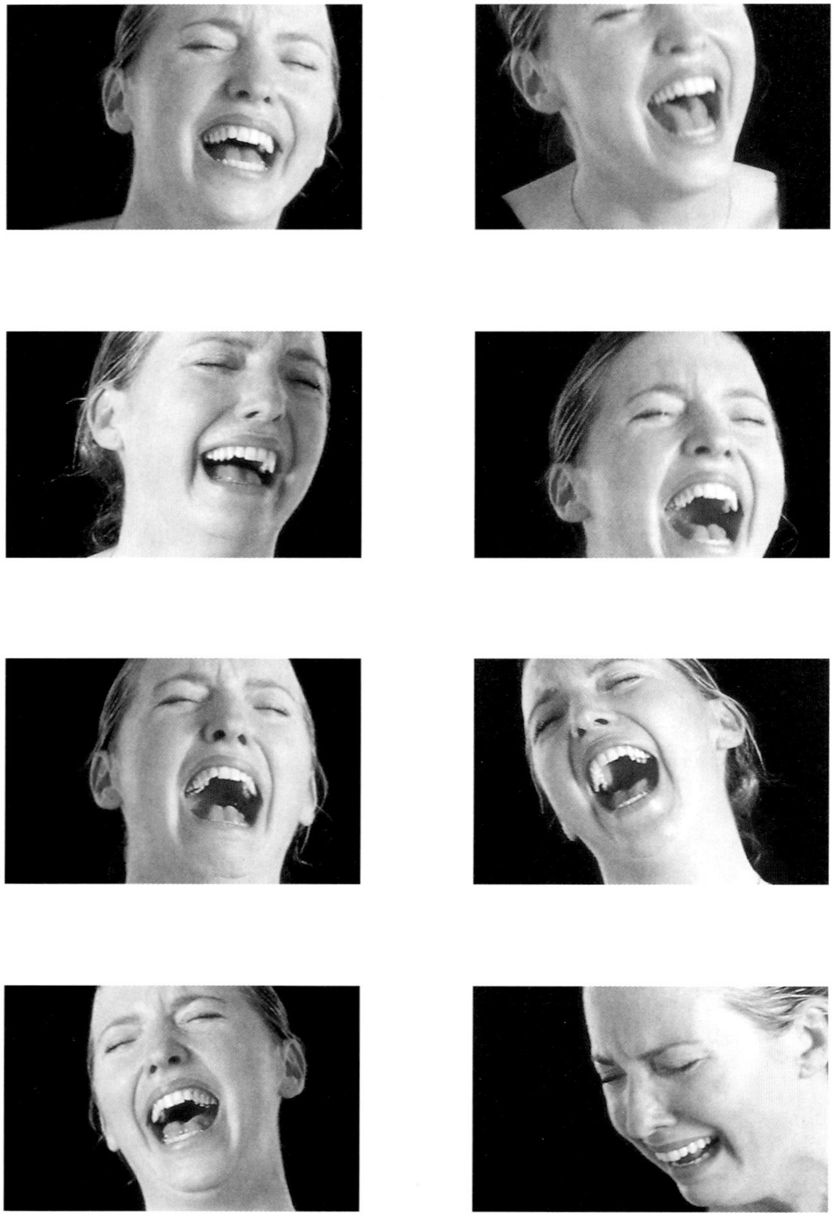

SAM TAYLOR-WOOD, HYSTERIA, 1997, 8-minute laser disc / HYSTERIE, 8-Minuten-Laserdisk.

Den Antagonismus aushalten

ELISABETH BRONFEN

Sam Taylor-Woods «Fünf revolutionäre Sekunden»

– weil eine Karte eben genau das ist – eine sichtbar gemachte Verbindung

Franco Moretti, *Atlas des europäischen Romans*

In einer neueren Laserdisk-Projektion mit dem Titel HYSTERIA zeigt uns Sam Taylor-Wood in extremer Nahaufnahme das verzerrte Gesicht einer Frau. Von einer heftigen Emotion ergriffen, hebt und senkt sich ihr ganzer Körper, der Kopf neigt sich nach hinten und nach vorne, der einzige Teil des Gesichts, den wir ständig sehen, ist der geöffnete Mund. Aufgrund der Zeitlupe und in Ermangelung einer Tonspur lässt sich praktisch nicht entscheiden, ob sie lacht oder weint. Die Künstlerin erklärt, sie habe diese beiden gegensätzlichen Zustände miteinander verschmelzen und den Unterschied zwischen ihnen so sehr verwischen wollen, dass sie deckungsgleich werden würden. Zugleich sollte die emotionale Aufgewühltheit der Schauspielerin auch den impliziten Betrachter ergreifen, der ebenfalls in Verwirrung gestürzt wird, da er oder sie ausserstande ist sich von dieser zermürbenden Artikulation eines extremen Gefühlsausbruchs zu distanzieren, weil dieser sich jeder unzweideutigen Interpretation verweigert. Mit der Einzelbild-Analyse dieser theatralischen Zurschaustellung eines zeitweiligen Verlusts der Selbstbeherrschung, die den Betrachter zwangsläufig in die Darbietung mit einbezieht und damit nicht nur die Konturen der dargestellten emotionalen Krise verwischt, sondern auch die Unterscheidung zwischen Betrachter und Spektakel, erweist Sam Taylor-Wood der Ikonographie der hysterischen Attacke, die der am Ende des 19. Jahrhunderts tätige Psychiater Jean-Martin Charcot erfand, ihre Reverenz. Berühmt sowohl für die öffentliche Zurschaustellung der psychosomatischen Symptome seiner Patient(inn)en während seiner berühmt-berüchtigten Dienstagsvorlesungen im Hörsaal der Pariser Salpêtrière als auch für die Photographien, die er als Teil seiner Bemühungen, die fünf von ihm konstatierten Phasen der Hysterie im Bild zu bannen, herstellte, war Charcot der erste, der sich die Visualität zur medizinischen Untersuchung leidenschaftlicher Gebärden zunutze machte.

Die Hysterie, diese schwer zu fassende und enigmatische psychosomatische Störung, für die sich keine organischen Verletzungen finden lassen, entwickelte sich rasch zu einem verbalen Platzhalter für

ELISABETH BRONFEN ist Professorin für Englische Literatur an der Universität Zürich. Zu ihren zahlreichen Publikationen gehört u.a. das Buch *Das verknotete Subjekt. Hysterie in der Moderne* (Volk & Welt, Berlin 1998).

den Ausdruck eines Unbehagens, das sich jeder Diagnose widersetzt, und wurde auf diese Weise auch zu einer kulturellen Trope. Ihre bevorzugten Symptome – eine theatralische Inszenierung krisenhafter Momente sowie die körperliche Darstellung des Umherschweifens der Phantasie – galten nicht nur als Ausdruck eines unbefriedigten Begehrens. Vielmehr formulierte Sigmund Freud in seiner revolutionären Neuinterpretation die These, dass die Selbst-Zurschaustellung der Hysterikerin das Leiden an der Fragilität verkünde, das den bürgerlichen Vorstellungen von Glück und Gesundheit innewohnt, und eine Artikulation des Unbehagens sei, das unter jedem harmonischen In-der-Welt-Sein lauert. Die provokatorische Inszenierung emotionalen Exzesses und emotionaler Lähmung seitens der Hysteriker sei, so Freuds These, ein Insistieren darauf, dass man sich der menschlichen Verwundbarkeit und den Ängsten, die unter allen glatten Selbstentwürfen schlummern, stellen muss. Doch wie Freud bei seinen eigenen Krankengeschichten so schmerzlich erfahren musste, ist das herausragendste Merkmal des hysterischen Subjekts dessen anhaltender Widerstand gegen jede eindeutige, geschweige denn abschliessende Klassifikation. Im Verlauf der hysterischen Inszenierung emotionaler Krisen werden nicht nur Grenzen durchlässig, sondern die beabsichtigte Verkündigung der Klage droht darü-

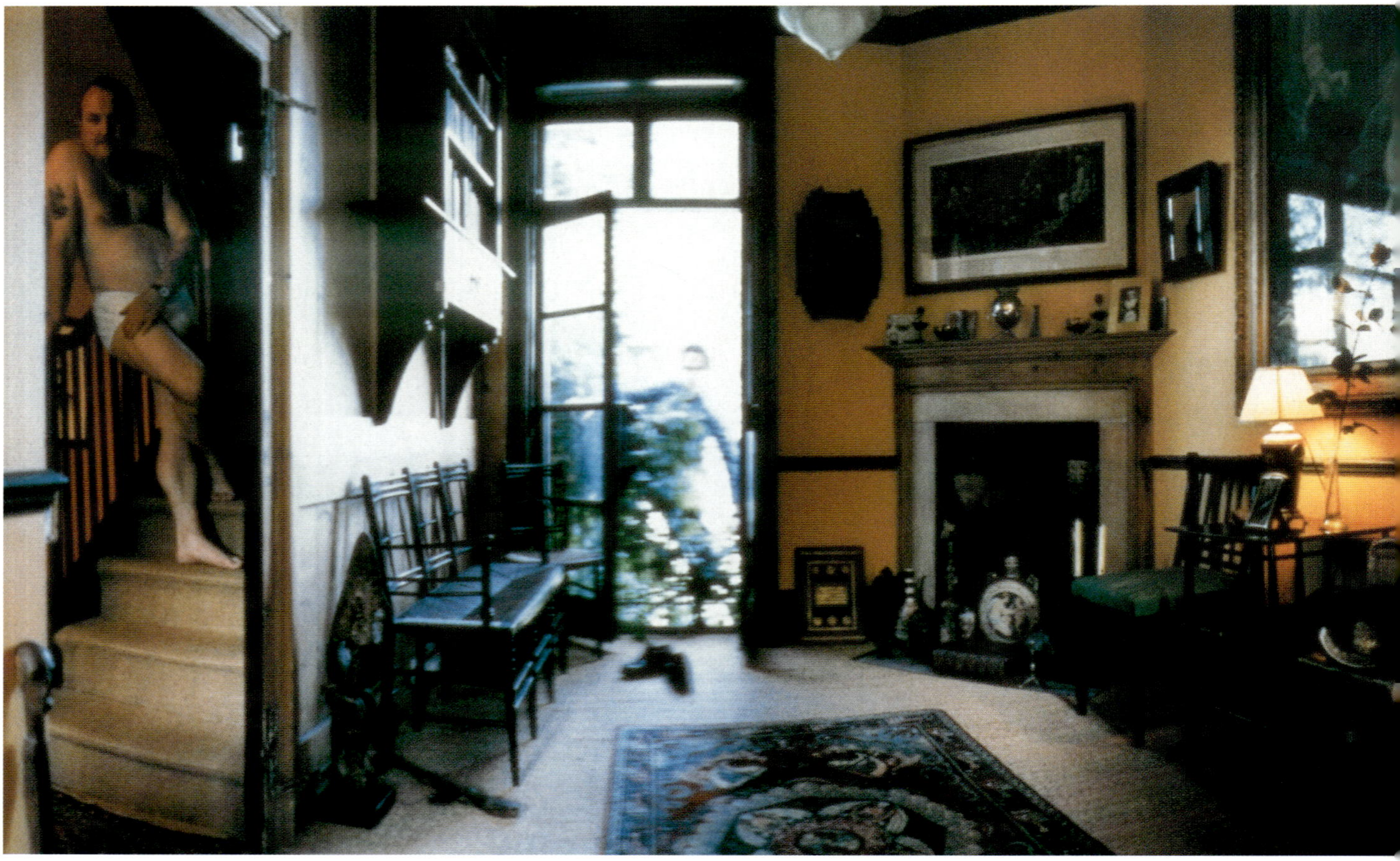

ber hinaus kein Ende zu finden. Der Antagonismus, den die Hysterikerin so eindringlich, wenn auch nur indirekt, verkündet, ist Teil jenes traumatischen Wissens, das das Subjekt ebenso sehr umtreibt wie das unbefriedigte Begehren: eine fundamentale Krise des emotionalen Wohlbefindens und der emotionalen Ausgeglichenheit, die sich niemals bewältigen, sondern lediglich aushalten lässt.

Auf nachgerade unheimliche Weise erweist sich die Hysterie so als besonders angemessene kritische Trope für Sam Taylor-Woods eigenes ästhetisches Projekt. Auch wenn sie im postmodernen Gewand daherkommen, rufen viele ihrer Protagonistinnen die leidenschaftlichen, auf Charcots Bühne in Szene gesetzten Gebärden in Erinnerung. Völlig von ihrer psychischen Realität in Beschlag genommen – entweder sind sie sich ihrer Umgebung überhaupt nicht bewusst oder sie setzen sich markant von ihren Mitmenschen ab, indem sie mit ihnen streiten oder sie unbarmherzig ignorieren – scheinen sie alle einer kulturellen Krankheit Ausdruck zu verleihen. Sam Taylor-Wood bemerkt in diesem Zusammenhang: «Man hat zurzeit den Eindruck, als fühlten sich die Menschen von der Welt, in der wir leben, abgeschnitten, als stünden sie nicht mehr so ganz im Einklang mit ihrer Umwelt.»[1] Zugleich konstatiert sie mittels des Bildes eine andere Einsicht, die Freud bereits in seinen frühen Schriften zur Hysterie for-

SAM TAYLOR-WOOD, FIVE REVOLUTIONARY SECONDS XIII, 1998, left half of image (for other half see next double-spread), c-print, 8¼ x 78¾" / FÜNF REVOLUTIONÄRE SEKUNDEN XIII, linke Bildhälfte (rechte Hälfte siehe nächste Doppelseite), C-Print, 21 x 200 cm.

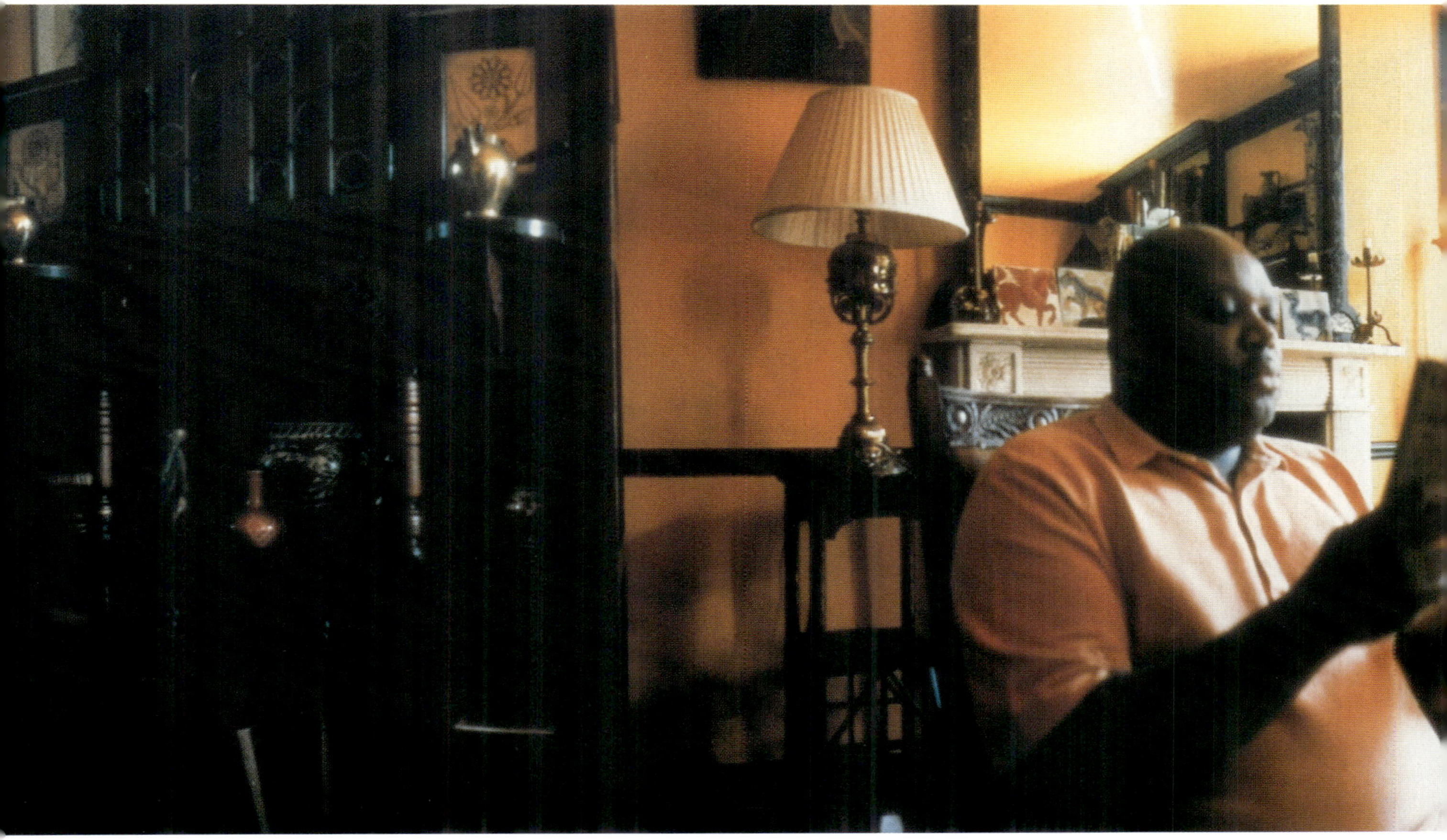

muliert hat: Auch wenn der psychische Apparat von der Angst vor der subjektiven Fehlbarkeit und Fragilität infiziert ist, ist dieses traumatische Wissen von jeder unbewussten oder bewussten Repräsentation durch eine Lücke in der Psyche abgegrenzt. Mit anderen Worten, auch wenn das Trauma all jene Schutzdichtungen heimsucht, die wir produzieren, um in unserer psychischen Realität leben zu können, verweisen diese Erzählungen auf einen fundamentalen Antagonismus, zu dem wir keinen direkten Zugang haben. Indem man die widersprüchlichen Erfahrungen zu einer zusammenhängenden Erzählung ordnet, lassen sich psychische Krisenmomente wieder in eine Situation scheinbarer emotionaler Kontrolle und Ausgeglichenheit integrieren. Doch wie Slavoj Zizek scharfsinnig bemerkt hat, sind solche beschwichtigenden Phantasien nicht nur nichts anderes als Schutzdichtungen, insoweit als sie «auf der Ausschliessung traumatischer Ereignisse beruhen und die von diesen Ausschliessungen hinterlassenen Lücken übertünchen», sondern «die Erzählung als solche kommt nur deswegen zustande, weil sie einen fundamentalen Antagonismus lösen soll, indem sie dessen Begriffe in eine zeitliche Abfolge bringt.»[2)]

In ihrer 1995 begonnenen Serie mit dem Titel FIVE REVOLUTIONARY SECONDS (Fünf revolutionäre Sekunden) spielt Sam Taylor-Wood mit der doppel-

SAM TAYLOR-WOOD, FIVE REVOLUTIONARY SECONDS XIII, 1998, right half of image (for other half see preceding page), c-print, 8¼ x 78¾" / FÜNF REVOLUTIONÄRE SEKUNDEN XIII, rechte Bildhälfte (linke Hälfte siehe vorhergehende Doppelseite), C-Print, 21 x 200 cm.

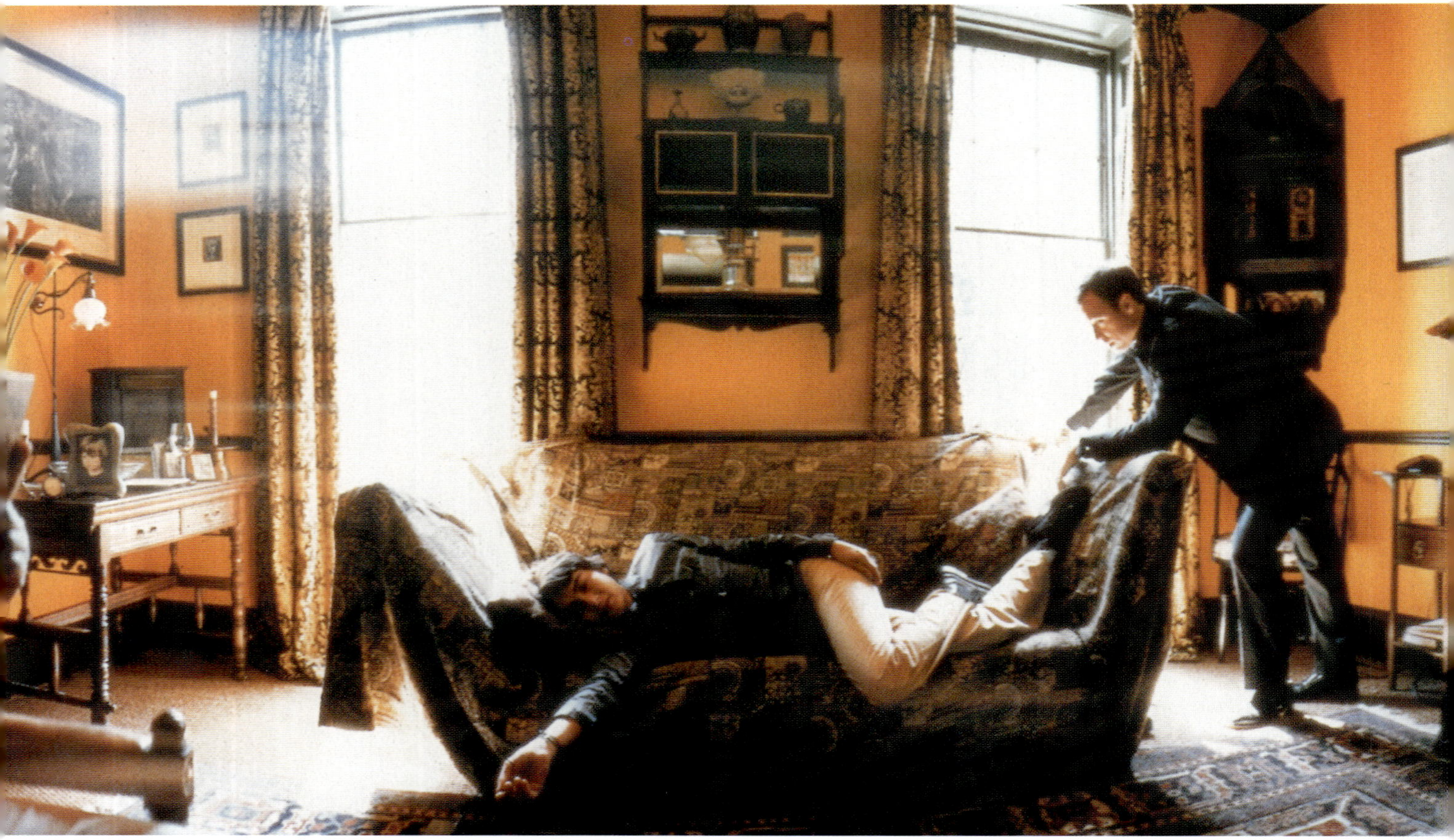

ten Bedeutung des Wortes «Revolution» (Revolution/Umdrehung) um uns mittels der Photographie Phantasieszenarien zu präsentieren, die das Übergreifen verdrängter Antagonismen auf eben jenes Repräsentationsmedium inszenieren, das diesen ursprünglichen toten Punkt verdecken sollte. Mit einer von der Royal Air Force entwickelten Kamera für Luftaufnahmen stellt sie sich selbst ins Zentrum eines Raums, den sie aufgrund seiner Grösse, seiner Eleganz oder auch seiner Dekadenz ausgewählt hat. Nachdem sie ihren Schauspielern Anweisungen gegeben hat, welche leidenschaftlichen Gebärden und Posen sie einnehmen sollen, macht sie eine 360-Grad-Panorama-Aufnahme des Raums mit einer Belichtungszeit von fünf Sekunden. Während die Kamera einmal um die eigene Achse schwenkt, zeichnet sie die verschiedenen im Raum befindlichen Personen auf, die, isoliert in ihrer eigenen psychischen Realität oder in einem emotionsgeladenen Austausch mit einer anderen Person begriffen, die anderen im Raum anwesenden Menschen gar nicht zur Kenntnis nehmen. Taylor-Woods «revolutionäre» Bewegung fängt einen «revolutionären» Moment ein, denn das von ihr aufgezeichnete Szenario ist in Wirklichkeit ein grausiges psychisches Schlachtfeld. Im äussersten linken Winkel von FIVE REVOLUTIONARY SECONDS XIII etwa steht ein nur mit Unterhosen bekleideter Mann auf der Treppe und starrt

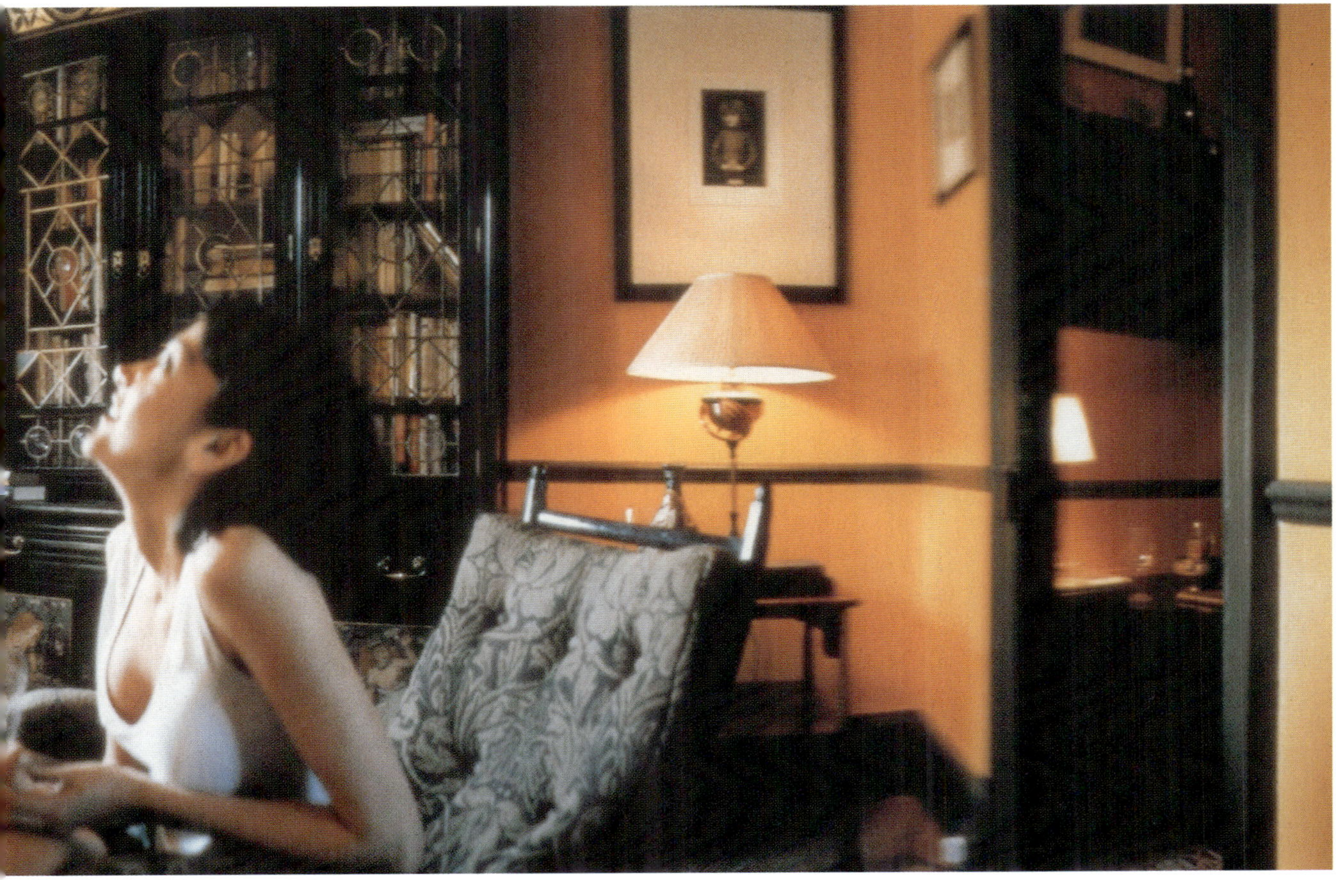

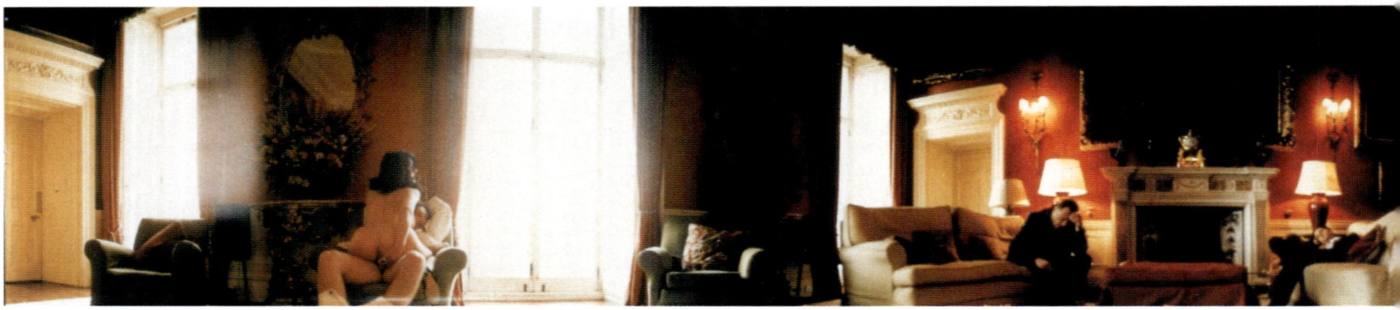

SAM TAYLOR-WOOD, FIVE REVOLUTIONARY SECONDS III, 1996, color photograph on vinyl with CD, 28⅜ x 298" / FÜNF REVOLUTIONÄRE SEKUNDEN III, Farbphotographie auf Vinyl mit CD, 72 x 757 cm.

uns durch eine offene Türe an. Doch aufgrund des Bildausschnitts können wir nicht feststellen, ob es sich dabei nur um ein Spiegelbild handelt, das auf eine Figur verweist, die sich weit rechts ausserhalb des Bildausschnitts befinden müsste. Bei näherer Prüfung der dargestellten Szene entdeckt unser Auge eine weitere männliche Gestalt, blau gekleidet, die auf den Baum draussen vor dem Fenster projiziert ist, sowie im Inneren des Raums ein verlassenes Paar Schuhe. Klar abgegrenzt gegen diese beiden verwirrenden Erscheinungen und zugleich durch die elegante Raumausstattung mit ihnen verbunden sind vier ganz und gar mit sich selbst beschäftigte Gestalten: ein in die Lektüre seines Buchs vertiefter Mann, eine junge Frau, die auf einer Couch liegt und uns verträumt anblickt, sowie ein weiterer Mann, der sich auf die linke Lehne der Couch stützt und den darauf liegenden Körper anstarrt; schliesslich noch eine Frau, die, ein leeres Weinglas in der rechten Hand, zur Decke starrt. Neben der Isolation dieser Figuren fällt uns ausserdem unweigerlich auf, dass jede von ihnen unseren Blick in eine andere Richtung lenkt, auf etwas, das nicht gezeigt wird, auf eine der Gestalten im Raum, auf ein implizites Tagtraum-Szenarium, einen angedeuteten Text, einen gespenstischen Schauplatz und schliesslich auf uns selbst als Objekt des direkten Blicks des spärlich bekleideten Mannes. Zugleich werden diese widerstreitenden Elemente als ein heikler Moment in der Zeit aufrechterhalten, arretiert wie an einem Wendepunkt. Denn was die Szene so unheimlich macht, ist neben der gespenstischen Figur im Baum das bedrohliche Gefühl, dass im nächsten Augenblick etwas geschehen wird. Doch der Antagonismus, den uns Sam Taylor-Wood mit der Inszenierung dieses fragilen Augenblicks präsentiert, besteht darin, dass dieser anscheinend immanenten Peripetie eine ebenso starke Vorahnung entgegenwirkt, dass sich die dargestellte emotionale Sackgasse nicht lösen lässt. Die Figuren sind für immer in der Ankündigung der «Revolution» gefangen, in dem, was Roland Barthes den «riskanten Moment» nennt, der den Abschluss einer narrativen Sequenz verheisst. Alles könnte und nichts wird passieren – das ist die affektive Botschaft dieser ganz unverblümt dramatischen Inszenierung der Nicht-Kommunikation.

Ein weiteres Beispiel: Im Zentrum von FIVE REVOLUTIONARY SECONDS V sehen wir drei um einen Tisch versammelte Männer; einer sitzt auf einem Stuhl, mit dem Rücken zu uns, einer lehnt über dem Tisch und bedroht dabei offensichtlich den Sitzenden, und der dritte, in geringem Abstand hinter ihm stehende Mann beobachtet den Streit. Die inszenierte Auseinandersetzung wird in einem Spiegel gebrochen. Dieser zeigt uns, rechts von der Gruppe postiert, das Gesicht des Sitzenden, das freilich fast völlig von seiner rechten Hand verdeckt wird, die seinen Kopf stützt. Den Kontrapunkt zu dieser konfliktgeladenen Szene bildet eine Frau, die auf einem zur Linken des Tisches stehenden Sofa lehnt, als posiere sie für eine Kamera, wobei ein Scheinwerfer auf ihr Gesicht gerichtet ist. Weiter links sehen wir einen einzelnen Mann, der auf einem Stuhl sitzt und mit auf dem Fenstersims ruhenden Beinen aus dem

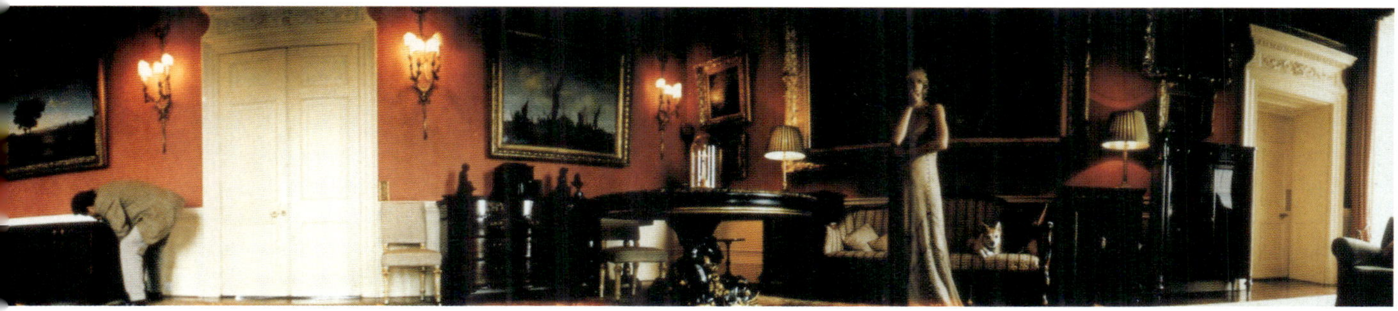

Fenster blickt. Hinter ihm befindet sich ein zweiter Spiegel, der keinen Körper reflektiert, sondern den freien Stuhl, auf dessen Rückenlehne ein Pullover hängt. Ganz links sehen wir die untere Hälfte eines von der Decke herabhängenden Körpers. Das Geschlecht dieser Figur lässt sich genauso wenig bestimmen wie die Bedeutung dieser Position. Zwischen Decke und Boden hängend, fungiert die Gestalt als Fremdkörper, ist zugleich Teil der Szene und auch wieder nicht. Ganz rechts flüchtet eine Frau in einem roten Kleid vor etwas oder zu etwas – womöglich zu dieser nur halb sichtbaren, hängenden Gestalt. Es lässt sich nicht mit Bestimmtheit sagen. Die Gestalt der Frau bleibt unscharf, ihre Beweglichkeit ist eine ausgleichende Gegenkraft zur Statik der anderen. Auch sie fungiert als unheimliches Element, eine Verkörperung der Unruhe, die unter der eleganten glatten Oberfläche der Szene lauert, obgleich ihre Flucht ebenso angehalten ist wie der Streit, der jeden Moment loszubrechen droht.

Sam Taylor-Wood hat erklärt, dass ihr thematisches Interesse bei der REVOLUTION-Serie von Anfang an «die Idee der Dekadenz [war] und wie die Leute damit umgehen. Und diese dysfunktionellen sozialen Situationen, in denen Menschen nicht miteinander interagieren. Jede Person ist innerhalb ihrer Gedanken, Worte und Handlungen isoliert, wird aber von dem Überfluss, der sie umgibt, zusammengehalten.»[3] Doch wie in der klassischen Szene der Hysterie, wo für die Inszenierung der psychischen Angst auf eine Ausdrucksweise zurückgegriffen wird, welche die Verwirrung spiegelt, die artikuliert werden soll, so reflektiert auch der Darstellungsmodus dieser Künstlerin die widerstreitenden Krisenmomente, die sie uns präsentiert. Nicht nur die dargestellte Situation, sondern die Erzählung selbst ist in ihrer Kohärenz beeinträchtigt. In ihrem Gespräch mit Bruce Ferguson fügt Sam Taylor-Wood hinzu: «Aber ich sehe sie als dysfunktionale Erzählungen. Sie sehen so aus, als seien sie der Anfang einer Geschichte; man kann versuchen, Assoziationen zwischen den Leuten und ihren Handlungen herzustellen, aber man findet nicht zwangsläufig eine Geschichte... Dasselbe gilt für das Format. FIVE REVOLUTIONARY SECONDS ist 7,5 Meter lang. Man betrachtet die Photographien also genau so, wie man sich einen Film ansehen würde, weil man das Bild nicht in einem Blick erfassen kann. Man wählt bewusst aus, was man sich ansieht, man springt zwischen den Leuten hin und her und gibt der Geschichte eine andere Struktur.»[4]

Man könnte dies in der Tat als eine Ästhetik der Hysterie bezeichnen. Denn Sam Taylor-Wood konstruiert einen nahtlosen, aber heterogenen Raum, in dem sich Menschen zugleich sehr nahe und unendlich weit voneinander entfernt sind, weil sie zwar eine Räumlichkeit miteinander teilen, sich aber in Wirklichkeit an einem ganz anderen Ort befinden, nämlich auf der Bühne ihres Privattheaters. Die photographische Präsentation der Künstlerin weckt also einerseits unser Begehren nach einer Erzählung, macht aber andererseits unsere Hoffnung auf narrative Schlüssigkeit und Geschlossenheit im selben Augenblick zunichte. Stattdessen wandern wir, gefangen in unseren einsamen Tagträumen, wie die dargestellten Figuren im Geiste umher und lassen unseren Blick innerhalb der Grenzen der dargestellten Welt hin und her schweifen, müssen dann jedoch feststellen, dass uns trotz der Fülle der sich anbietenden möglichen und widersprüchlichen Deutungen die Aufdeckung des wahren Grundes für den vorgeführten emotionalen Zwiespalt, ja jedes Verständnis des Inhalts der Szene überhaupt, verwehrt bleibt. Stattdessen wird die Bühne der leidenschaftlichen Gebärden anderer zu einem Spiegel, der unsere eigenen Wünsche, aber auch Ängste reflektiert. Zum Teil, weil die dargestellten Szenen unsere eigene unersättliche Vorstellungskraft anregen und uns zum Dialog mit unseren unbewussten Phantasien einladen; zum Teil, weil wir – unfreiwillig an der unmöglichen Aufgabe beteiligt, den uns präsentierten emotionalen Krisenmoment in eine kohärente Erzählung aufzulösen – unsere eigene hermeneutische Fehlbarkeit feststellen müssen. Während wir noch zwischen träumerischer Teilnahme und selbst-bewusster Analyse hin und her schwanken, zeigt sich, dass in Wirklichkeit die Kehrseite der Phantasie heraufbeschworen wird: das traumatische Wissen um Verwundbarkeit, Fragilität und Unvollkommenheit. Die «revolutionäre» Bewegung der Kamera inszeniert die Tatsache, dass narrative Kohärenz eine Schutzdichtung ist, die eine Lücke zudeckt. Doch diese Bresche entspricht nicht einfach nur den unsichtbaren Grenzlinien zwischen den verschiedenen einsamen Figuren, sondern wird auch an den Rändern der einzelnen Panoramabilder sichtbar gemacht, wo diese sich eigentlich aneinander fügen sollten: Denn weil das photographische Bild als gewaltiger flacher Streifen erscheint, öffnet sich die dargestellte Szene über den Rahmen hinaus und fliesst in den Raum des Betrachters.

Der Antagonismus, der in allen FIVE REVOLUTIONARY SECONDS aufrechterhalten bleibt, unterminiert so auf unheimliche Weise eben jene Idee der panoramahaften Totalität, die Sam Taylor-Wood ebenfalls anvisiert. Einerseits erklärt sie: «Ich versuche eine vollständige Serie der menschlichen Gefühle zusammenzutragen, auch wenn sie über mehrere Personen verteilt zum Ausdruck kommen. Ein und derselbe Raum wird zum Schauplatz für Erotik, Wut, Nachdenklichkeit, Kreativität, Abneigung, Angst, Freude, Qual, Lust. Es ist, als ob ich die ganze Skala der emotionalen oder existenziellen Welt erklären wollte.»[5] Und doch lässt sich diese Totalität nur im Duo mit der entgegengesetzten rhetorischen Figur der Auflösung darstellen. Denn die Künstlerin erklärt zugleich: «Ich versetze viele Figuren in FIVE REVOLUTIONARY SECONDS in einen Zustand des Unbehagens, durch Nacktheit oder gesellschaftlichen Status, manchmal aber auch wieder in eine luxuriöse Situation. Ich habe sozusagen sowohl ein persönliches als auch ein soziales Interesse daran, die Szene ‹aus dem Leim gehen› zu lassen.»[6] Man kann also nicht nur aufgrund der Entsprechung zwischen der dysfunktionalen sozialen Szene und der dysfunktionalen visuellen Erzählung, die das ent-

SAM TAYLOR-WOOD, FIVE REVOLUTIONARY SECONDS I, 1995, color photograph on vinyl with cassette tape, 28 5/16 x 219 5/16" / FÜNF REVOLUTIONÄRE SEKUNDEN I, Farbphotographie auf Vinyl mit Videokassette, 72 x 757 cm.

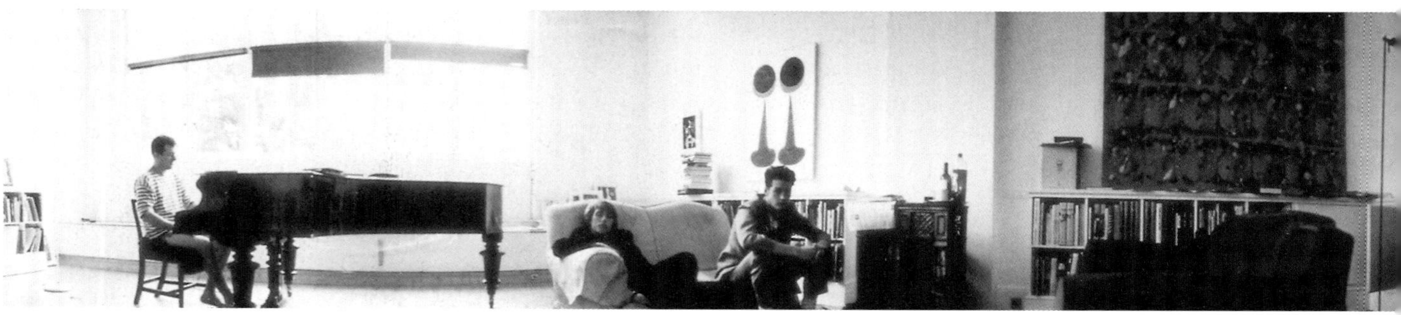

worfene Szenarium gleich wieder unterminiert, von einer Ästhetik der Hysterie sprechen; und nicht nur, weil diese Bilder unsere Gewissheit als Betrachter in Frage stellen, sondern auch, weil sich die Visualisierung von extremen psychischen Zuständen als Geste der Selbsterkenntnis erweist. Obwohl Sam Taylor-Wood die Betrachterin einer Szene ist und sie die Phantasien der von ihr ausgewählten Protagonisten inszeniert, handelt es sich in struktureller Hinsicht auch um ihr eigenes inneres Privattheater. Sie erläutert dies folgendermassen: «Ich spüre, dass der Wahnsinn in jedem steckt. Kunst zu machen bedeutet für mich, das Gleichgewicht zwischen meiner Neurose und meiner Psychose zu finden. Ich kann die Balance nur halten, weil ich mich ständig mit meinen Befürchtungen und Ängsten auseinander setze.»[7]

Ihre Sorge darum, nicht nur die kritische Grenze zwischen Neurose und Psychose aufrechtzuerhalten, sondern auch die Fragilität dieser Grenze zu bewahren, erinnert an eine weitere revolutionäre Wende, nämlich jene, die Julia Kristeva als den Übergriff des Semiotischen auf das Symbolische beschreibt. Unser Bedürfnis, archaisches psychisches Material abzuwehren, dessen Nähe das Gleichgewicht unseres psychischen Apparats ernsthaft gefährden würde, ist nicht nur in jenem Bereich lokalisiert, den die französische Kulturkritikerin als das Semiotische bezeichnet um anzudeuten, dass es zwar affektiv markiert, aber nicht symbolisch verschlüsselt ist. Sondern es findet auch einen Kontrapunkt in der poetischen Sprache als dem Medium, durch welches dieses verdrängte Material zurückkehrt um das Gleichgewicht der symbolischen Systeme aufzubrechen, gleichviel, ob diese psychisch oder sozial sind. Wie der Borderline-Schizophrene, der Melancholiker und der Liebende haben auch Künstler, so Kristevas These, seit der Antike versucht, sich dem Reich des Wahnsinns zu stellen, auch wenn sie ihm damit erneut Gestalt verleihen: Sie reissen Lücken in die Starrheit der symbolischen Kodes, aber ohne diese jemals völlig preiszugeben. In ihrer Revolution der photographischen Sprache greift Sam Taylor-Wood nicht nur diese antike Weisheit auf, sondern auch die andere Seite der Gleichung, selbst wenn sie es vielleicht auf eine weniger kathartische Weise tut, als von den antiken Ästhetikern gefordert. Auch uns platziert sie auf der Schwelle, auch wir müssen den Antagonismus aushalten.

(Übersetzung: Nikolaus G. Schneider)

1) Zitiert in «Happening Artist Sam Taylor-Wood», in: *Interview,* Oktober 1998, S. 72.
2) Slavoj Zizek, *The Plague of Fantasies,* London 1997, S. 10f.
3) In: «Bruce Ferguson», «Sam Taylor-Wood», *Bomb,* Herbst 1998, S. 48.
4) Ebenda, S. 45.
5) Zitiert nach dem Interview zwischen Germano Celant und Sam Taylor-Wood im Ausstellungskatalog *Sam Taylor-Wood,* Fondazione Prada, Mailand 1998, S. 270.
6) Ebenda, S. 210.
7) Zitiert von Philip Hoare, «?.», in: *Frank,* November 1998, S. 159.

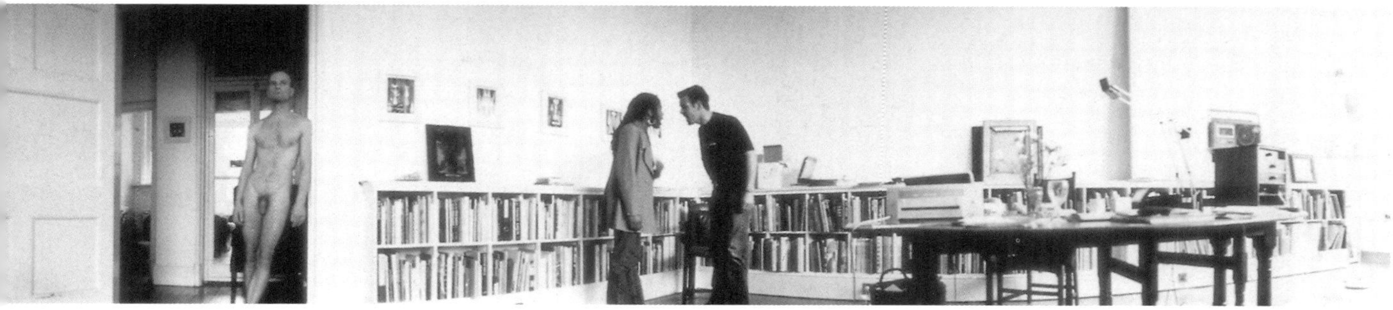

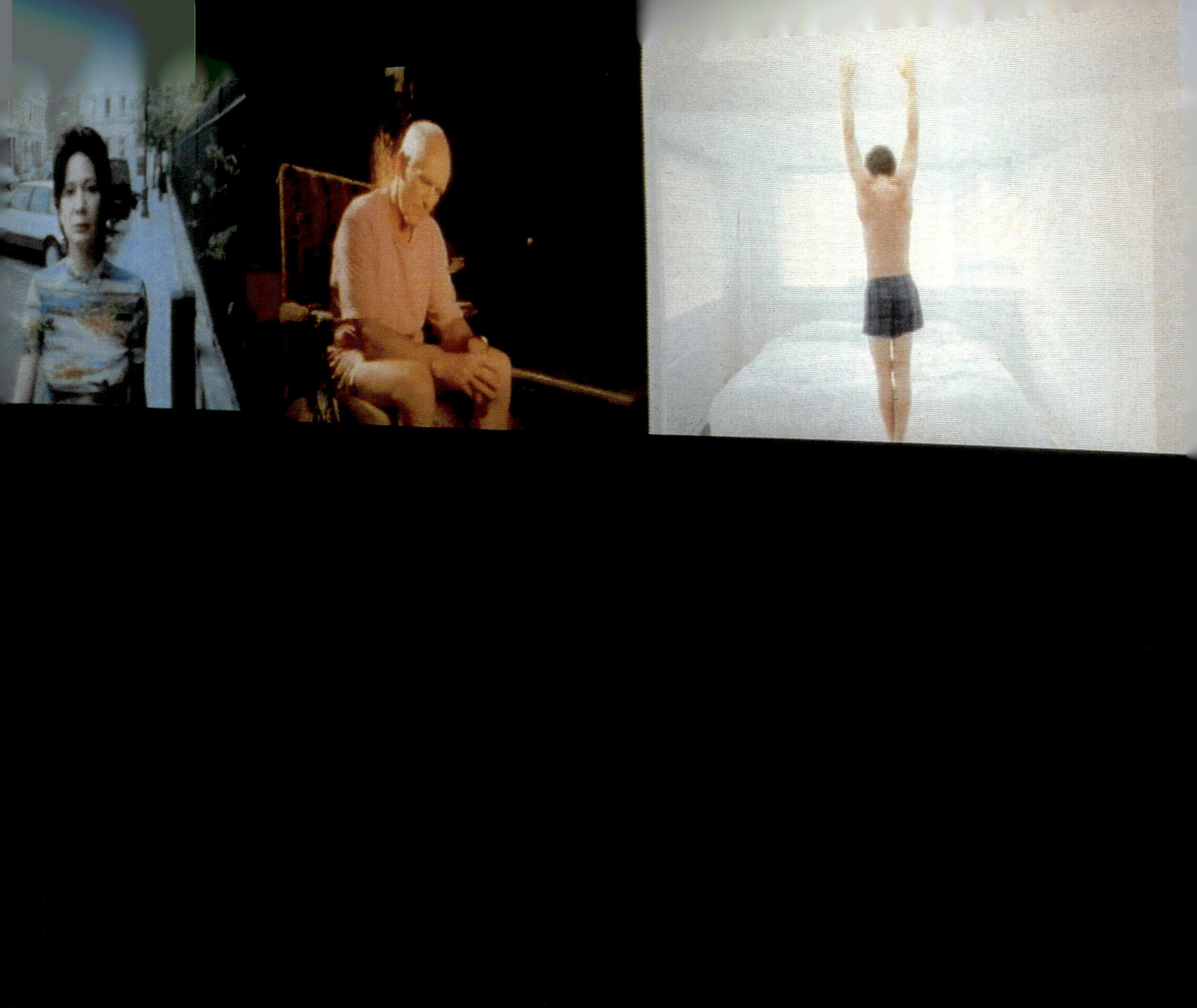

SAM TAYLOR-WOOD, PENT UP, 1996, 5-screen laser-disc projection with sound, shot on 16-mm film, 10 mins. 30 secs., installation view, Chis

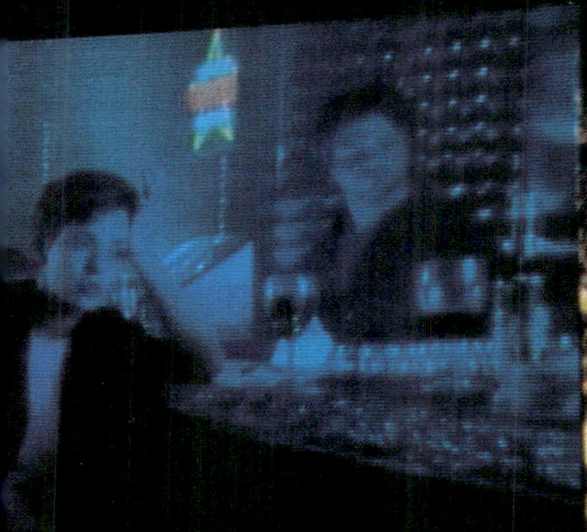

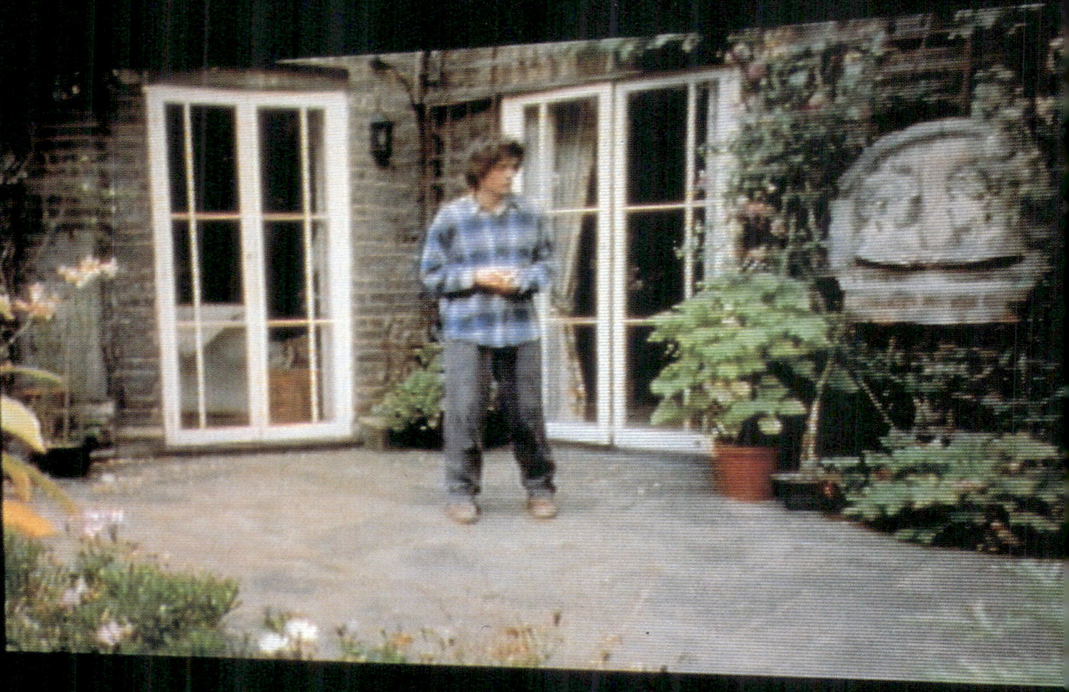

FRANCESCO BONAMI

SLIDING............S

SAM TAYLOR-WOOD'S INVENTION OF THE DIALOGUE

On the first page of his 745-page-long book, *Shakespeare: The Invention of the Human*, Harold Bloom writes that Shakespeare's characters develop rather than unfold; that is why they reconceive themselves. According to Bloom, they do so because at times they overhear themselves talking, and this self-witnessing brings them to individuation. Now Sam Taylor-Wood is no Shakespeare, but her works reflect and develop a theatrical dimension that unfolds in front of the viewer and allows her characters to individuate themselves in relation to each other, and to the space containing both them and the viewer. The people appearing in her video installations seem to have already decided upon their independence from the work itself, expressing a desire to play out their secrets and anguish, building a kind of objective theater of passions. At every moment the work offers the viewer a spectacle of his or her own appetites and contradictions. Yet, as in a Robbe-Grillet novel or film, the viewer's position never remains the same. The stage moves around or in front of us, forcing the vanishing point of the piece to converge from characters to spectator, moving from one side of the narrational spectrum to the other, pushing the viewer, outside the projection, from the role of analyst to that of analysand. Once the characters have individuated their relationships within the work, they start reflecting upon their relationships outside the screen, underlining their limitations, beginning to overhear their dialogues as reflections of the viewer's mind.

Sam Taylor-Wood's early works achieve the impossible task of visualizing mental anxiety while neither abandoning the scene nor entering a metaphysical environment, but remaining still in front of reality's other side. They ape life, as we all have to do in order to complete the same process of the individuation of our defaulting identities. Four characters surround the viewer in KILLING TIME (1994); their boredom fences us in; we have to listen in order to escape. In TRAVESTY OF A MOCKERY (1995) the gate is open, yet we've been transformed into the missing two walls of a kitchen, we're the completing factor of this couple's claustrophobic reality, the mysterious reason for their fight. They confront each other about our presence, our role in the dynamic narrative of their dysfunctional relationship. We don't understand, but feel that our presence is the disruptive cause of their reciprocal hatred. In ATLANTIC

FRANCESCO BONAMI is Senior Curator at the Museum of Contemporary Art, Chicago.

SAM TAYLOR-WOOD, TRAVESTY OF A MOCKERY, 1995, detail of 10-min. color projection with sound / KARIKATUR EINER POSSE, Ausschnitt aus 10-Min.-Farbvideoprojektion mit Ton.

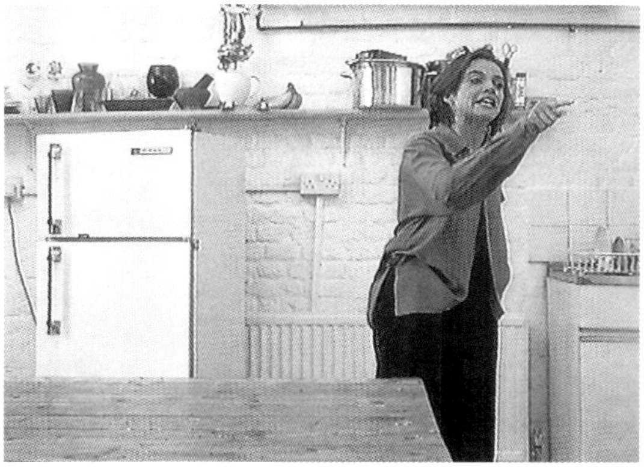

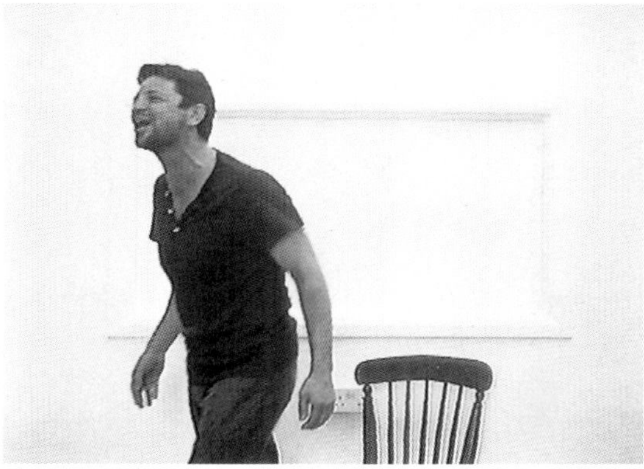

(1997), viewer and character overlap and exchange positions according to the camera's point of view. Again, we find ourselves in the absurd position of trying to understand and actually visualize feelings.

These three video installations are the first three acts of a four-act play. Up until this point, Taylor-Wood's characters have attempted to negotiate the narratives grafted onto their relationships with those of the viewer. By surrounding the viewer, or including him or her in a mental space, they awkwardly attempt to negotiate the failure of their roles outside the conventional structure of the screen/stage. These characters vicariously live the parochial experience of some kind of third generation Brechtian or Grotowskian disciple. They ask us to perform as a condescending audience, the extraneous public that might empower their otherwise powerless performances.

When the curtain rises on the final act, PENT UP (1996), the fence that had surrounded the public and actors is gone. These characters are aggressively coming to terms with the collapse of the mystifying concept of "relationship." They are all alone, moving forwards and sideways, toward each other and to the edges of the frame, against us. All of them are talking, none are listening, all are answering. The fence is now linear, invisible, but more than ever a protection against the growing rage of their discontent, the revolt against roles. With PENT UP, Taylor-Wood succeeds in Brecht's effort to estrange the viewer, producing a distance that cannot be intellectualized, only painfully experienced.

Yet, once we overcome our feelings of estrangement, we realize that in the process something else quite specific has happened which delineates the roles into the clear functions of gender throughout Taylor-Wood's work. In the characters' sequences—a woman walking down the street, an old man mumbling on a chair in a dark room, a man in his bedroom, a woman in a bar, a man in a courtyard—the dialogic structure is sustained by the two women who occupy public spaces, the street and the bar. They are the vectors through which the entire structure of the work builds its own syntax. The men appear to be devoured by the solipsistic and hedonistic dimensions of their enclosed spaces. Their language sinks into the quicksand of convoluted thought. While the women seem to accept the necessity of looking for an unlikely hole in the fence of communication, the men recede into a sort of confused and endless rehearsal, obsessing about their own and each others presence.

These men seem to share Robbe-Grillet's idea that "our thoughts do not choose to be thoughts of our life. We watch things pass by in order to forget that they are watching us die."[1] While for the women another Robbe-Grillet question clearly leads their search for individuation: "Is it possible to escape tragedy? Today its rule extends to all my feelings and all my thoughts, it conditions me utterly. My body can be satisfied, my heart content, my consciousness remains unhappy."[2] For Sam Taylor-Wood, man is a sick animal. In the naive attempt to cure him, she creates different stages upon which the process of individuation might also be healing. She puts the world between parentheses in order to talk about reality. In PENT UP, her characters exchange bits of reality like a relay baton; they come on stage to find one another and finish the game. Communication swings relentlessly, yet unsuccessfully back and forth. Eventually, they remain within the frame of their minds, letting the viewers slip back into their own.

In this final act of her most accomplished production to date, Sam Taylor-Wood moves us not with images chosen for their potential to move us, but with relations of images that animate the characters. She strives to mechanize her models externally while allowing them internally to be free. The camera overlaps with the viewer's gaze, mesmerized and unmoving. Women come forward, men reverse. They all seek contact with the space and with themselves, in a process that transforms the human into a character, an actor. Then they stop the action to begin anew, again and again. They listen to the artist as a young director, reminding us that to be truly fictional we must correct all the mistakes of our fantasies, and be human in our desire for perfection, pushing the constant and the eternal under the accidental.

1) Alain Robbe-Grillet, *For a New Novel: Essays on Fiction*, transl. by R. Howard (New York: Grove Press, 1965), p. 105.
2) Ibid., p. 75.

SAM TAYLOR-WOOD, ATLANTIC, 1997, 3 laser discs for 3 10-min. projections / 3 Laserdisks für 3 Projektionen à 10 Min.
(PHOTO: STEPHEN WHITE)

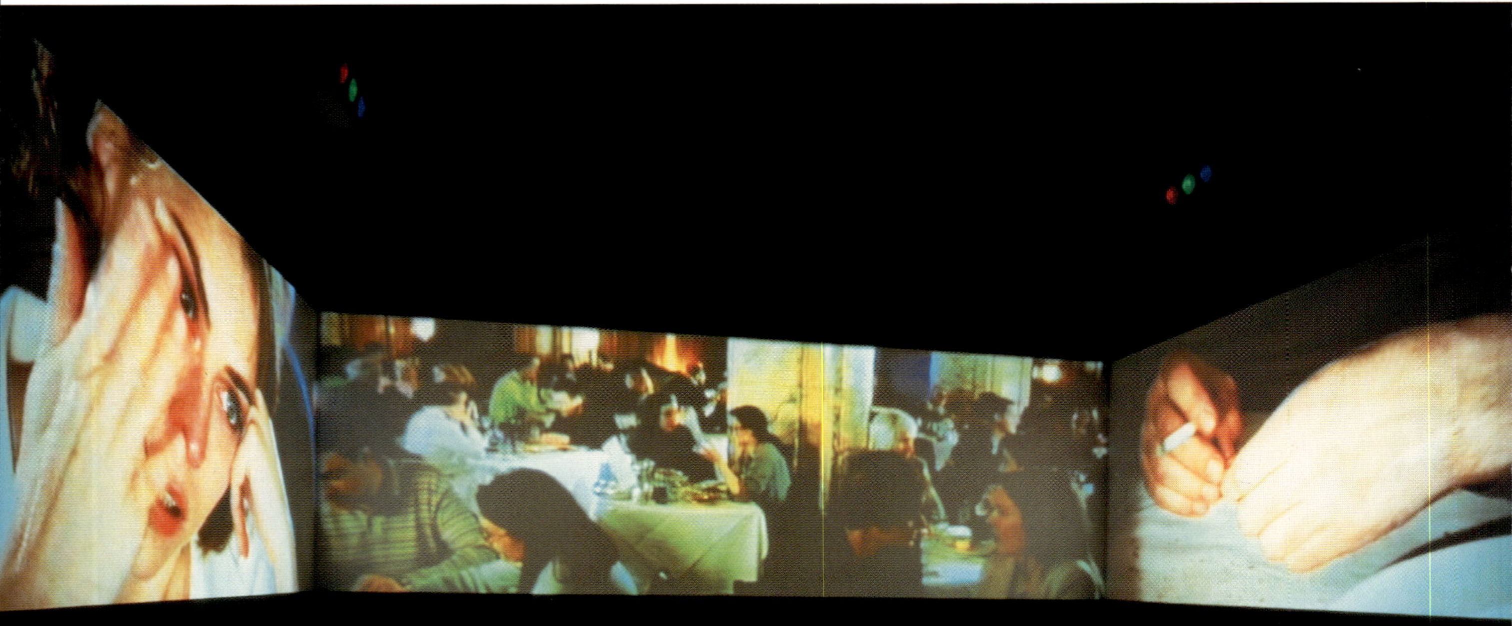

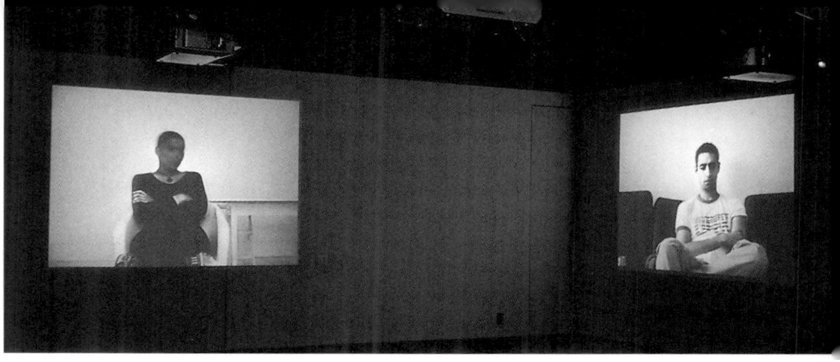

SAM TAYLOR-WOOD, KILLING TIME, 1994, 60-min. video projection and sound / ZEIT TOTSCHLAGEN, 60-Min.-Videoprojektion mit Ton.

GLEITENDE ÜBERGÄNGE

SAM TAYLOR-WOODS ERFINDUNG DES DIALOGS

FRANCESCO BONAMI

Auf der ersten der 745 Seiten seines Werks, *Shakespeare: The Invention of the Human*, schreibt Harold Bloom, dass Shakespeares Charaktere sich eher entwickeln als entfalten und dass sie deshalb sich selbst immer wieder neu begreifen. Laut Bloom tun sie das, weil sie manchmal ob ihrer eigenen Worte stutzen und weil diese Selbstwahrnehmung der Individuation förderlich ist. Zugegeben, Taylor-Wood ist nicht Shakespeare, aber ihre Arbeiten schaffen und reflektieren eine Theatersituation, die vor Publikum spielt und ihren Figuren erlaubt sich individuell zu entwickeln, und zwar in Beziehung zueinander und in Bezug auf den Raum, den sie mit dem Betrachter teilen. Die Menschen, die in ihren Videoinstallationen auftreten, scheinen sich von dem Werk bereits emanzipiert zu haben; sie wollen ihre Geheimnisse und Ängste ausagieren und erzeugen so eine Art objektives Theater der Leidenschaften. Dem Betrachter werden ohne Unterlass seine eigenen Gelüste und Widersprüche vorgeführt. Doch wie in einem Roman von Robbe-Grillet (oder dessen Verfilmung) ändert sich der Standort des Betrachters ständig. Die Bühne bewegt sich vor oder um uns herum, so dass sich der Fluchtpunkt des Werks von den Protagonisten auf den Betrachter verschiebt und beide konvergieren; das erzählerische Spektrum wird in seiner ganzen Breite ausgeschöpft und der Betrachter aus der Rolle des Analytikers in jene des Analysanden gedrängt. Kaum haben die Charaktere ihre jeweiligen Beziehungen innerhalb des Werkes herausgearbeitet, beginnen sie über ihre Beziehungen ausserhalb des Bildschirms nachzudenken, verweisen auf ihre Grenzen und beginnen ihre Dialoge als Spiegelungen der Gedanken des Betrachters zu verstehen.

Sam Taylor-Wood gelingt in ihren frühen Arbeiten das Unmögliche, innere Ängste sichtbar zu machen, ohne dabei die Bühne zu verlassen oder in eine metaphysische Dimension überzuwechseln; trotzdem verliert sie die andere Seite der Realität nie aus den Augen. Ihre Arbeiten imitieren das Leben, wie wir alle es tun müssen, um den Individuations-

FRANCESCO BONAMI ist Kurator am Museum of Contemporary Art, Chicago.

prozess unserer unvollkommenen Identitäten zu vollenden. In KILLING TIME (Zeit totschlagen, 1994) sieht sich der Betrachter von vier Personen umgeben. Ihre Langeweile wirkt einengend; wenn wir ihr entfliehen wollen, müssen wir zuhören. In TRAVESTY OF A MOCKERY (Karikatur einer Posse, 1995) steht die Tür zwar offen, doch werden wir in die fehlenden beiden Wände einer Küche verwandelt; wir sind das ergänzende Teil im Puzzle der klaustrophobischen Wirklichkeit dieses Paares und der rätselhafte Grund für seine Auseinandersetzungen. Sie streiten sich wegen unserer Gegenwart, wegen unserer Rolle in der bewegten Geschichte seiner gestörten Beziehung. Wir verstehen es nicht, spüren aber, dass unsere Gegenwart auslösendes Moment seines gegenseitigen Hasses ist. In ATLANTIC (Atlantisch, 1997) verwischt sich die Grenze zwischen Betrachter und Protagonist und sie tauschen je nach Kameraperspektive ihre Positionen. Wieder befinden wir uns in der absurden Lage Gefühle verstehen, ja sogar visualisieren zu wollen.

Diese drei Videoinstallationen bilden gleichsam die ersten drei Akte eines Vierakters. Bis zu diesem Punkt haben Taylor-Woods Protagonisten versucht die auf ihren Beziehungen beruhenden Geschichten mit jenen des Betrachters in Einklang zu bringen. Das Einkreisen des Betrachters und dessen Miteinbezug auf der geistigen Ebene war der peinliche Versuch das Scheitern ihrer Rollen ausserhalb der konventionellen Struktur von Bildschirm/Bühne zu vertuschen. Die Figuren durchlebten gewissermassen stellvertretend die einengende Erfahrung einer Art Brecht- oder Grotowski-Schüler der dritten Generation. Sie wollten, dass wir die Rolle des geneigten Publikums übernehmen und den aussenstehenden Zuschauer spielen, der ihren sonst ziemlich schwachen Auftritten Kraft verleiht.

Wenn sich der Vorhang zum vierten und letzten Akt, PENT UP (Aufgestaut, 1996), hebt, ist der Zaun, der Zuschauer und Akteure umgab, verschwunden. Die Figuren setzen sich jetzt unerschrocken mit dem Scheitern des rätselhaften Konzepts «Beziehung» auseinander. Sie sind völlig allein, laufen nach vorn, zur Seite, aufeinander zu und zum Bildrand, auf uns zu. Alle sprechen, keiner hört zu, doch alle antworten. Der Zaun verläuft jetzt gerade, unsichtbar, ist aber mehr denn je ein Schutz gegen die wachsende Wut und Unzufriedenheit und den Aufstand der Figuren gegen ihre Rollen. Mit PENT UP gelingt Sam Taylor-Wood der Brechtsche Verfremdungseffekt: Sie schafft eine Distanz, die nicht intellektuell begriffen, sondern nur schmerzlich erfahren werden kann.

Sobald wir jedoch dieses Gefühl der Verfremdung überwinden, erkennen wir, dass sich in diesem Prozess noch etwas anderes, Besonderes ereignet hat, etwas, was die Rollen in Taylor-Woods gesamtem Werk eindeutig als geschlechtsspezifisch ausweist. In den Personensequenzen – eine Frau geht eine Strasse entlang, ein alter Mann auf einem Stuhl murmelt in einem dunklen Raum vor sich hin, ein Mann in seinem Schlafzimmer, eine Frau am Tresen, ein Mann in einem Hof – wird die dialogische Struktur von den beiden Frauen aufrechterhalten, die sich im öffentlichen Raum befinden (auf der Strasse, in einer Bar). Sie sind das richtungsweisende Strukturelement, auf dem die werkeigene Syntax aufgebaut ist. Die Männer scheinen von den solipsistischen und hedonistischen Dimensionen ihrer geschlossenen Räume verschlungen zu werden. Ihre Sprache versinkt im Treibsand der verworrenen Gedanken. Während die Frauen anscheinend die Notwendigkeit erkannt haben, nach der unwahrscheinlichen Lücke im Kommunikations-Zaun zu suchen, ziehen sich die Männer in die chaotische, endlose Wiederholung zurück, besessen von ihrer eigenen und der Anwesenheit der anderen.

Diese Männer scheinen Robbe-Grillets Vorstellung zu teilen, dass unser Denken nicht das Denken unseres Lebens sein will; dass wir beobachten, wie die Dinge an uns vorüberziehen, um zu vergessen, dass sie uns beim Sterben zusehen.[1)] Was die Frauen betrifft, so scheint ihr Streben nach Individualität ebenfalls von einer Frage Robbe-Grillets geleitet zu werden, nämlich der, ob man der Tragödie entrinnen könne, die heute all unsere Gefühle und Gedanken beherrscht und uns vollkommen bestimmt. Denn, so Robbe-Grillet, selbst wenn unser Körper zufrieden, unser Herz froh ist, bleibt doch unser Bewusstsein unglücklich.[2)] Für Sam Taylor-Wood ist der Mensch ein krankes Tier. Im natürlichen Bestreben ihn zu heilen schafft sie verschiedene szenische

SAM TAYLOR-WOOD, PENT UP, 1996, 5-screen laser-disc projection with sound, shot on 16-mm film, 10 min. 30 sec. / AUFGESTAUT, Laserdisk-Projektion mit Ton auf 5 Leinwänden, aufgenommen auf 16-mm-Film, 10 Min. 30 Sek.

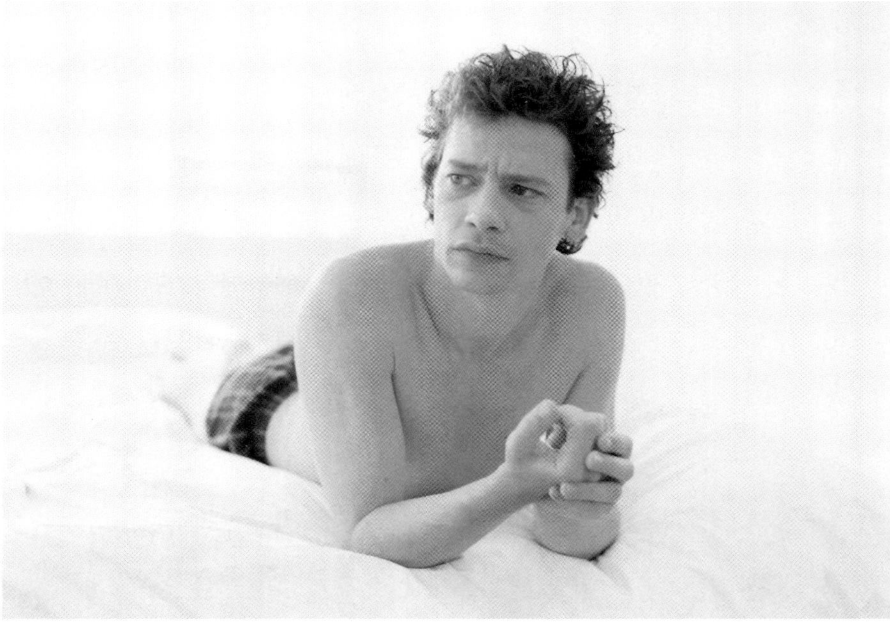

Situationen, in denen der Individuationsprozess zugleich zum Heilungsprozess werden könnte. Sie klammert die Welt aus um über die Realität zu sprechen. In PENT UP reichen die Protagonisten einander kleine Wahrheiten weiter wie Stäbe im Stafettenlauf; sie kommen auf die Bühne um einander zu finden und das Spiel zu beenden. Die Kommunikation wogt erbarmungslos hin und her, aber sie gelingt nicht. Schliesslich bleiben alle in ihrem eigenen Denken gefangen und lassen auch den Betrachter wieder in das seine schlüpfen.

In diesem letzten Akt ihrer bisher besten Arbeit fesselt uns Sam Taylor-Wood nicht mit Bildern, die eben wegen dieses fesselnden Potenzials ausgesucht wurden, sondern mit Beziehungen zwischen Bildern, die die Figuren lebendig werden lassen. Sie unterwirft ihre Darstellerinnen und Darsteller äusserlich mechanischen Zwängen, gesteht ihnen aber innere Freiheit zu. Der Blick der Kamera, gebannt und bewegungslos, fällt mit dem Blick des Betrachters zusammen. Frauen treten vor, Männer wenden sich ab. In einem Prozess, der die Menschen in bestimmte Charaktere, in Schauspieler verwandelt, suchen alle den Kontakt mit dem Raum und mit sich selbst. Dann hören sie auf zu agieren um gleich darauf wieder von vorn anzufangen, immer und immer wieder. Sie hören auf die Künstlerin als junge Regisseurin und erinnern uns daran, dass wir um wirkliche Fiktionen zu schaffen all unsere falschen Vorstellungen korrigieren und in unserem Streben nach Vollkommenheit so menschlich sein müssen, das Bleibende und das Ewige dem Zufälligen unterzuordnen.

(Übersetzung: Uta Goridis)

1) «Notre pensée ne veut pas être la pensée de notre vie. Nous regardons passer les choses pour oublier qu'elles nous regardent mourir.» Alain Robbe-Grillet, *Pour un nouveau roman*, Les éditions de minuit, Paris 1961, S. 90.
2) «Est-il possible d'échapper à la tragédie? Aujourd'hui son règne s'étend sur tous mes sentiments et toutes mes pensées, elle me conditionne du haut en bas. Mon corps peut être satisfait, mon cœur content, ma conscience reste malheureuse.» Ebenda, S. 67.

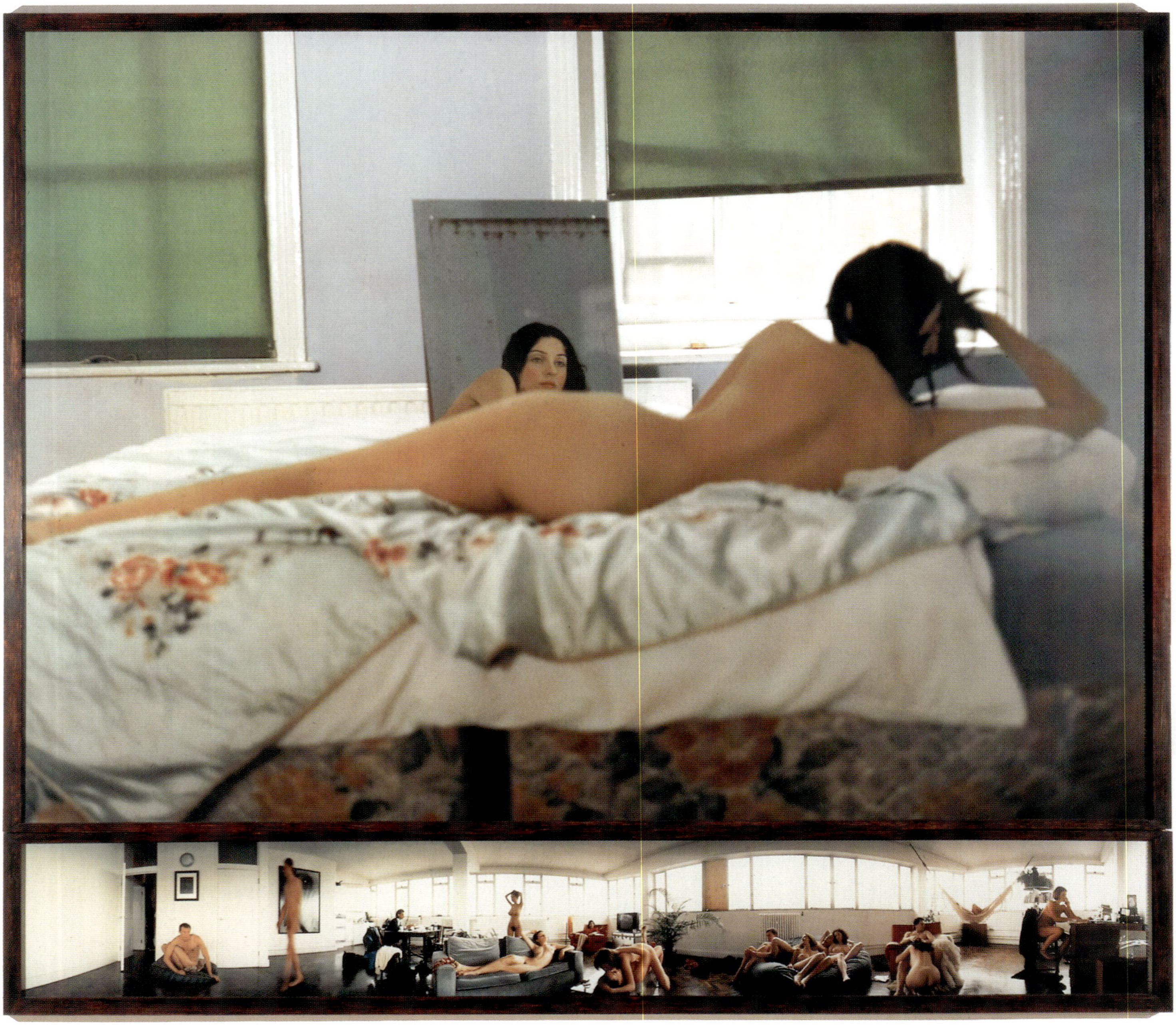

SAM TAYLOR-WOOD, SOLILOQUY III, 1998, framed c-print, 89⅜ x 101³⁄₁₆" / MONOLOG III, gerahmter C-Print, 227 x 257 cm.
(PHOTO: ATTILIO MARANZANO)

EWA LAJER-BURCHARTH

The Soliloquious Vision

Intriguing spaces open up for your view in Sam Taylor-Wood's series of photographic installations, FIVE REVOLUTIONARY SECONDS (1995). Photographed with a special rotating camera that registers a 360-degree view in one continuous take—the five-seconds-long revolution to which the title of these works refers—the interior views of private lofts, these once bohemian quarters of the artists, now spacious and stylish realms of urban affluence and decorating ambition, stretch for your perusal on the gallery walls.[1] While panoramic in scope, the photographs are presented as flat, extended rectangles of vision attached to the walls—one interior to each wall, three views to one installation—without any attempt to recreate the circular ambience of the rotundas in which panoramas were originally housed in the late eighteenth and early nineteenth centuries. Circumambient, yet flattened out, these are at once seamless and discontinuous visions. The spatial distortions produced by the eye of the camera traveling around the rooms remind one of Borromini's architecture, with its disruptive interplay of concave and convex shapes—only here they are more exaggerated. The architectural interior is thus represented as an open-ended, continuously unravelling fold.

These architectural folds are inhabited by the oddly monadic, self-absorbed subjects whose detachment further underscores the internal heterogeneity of these spaces. Not only do these figures rarely interact with one another, except on those rare occasions when they engage in a sexual act or a shouting match, episodes that are disruptive and incongruous with the larger human continuum on view; it is also that these characters could hardly be imagined as actually living together in any of these spaces, coming as they evidently do from socially and often also sexually divergent (and non-convergent) contexts, each of them sealed, moreover, in the invisible envelope of his or her own emotional universe. What, for instance, does a woman in a white evening gown whirling like a dervish; a young dandy standing immobile by the kitchen counter, caught in a reverie, his vest thrown nonchalantly over his shirtless shoulders; a female giant in a red satin dress posing in an armchair; two guys enacting some sado-masochistic scenario; a nondescript man in a suit gazing at the imaginary flies on the ceiling; and other assorted types making their appearance in FIVE REVOLUTIONARY SECONDS IX have to do with one another? And

EWA LAJER-BURCHARTH teaches modern art and critical theory at Harvard University. She is the author of *Necklines: The Art of Jacques-Louis David After the Terror* (New Haven: Yale University Press, 1999).

what are we to make of such oblivious figures as the totally naked man leaning pensively against the door frame in a room otherwise filled with thoroughly dressed people, his anatomical details offered in full view to our inspection?

Clearly, these are not real but imaginary, constructed spaces, a point missed by those critics who, taking them at their sociological face value, scoffed at Taylor-Wood's snobby immersion in the chic world of the upper-crust crowd. Yet, it seems to me that it is not "having" but rather "being" that these well-to-do locations are really about. Caught up in their own separate worlds, the monad-like beings featured in these spaces point, beyond themselves, to the notion of the pose. Unfolding through their habitus, at once distended and condensed, is a subjective space—a panoramic theater of the self. The question is what kind of self is being thus envisioned?

It may be tempting to identify this self as a subject of fashion. There is some resemblance between Taylor-Wood's staged locations and the arenas of sophisticated fashion photo shoots. Yet, to simply collapse the artist's project onto the paradigm of fashion photography is, in my view, to miss the scope and nature of her visual ambition. Engaging the conventions of photography, panorama, and avant-garde film, Taylor-Wood concocts morphologically complex visual images that address the issue of subjectivity in the era of screen. At stake here is, in other words, the subject at that historical juncture in which the ubiquity and pervasiveness of the technological means for generating cultural image-repertoire—from the computer monitor, to the proliferating folds of the advertising spread in a magazine, to the forever multiplying film screens in your local multiplex—rendered the boundaries between the self and such images increasingly porous.[2] The quality of a fashion shoot in Taylor-Wood's work speaks to this condition: It is fashion photography as a mode of being that it explores. Thus, rather than being panoramas of fashionable social types, her galleries of self-absorbed eccentrics may rather be seen to stand for different subject positions, different fantasies of the self already i n h a b i t e d by the screen, while her interiors may be seen to represent interiority in a particular sense, as a topography of one's—plural—identifications.[3] The constructed nature of this imaginary subjective realm is emphasized by the mode of installation, with the loudspeakers suspended between the photographs from which the acoustic relics of the shoot—the voices and sounds of the visual space in the making—may be heard.

While FIVE REVOLUTIONARY SECONDS may be seen to continue the critical tradition represented by the photography-based aesthetic practice of the previous decade, and the discourse of cultural construction that subtended this practice, it departs from it in several key aspects. One is the sheer diversity and richness of human types that appear in this work and the categories of identity that it helps to articulate—the whole array of bodily sizes and colors, of affects, and what in another century would be called "temperaments," and of sexual orientations. This subjective plurality moves the notion of difference—psychic and sexual—to another register, beyond the familiar binaries.

Another is the personal dimension that these diversified actors give to the idea of the pose. While the conspicuous way in which they are staged foregrounds posing as an act of claiming one's place in the field of vision and meaning, it does not always seem to guarantee these actors' intelligibility. Looking at some of these enigmatic figures one is reminded of the frustrated Delacroix who, confronted by the radically new and incomprehensible language of the body in Courbet's BATHER, exclaimed: "But what does it mean?!" The didactic or normative dimension of the pose seems to be entirely lacking from these exercises of self-display. Though they seem to share an allegorical stasis with Sherman's UNTITLED FILM STILLS, these images are not about aspiring to or measuring oneself up against the pose understood as a culturally generated, normative ideal of the self (in Sherman's case, femininity). Rather it is a retreat from the pose into the private realm of reverie that is visualized here. While flaunting their stances, the protagonists of Taylor-Wood's vision seem detached, absorbed by some internal negotiation. This is epitomized, of course, by all these withdrawn, pensive figures that so frequently pop up in her interiors.[4] What they are engaged in is not exactly a narcissistic self-absorption—it does not involve the confrontations with one's image—but rather in another kind of self-reflective activity: a silent psychic dialogue with oneself.

Last but not least, what distinguishes Taylor-Wood's work are the dimensions of space and time in her vision. Because of the optical revolution of her camera which needs five seconds to "take in" the whole room, time is from the start inscribed—visibly—in this space. It is not, however, the narrative time of linear progression in space that connects one event to another in a visual chain-like production of a plot, but rather a corrosive kind of time that ruins the story. Temporal dimension amounts to interference within the narrative fabric of Taylor-Wood's image, a disruption that stops short, though, from tearing this vision apart. Space unfolds thus through a structural development that acts like a Deleuzian fold: a proliferation of singularities.[5] Internally creased by a series of subjective instances, each of them an irreducible monadic being enclosed in the realm of its own pose, the visual architecture of FIVE REVOLUTIONARY SECONDS amounts to a sequence of spatial pockets that both disturb and differentiate it from within.

As such, Taylor-Wood's panoramas of the self may be seen as an effort to reposition the individual subject within the realm of vision, or to reformulate visuality in order to make space for the private self. This, however, does not seem to be a matter of returning to some naive notions of individualism as a mode of existing outside culture, outside vision, but rather of remapping the relation between vision and self. On one hand, Taylor-Wood's camera reclaims a central position for the subject in the visual realm unfolded through the circumambient perusal of the single camera eye. On the other, this ocularcentric vision does not construct a panoptical space, with an inviolable surveying subject at its core (the eye as I), for it is pluralized by the different folds of subjectivity nestling inside it and creasing it from within. The result is a polyphonic visuality that confounds and exceeds the disciplinary register of vision. A space that thus also invites us to reimagine the specular foundations of the self.[6]

The SOLILOQUIES series (1998) speak to this project eloquently. In it, the self is imagined explicitly in a psychic dialogue with itself that we could only suspect in the characters of FIVE REVOLUTIONARY SECONDS. The series comprises five giant photographic tableaux each consisting of a main panel and a narrow predella placed underneath. Within this structure of a Renaissance altar, two different modalities of vision were deployed to represent the dual registers of subjective functioning—bodily and psychic. The upper panels are more or less straightforward, high-art kind of photographs, often stylized after a well-known painting; the predellas below were shot with the same panoramic camera the artist used in her previous work. These two different modes of vision represent a subject split by fantasy or dream: in the upper part we see the physical body of an individual sleeping, daydreaming or otherwise caught in a moment of self-reflection that brackets him or her from the surrounding reality. In the predellas, an imaginary world unfolds as the oneiric space of sexual fantasy. The de-realizing spatial effects produced by the panoramic camera were enhanced by some local digital manipulation of the image to represent the work of condensation and disfiguration of reality in fantasy or dream.

In SOLILOQUY III a woman is shown taking pleasure in looking at her mirror reflection, her body arranged like Velasquez's ROCKEBY VENUS, her gaze glazed with reverie, as is the photograph itself, slightly grainy as if shot through a semi-transparent veil. Grays, pinks, and citron yellows prevail. In the predella below we see a phantasmatic scene of orgy that this "Venus" imagines: a sparsely furnished studio full of naked people, men and women, some making out, others splayed languorously on sofas and cushions, as if awaiting their turn, not without ennui. One naked man squats on a mat by the door like a dog. Another, a blurred elongated, Giacometti-like sentinel of flesh, promenades without purpose across the room. An odalisque straight from Ingres stretches her languid corpus on a couch. Someone's legs emerge from a hammock. A fully dressed man sits by his desk clearly not looking at a nude displaying herself in front of him. A naked woman speaks on the phone at another desk. Finally, the "Venus" herself appears in the back of the room, sitting in an armchair, dressed in red, her eyes closed, indifferent to the orgy. It is the contrast between the gently outlined feminine body filtered through the aesthetic screen of the culturally acceptable nude and the scene below, the product of her imagination, that is most striking here.

In SOLILOQUY IV, the foreshortened naked torso of a giant breasty woman in deep sleep, her mouth agape, spreads on a sofa, her soft reddish flesh sunk deep into the ornamented pillows. Here, Taylor-Wood exploits the contrast between the slumbering feminine body and the activity of her psyche differently: It is not the genteel misty look of the dreaming subject but her obtrusive fleshiness that is juxtaposed with the products of her imagination envisioned below. In an empty room of an old house, picturesque windows, stripped wallpapers, and traces of furniture on the wall, three dwarves and a child gaze intently upward, perhaps at the female giant's elbow that crosses the border of the upper panel and intrudes into the predella. Chubby male twins stand to the right flanking a mantelpiece. For those who recognize the giant woman as Sue Tilly, Lucien Freud's favorite model, the transformative effect of Taylor-Wood's vision is the more obvious: What in Freud appears as the unredeemable materiality of flesh, in Taylor-Wood's is imagined as a seat of subjectivity—and desire.

It is the unconventional definition of the male body as an object of desire that is most compelling in SOLILOQUY II, envisioned in an outdoor, wooded setting of autumn yellows, ochres, and golds. A sexy young man, shirtless, unshaven, the belt of his pants suggestively unbuckled, strikes a tentative pose amidst stray dogs. Standing, laying about, attending to their hides, his canine attributes are laden with invisible yet clearly sensed obscenity. Below him, the predella reveals a subterranean landscape of pornographic fantasy, a bathhouse peopled with naked characters, some couples having sex, other solitary figures leaning restlessly against the walls of the tiled chambers. The protagonist himself appears in one corner, sitting, somewhat resigned, on the floor with a dog lying by his side.

Explaining her understanding of the term "soliloquy," Taylor-Wood refers to a condition of detachment that an actor experiences in relation to both

SAM TAYLOR-WOOD, SOLILOQUY II, 1998, framed c-print, 81½ x 101 3/16" / MONOLOG II, gerahmter C-Print, 207 x 257 cm. (PHOTO: ATTILIO MARANZANO)

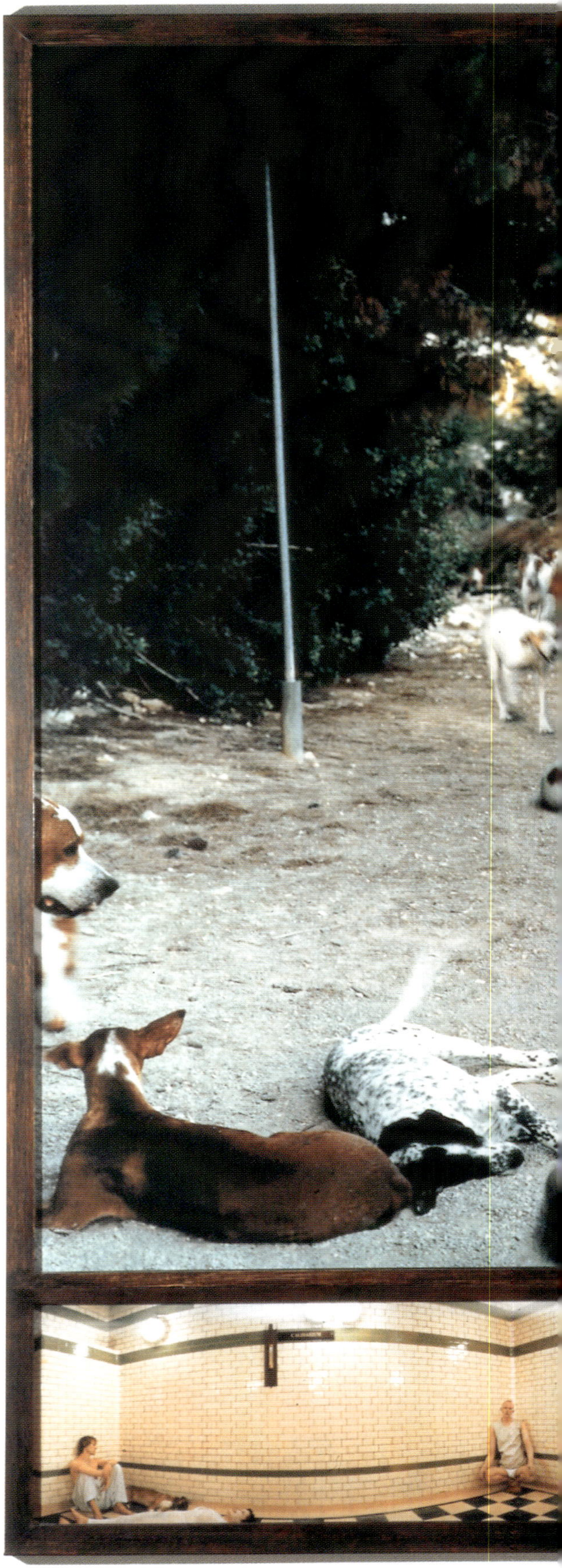

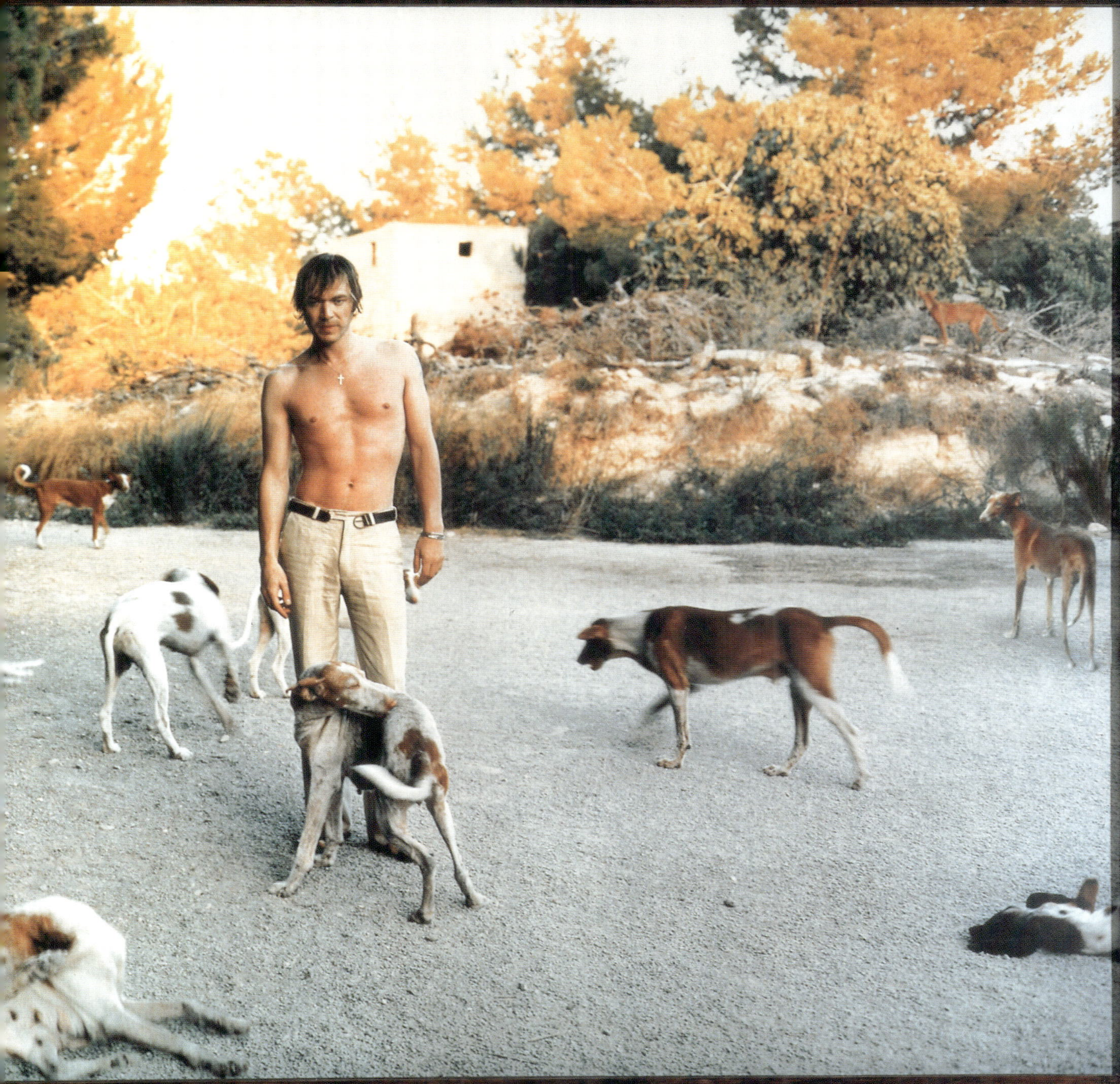

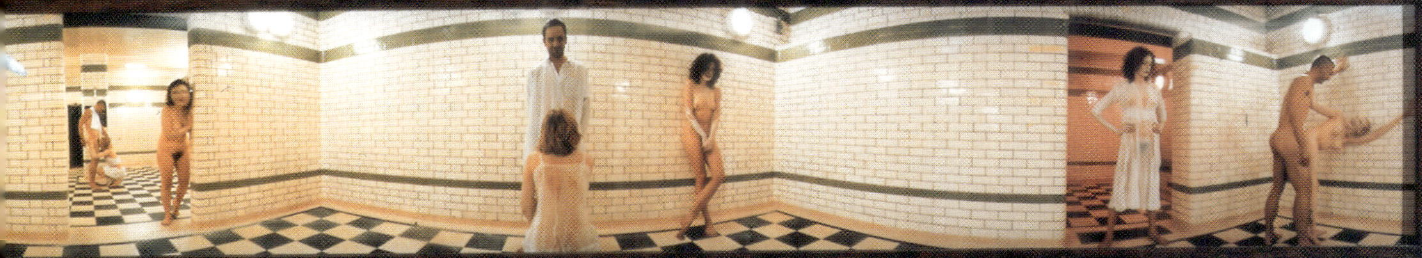

his character and the play in which he performs, a mode in which, as it often happens in Shakespeare, the actor steps out of the play to deliver an authorial commentary on it directed to an audience.[7] One can see this notion thematized explicitly via the figures of detachment such as, for instance, the three dwarves looking out from the oneiric space of the giant woman, or the woman in the center of the dog man's pornographic vision, her facial features liquified through digital manipulation to mark her disengagement both from the scene and from her own body. But one may also see detachment as the very logic that governs these images. Thus soliloquial is the very structure of Taylor-Woods vision, the structural split between the subject and its fantasy that it represents as a spatial condition of her subjects psychic conversations with their own selves.

It is not so much the prominence of sex in these dreams and fantasies—Sigmund Freud would concur—but the way in which it is configured that is most original. Of particular interest is the way in which these libidinally saturated fields of fantasy are traversed yet unstructured by sexual difference. Men and women appear in them interchangeably, as both subjects and objects of desire. While this may seem entirely natural, it is enough to think of any recent Hollywood screen romance to be reminded of the persistent ways in which predictable gender hierarchy (woman-object/man-subject of desire) continues to be cherished by the dominant visual culture. It is precisely the task of denaturalizing such hierarchy that informed feminist aesthetic practice of the last two decades. Arriving on the art scene in its wake clearly enables Taylor-Wood to make a lusting woman her working assumption—something her work takes for granted, and then seeks to complicate. Let us recall that the artist began her career with a saucy, in-your-face self-portrait, pants down, wearing aviator glasses and a T-shirt reading FUCK, SUCK, SPANK, WANK (1993)—a male gay slogan that added ambivalence to her self-definition as a sexual being.

Another striking aspect of lust in her vision is its ambiguity. Her sexual scenarios are consistently unresolved, displacing binary oppositions—often simply by their endless proliferation—and refusing any closure. The critical postulate to destabilize the binary distinctions within which visual culture tends to lock the collective imagination of sex is, of course, not new but what an alternative, unfettered field of desire might actually look like has rarely been shown. SOLILOQUIES propose a view of just such a field.

And this is where I see the enabling dimension of this work: a vision unraveled from within itself in a manner that extends and expands the cultural limits of representability. They are not just the representations of dream, but scenes of fantasy about what

SAM TAYLOR-WOOD, WRECKED, 1996, c-print, 60 x 156" / AM ENDE, C-Print, 152,4 x 396,2 cm.

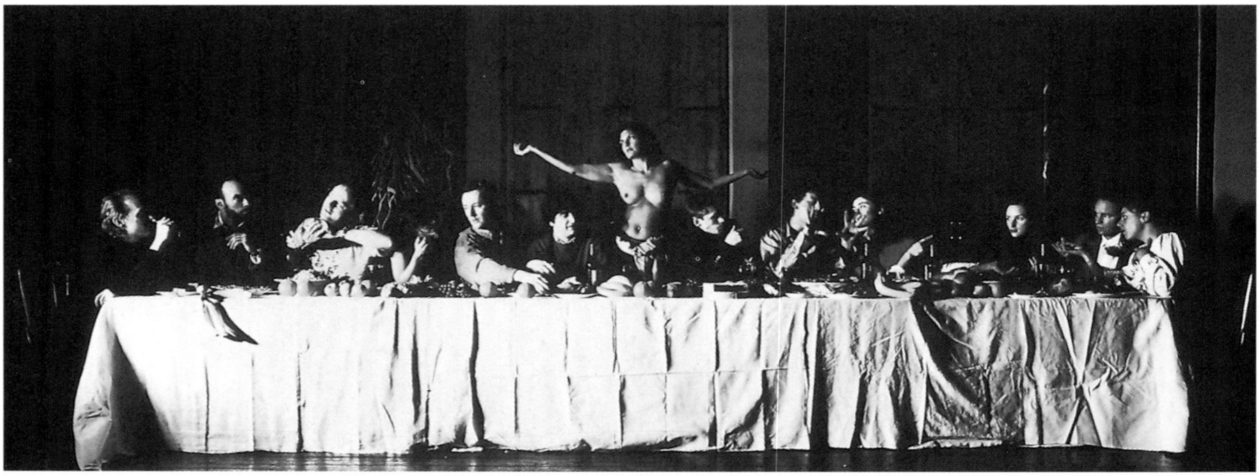

dreaming might amount to: stretching the pose, distending the visual field, and opening it up to the endless play of desire. This is where the "revolutionary" dimension of Taylor-Wood's vision resides: It is a soliloquial remedy for the visual hegemony of the screen.

1) The artist uses an Alpha Rota Camera equipped with an electronic motor and a 220 film to produce a color negative from which the prints are made. It takes five seconds to complete one rotation.
2) For a more extensive discussion of this point in relation to contemporary art see my "Real Bodies: Video in the 90s," *Art History* (June 1997), vol. 20, no. 2, pp. 185–213.
3) From the psychoanalytic point of view, as Diana Fuss has argued, "subjectivity can be most concisely understood as a history of one's identifications." See her *Identification Papers* (New York & London: Routledge, 1995), p. 34.
4) Taylor-Wood's video work BRONTOSAURUS (1995), featuring a naked man dancing to inaudible music, withdrawn into his own space, visibly, rhythmically separate from the space of music we are hearing, Barber's *Adagio for Strings,* is another figure of this subjective detachment that we witness in the actors of the FIVE REVOLUTIONARY SECONDS series.
5) See Gilles Deleuze, *The Fold. Leibniz and the Baroque.* Forword and transl. Tom Conley (Minneapolis: Minnesota University Press, 1993).
6) For the most extensive recent theoretical discussion of the specular bases of subjectivity see Kaja Silverman, *The Threshold of the Visible World* (New York and London: Routledge, 1997).
7) "Germano Celant/Sam Taylor-Wood: Soliloquy. Essay/Interview," in: *Sam Taylor-Wood,* ex. cat., Fondazione Prada, Milan, 1998, p. 156.

Erratum in Parkett No. 53

We apologize to Ewa Lajer-Burcharth for omitting a line in her essay on Tracey Moffatt, "A Stranger Within."

From line six the last paragraph on page 43 should read: "What the series makes clear is that for Moffatt, this project is inseparable from the process of distinguishing oneself as a daughter from a mother. Dissimilation is thus envisioned here as a psychic act that structures the daughter/mother relation in particular, referring to the fact that the girl's, unlike the boy's, development of her own distinct self involves the difficult task of separating from her mother while at the same time identifying with her."

SAM TAYLOR-WOOD, BRONTOSAURUS, 1995, 10 min. video projection and sound / 10 Min. Videoprojektion mit Ton.

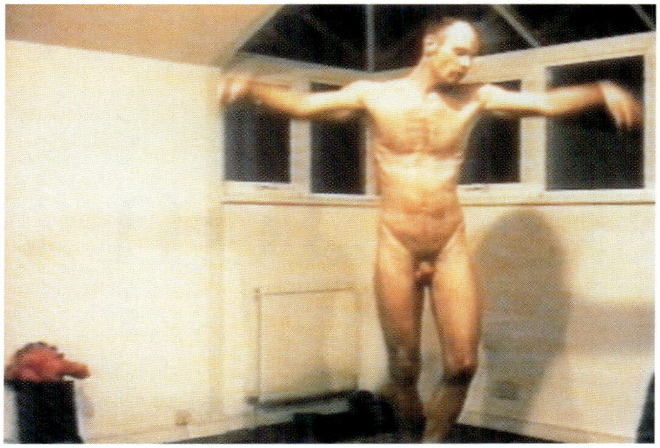

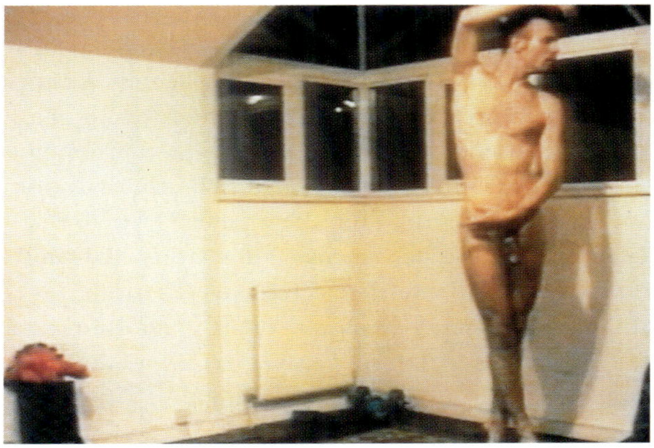

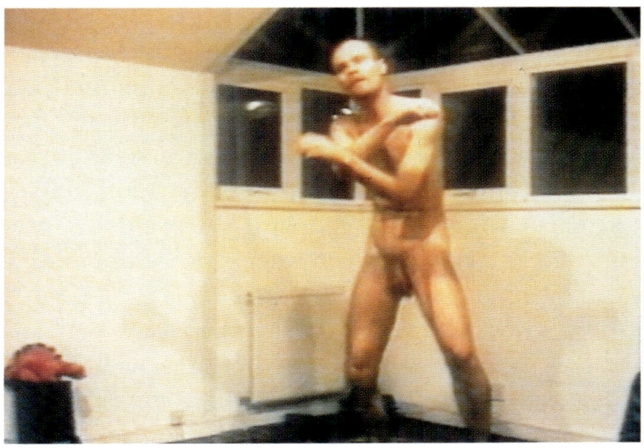

EWA LAJER-BURCHARTH

Die monologische Vision

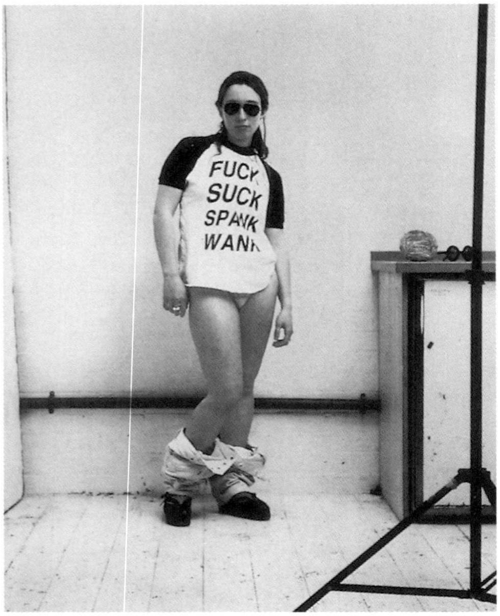

SAM TAYLOR-WOOD, FUCK, SUCK, SPANK, WANK, 1997, screen print, 38½ x 29½" / FICK, SCHLECK, SCHLAG, WICHS, Siebdruck, 98 x 75 cm. (PHOTO: STEPHEN WHITE)

Sam Taylor-Woods FIVE REVOLUTIONARY SECONDS (Fünf revolutionäre Sekunden, 1995), eine Serie photographischer Installationen, erschliesst dem Blick faszinierende Räume: Es sind Innenansichten privater Lofts, die früher die Künstlerboheme beherbergten, inzwischen aber einer reichen Kulturschickeria mit einem Faible für Innendekoration als stilvoll geräumiges Ambiente dienen. Sie wurden mit einer Spezialkamera gedreht, die sich innerhalb von fünf Sekunden einmal um die eigene Achse dreht – daher der Titel der Arbeit.[1] Obwohl es 360-Grad-Panoramen sind, werden diese Ansichten als zweidimensionale, langgestreckte, rechteckige Bilder an den Wänden der Galerie gezeigt, an jeder Wand ein Interieur, drei Ansichten pro Installation, ohne dass dabei die spezifische Wirkung der im späten achtzehnten und frühen neunzehnten Jahrhundert für Panoramen üblichen Rotunden angestrebt würde. Einen Kreis im Raum beschreibend und flach ausgebreitet, wirken sie nahtlos und uneinheitlich zugleich. Die räumlichen Verzerrungen, die das umherschweifende Auge der Kamera erzeugt, erinnern mit ihren abwechselnd konkaven und konvexen Formen an die Architektur Borrominis – nur sind sie hier noch extremer. Der Innenraum erscheint als eine einzige endlose Abfolge von Falten.

Diese architektonischen Falten werden von seltsamen, selbstvergessenen monadischen Wesen bevölkert, deren Distanziertheit die innere Heterogenität dieser Räume noch unterstreicht. Abgesehen von gelegentlichen Beischlafszenen oder lautstarken verbalen Auseinandersetzungen – Episoden, die im krassen Gegensatz zum sonst dargestellten menschlichen Tun und Treiben stehen – findet zwischen ihnen praktisch keine Interaktion statt. Man kann sich auch kaum vorstellen, dass diese Charaktere, die offensichtlich aus ganz unterschiedlichen gesellschaftlichen Schichten, häufig auch aus sexuell divergierenden Kontexten kommen und ausserdem noch im unsichtbaren Kokon ihres eigenen emotio-

EWA LAJER-BURCHARTH lehrt zeitgenössische Kunst und Kritik an der Harvard University. Sie ist Autorin des Buches *Necklines: The Art of Jacques-Louis David After the Terror* (New Haven: Yale University Press, 1999).

nalen Universums eingesponnen sind, tatsächlich in einem dieser Räume zusammenleben. Was könnte sie verbinden? Diese wie ein Derwisch herumwirbelnde Frau im weissen Abendkleid; den reglos am Küchentresen lehnenden, vor sich hin träumenden jungen Dandy, die Weste achtlos über die hemdlose Schulter geworfen; die in einem Sessel thronende Riesin in rotem Satin; die beiden in ihre sadomasochistischen Spielchen vertieften jungen Männer; den unauffälligen Mann im Anzug, der auf unsichtbare Fliegen an der Decke starrt, und all die anderen zusammengewürfelten Typen, die in FIVE REVOLUTIONARY SECONDS IX auftreten? Wie erklären wir uns so selbstvergessene Figuren wie diesen splitternackten, nachdenklich im Türrahmen lehnenden Mann in einem Raum voll korrekt gekleideter Menschen, dessen anatomische Details unserem Blick schutzlos preisgegeben sind?

Dies sind eindeutig keine realen, sondern imaginäre, konstruierte Räume, eine Feststellung, die ich bei Kritikern vermisse, die Taylor-Woods Arbeit unbesehen als soziologische Studie auffassen und abschätzig von ihrem Eintauchen in die snobistische Welt der Kulturschickeria sprechen. Meiner Meinung nach geht es in diesen schicken Interieurs weniger ums Haben als ums Sein. Die in ihrer eigenen Welt gefangenen monadischen Wesen, die in diesen Räumen auftreten, weisen über sich selbst hinaus, auf den Begriff der Pose. Durch ihr Verhalten entsteht ein subjektiver Raum, Dehnung und Verdichtung zugleich – ein panoramisches Schauspiel des Ich. Die Frage ist nur, was für ein Ich hier im Blick ist.

Man könnte versucht sein es als ein Ich der Modewelt zu betrachten. Zwischen Taylor-Woods Szenarien und den Schauplätzen der raffinierten Modephotographie gibt es Ähnlichkeiten. Meiner Meinung nach wird man jedoch weder der Bandbreite noch dem Wesen ihrer visuellen Intention gerecht, wenn man das Vorgehen der Künstlerin als mit der Modephotographie übereinstimmend betrachtet. Indem sich Taylor-Wood der Konventionen der Photographie, des Panoramas und des Avantgardefilms bedient, schafft sie formal komplexe Bilder, die die Frage nach der Subjektivität im Zeitalter des Bildschirms aufwerfen. Mit anderen Worten, es geht hier um das Subjekt an einem historischen Wendepunkt, an dem die Allgegenwart und Grenzenlosigkeit der technischen Mittel zur Schaffung eines kulturellen Bildrepertoirs – vom Computerbildschirm, den überhand nehmenden Werbeseiten von Zeitschriften bis zur ständig wachsenden Zahl der Leinwände im Kinocenter um die Ecke – die Grenze zwischen Ich und Bild immer durchlässiger werden lässt.[2)] Dass Taylor-Woods Arbeiten die hohe Qualität von Modephotos aufweisen, ist nur folgerichtig: Die Modephotographie als Seinsform ist hier Gegenstand der Untersuchung. Diese Galerie der selbstvergessenen Exzentriker zeigt daher weniger ein Panorama der Schickeria als unterschiedliche Positionen und Phantasien des bereits vom Bildschirm besessenen Ich; die Innenräume stehen für Innerlichkeit in einem besonderen Sinn, als Topographie unserer – mehrfachen – Identifikationen.[3)] Das Konstruierte dieses imaginären Subjektraums wird durch die Art der Installation noch verstärkt: Aus zwischen den Photographien angebrachten Lautsprechern sind akustische Spuren der Dreharbeiten zu hören – die Stimmen und Geräusche während der Arbeit am sichtbar gemachten Raum.

Man könnte FIVE REVOLUTIONARY SECONDS als Fortführung jener kritischen Tradition betrachten, die im vergangenen Jahrzehnt die ästhetische Praxis der Photographie und den ihr zugrunde liegenden Diskurs über die Konstruktion von Kultur beherrschte. In entscheidenden Punkten weicht die Arbeit aber auch davon ab: Dazu gehört die pure Vielfalt, der Reichtum menschlicher Charaktere und Identitäten, die sie zum Ausdruck bringt – die ganze Palette der Körpergrössen, Farben, Affekte und dessen, was man früher «Temperamente» genannt hätte, und der sexuellen Neigungen. Diese subjektive Pluralität verschiebt den Begriff der Differenz – der psychischen wie sexuellen – auf eine andere Ebene, jenseits der gewohnten Dualitäten.

Ein weiterer Aspekt ist die persönliche Dimension, die die sehr unterschiedlichen Darstellerinnen und Darsteller dem Begriff der Pose verleihen. Während die demonstrative Art der Inszenierung das Posieren als einen Akt der Selbstbehauptung – «Seht her, ich bin von Bedeutung!» – in den Vordergrund rückt, ist das Verständnis keineswegs gewährleistet. Der Anblick der rätselhaften Gestalten lässt einen an den frustrierten Delacroix denken, der, mit der radikal neuen und unverständlichen Körpersprache von Courbets BADENDER konfrontiert, ausrief: «Aber was bedeutet das?!» Die didaktische oder normative Dimension der Pose scheint diesen Selbstdarstellungen völlig zu fehlen. Obwohl sie mit Shermans UNTITLED FILM STILLS die allegorische Stasis zu teilen scheinen, geht es in diesen Bildern nicht um das Einnehmen einer Pose oder um ein Sichmessen mit der Pose als einem kulturbedingten, normativen Ideal des Ich (bei Sherman: der Weiblichkeit). Sie veranschaulichen vielmehr die Abkehr von der Pose und den Rückzug in den privaten Bereich der Träumereien. Selbst in ihren Posen erscheinen die Protagonisten in der Sicht dieser Künstlerin selbstvergessen und gedankenverloren. All die introvertierten, nachdenklichen Gestalten, die in Taylor-Woods Interieurs auftauchen, bestätigen das nur.[4] Sie sind jedoch nicht wirklich in narzisstischer Selbstbetrachtung vertieft – es geht nicht um eine Konfrontation mit dem eigenen Bild –, sondern eher in einer Art selbstreflektierender Tätigkeit: in der stummen Zwiesprache mit sich selbst.

Last but not least wäre da noch die besondere Sicht der Dimensionen Raum und Zeit: Wegen der 360-Grad-Umdrehung der Kamera, die fünf Sekunden benötigt um den ganzen Raum «wahrzunehmen», ist die Zeit von Anfang an sichtbar in diesem Raum verzeichnet. Es ist jedoch nicht die narrative Zeit einer linearen Progression im Raum, die wie eine sichtbare Handlungskette ein Ereignis mit dem anderen verknüpft, sondern eher eine korrosive Zeit, die die Geschichte zerstört. Innerhalb des narrativen Gewebes von Taylor-Woods Bild kommt die zeitliche Dimension einer Störung gleich, einem Bruch, der das Ganze um ein Haar auseinander reisst. Der Raum entfaltet sich durch eine strukturelle Entwicklung, die sich wie eine Deuleuze'sche Falte verhält: eine Proliferation von Singularitäten.[5] In sich gekrümmt durch eine Reihe subjektiver Momente, jedes davon eine irreduzible, in ihrer eigenen Pose eingeschlossene Monade, entspricht die visuelle Struktur von FIVE REVOLUTIONARY SECONDS einer Reihe räumlicher Taschen, die das Werk von innen heraus differenzieren und in Frage stellen.

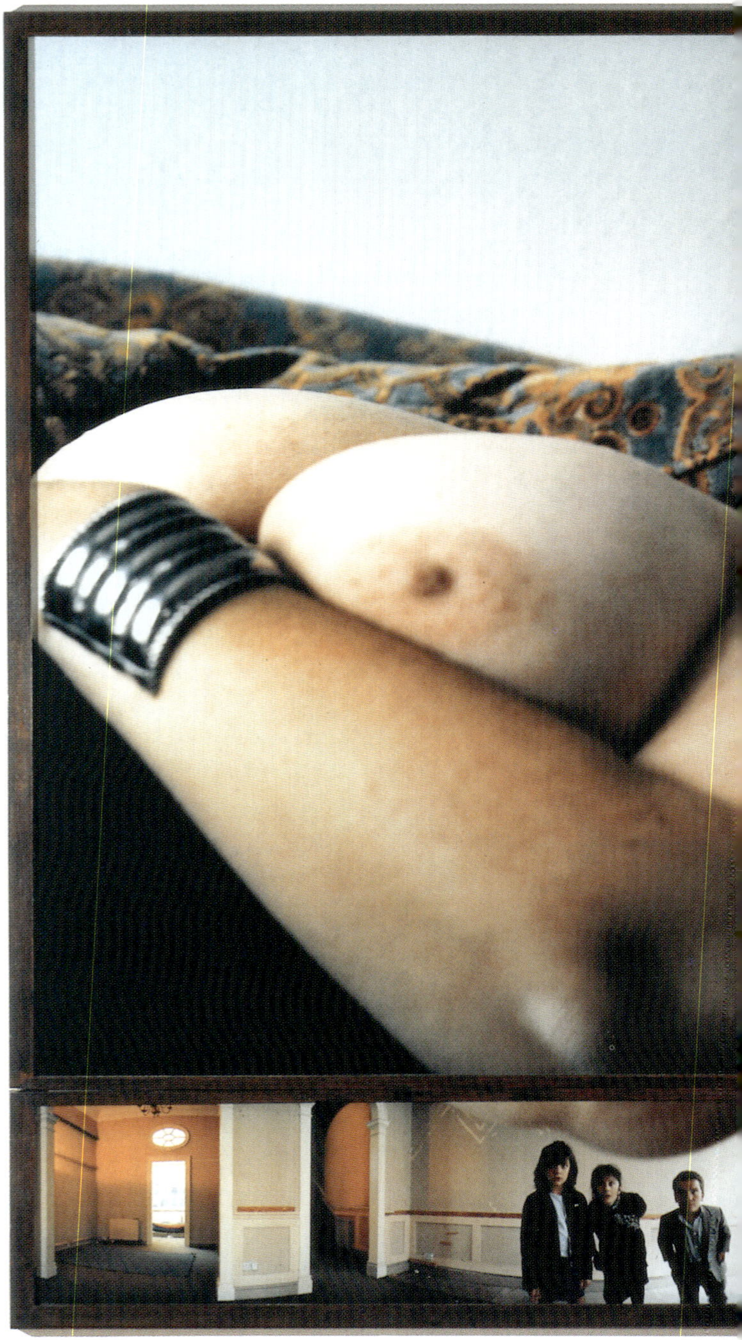

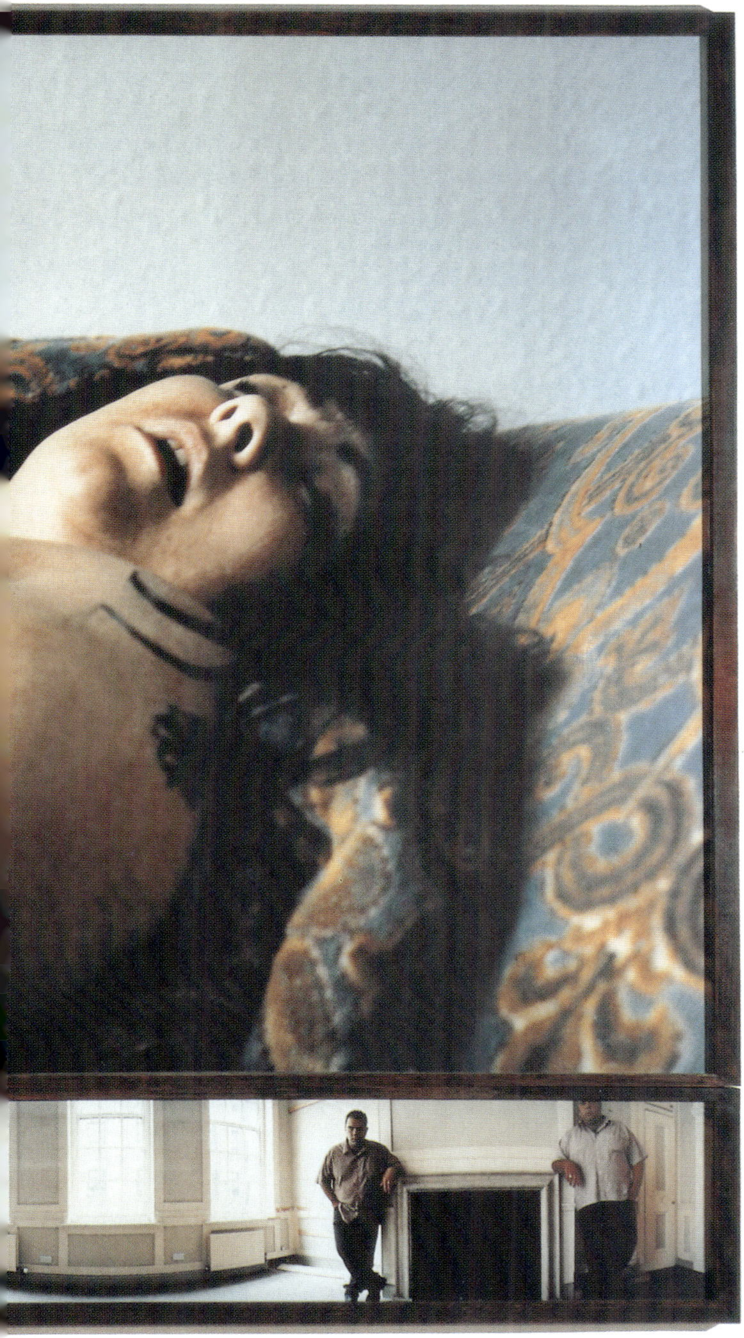

SAM TAYLOR-WOOD, SOLILOQUY IV, 1998, framed c-print, 87⅜ x 101$^{3}/_{16}$" / MONOLOG IV, gerahmter C-Print, 222 x 257 cm. (PHOTO: ATTILIO MARANZANO)

Als solche können Taylor-Woods Panoramen des Selbst als visuelle Neubestimmung des individuellen Subjekts im Bereich des Visuellen oder auch als Neudefinition des Visuellen gelten, die für das private Ich Platz schafft. Keineswegs sind sie ein Rückgriff auf naive Vorstellungen von Individualismus als etwas, was ausserhalb der Kultur, ausserhalb einer bestimmten Sicht existiert, sondern ein Überdenken der Beziehung zwischen Sehen und Ich. Einerseits will Taylor-Woods Kamera dem Subjekt seine zentrale Position in dem durch das Kreisen des Kamera-Auges erschlossenen visuellen Bereich zurückgeben, andererseits konstruiert das Auge keinen allumfassenden optischen Raum mit einem unangreifbaren, dominierenden Subjekt in seiner Mitte (das Auge als Ich / the eye as I), denn es wird durch die verschiedenen Falten der Subjektivität in seinem Innern gebrochen und vervielfältigt. Das Ergebnis ist eine visuelle Polyphonie, die über die normale Sichtweise hinausgeht und sie in Frage stellt. Ein Raum, der uns einlädt, die spekulativen Grundlagen des Ich neu zu erfinden.[6)]

Die Serie SOLILOQUIES (Monologe, 1998) ist ein beredter Kommentar hierzu. Das Ich ist hier eindeutig in einen inneren Dialog mit sich selbst vertieft, was wir bei den Charakteren von FIVE REVOLUTIONARY SECONDS nur vermuten können. Die Serie umfasst fünf riesige Tableaux, die aus jeweils einem Hauptteil und einer schmalen Predella darunter bestehen. Innerhalb dieser Struktur eines Renaissance-Altars werden zwei verschiedene Blicke entwickelt um das duale System subjektiver Abläufe darzustellen – ein körperlicher und ein geistiger. Die oberen Tafeln sind mehr oder weniger einfache, bekannten Gemälden nachempfundene Kunst-Photographien; die Predellen darunter wurden mit derselben Panorama-Kamera aufgenommen, die wir bereits von früheren Arbeiten kennen. Diese beiden unterschiedlichen Sehweisen stehen für das durch Phantasie oder Traum gespaltene Subjekt: Im oberen Teil sehen wir den physischen Leib eines Individuums, das entweder schläft, seinen Tagträumen nachhängt oder vor sich hin sinniert; jedenfalls ist es irgendwie seiner Umgebung enthoben. In den Predellen entfaltet sich die imaginäre Welt als Traumsphäre sexueller Phantasien. Die durch die Panorama-Kamera bewirkten räumlichen Verfremdungseffekte wurden durch partielle digitale Manipulationen verstärkt um die in der Phantasie oder im Traum durchgeführte Verdichtung oder Verfremdung der Realität darzustellen.

In SOLILOQUY III betrachtet eine Frau voller Wohlgefallen ihr Spiegelbild, hingestreckt wie Velázquez' VENUS IM SPIEGEL, der Blick so entrückt wie das Photo selbst, dessen Grobkörnigkeit den Eindruck erweckt, es sei durch einen Schleier hindurch aufgenommen. Grau-, Rosa- und helle Gelbtöne herrschen vor. In der Predella darunter erkennt man eine phantasmagorische Orgie, die sich diese «Venus» vorstellt: eine spärlich möblierte Wohnung voll nackter Männer und Frauen, manche ineinander verknäult, andere aufreizend auf Sofas und Polstern ausgestreckt, als warteten sie leicht gelangweilt darauf, dass sie an die Reihe kämen. Wie ein Hund liegt auf der Türmatte ein nackter Mann. Ein anderer, langgestreckt wie eine Figur von Giacometti und leicht verschwommen, wandert ziellos durch den Raum. Auf einer Couch räkelt eine Odaliske im Ingres-Stil ihren lasziven Leib. Aus einer Hängematte ragen ein Paar Beine. Ein vollständig bekleideter Mann sitzt an seinem Schreibtisch, ohne die vor ihm ausgestreckte Nackte zu beachten. An einem anderen Schreibtisch telefoniert eine nackte Frau. Schliesslich taucht im hinteren Teil des Raums die «Venus» selbst auf: Sie sitzt in einem Sessel, ganz in Rot, die Augen geschlossen, unbeeindruckt von der Orgie. Am auffälligsten ist der Kontrast zwischen den sanften Konturen dieses, durch den Schleier des kulturell Akzeptablen gefilterten, weiblichen Körpers und seinen Phantasien in der Szene darunter.

SOLILOQUY IV zeigt den verkürzten nackten Torso einer Frau mit riesigen Brüsten, die mit geöffnetem Mund tief und fest auf einem Sofa schläft, das weiche, rosa Fleisch tief in die reich verzierten Kissen gebettet. Hier ist der Kontrast zwischen dem schlafenden weiblichen Fleisch und der Bewegung der Psyche anders dargestellt: Nicht der vornehm verschleierte Blick des träumenden Subjekts, sondern seine penetrante Fleischlichkeit kontrastiert mit den darunter dargestellten Phantasien. Im leeren Zimmer eines alten Hauses mit malerischen Fenstern, heruntergerissenen Tapeten und Spuren von Möbeln an den Wänden starren drei Zwerge und ein Kind angestrengt nach oben, vielleicht auf den Ellbogen der Riesin, der über die obere Tafel auf die Predella quillt. Rechts neben einem Kamin stehen pausbäckige männliche Zwillinge. Für diejenigen, die in der Riesin Sue Tilly, das Lieblingsmodell des Malers Lucien Freud erkennen – manche tun das –, ist der Verwandlungseffekt von Taylor-Woods Sicht noch augenfälliger: Was bei Freud unerlöstes Fleisch ist, wird bei Taylor-Wood als Sitz der Subjektivität – und des Begehrens – vorgestellt.

Das Bestechendste an SOLILOQUY II ist die unkonventionelle Definition des männlichen Körpers als Objekt der Begierde, das in einer Herbstidylle aus Gelb-, Ocker- und Goldtönen platziert wird. Ein unrasierter, attraktiver junger Mann ohne Hemd und mit provozierend geöffneter Gürtelschnalle posiert zwischen einem Rudel streunender Hunde. Ob er nun stehend oder liegend mit ihrem Fell beschäftigt ist, die Eigenschaften, die er mit diesen Hunden teilt, sind zwar nicht sichtbar, aber doch spürbar obszöner Natur. Die Predella darunter zeigt eine unterirdische Landschaft, eine obszöne Phantasie: ein mit Nackten bevölkertes Badehaus, die entweder miteinander kopulieren oder unruhig an den Wänden der gekachelten Räume lehnen. Der Protagonist selbst erscheint in einer Ecke, niedergeschlagen mit einem Hund an seiner Seite auf dem Boden sitzend.

Nach der Bedeutung des Ausdrucks SOLILOQUIES gefragt, verwies Taylor-Wood auf die Distanz, die ein Schauspieler sowohl in Bezug auf die eigene Rolle wie auch auf das Stück empfindet, in dem er spielt, eine Distanz, die, wie das häufig in Shakespeares Dramen geschieht, einen Schauspieler an die Rampe treten und einen Kommentar des Autors an die Adresse des Publikums sprechen lässt.[7] Thematisiert wird dieser Begriff anhand völlig losgelöster Figuren, wie jener der drei Zwerge, die aus dem Traumbereich der Riesin herausblicken, oder der Frau, die im Mittelpunkt der obszönen Phantasie des Mannes mit den Hunden steht, und deren Gesichtszüge durch digitale Manipulation verflüssigt erscheinen, was sowohl ihre Distanz zur Szene wie zum eigenen Körper andeutet. Aber man kann diese Distanz auch als die Logik dieser Bilder begreifen. So gesehen ist der Monolog das tragende Moment in Taylor-Woods Arbeiten, der strukturelle Bruch zwischen dem Subjekt und seinen Phantasien, den sie räumlich als innere Zwiesprache der Figuren mit sich selbst darstellen.

Nicht sosehr die Sexualität selbst (Freud würde da beipflichten), sondern die Art und Weise, wie sie in den Träumen und Phantasien zum Ausdruck kommt, macht die Originalität dieser Arbeiten aus. Interessant ist auch, wie die Geschlechterdifferenz den libidinösen Bereich der Phantasie zwar durchzieht, aber nicht bestimmt. Männer und Frauen sind sowohl als Objekte wie auch als Subjekte der Begierde austauschbar. Das mag einem selbstverständlich vorkommen, wenn man sich jedoch die neuesten Leinwandschnulzen aus Hollywood ansieht, wird einem die ebenso penetrante wie vorhersehbare Geschlechterhierarchie (Frau Objekt, Mann Subjekt der Begierde) innerhalb der herrschenden Kultur der Bilder vor Augen geführt. Diese Hierarchie zu unterminieren hatte sich die feministische Ästhetik der letzten beiden Jahrzehnte zur Aufgabe gemacht. Taylor-Wood, die in ihrem Gefolge die Kunstszene betrat, verdankt ihr, dass sie in ihren Arbeiten weibliche Geilheit als eine Selbstverständlichkeit voraussetzen kann – etwas, was sie in ihren Arbeiten tut und anschliessend zu differenzieren sucht. Erinnern wir uns, dass die Künstlerin ihre Karriere mit einem rotzig-aggressiven Selbstporträt begann, in dem sie mit heruntergelassenen Hosen, Fliegerbrille und einem T-Shirt mit der Aufschrift FUCK, SUCK, SPANK, WANK (1993) auftrat, einem Schwulen-Slogan, der ihre geschlechtliche Selbstdefinition noch ambivalenter erscheinen liess.

Auffällig ist auch das Schillernde der Lust in Taylor-Woods Darstellung. Die sexuellen Szenarien bilden regelmässig unaufgelöste, irritierende Gegensätzlichkeiten – häufig einfach durch ihr endloses Fortdauern – und verweigern jede Lösung. Das kritische Postulat, die Dualitäten zu destabilisieren, an denen die visuelle Kultur die kollektiven sexuellen Phantasien festzumachen sucht, ist natürlich nicht neu. Wie jedoch die Alternative, das uneingeschränkte Begehren, tatsächlich aussehen könnte, ist selten dargestellt worden. SOLILOQUIES macht hierzu einen Vorschlag.

Und darin sehe ich die eigentliche Dimension dieses Werkes. Es vermittelt eine Sicht, die sich von innen heraus entwickelt, die die kulturellen Grenzen der Darstellbarkeit erweitert und expandieren lässt. Es handelt sich dabei nicht nur um die Darstellung von Träumen, sondern auch um Phantasien darüber, was Träumen heissen könnte: eine Erweiterung der Pose, ein Ausdehnen des Gesichtsfeldes und seine Öffnung für das endlose Spiel des Verlangens. Darin liegt die «revolutionäre» Dimension von Taylor-Woods Vision, der Monolog als Gegenmittel gegen die Hegemonialmacht des Bildschirms.

(Übersetzung: Uta Goridis)

1) Die Künstlerin benützt eine Alpha-Rota-Kamera mit elektronischem Motor und einem 220er-Film um ein Farbnegativ herzustellen, von dem danach Abzüge gemacht werden. Eine volle Umdrehung dauert fünf Sekunden.

2) Für eine ausführlichere Erörterung dieses Gesichtspunktes vgl. meinen Artikel «Real Bodies: Video in the 90s», in: *Art History*, Juni 1997, Bd. 20, Nr. 2, S. 185–213.

3) Aus psychoanalytischer Sicht kann Subjektivität am exaktesten als «Geschichte der Identifikationen» beschrieben werden. Vgl. dazu: Diana Fuss, *Identification Papers*, Routledge, New York & London 1995, S. 34.

4) Taylor-Woods Videoarbeit BRONTOSAURUS (1995) – sie zeigt einen nackten Mann, der zu einer unhörbaren Musik tanzt, ganz in seinen eigenen Raum zurückgezogen, sichtbar, rhythmisch getrennt vom Raum der Musik, die wir hören, Barbers *Adagio für Streicher* – ist ein weiteres Beispiel für diese Selbstversunkenheit des Subjekts, das wir bei den Darstellern in FIVE REVOLUTIONARY SECONDS feststellen.

5) Vgl. dazu Gilles Deleuze, *Die Falte. Leibniz und der Barock*, Suhrkamp, Frankfurt am Main 1995.

6) Vgl. dazu: Kaja Silverman, *The Threshold of the Visible World*, Routledge, New York & London 1997.

7) «Germano Celant/Sam Taylor-Wood: Soliloquy. Essay/Interview», in: *Sam Taylor-Wood*, Ausstellungskatalog, Fondazione Prada, Milano 1998, S. 156.

Edition for Parkett **SAM TAYLOR-WOOD**

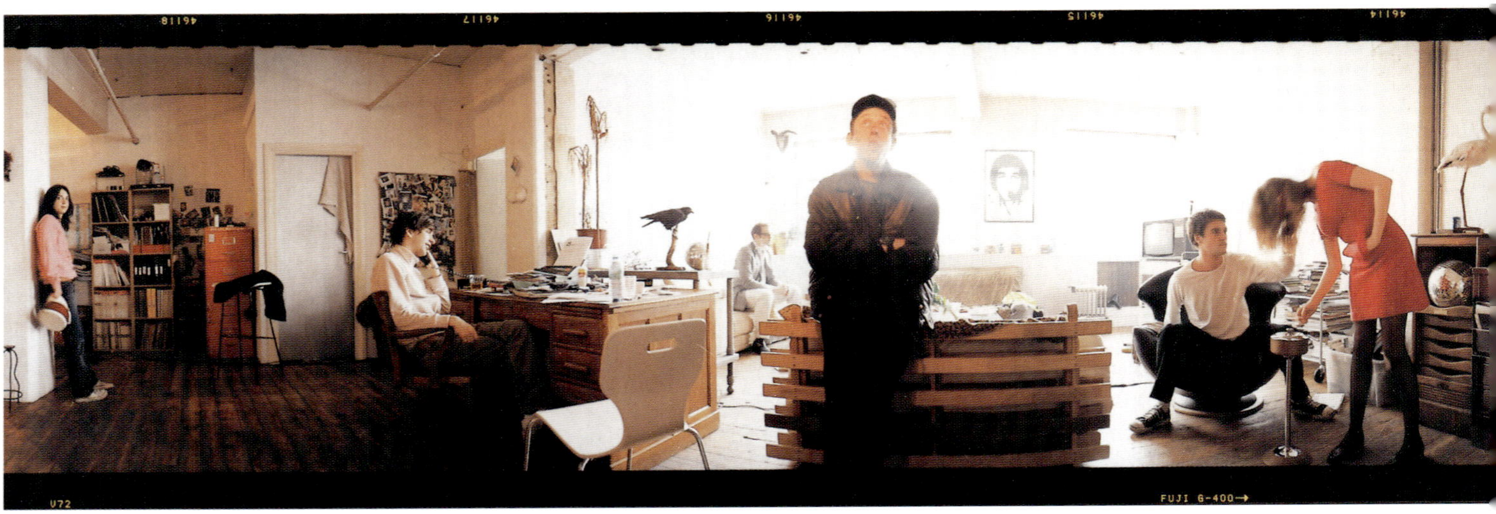

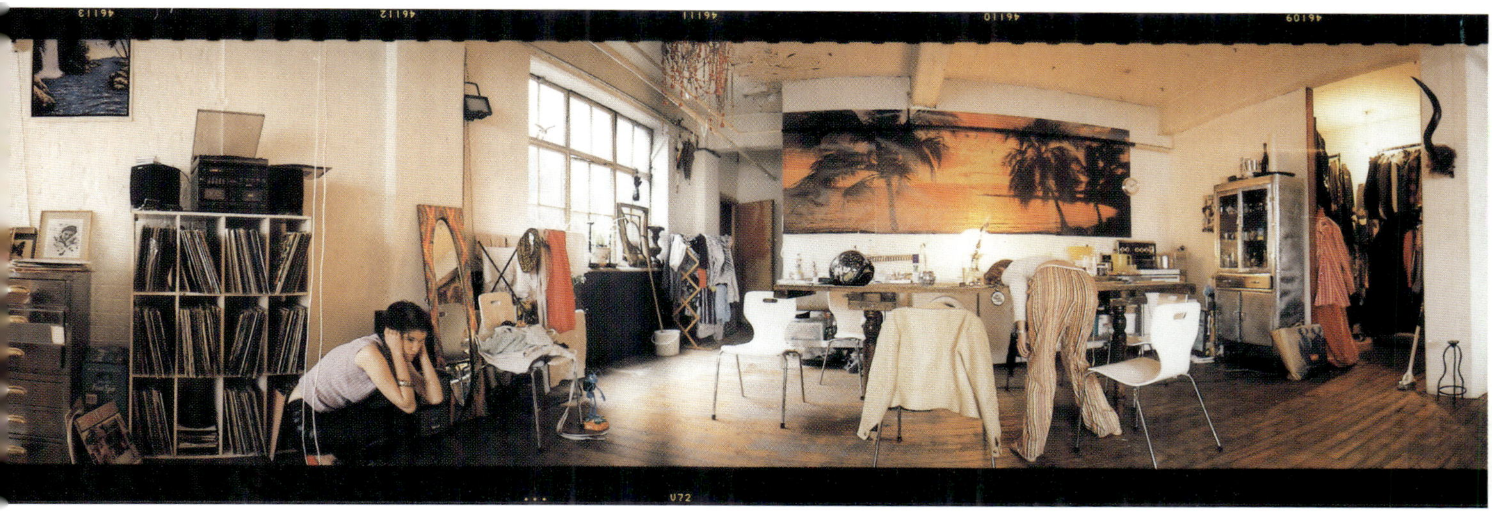

FIVE REVOLUTIONARY SECONDS XIV (SKETCH), 1999
C-print, 360-degree panorama shot, 2¾ x 16½"
Edition of 50, signed and numbered

FÜNF REVOLUTIONÄRE SEKUNDEN XIV (ENTWURF), 1999
C-Print, 360-Grad-Panorama-Aufnahme, 7 x 42 cm
Auflage: 50, signiert und nummeriert

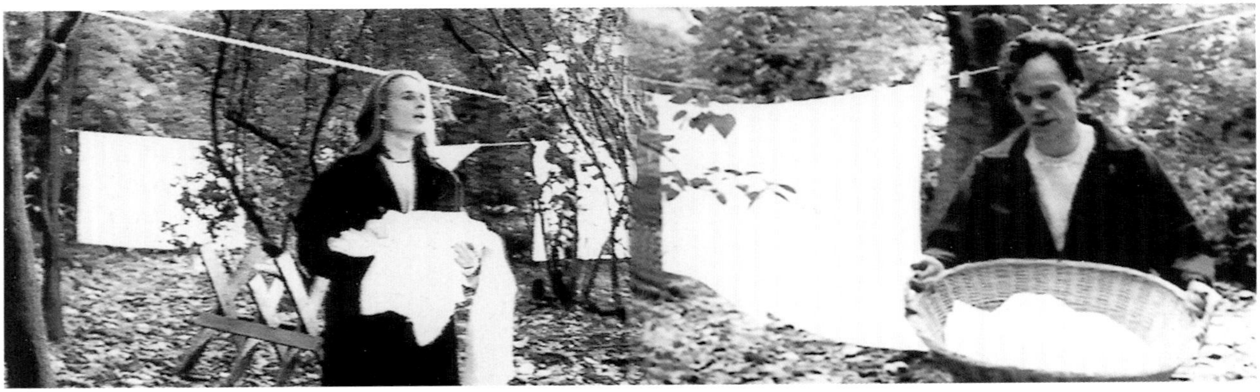

HYBRIDE WIRKLICHKEITEN

DIE «MENSCHLICHEN DRAMEN» DER EIJA-LIISA AHTILA

BEATRIX RUF

«Heute weint mein Vater. Sein Vater wurde spät gestern Nacht von einem Auto überfahren. Er war sofort tot.» So beginnt der Text des jungen Mädchens in Eija-Liisa Ahtilas dreiteiligem Film TODAY. Und er endet mit: «Vielleicht ist es gar nicht mein Vater, der weint, sondern der Vater von jemand anders. Sannas Vater, Mias Vater, Markos Vater, Pasis Vater – oder Veras Vater. Ich sitze in einem Sessel. Ich habe einen Freund. Ich habe etwas auf meinem Schoss. Ich bin 66 Jahre alt.»[1] Diese Zitate umreissen auch schon, was Eija-Liisa Ahtilas auf Film basierende künstlerische Arbeit ausmacht: Unpathetisch und erschreckend direkt behandeln ihre Filme Szenen vielleicht realer, immer aber möglicher alltäglicher Lebenssituationen und -ereignisse, in deren logische Abläufe und Erfahrungen das Surreale, das Asynchrone und das Alogische einbrechen.

BEATRIX RUF ist Konservatorin am Kunsthaus Glarus. Sie lebt in Glarus und Zürich.

Video, Film, die neuen digitalen Bildmedien sind für viele Künstlerinnen und Künstler und vor allem für die Generationen, die mit der allgegenwärtigen Präsenz von Fernsehen, Kino, Werbefilmen und MTV aufgewachsen sind und aufwachsen, gängige Ausdrucksmittel. Die Beeinflussungen unserer Selbst- und Wirklichkeitserfahrung durch die zeitgenössische visuelle Kultur sind vielfältig. Die Bildwelten sind ein konstitutiver Teil unserer Wirklichkeit. Der Wirklichkeitsverlust durch die Medien wird zwar schon seit Anfang unseres Jahrhunderts problematisiert, die Perfektionierung der Massenmedien, die Privatisierung der Möglichkeit Bilder zu produzieren, die Wirklichkeit ins Filmische, ins Bild zu verwandeln, wird aber zunehmend präsenter. Baudrillard hat von einer pornographischen Dimension der Allgegenwart des Abbildbaren gesprochen. Pornographisch deshalb, weil unbegrenzte Darstellung möglich geworden ist: das Bild als Verfügung/Verfügbarmachung der Wirklichkeit, des Privaten wie

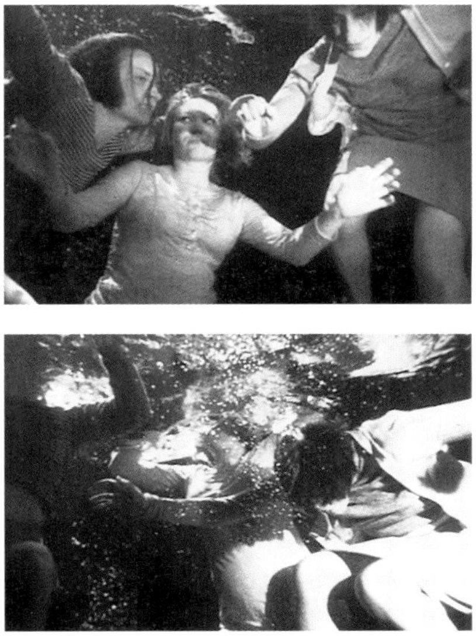

EIJA-LIISA AHTILA, ME/WE, OKAY, GREY, 1993, video stills / ICH/WIR, OKAY, GRAU.
(PHOTOS: CRYSTAL EYE LTD, HELSINKI)

des Öffentlichen. Fiktion und Realität sind hier obsolete Kategorien. Betroffen davon ist nicht zuletzt die Konstruktion unseres Selbst, das sich angesichts ambivalenter Realitäten positionieren muss: zwischen privaten und medial vermittelten, öffentlichen Bildern des Subjekts, zwischen Realitätskontrolle und individueller Wirklichkeitskonstruktion. Ein Subjekt, das uns als aus multiplen Elementen geschnürtes Bündel von Konstellationen, Konzepten und Dramaturgien und vor allem erst als Relation zu den medialen Darstellungen fassbar wird.

Die finnische Künstlerin Eija-Liisa Ahtila (geb. 1959) arbeitet mit den Bedingungen und Wirkungsweisen unserer visuellen Kultur und stellt Fragen an die Positionierung des Subjektes heute. Seit Ende der 80er Jahre ist sie mit einem komplexen Werk hervorgetreten, das die ganze Breite visueller Kultur bespielt und – neben Photographie, Performance und Film im Videoformat – in den letzten Jahren vor allem durch ihre Videoinstallationen aufgefallen ist. Die «menschlichen Dramen» (Eija-Liisa Ahtila) ihrer letzten vier im Filmformat gedrehten und ins Videoformat übertragenen Kurzfilme ME/WE, OKAY, GRAY (1993, 90 Sekunden), IF 6 WAS 9 (1995, 10 Minuten), TODAY (1996/1997, 10 Minuten) und ANNE, AKI AND GOD (1998, 2 x 15-Minuten-Loop) präsentiert sie in parallelen Bildspuren, die die Erzählung in mehrere Episoden fragmentieren und zu komplexen Stücken komponieren. Die Künstlerin spielt mit der visuellen Überladung, der erschwerten Erfassbarkeit der Erzähllinien. Orte, Menschen, Stimmen, Rhythmen wechseln von einer Filmebene in die andere und erzeugen einen nicht linearen Erzählfluss. Text, Tonspur und Bilder sind in einem lang andauernden Prozess mit grosser Präzision ausgearbeitet. Die filmischen Ebenen entwickeln dabei ihre je eigenen, widersprüchlichen Wirkungen, die die Logik der anderen Elemente brechen oder Bedeutungen neu konstituieren. Bilder und Texte spielen ihre Fähigkeit aus zu lügen oder die Wahrheit zu sagen; die originale Texttonspur des Finnischen klingt verführerisch und fremd. In den übersetzten Untertiteln werden die Texte zum visuellen Element, das die parallelen Bildebenen zusammenbindet.

Die Fragmentierung der Erzählebenen und die Installationsformen ihrer Arbeiten reflektieren formal auf das veränderte Verständnis des Subjektbegriffes und der Idee eines ungeteilten Selbst, das sich seine Rollen, Muster und Formen im Zusammenspiel mit den globalen gesellschaftspolitischen Zusammenhängen neu fassen muss.

Eija-Liisa Ahtilas Filme berühren den Erfahrungsschatz jedes Menschen. Sie sind zugleich persönlich und allgemeingültig, weil ihre Geschichten und Ereignisse überall spielen könnten. Das Leben in Städten, die Schulzeit, das Elternhaus, Pubertät, Sexualität, Ehe, Freizeitbeschäftigungen. Sie machen Normalität in ihrer Brüchigkeit erlebbar: Normalität befremdet. Ahtilas Protagonisten sprechen in der Stimme ihres fiktiven Gegenübers, sie spielen sich selbst und wenden sich an das Publikum. Sprachformeln werden zu musikalischen Rhythmen, gescheiterte Kommunikation führt zu grotesken Interpretationen und Rollenwechseln. Einschränkungen durch Konventionen, emotionale Bindungen und Einsamkeit sind genauso bedrohlich wie eine atomare Katastrophe. Die Menschen sind getrieben durch die heterogenen Aspekte der Realität: Verunsicherung der Lebensstile und Rollenmodelle, Nachrichtenflut, zweifelhaft gewordene Wirklichkeiten.

Die heutige Beschaffenheit alltäglicher Erfahrungen wird in ihren Texten und scharf komponierten Bildwelten offen gelegt. Wie andere Künstlerinnen und Künstler der 90er Jahre thematisiert auch Eija-Liisa Ahtila die aufgehobene Grenze zwischen dem Privaten und Öffentlichen sowie die Medienerscheinungen, die diese Aufhebung mitbestimmen: Bekennershows, Seifenopern, Realtime-Serien. In ihren Arbeiten wird das Private dabei zu einer Instanz des Politischen, das von ihren präzisen Mitteln getragen ist. Veröffentlichung des Privaten, des alltäglich Normalen oder Profanen ist hier nie Intimitätsschleuder, Privatheitsorgie oder identifikationsträchtiger Mitleidsgag. Auf der Ebene der Filmsprache verwebt die Künstlerin die Wirkungsweisen und Stile gängiger Filmgenres wie Kurzfilm, Werbefilm, Dokumentarfilm oder auch das Format der Hollywood-Fiktion zu neuen und eigenen Bildwelten, die Vertrautes unbekannt werden lassen und eine eindeutige Kategorisierung verunmöglichen. Ihre Überschreitungen der klassischen Medien machen sie «inkompatibel» für die üblichen Vermarktungsstrategien von Film, Video oder Kunst, aber auch für jede schnelle Kategorisierung der Wahrnehmung: Fiction, Dokumentarkino, Avantgardefilm? Eija-Liisa Ahtila arbeitet mit kinematographischem Formensinn. Bekannte scheinen auf: Jean-Luc Godard, Chantal Akerman, aber auch Aki Kaurismäki. Geläufige kollektive filmische Sprachen werden gekonnt benutzt und dennoch kann man an ihren Bildwelten keinen «Stil» festmachen. Ihre Filme sind präzis konstruierte Hybride, die sich ihre Autonomie in den bekannten Kontexten erhalten. Die Arbeiten bestehen so folgerichtig in unterschiedlichen Formaten, sei es als Film, der über die üblichen Medienkanäle Fernsehen und Kino verbreitet werden kann, sei es als für jedes filmische Stück eigens entwickelte Installationen im Kunstkontext, die Situationen schaffen, in denen wir die bewegten Bilder als lebensgrosses Gegenüber erleben, oder die uns in erzählerische Ensembles eintauchen lassen. Eija-Liisa Ahtilas Arbeiten setzen genau da an, wo der Film seine Ambivalenz entwickelt, zwischen der Möglichkeit zur Fiktion und dem dokumentarischen Versprechen der Photographie. Das filmische Bild setzt sich in ihren Arbeiten vom Film ab.

Meist geht Eija-Liisa Ahtila von einem «Dokument» der Realität aus: einer Erzählung, einem Zeitungsausschnitt, einem historischen Ereignis... Vergleicht man die Werke Eija-Liisa Ahtilas etwa mit den Videoarbeiten ihrer Künstlerkollegin Sam Taylor-Wood, steht, verkürzt gesagt, dem dort thematisierten «Theatralischen» der menschlichen Realität hier das problematisierte Authentische als das Super-Reale gegenüber, das ins Surreale mutiert.

Die jüngste Arbeit ANNE, AKI AND GOD scheint exemplarisch für Eija-Liisa Ahtilas künstlerischen Ansatz. Das auf aufgezeichneten Therapiesitzungen beruhende Skript zum Film greift konkret eine zeitgenössische Version der Identitätsstörung auf. Als eigenständige Videoinstallationsversion bildet sie die Grundlage für einen abendfüllenden Kinofilm, den die Künstlerin unter dem Titel *A Quest for a Woman* zurzeit erarbeitet. Basierend auf den Erlebnissen des Mannes Aki, der an einer medizinisch nicht vollständig erfassbaren neuen Version der Schizophrenie leidet und sich im Zustand einer Psychose eine «Frau» erschuf, kreiert die Arbeit eine multiple Identität in Form einer Casting-Situation, in der unterschiedliche Schauspieler Akis Rolle übernehmen, frappierend im Gleichklang ihrer Texte und flankiert von den imaginiert wirklichen Frauenmodellen. «Aki V kündigte seine Stelle als Programmierer bei Nokia, erkrankte an Schizophrenie und isolierte sich in seinem Einzimmer-Apartment. Sein Geist begann sich in Bild und Ton eine eigene

EIJA-LIISA AHTILA, TODAY / TÄNÄÄN, 1996–97, installation view, left screen / HEUTE, Installationsansicht, linke Leinwand.

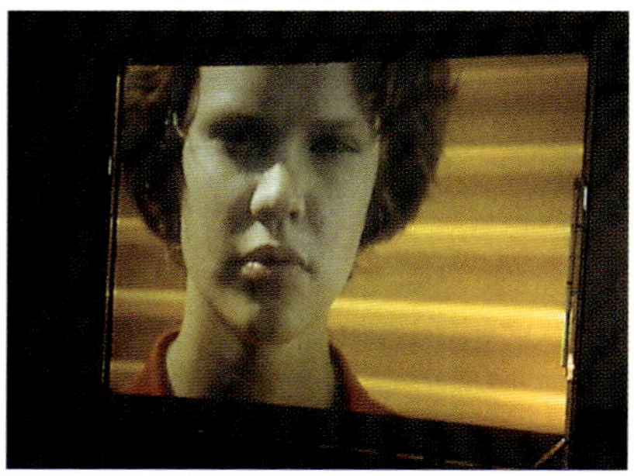

Wirklichkeit zu schaffen. Nach und nach wurde diese Fiktion zu Fleisch und Blut, die Grenze zwischen Realität und Fiktion verschwamm. Eingebildete Personen und Ereignisse traten aus Aki Vs Kopf heraus und lebten parallel zu der ihn umgebenden Realität. Die Hauptperson in dieser neuen Welt war Anne Nyberg, Akis Verlobte.»[2] Akis von Gott aufgetragene Aufgabe beschränkt sich aber nicht nur auf die Suche nach seiner Verlobten, sondern sein Zustand soll ihn auch auf eine zukünftige Aufgabe vorbereiten: «Dann wurde Aki informiert, dass seine wichtigste Pflicht in der Zukunft die Verantwortung für Hollywood sei, da Hollywood alle emotionalen Phantasien der Menschen kontrolliere.»[3] Madonna, Marlon Brando, Elizabeth Taylor, Montgomery Clift besuchen ihn als Lehrmeister.

TODAY (1996/1997) lehnt sich ebenfalls am Fiction-Genre an. Die Protagonisten sprechen direkt zum Publikum, aber ihre scheinbar informativen Monologe sind absurd, offenbaren Brüche, überzeichnen die Wahrnehmung ins Unermessliche. Stille wird zur Katastrophe, der Plot scheitert – was ist wirklich passiert? In drei Episoden erzählen drei Personen ihre Version der Erinnerung und ihre Gefühle. Das scheinbar gleiche Erlebnis wird zum Auslöser widerstreitender Wirklichkeiten: Rollenkonflikte, Erinnerungen, das Hadern mit Konventionen und Lebensbedingungen in einer Kleinstadt, Kindheitserinnerungen und Beziehungen zwischen Vater und Tochter… Die Episoden sind in drei «Farben» gestimmt. Eine verzerrte Maske reisst uns in die Geschichte des Mädchens. Sie wirft einen Ball gegen eine gelbe Wand und erzählt lakonisch, trocken, abgeklärt, eigentümlich gefasst vom Unfall, ihrem Vater und seinem exaltierten Weinen, das seine Emotionen zu abgekapselten Entitäten, zum Spektakel werden lässt. Ihr Text richtet sich ans Publikum und mit ihr schauen wir dem Psychodrama des Vaters und ihren eigenen Widersprüchen zwischen kindlichem Spiel und abgeklärtem Statement zu: «Grossvater wurde alt. Er hat sich schon lange aus dem Berufsleben zurückgezogen. Mein Dad hat sich aus dem Leben zurückgezogen.»[4]

Veras Welt ist in Rot getaucht. Der Tod des Vaters überfällt sie in atemloser Bedrängnis über das versteinerte Leben in der Kleinstadt, das die Menschen

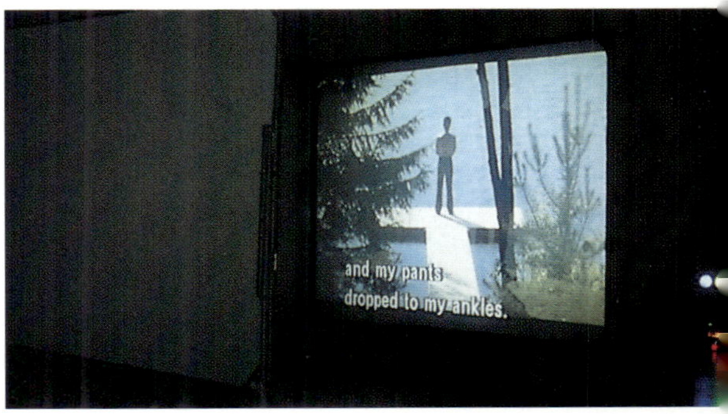

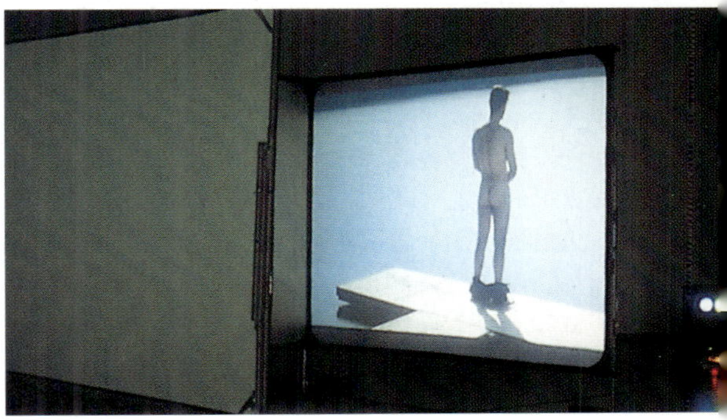

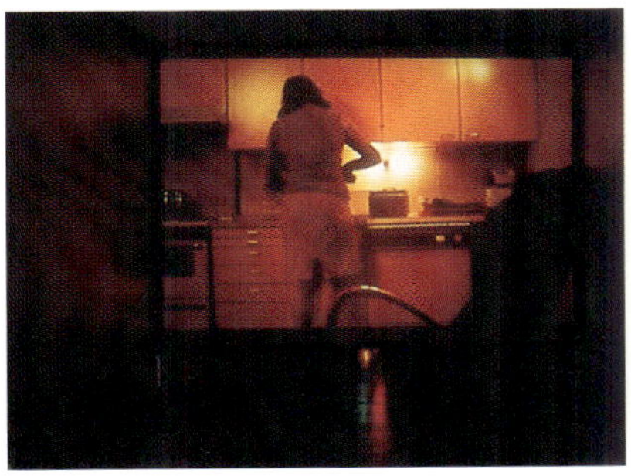

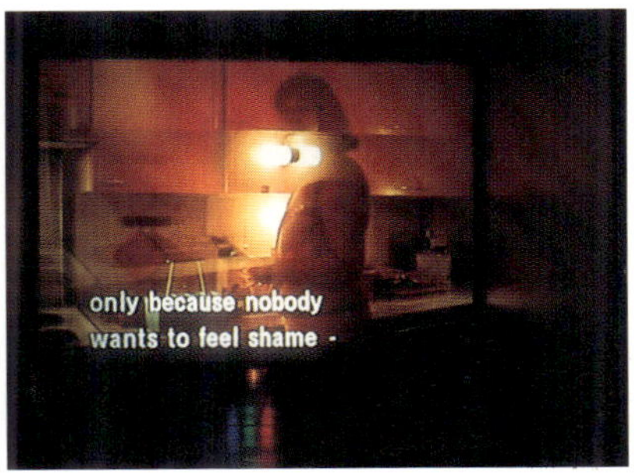

EIJA-LIISA AHTILA, TODAY / TÄNÄÄN, 1996–97, installation view, Kunsthaus Glarus, Switzerland, 1998, central screen (on the left) and righthand screen (above) / HEUTE, mittlere Leinwand (links) und rechte Leinwand (oben).

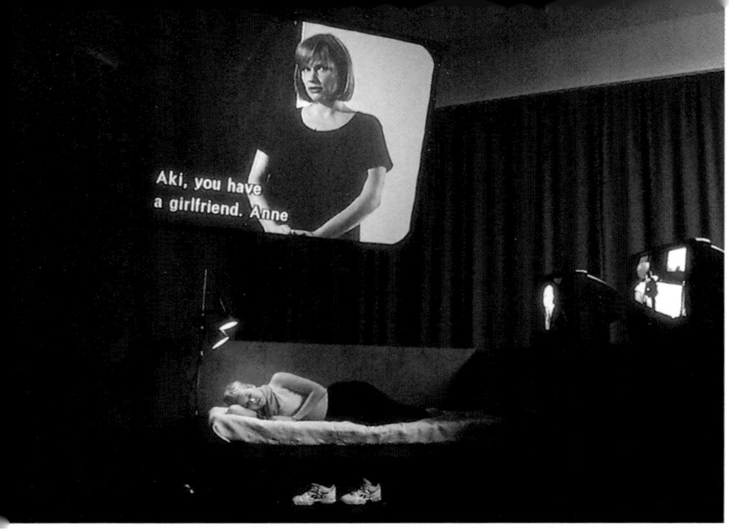

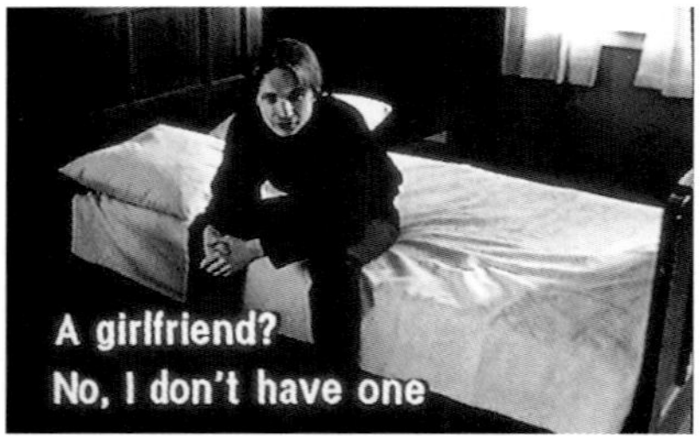

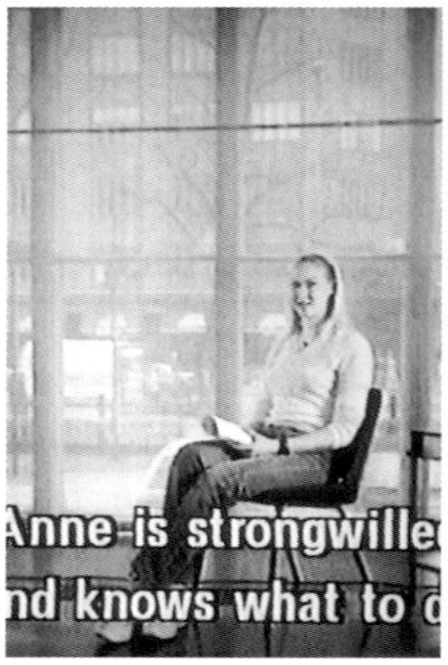

EIJA-LIISA AHTILA, ANNE, AKI & GOD, 1998, installation view at KIASMA, Museum for Contemporary Art, Helsinki, 1998, and film stills / Installationsansicht und Filmstills.

zu Masken ihrer selbst werden lässt und Gefühle, Begehren hinter automatisierten Handlungen versteckt. Sie raucht, hält den kleinbürgerlichen Haushalt in Ordnung: «Die Leute schlafen mindestens zweimal in der Woche miteinander, nur weil sich niemand schämen will – damit es halt getan ist.»[5] Im blau gestimmten Monolog des Vaters erscheint der Todesfall des Vaters wie eine verspätete Rache: «Und er erzählte mir wieder, dass mein Leben von einem Unfall zum nächsten treibt. Du kannst keine Entscheidungen treffen. Du kannst nicht einmal entscheiden, ob es gut oder schlecht war. (...) Und dann, wieder, geschah ein Unfall.»[6] Männliche Rollenmodelle scheitern, Berührungen und Gefühle sind verbotenes Gebiet. Die Füsse des Vaters werden von einem Hund geleckt, was er für seine Tochter sein soll, weiss er nicht. Wir schauen mit dem Mädchen zu, wie ihm am Wasser stehend die Hosen von den Hüften fallen...

Die wohl bekannteste Arbeit der Künstlerin IF 6 WAS 9 erinnert an Serienformen, die das Fernsehen «aus dem Leben» greift, in denen private Erlebniswelten veröffentlicht werden. Scheinbar authentisches Dokument, erzählen fünf junge Mädchen, Teenager, von ihrer ersten sexuellen Erfahrung oder Phantasie in drei parallelen Bildspuren. Ihre Handlungen, Texte und Bilder wandern von einer Bildspur zur nächsten, verbinden sich über die Tonspur oder greifen von einem Film in den anderen. Ihre Phantasien und Erzählungen verdichten sich zu einem grossen Text widersprüchlicher Rollenmodelle und Identitäten. Wohlerzogenes Klavierüben, Schulsport und gesellige Nachmittage im Spiel sind durchzogen von den sprachlich ebenso ernüchternd präzisen wie poetischen Schilderungen. Allesamt Laienschauspielerinnen sprechen sie Texte, die authentisch sein könnten, es aber nicht sind. Sie sprechen Texte, die das Archiv allgemeiner kultureller und medialer Prägungen spiegeln, die zwischen Altklugheit und Naivität oszillieren und das gesamte Feld von halbwissender Phantasieleistung, Mediengeprägtheit und pubertierender Versponnenheit abstecken. Ihre unmaskierte und unverblümte Direktheit kollidiert mit dem beschaulichen Alltag braver Schulmädchen, aber auch mit den Phantasien der Betrachter, die sich in der Unschuld, Offenheit und aufblühenden Weiblichkeit verfangen. Vorstellungen, Erfahrungen, Reife und Unschuld vermischen sich in einem ungeklärten, aber gleichzeitig abgeklärten Rollenverständnis. Denn die erste Erfahrung realisiert das gesamte Repertoire kultureller Kenntnisse und Erkenntnisse, man ist dann «älter», so alt wie Rollenmodelle und Konventionen eben sind. «Hier sitze ich, die Beine gespreizt, wie ein kleines Mädchen, das noch nichts über Sex weiss, das keine Ahnung davon hat, dass eine Frau ihre intimen Bereiche und ihre Lust verbergen muss. Tatsächlich bin ich 38 Jahre alt. Ich habe die Brüste einer Frau und Lippen, die sich reizvoll öffnen. Ich tarne meine Aggressionen auf sehr weibliche Art.»[7]

Die drei Schwarzweissfilme ME/WE, OKAY und GRAY machen Anleihen beim Werbeclip: Während

90 Sekunden überfallen drei atemlose Kurzfilme den Betrachtenden, danach ist lange Pause, bis der nächste Super-GAU der Wahrnehmungsüberforderung einsetzt. Der Ausgangsplot ist das Ereignis eines Atomunfalls. Angesiedelt zwischen Waschmittelwerbung und Heimvideo breiten sich die surrealen Dialoge, misslungenen Kommunikationsmuster und Beziehungen aus, die eine Frau, ein Mann und eine Gruppe von Frauen im Niemandsland ihrer persönlichen Erfahrung dabei durchleben. Der Ort: überall. Die psychische Befindlichkeit: zeitgenössische Unmöglichkeit. Mit sich überschlagender Geschwindigkeit vermischen sich Realität, Fiktion und die Identitäten der Protagonisten. Die äussere Krise ist die Krise der Identität. In ME/WE spricht ein Mann über die Veränderungen, die seine Familie, seine Beziehungen durch das Ereignis erfahren haben. Aber alle Beteiligten leben nur seinen Text. Die Tochter, der Sohn, die Frau sprechen lippensynchron in der Stimme des Mannes, sie sind Spiegel seines Selbst, besetzt mit s e i n e n Emotionen, s e i n e n Wahrnehmungen, s e i n e n Interpretationen. Sie sind all die anderen, die eine Rolle spielen im eigenen Selbst. In OKAY steigern sich das Eingeschlossensein in den häuslichen Kontext, unerfülltes sexuelles Begehren, die Grenzen sprachlicher Mitteilung zu einer surrealen Version von Rilkes Gedicht vom Panther, der im Käfig seine sinnlosen Kreise zieht. Die Frau spricht in der eigenen und der Stimme des Mannes: «Wenn ich nur könnte, würde ich mich in einen Hund verwandeln. Ich würde bellen und alles beissen, was sich bewegt. Wauwau. Wauwau. Wauwau.»[8] Aggression, Selbstverurteilung, Hass, Verzweiflung stimmen ein in den monotonen Singsang des «It's okay. It's okay. It's okay», das als musikalisches Moment die drei Filmspuren zusammenbindet und den atemlosen Rhythmus zu beruhigen versucht. In GRAY sind drei Frauen nach der Katastrophe an einem Unort, in einer Art Aufzug, gefangen, was sie gezwungenermassen zu einer Gruppe zwischen wissenschaftlicher Analyse und persönlichem Ausgeliefertsein zusammenschweisst. Hier sind «Alle beruhigenden Geräusche (...) ungenügend.»[9] Eine Tasse fällt in Zeitlupe, ein weisses Laken breitet sich aus, Frauen schweben im Wasser.

Die Erwartung, im Kino würde über das Leben erzählt, verknüpft mit der Illusion des Kinos auch die Vorstellung, dass sich die Erzählung des Films anderswo – etwa im Leben – fortsetzen lässt. Das Erzählen in Bildern jedoch stösst an die Grenzen der Schrift, die unsere Gedächtnisleistungen an die Ordnung des Sukzessiven bindet. In den sprachlich, bildlich und auditiv komplexen Filmwerken Eija-Liisa Ahtilas erzählt das «Kino» nicht vom Leben, sondern es konstruiert Symbole, Konstellationen von Bedeutungen und Modellen, die das Reale so geschickt überzeichnen und als Surreales offenbaren, dass wir auf die Realität gestossen werden. Die «Macht» ihrer Bilder verführt nicht a u s der Wirklichkeit, sondern führt ü b e r sie hinaus zu einem möglichen neuen Massstab subjektiver Wirklichkeit. «It's okay. It's okay. It's okay.»

1) "Today my dad's crying. Last night a car drove over his dad who died instantly. (...) Maybe it's not my dad who's crying—but someone else's dad. Sanna's dad, Mia's dad, Marko's dad, Pasi's dad—or Vera's dad. I'm in an armchair. I have a boyfriend. I have something on my lap. I'm 66 years old."
2) "Aki V resigned from his work as a computer application support with Nokia Virtuals, became ill with schizophrenia and isolated himself in his one room flat. His mind started to produce a reality of its own in sounds and visions. Little by little this fiction became flesh and blood, the line between reality and imagination became blurred. Fantasized persons and events stepped out of Aki V's head and became parallel with the reality around him. The leading character in this new world was Anne Nyberg, Aki's fiancée."
3) "Then Aki was informed that his main duty in the future would be being in charge of Hollywood because Hollywood controlled all emotional fantasies of human beings."
4) "Granddad had lived to be old. He had long retired from working life. My dad had retired from life."
5) "People make love at least twice a week—only because nobody wants to feel shame—and that it's done."
6) "And he talked to me again—that 'your life is just drifting from one accident to another,' you can't even decide, you can't even decide—whether they've been good or bad. (...) And then, again, an accident happened."
7) "Here I sit with my legs apart—like a small girl who has not learned anything about sex. Who has no idea of the fact—that a woman must hide her private parts and lust. In fact I am 38 years old, I have a woman's breasts and labia which open beautifully. I tend to disguise my aggression in a very feminine fashion."
8) "And I think that if I could only change myself, I would transform myself into a dog and I would bark and bite everything that moves... Woof Woof...Woof Woof..."
9) "All the sounds of comfort are insufficient."

EIJA-LIISA AHTILA, IF 6 WAS 9, 1995, installation view, Kunsthaus Glarus, Switzerland, 1998 / WENN 6 9 WÄRE.

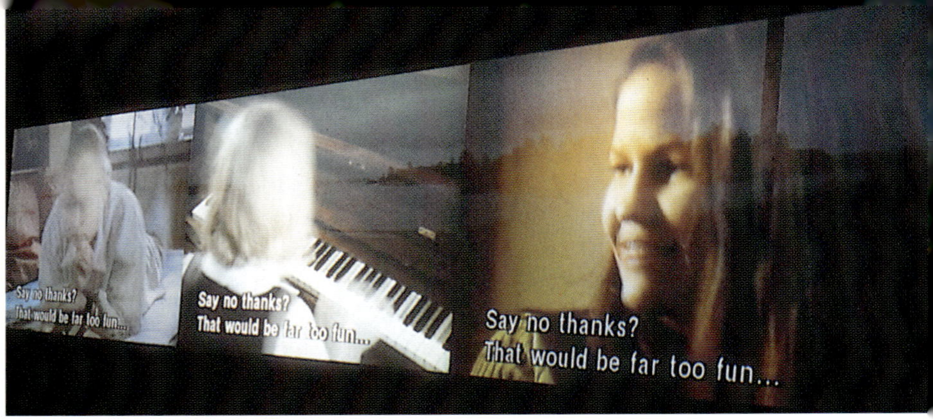

HYBRID REALITIES

EIJA-LIISA AHTILA'S "HUMAN DRAMAS"

BEATRIX RUF

"Today my dad's crying. Last night a car drove over his dad who died instantly." These are the first words spoken by the young girl in Eija-Liisa Ahtila's film trilogy, TODAY. Her last words are: "Maybe it's not my dad who's crying—but someone else's dad. Sanna's dad, Mia's dad, Marko's dad, Pasi's dad—or Vera's dad. I'm in an armchair. I have a boyfriend. I have something on my lap. I'm 66 years old." The quotations embrace the entire scope of Eija-Liisa Ahtila's film-based artistic work: Her unsentimental and disarmingly direct scenes show real or potentially real situations of ordinary life, whose logical processes and experiences are broken by surreal, asynchronous, and alogical sequences.

Video, film, and the new digital media are familiar means of expression for many artists and above all for the generations that have grown up with the ubiquitous presence of television, movies, commercials, and MTV. Our experience of ourselves and reality has been influenced by contemporary visual culture in myriad ways. Pictures have become a constitutive part of our reality. The loss of reality through the media was already an issue at the beginning of this century but the perfection of the mass media, the privatization of producing images, of transferring reality to films and pictures have since seen rampant growth. Baudrillard spoke of a pornographic dimension in the omnipresence of potential reproduction—pornographic because of the possibility of unlimited depiction: the picture as the determining factor of reality, both private and public. The categories of fiction and reality have become obsolete. Even the construction of our self is affected, for it has to stake out a position in the face of ambivalent realities: between private and medially transmitted public pictures of the subject, between controlled reality and the individual construction of reality. The subject can now be grasped only as a bundle of multiple configurations, concepts, and dramaturgical elements and, above all, only in relation to its medial representations.

The Finnish artist Eija-Liisa Ahtila (b. 1959) works with the conditions and consequences of our visual culture and questions today's positioning of the subject. Since the end of the eighties she has produced a

BEATRIX RUF is the director of the Kunsthaus Glarus. She lives in Glarus and Zurich.

complex oeuvre that covers the entire range of visual culture. She has made a name for herself in photography, performance, films in video format, and most recently in video installations. Her last four film shorts—ME/WE, OKAY, GRAY (1993, 90 seconds), IF 6 WAS 9 (1995, 10 minutes), TODAY (1996/1997, 10 minutes) and ANNE, AKI AND GOD (1998, 2 x 15 minute loops)—were shot with a film camera and transferred to video. Ahtila presents these "human dramas," as she calls them, in parallel tracks that fragment the narrative into several episodes and intricately composed pieces. The artist works with visual overkill and an obscurity of narrative line. Places, people, voices, rhythms change from one film level to another and create a nonlinear narrative flow. The combination of text, soundtrack, and image is the result of great deliberation and meticulous implementation, in which the film levels each exert an independent and contradictory impact that may break up the logic of the other elements or generate new meanings. Pictures and words toy with their ability to lie or tell the truth. The original Finnish soundtrack sounds seductive and strange, while the text in the translated subtitles becomes a visual component that unites the parallel pictorial levels.

The fragmentation of the narrative level and the installative form of her works formally reflects on a changed understanding of the concept of the subject and the notion of an undivided self, which must reconfigure its roles, patterns, and forms in the context of social and political globalization.

Eija-Liisa Ahtila's films explore the treasure chest of human experience. They are both personal and universal because her stories, her incidents could happen anywhere. Life in cities, school, home, puberty, sexuality, married life, recreation. We experience the fragility of normality: normality alienates. Ahtila's protagonists speak in the voice of their fictional others, they play themselves and address the public. Rituals of speech become musical rhythms; floundering communication leads to grotesque interpretations and switching of roles. The constraints of convention, emotional ties, and loneliness are just as menacing as the threat of nuclear catastrophe. People are harried by the heterogeneous array of reality: the uncertainty of life styles and role models, the flood of information, and questionable realities.

The nature of contemporary daily experience is exposed in her texts and incisively composed pictorial worlds. Like other artists of the nineties, Eija-Liisa Ahtila explores the crumbling boundary between public and private, and the media productions that contribute to it: confessional talk shows, soap operas, real-time series. A taut precision of means moves the private world of her works into the political arena. Her public disclosure of ordinary personal worlds never sinks into intimate revelations, confessional orgies, or melodramatic faux catharsis. In cinematic terms, the artist weaves the effects and styles of common genres—the short, the commercial, the documentary, the Hollywood feature film—into a new world of her own invention, which alienates the familiar and eludes classification. Ahtila's transgression of the classical media makes her work "incompatible" with the conventional marketing strategy of film/video/art media, but also with the preconceived categorization of perception: fiction, documentary, avant-garde cinema? Eija-Liisa Ahtila works with a cinematographic sense of form. Familiar figures crop up: Jean-Luc Godard, Chantal Akerman, but also Aki Kaurismäki; prevailing collective cinematic idioms are exploited and yet the imagery resists stylistic determination. Ahtila's films are precisely constructed hybrids, which preserve their autonomy in familiar contexts. This leads to the logical consequence of works in different formats: as a film, for example, that can be distributed via the usual channels of television and cinema, or as separate installations that create situations in the art context in which we experience the moving images as life-sized others or are immersed in narrative ensembles. Eija-Liisa Ahtila's works set in at the exact interface of the filmic ambivalence between the possibility of fiction and the promise of photography to document reality. The filmic image in her works is set off against the film.

As a rule the artist starts with a "document" of reality: a story, a newspaper clipping, a historical event... If we compare Ahtila's works to the videos of her artist colleague Sam Taylor-Wood, one might speak of the "theatricality" of human reality in the latter oeuvre as opposed to the issue of authenticity as a super-reality that mutates into sur-reality in the former.

Eija-Liisa Ahtila's most recent production, ANNE, AKI AND GOD, epitomizes her artistic approach. Based on recordings of therapy sessions, the film script explicitly addresses a contemporary version of identity disturbance. This self-contained video installation also provides the source material for a full-length feature film, now in production, titled *A Quest for a Woman*. Drawing on the experiences of Aki, who is suffering from a new form of medically uncharted schizophrenia and has created his own "woman" in a state of psychosis, the film sets up a multiple identity in the form of a casting situation in which several actors play the part of Aki. Flanked by the live women models of their imagination, they recite their lines with a disturbing uniformity. "Aki V resigned from his work as a computer application support with Nokia Virtuals, became ill with schizophrenia, and isolated himself in his one room flat. His mind started to produce a reality of its own in sounds and visions. Little by little this fiction became flesh and blood, the line between reality and imagination became blurred. Fantasized persons and events stepped out of Aki V's head and became parallel with the reality around him. The leading character in this new world was Anne Nyberg, Aki's fiancée."

But Aki's task, assigned to him by God, is not restricted to looking for his fiancée; he must also prepare himself for a future responsibility: "Then Aki was informed that his main duty in the future would be being in charge of Hollywood because Hollywood controlled all emotional fantasies of human beings." He is instructed by Madonna, Marlon Brando, Elizabeth Taylor, and Montgomery Clift.

TODAY (1996/1997) is also indebted to the genre of fiction. The protagonists speak directly to the audience, but their seemingly informative monologues are absurd, obvious ruptures of immeasurably exaggerated perceptions. Silence becomes a catastrophe, the plot fails—what really happened? In three episodes, three people talk about their version of memory and their feelings. The same experience yields contradictory realities: conflicting roles, memories, contending with the conventions and living conditions in a small town, childhood memories, and the relationship between father and daughter... The episodes are tuned in three "colors." A distorted mask thrusts us into the girl's story. She is throwing a ball at a yellow wall (this activity runs through all three tracks). Laconically detached and unsettlingly self-controlled, she tells us about the accident, about her father and his exalted tears so that the emotions become encapsulated entities, mere spectacle. Her words are directed to the audience and we join her in looking at her father's psychodrama and at her own contradiction between child's play and aloof statement: "Granddad had lived to be old. He had long retired from working life. My dad had retired from life."

Vera's world is bathed in red. The death of her father overwhelms her in the breathless constraints of fossilized small town life, which turns people into masks of themselves and hides feelings and desires behind automated actions. She smokes and keeps house: "People make love at least twice a week—only because nobody wants to feel shame—and that it's done." In the father's blue-toned monologue, his father's death appears as belated revenge: "And he talked to me again—that 'your life is just drifting from one accident to another,' you can't even decide, you can't even decide—whether they've been good or bad. (...) And then, again, an accident happened." Male role models fail; feelings and touch are forbidden territory. A dog licks his father's feet; he himself does not know what he is supposed to be for his daughter. Together with the girl, we watch him standing at the water's edge with his pants falling down.

The artist's best-known piece, IF 6 WAS 9, is reminiscent of "live" TV series in which private worlds are made public. In what appears to be an authentic document, five teen-age girls recount their first sexual experience or fantasy in three parallel visual tracks. Their actions, words, and the pictures wander from one track to the next, are linked together via the soundtrack, or interfere with each other from one film to another. Their individual fantasies and stories merge into one overriding statement on contradictory role models and identities. Obedient piano practice, school athletics, and social afternoons at play alternate with descriptions as soberingly precise as they are poetic. These lay performers all speak lines that could be authentic but aren't. Their lines mirror the inventory of general cultural and medial conditioning which oscillates between precocity and naïveté and covers the entire field of semi-knowledgeable fantasy, media indoctrination, and adolescent quirkiness. Their undisguised and uninhibited directness clashes with the uneventful life of the well-behaved schoolgirl but also with the fantasies of viewers who become enmeshed in their innocence, openness, and blossoming womanhood. Imagination, experience, maturity, and innocence merge in a still ambivalent though detached understanding of role because the first experience embodies the entire repertoire of cultural knowledge and insight. The experience has made them "older," as old as the role models and conventions they have grown up with. "Here I sit with my legs apart—like a small girl who has not learned anything about sex. Who has no idea of the fact—that a woman must hide her private parts and lust. In fact I am 38 years old, I have a woman's breasts and labia which open beautifully. I tend to disguise my aggression in a very feminine fashion."

The three black and white films ME/WE, OKAY, GRAY are indebted to the genre of the commercial: the viewer is bombarded for 90 seconds by these breathless shorts shown simultaneously on separate monitors, followed by a long break before the catastrophic assault on perception repeats itself again. The point of departure is a nuclear disaster. In something like a cross between a commercial for a detergent and a home video, the personal experiences of people involved in the catastrophe emerge in an array of surreal dialogues, patterns of breakdowns in communication, and deteriorating relationships. The place: everywhere; the psychic condition: contemporary impossibility. Reality, fiction, and the identities of the protagonists blend into each other at breakneck speed. The external crisis is the crisis of identity. In ME/WE, a man describes how his family and his relationships have changed since the event. But the members of his family live only in his text. The daughter, the son, the wife lip-synch the voice of the man; they are mirrors of his self, fitted with *his* emotions, *his* perceptions, *his* interpretations. They are all those others who play a role in our own selves. In OKAY, the confinement of domesticity, unfulfilled sexual desire, and the limitations of verbal communication converge in a surreal version of Rilke's poem of a caged panther forever pacing in meaningless circles. A woman speaks in her own and in her husband's voice: "And I think that if I could only change myself, I would transform myself into a dog and I would bark and bite everything that moves... Woof Woof... Woof Woof..." Aggression, self-condemnation, hate, and despair resonate in the singsong monotony of "It's okay. It's okay. It's okay"—the musical factor that unites all three tracks and attempts to calm the frantic rhythm. In GRAY, three woman are in a non-place after the catastrophe, caught in a kind of elevator which forces them into a togetherness that sways between scientific analysis and the consequences of being at their own mercy where "all the sounds of comfort are insufficient." A cup falls in slow motion, a white sheet spreads out, women float in the water.

The assumption that the movies tell us about life links cinematic illusion with the idea that the story of the film might continue elsewhere, in real life, for instance. However, narration in pictures shares with writing the limitation of binding the mnemonic performance to a successive order. Eija-Liisa Ahtila's complex linguistic, visual, and aural "movies" do not tell us about life; they construct symbols, clusters of meanings and models, which so skillfully exaggerate and reveal the sur-reality of reality that reality is thrust upon us. The "power" of her imagery does not lure us away from reality but beyond it back to a potential measure of subjective reality. "It's okay. It's okay. It's okay."

(Translation: Catherine Schelbert)

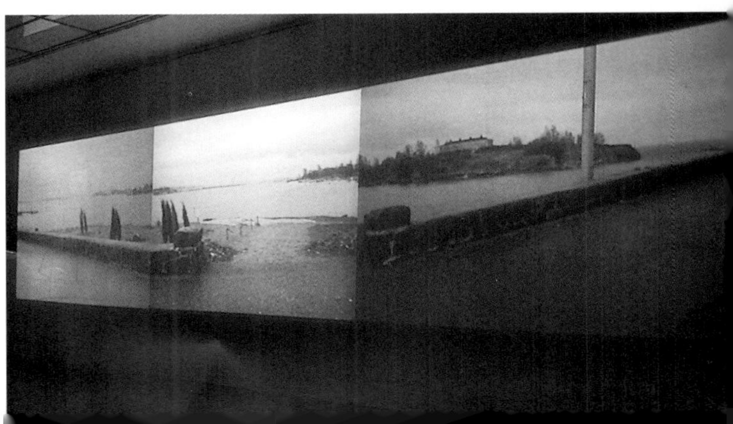

EIJA-LIISA AHTILA, IF 6 WAS 9, 1995, installation view, Kunsthaus Glarus, Switzerland, 1998 / WENN 6 9 WÄRE.

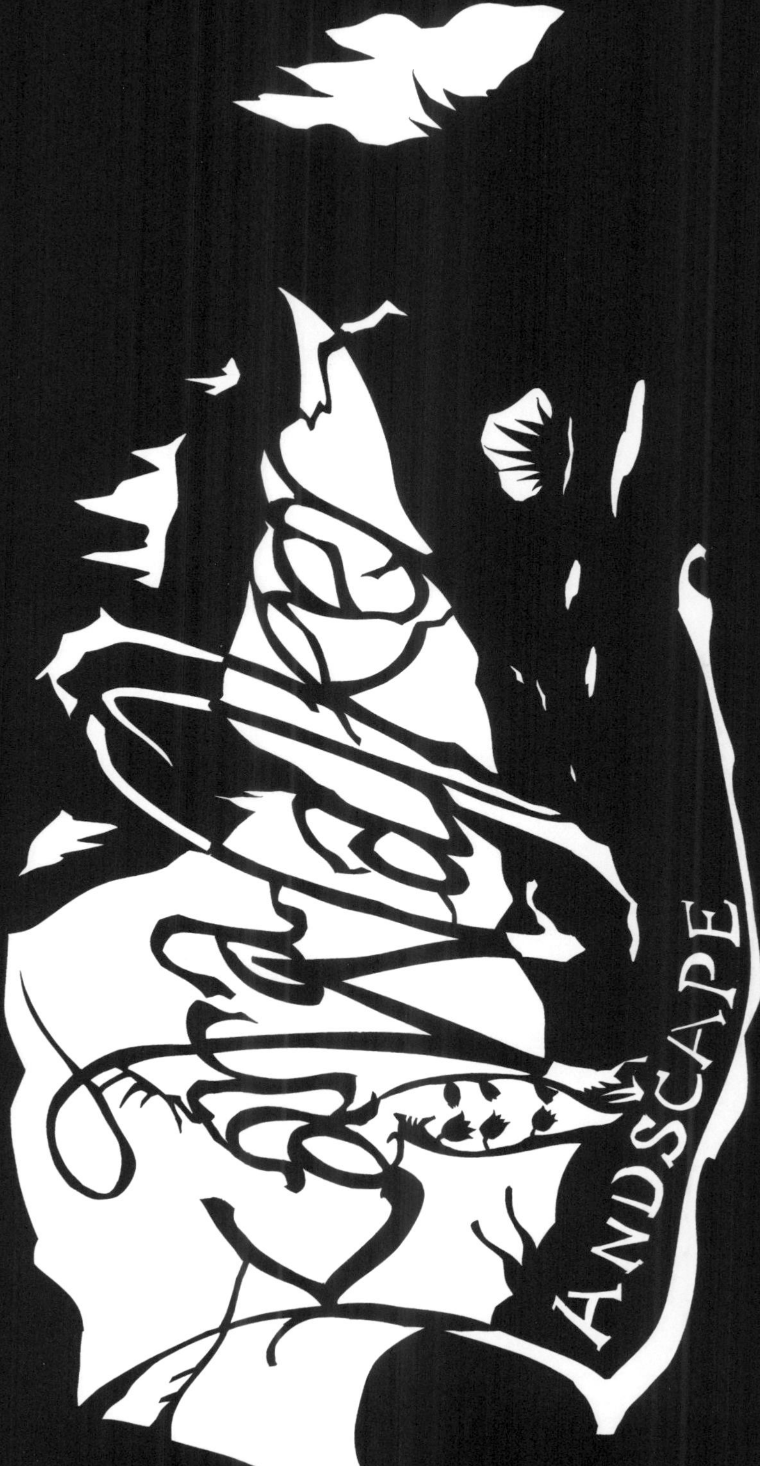
ANDSCAPE

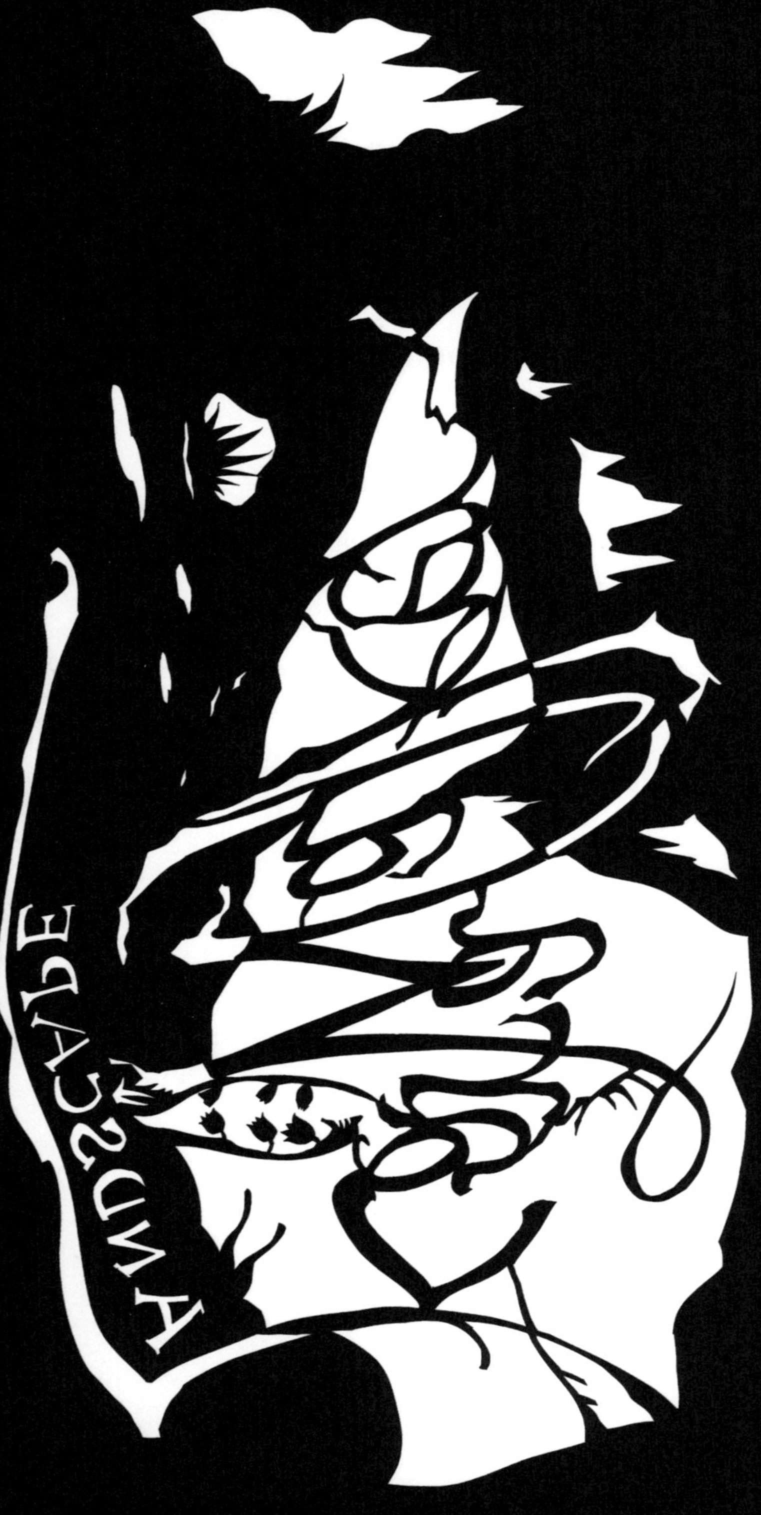
LANDSCAPE

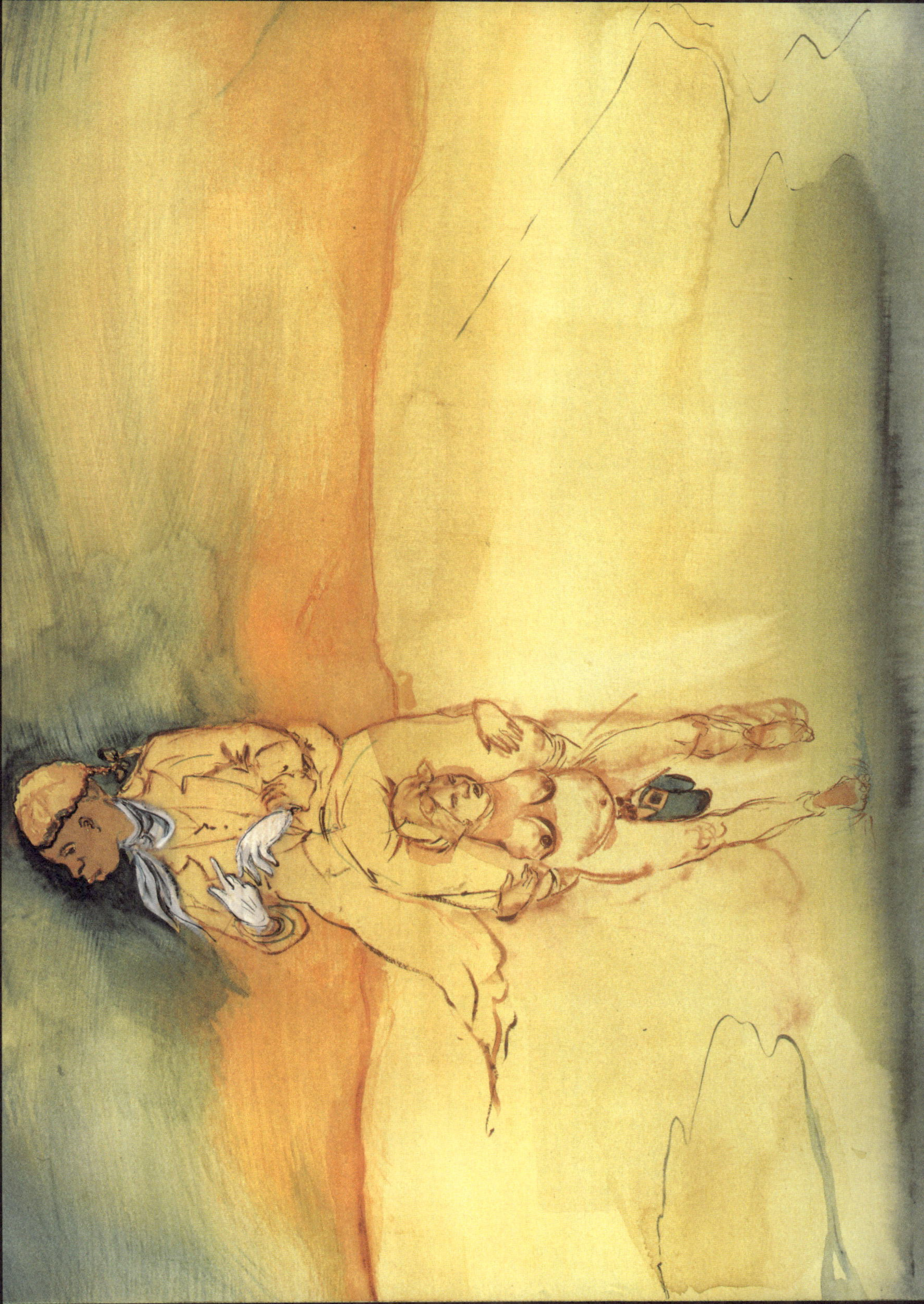

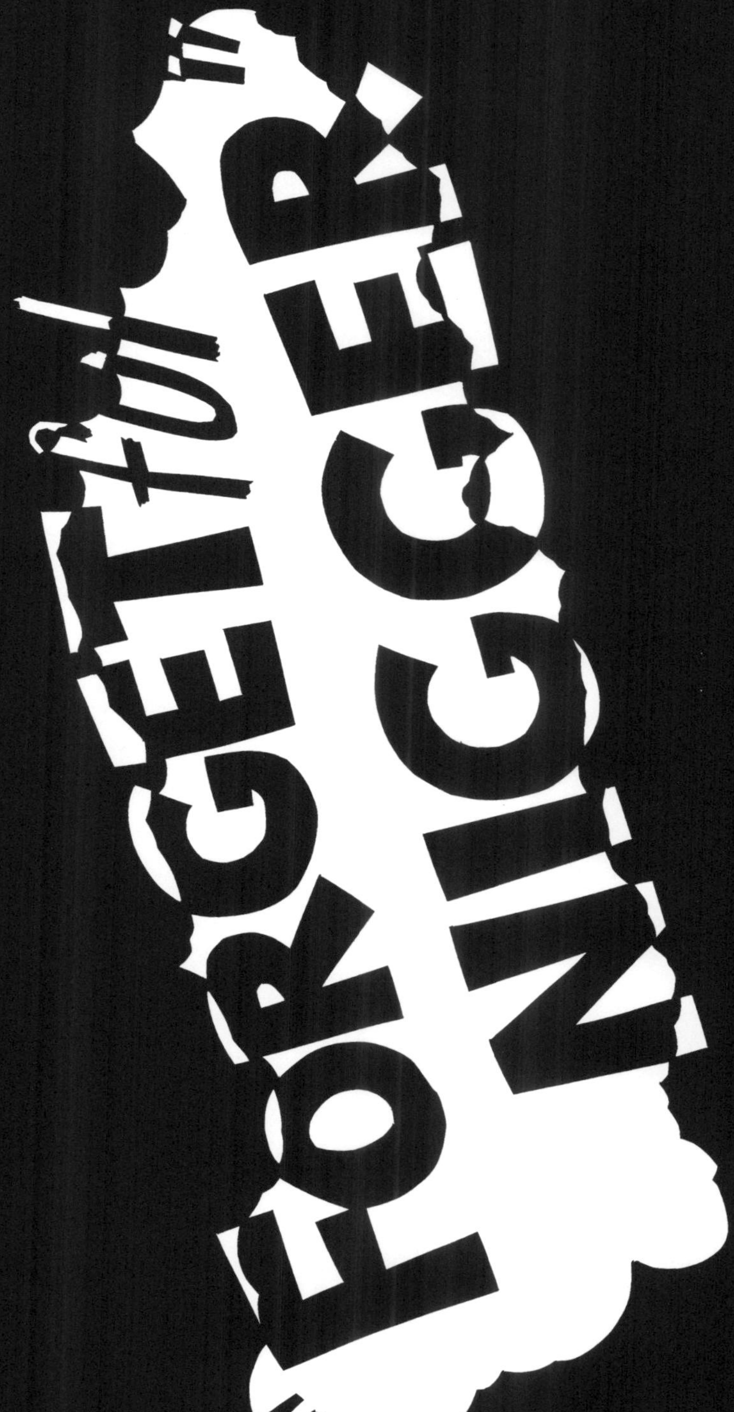
FÖRGETful
NIGGER

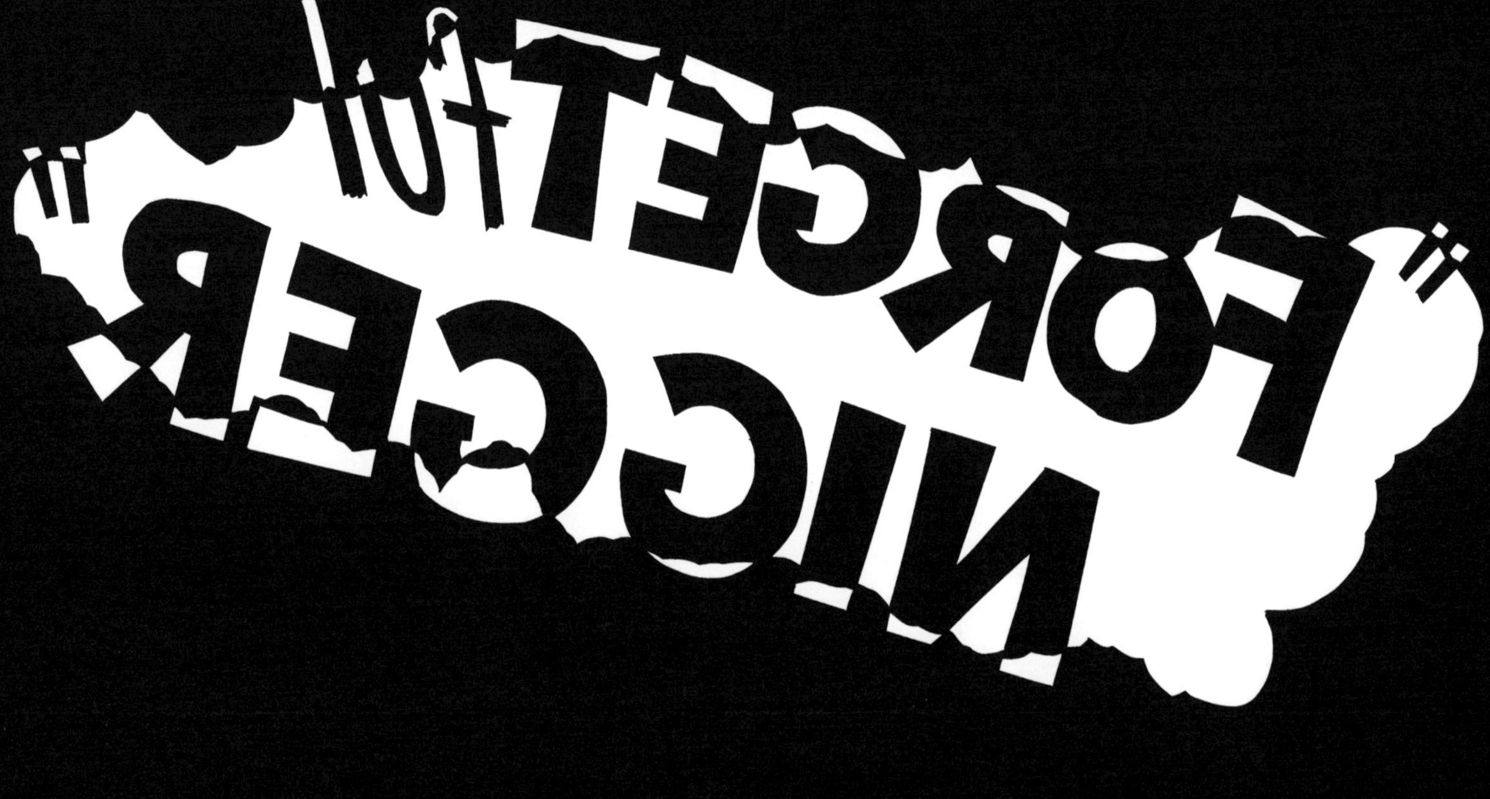
NIGGER, FORGET

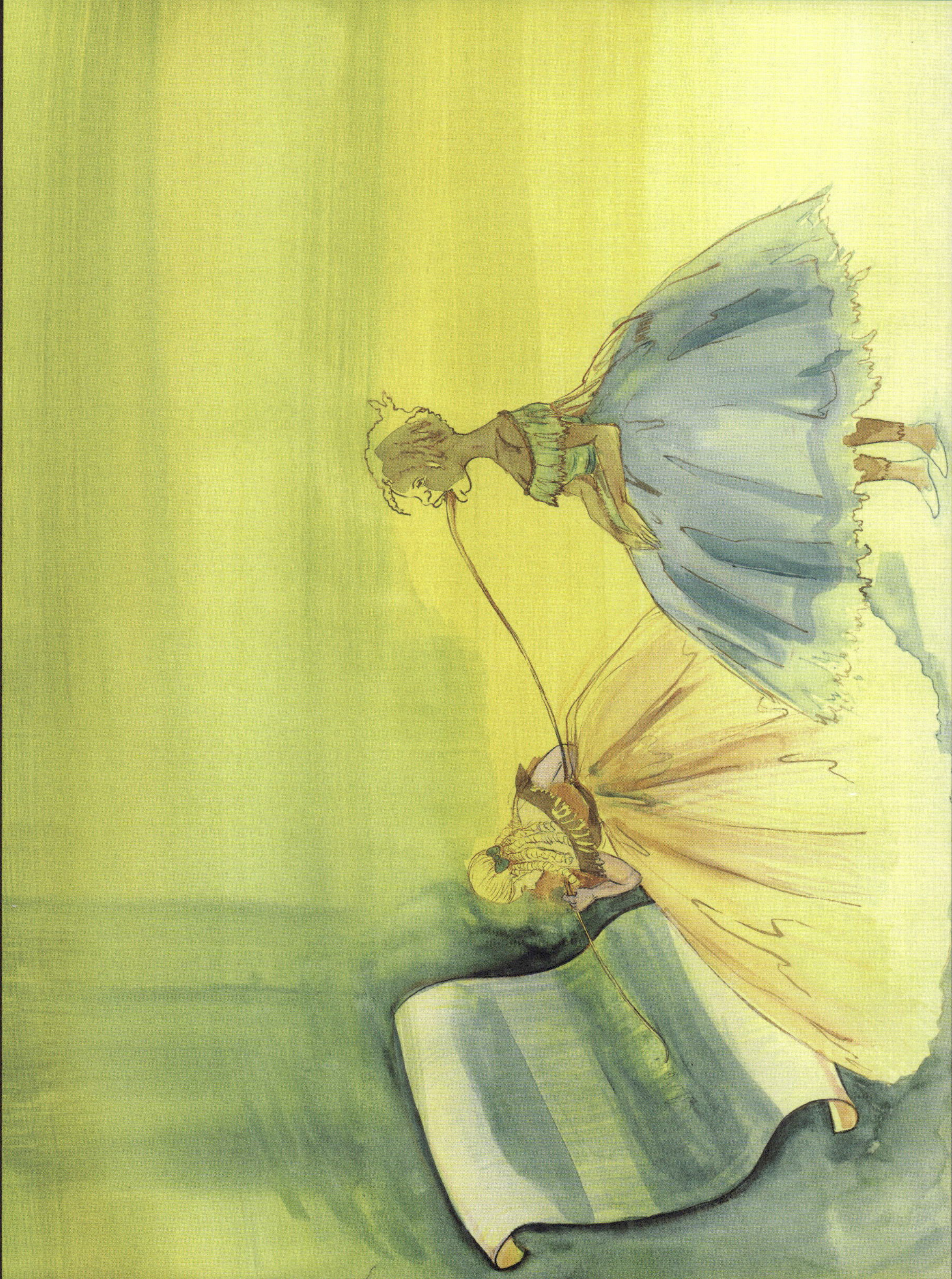

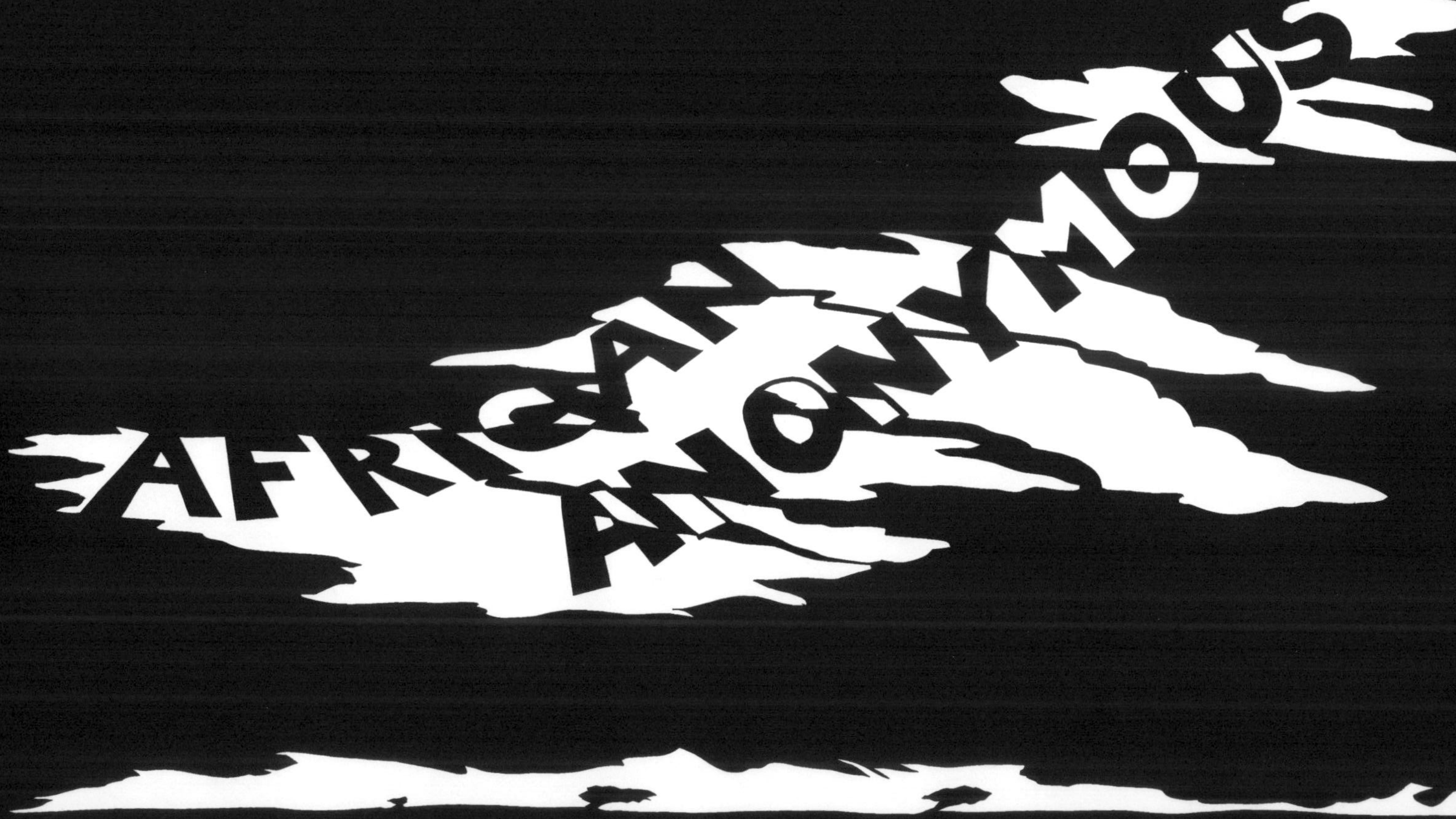
AFRICAN
ANONYMOUS

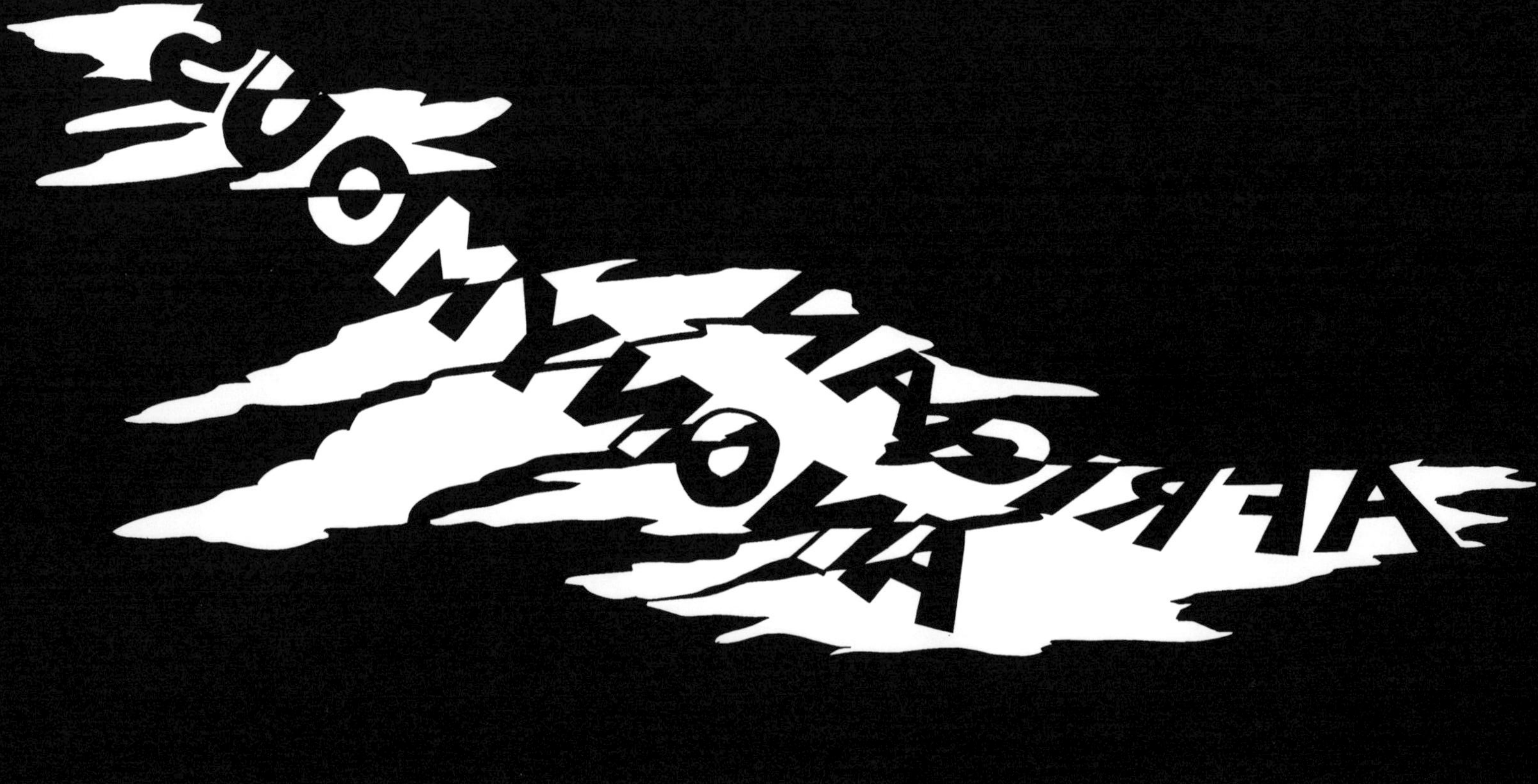
AFRICAN
ANONYMOUS

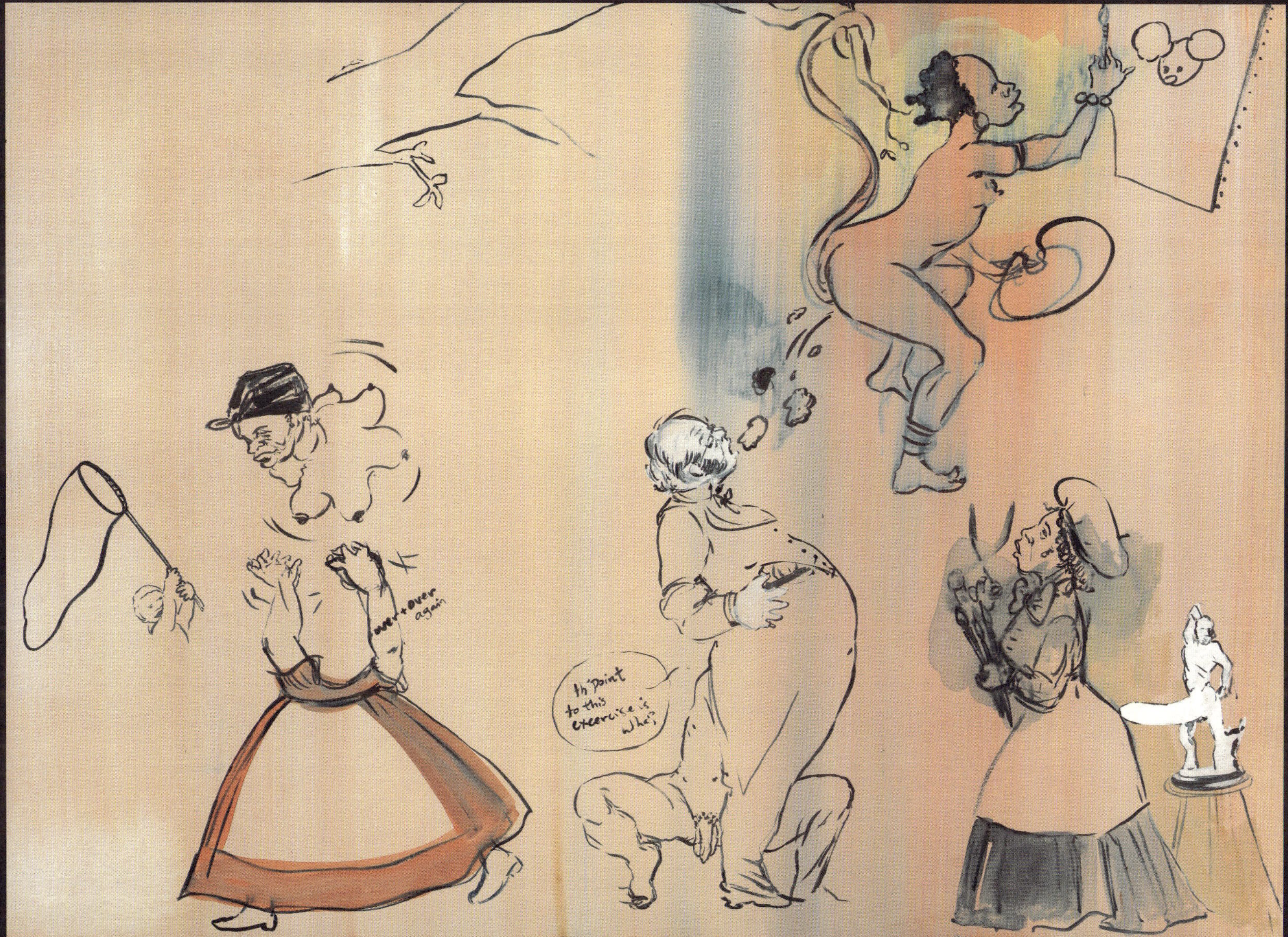
over + over again
th' point to this exercise is what?

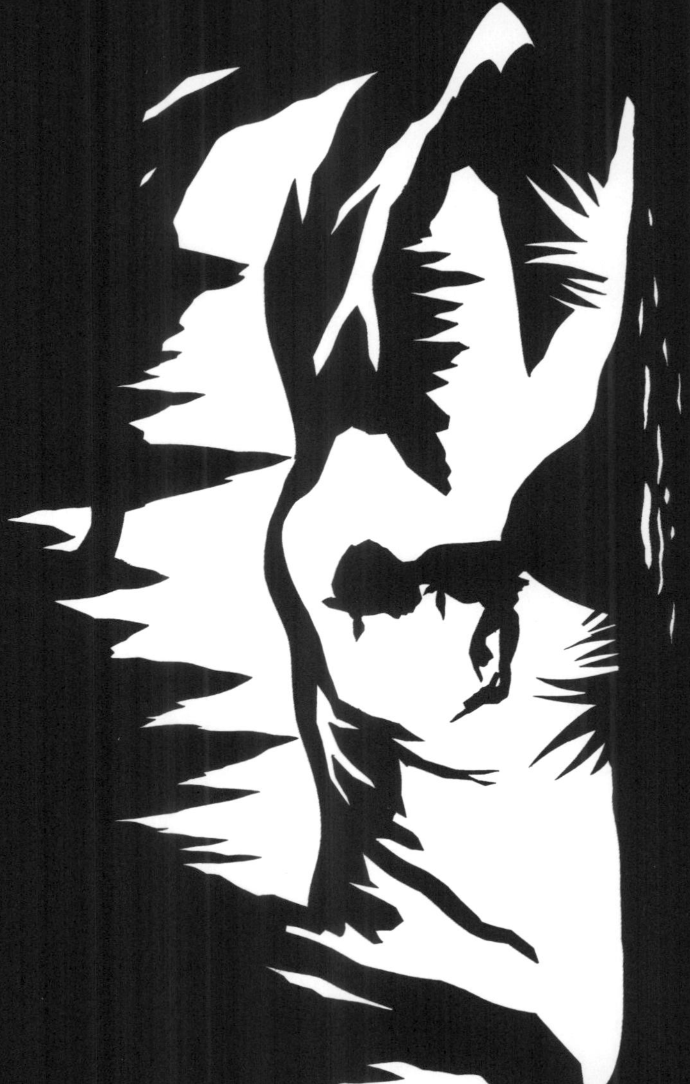

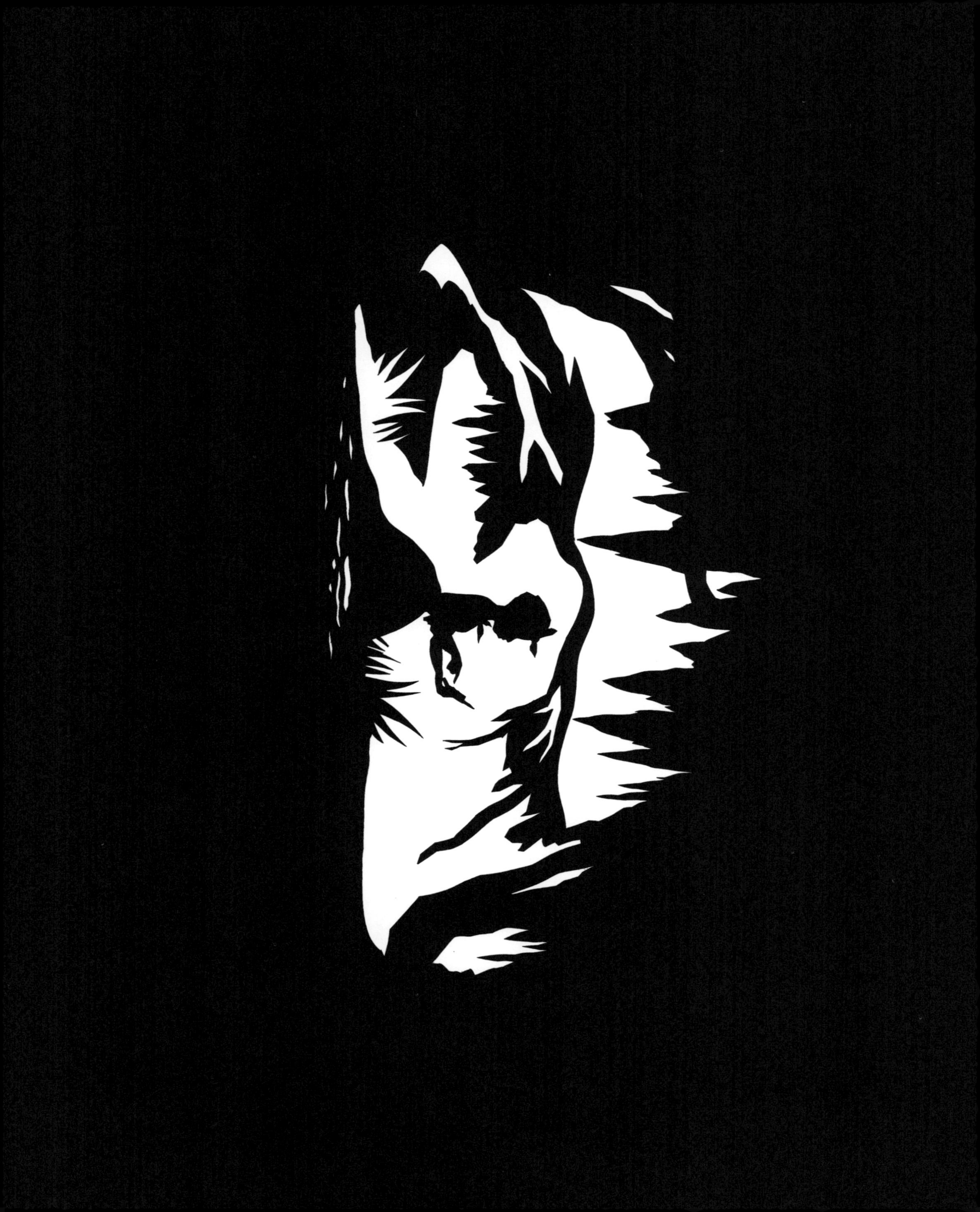

KARA WALKER, INSERT FOR PARKETT NO. 55, 1999

CUMULUS

Aus Europa

IN JEDER AUSGABE VON PARKETT PEILT EINE CUMULUS-WOLKE AUS AMERIKA UND EINE AUS EUROPA DIE INTERESSIERTEN KUNSTFREUNDE AN. SIE TRÄGT PERSÖNLICHE RÜCKBLICKE, BEURTEILUNGEN UND DENKWÜRDIGE BEGEGNUNGEN MIT SICH – ALS JEWEILS GANZ EIGENE DARSTELLUNG EINER BERUFSMÄSSIGEN AUSEINANDERSETZUNG.

IN DIESEM HEFT ÄUSSERN SICH MICHELLE NICOL, KUNSTKRITIKERIN UND FREIE KURATORIN AUS ZÜRICH, UND SUELY ROLNIK, PSYCHOANALYTIKERIN UND PROFESSORIN FÜR KLINISCHE PSYCHOLOGIE AN DER KATHOLISCHEN UNIVERSITÄT VON SAÕ PAULO.

Der Originalbegriff ist obsolet geworden

MICHELLE NICOL

Wurm versus Forester

Was jetzt kommt, ist eine Geschichte, die die unermüdlich beschworene Gültigkeit des Originalitäts-Axioms befragen will – ein allerletztes Mal. Kennen Sie *Self Service*? Wenn Sie Kleidermoden, die Vorführung von Lebensstilen und deren ironisierte Heilsversprechen mögen, wenn es Sie amüsiert, Menschen abgebildet zu sehen, die auf ihrem eigenen Balkon lange braune Lederhandschuhe von Hermés tragen, dann lautet die Antwort wahrscheinlich: Ja. *Self Service* ist eine Zeitschrift, die von den aktuellsten Moden ausgeht, sie zu absurden Höchstleistungen provoziert und dabei deren Widersprüchlichkeiten aufzeigt.

Die im Oktober 1998 erschienene Ausgabe Nr. 8 bearbeitete das Thema Absurdität. Hier findet sich eine Photostrasse mit dem lapidaren Titel «A bit of fur on a jacket or a skirt adds a little rock and roll» (Etwas Pelz auf Jacke oder Jupe verleiht dem Ganzen einen Hauch von Rock'n'Roll). Ihre erste Absicht besteht nicht weiter überraschend darin, Markenwerte zu standardisieren und Konsumpräferenzen festzulegen. Diese Bilder agieren mit einer minimal gesetzten Situationskomik, mit der Defunktion von Alltagsgegenständen und mit der Beweisführung, dass die abgebildeten Models/Menschen nichts als eine beliebige anthropomorphe Skulpturmasse sind. Die Absurdität und absolute Sinnlosigkeit der gestelzten Posen, die mit Ernsthaftigkeit vorgetragen werden, erheitern. Aber gleichzeitig führen sie Kleider vor,

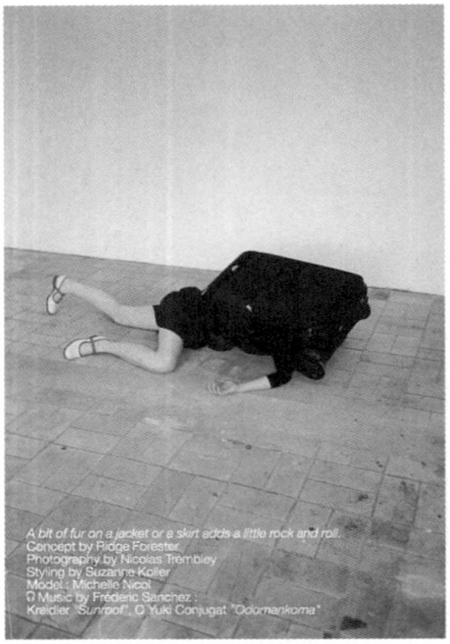

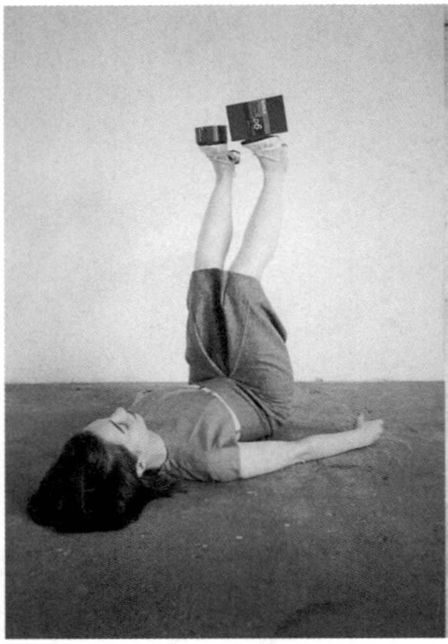

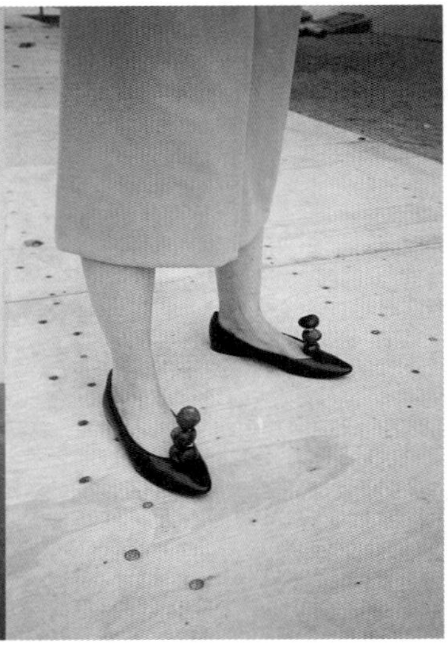

einfach so. Bild 1: Eine Frau liegt mit verrenkten Gliedmassen auf einem Steinboden. Sie trägt ein schwarzes Top und einen schwarzen Faltenjupe von Martine Sitbon, dazu flache Mary Janes in Beige, Grau, Rot. Oberkörper und Kopf sind von einem schwarzen Reisekoffer bedeckt. Bild 2: Ein Betonboden mit einer Frau, die auf dem Rücken liegt. Sie hält die Beine in die Höhe. Auf ihren waagrecht gehaltenen Füssen stehen eine Rolle braunes Klebeband und eine graue Videokassetten-Hülle. Sie trägt ein bläulich grünes Wollkleid mit hoher Taille von Alexander McQueen für Givenchy und elastische Schuhe in gebrochenem Weiss von Zucca. Bild 3: Zu sehen sind zwei Beine, die Füsse stehen in schwarzen Comme-des-Garçons-Ballerinas aus Gummi, darauf balancieren je drei aufeinander getürmte Kastanien. Von oben hängt ein grauer Jupe von Louis Vuitton ins Bild. Bild 4: Eine Frau steht vor einem Tisch, auf ihren Füssen stehen zwei Tischbeine. Sie trägt weisse Lackschuhe mit schwarzen Absätzen, einen weissen knielangen Jupe und ein rotes Oberteil, alles von Miu Miu. Bild 5: Eine Frau liegt mit dem Kopf nach unten auf einem Parkettboden. Auf ihrem Kopf liegt die Ecke eines roten Sofas. Ihr rückenfreies Balenciaga-Outfit wirkt dabei ziemlich dekorativ. Bild 6: Eine Frau von hinten. Sie hält das Gleichgewicht auf Plastikbällen stehend. Gar nicht so einfach, schon gar nicht in diesen Jil-Sander-Pantoffeln. Bild 7: Ein Mann im Tweedmantel von APC. In seinem Mund hängt ein Kleiderbügel mit einer Jacke von Yoshij Yamamoto. Bild 8: Ein vornübergebeugtes weibliches Hinterteil in rekonstruierten Jeans von Martin Margiela. Darauf steht eine Halbliterflasche Mineralwasser von Evian.

Natürlich kommen Ihnen diese Bilder bekannt vor. Unheimlich bekannt. Und das soll auch so sein. Denn sie sind allesamt Erwin Wurms photographischer Serie ONE MINUTE SCULPTURES nachempfunden. Das Konzept stammt von Ridge Forester, Künstler und Gebrauchsphotograph. Weil er die Anonymität von Bildern liebt, arbeitet er zum Beispiel für Image-Banken, stellt Landschaftsaufnahmen her, die von ihrer totalen Austauschbarkeit leben. Weil Forester mit Verve die totale Nicht-Identifizierbarkeit von Stilen verfolgt, betreute er einen Photographen mit der praktischen Ausführung. Mit dieser Strategie können seine Bilder stiltechnisch erst recht nicht auf eine Handschrift, auf einen spezifischen Macher zurückgeführt werden. Ist Forester ein gewissenloser Kupferer, ein schamloser Plagiator, ein wildernder Imitator? Nein. Räumlich unmittelbar nach der besagten pseudo-Wurm'schen Photostrasse platzierte der Art Editor von *Self Service* ein offenbarendes Gespräch zwischen einer Kritikerin und dem Künstler-Täter Forester. Erwin Wurm wird als Bilderlieferant genannt, die Strategie als eine Art von Hommage deklariert und die Arbeit als eine «Relecture».

«Der Originalbegriff ist obsolet geworden.» Das hört sich an dieser Stelle des Textes noch immer gut an. Ridge Foresters «A bit of fur on a jacket or a skirt adds a little rock and roll» könnte paradigmatisch dafür stehen,

S. 182–185: Bilder der von RIDGE FORESTER konzipierten Photostrasse in «Self Service», Nr. 8, Oktober 1998: A BIT OF FUR ON A JACKET OR A SKIRT ADDS A LITTLE ROCK AND ROLL (im Original farbig und ganzseitig). Photos: Nicolas Trembley; Styling: Suzanne Koller; Model: Michelle Nicol.

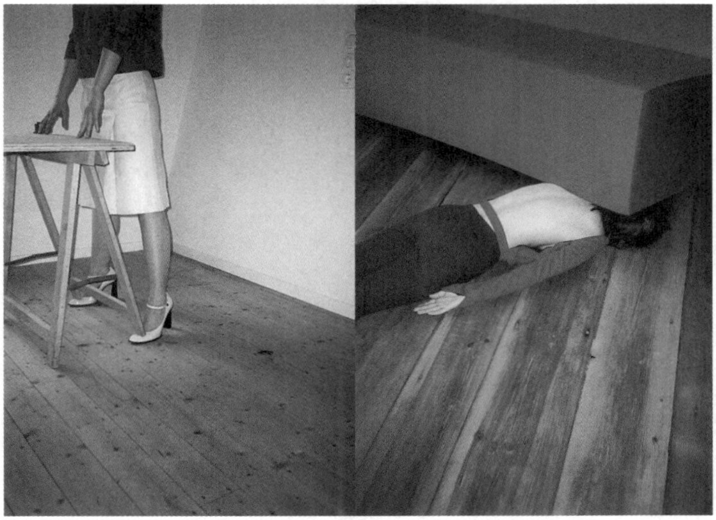

dass dieser so oft und so leichthin beschworene Mythos tatsächlich existiert. Um historische Rechtfertigung ringend mag man sich fragen: Ist es denn eine Appropriation? Die Appropriation-Art beinhaltet im Wesentlichen die Aneignung einer fremden Bildwelt durch Imitation oder Reproduktion. Zusammen mit einem latenten Begehren für das Original impliziert sie immer auch eine Form von Kritik. Als zum Beispiel Sherrie Levine 1981 eine Photographie von Edward Weston noch einmal photographierte und wiederum präsentierte, glich ihr Bild formal-ästhetisch exakt demjenigen von Weston. Was Inhalt, Konzeption, Absicht und Kontext betraf, bezeichneten diese Photographien jedoch eine strategische Differenz und in dieser Differenz machte sich Kritik fest.

Forester? Er begehrt Erwin Wurms Vorlage und produziert eine beliebige Nachzeichnung. Formal-ästhetisch interessiert ihn das visuelle Resultat allerdings wenig. Und am Aufzeigen einer inhaltlichen Differenz ist ihm ebenfalls nicht gelegen. Er verfolgt die Prinzipien der Ähnlichkeit und der Wiedererkennung. So stört es ihn zum Beispiel überhaupt nicht, dass die aufgetürmten Kastanien von Bild 3 nicht kunstvoll auf dem Schuh balanciert werden, sondern mit grobem Klebeband befestigt sind. Natürlich ist das auf dem Bild sichtbar und diese Transparenz ist Forester nur recht. Seine Transposition führt von der bedeutungsvollen Welt der Kunst in die sinnentleerte Welt der Mode, wo Begehren an Labels festgemacht wird.

Amüsant ist, dass Erwin Wurm Kleider und Menschen als Material einsetzt, an Moden und Stilen aber niemals wirklich interessiert ist. So kann Foresters Arbeit auch als eine Rückführung verstanden werden. «Wieder-Photographen» wie Levine fühlten sich subversiv, weil sie sich dem Autonomie- und Originalitätscode der institutionalisierten Kunstwelt widersetzten. Forester ist hingegen ein Verarbeiter und seine Strategie ist so subversiv wie eine Dose Ravioli und also höchstens als post-appropriationistisch zu bezeichnen. Im erwähnten Gesprächstext meint Forester: «Ich versuche mich selbst davon zu überzeugen, dass alles reproduzierbar ist.»

Unter dem Titel «Alles ist Reproduktion» veröffentlichte ich im Lebensart-Bund einer Schweizer Tageszeitung einen kurzen Text zu Ridge Foresters kopistischem Tun als Modephotograph. Dazu erschien «Bild 8» mit der Margiela-Jeans und der Evian-Flasche. Wie mir Erwin Wurm erzählte, wurde ihm dieser Artikel gleich mehrfach von empörten Freunden zugeschickt. Das Ergebnis? Erwin Wurm kokettierte mit der Drohung, rechtliche Schritte gegen die Zeitschrift *Self Service* einzuleiten. Weil wir aber alle wissen, dass der Originalbegriff obsolet ist, kam es zu einer aussergerichtlichen und sogar durchaus fröhlichen Einigung. Der im Namen von Ridge Forester agierende Photograph, gleichzeitig Art Editor von *Self Service*, darf nun von Erwin Wurm als Skulpturenmaterial eingesetzt werden. Das Resultat wird photographisch festgehalten und ist in einer der nächsten *Self Service*-Ausgaben zu besichtigen.

The Concept of the Original Is Obsolete

MICHELLE NICOL

Wurm v. Forester

What follows is a story that questions the indefatigably invoked validity of the obsolescence of originality as a concept. Ever heard of *Self Service?* If you like fashion, the presentation of lifestyles, and the sending up of their manifest destinies, if it tickles you to see people wearing long brown leather gloves by Hermés on their own balconies, then the answer is probably yes. *Self Service* is a magazine that pushes the latest fashions to absurd extremes and calls their bluff.

The October 1998 issue, No. 8, probes the subject of absurdity. There's a fashion story in it laconically titled: "A bit of fur on a jacket or a skirt adds a little rock and roll." The first priority consists, not surprisingly, of standardizing brand-name values and conditioning consumer preferences. The pictures operate with minimally dramatized situation comedy, with dysfunctional everyday objects, and with evidence to prove that the models-cum-humans in the pictures are nothing but random anthropomorphic sculptural materials. The absurdity and absolute meaninglessness of stilted poses, apparently intended to be taken seriously, are not conducive to keeping a straight face. They are also meant to model fashions. That's all. Picture 1: A woman with contorted limbs is lying on a stone floor. She is wearing a black top and a black pleated skirt by Martine Sitbon, and Mary Janes in beige, gray, and red. A black suitcase covers chest and head. Picture 2: A concrete floor with a woman lying on her back, legs raised perpendicular to her body. A roll of brown tape and a gray plastic video slipcase sit on the soles of her horizontal feet. She's wearing a bluish green, high-waisted wool dress by Alexander McQueen for Givenchy and off-white elastic shoes by Zucca. Picture 3: Two legs, black rubber Comme des Garçons ballerina slippers on the feet, a stack of three chestnuts balanced on each one. A gray skirt by Louis Vuitton dangles into the picture inches above the chestnuts. Picture 4: A woman standing in front of a table. Two table legs rest on her feet. She's wearing white patent-leather shoes with black heels, a white, knee-length skirt, and a red top, all by Miu Miu. Picture 5: A woman is lying face down on bare floorboards. The corner of a red couch resting on her head makes her bare-backed Balenciaga top look rather decorative. Picture 6: A woman standing on plastic balls. No mean feat in her Jil Sander slippers. Picture 7: A man in a tweed coat by APC. On a clothes hanger suspended from his mouth is a jacket by Yoshij Yamamoto. Picture 8: View of reconstructed jeans by Martin Margiela confined to the rear end of a woman bending over, which also serves as a perch for a half-liter bottle of Evian water.

Of course, all of these pictures ring a bell. A loud bell. And they're supposed to. They're takeoffs on Erwin Wurm's photographed series of ONE MINUTE SCULPTURES. The concept is Ridge Forester's, artist and commercial photographer. He loves the anonymity of pictures, which is why he works for image banks and shoots pictures of landscapes that are unique for being so utterly interchangeable. Since Forester deftly champions non-identifiable style, he hired a photographer to do the Wurm job. His strategy foils the rise of a signature style or technique and thus defies ascription to a specific maker. Does that make Forester a ruthless epigone, an unscrupulous plagiarizer, a

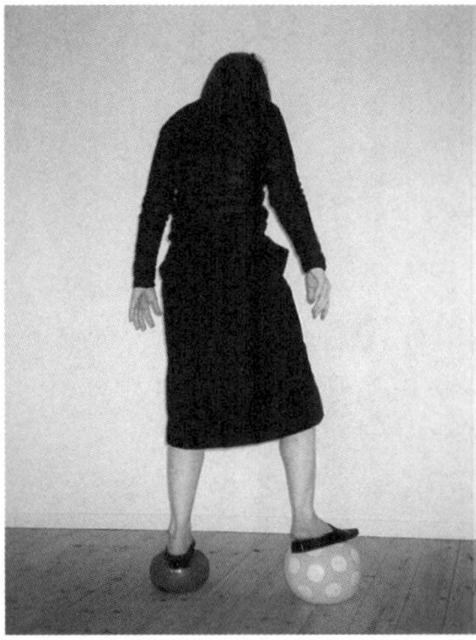

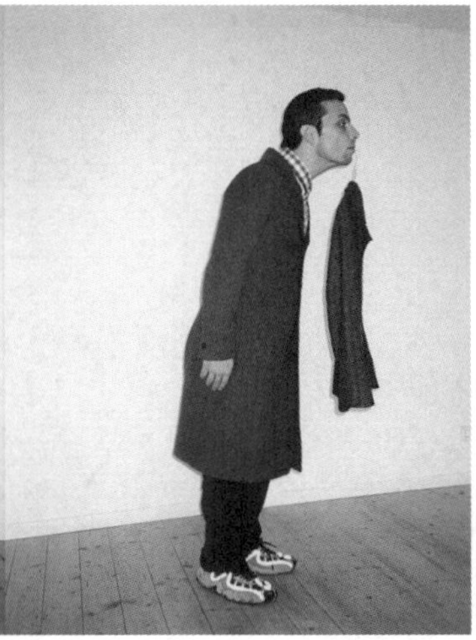

Pp. 182–185: Images of RIDGE FORESTER's fashion shoot in "Self Service," no. 8, October 1998: A BIT OF FUR ON A JACKET OR A SKIRT ADDS A LITTLE ROCK AND ROLL (all images originally in color and full page). Photography: Nicolas Trembley; styling: Suzanne Koller; model: Michelle Nicol.

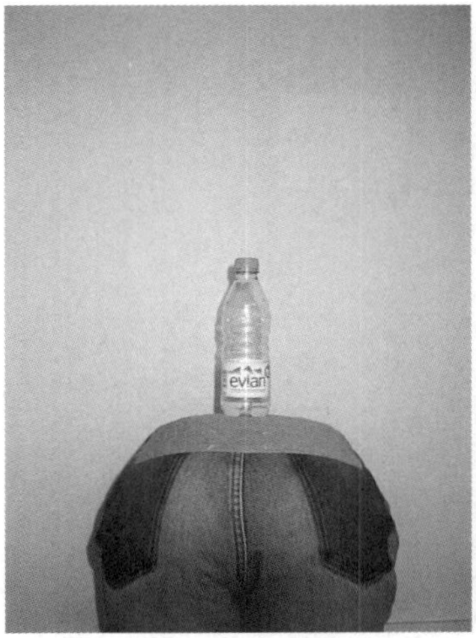

poaching imitator? No, it does not. Physically adjacent to said pseudo-Wurmian fashion story, the art editor of *Self Service* printed an enlightening conversation between a critic and artist-lawbreaker Forester. Erwin Wurm is mentioned as image source and supplier, the strategy explicitly declared as an homage of sorts, and the essay as a "rereading."

"The concept of the original is obsolete." Still sounds pretty good at this point. Ridge Forester's "A bit of fur on a jacket or a skirt adds a little rock and roll" could be paradigmatic evidence of the factuality of this much—and so glibly—vaunted myth. Struggling to find historical justification, one might pose the question: Well then, is it appropriation? Appropriation art essentially entails the use of somebody else's images through imitation or reproduction. Along with the latent desire for the original, it also always implies a kind of critique. For instance, when Sherrie Levine rephotographed a photograph by Edward Weston in 1981, the resulting work of art that she put on view was formally and aesthetically identical to Weston's. But in terms of content, concept, intention, and context, the photographs staked out a strategic difference, and in this difference lodged critique.

Forester? He desires Erwin Wurm's "original" and produces an arbitrary impersonation. He is not particularly interested in the formal, aesthetic outcome. Nor is he keen on pointing out a difference in content. He follows the principles of similarity and rediscovery. So it does not bother him in the least to have the chestnuts in picture 3 not skillfully balanced on top of each other but unceremoniously taped together. And of course, the tape is patently obvious, which is right up Forester's alley. He transposes the meaningful world of art into the meaningless world of fashion, where labels define desire.

Amusingly, Erwin Wurm's clothes and people are his materials; fashions and style are of no interest whatsoever. Thus Forester's work could be read as reclamation. Re-photographs like Levine's feel subversive because they undermine the institutionalized art world's code of autonomy and the original. But Forester is a processor and his strategy is as subversive as a can of ravioli; so, if anything, it would have to be called post-appropriative. In the above mentioned conversation, Forester opines, "I'm trying to convince myself that everything is reproducible." In the lifestyle section of a Swiss daily I recently published a short text titled "Everything Is Reproduction" on Ridge Forester's imitative activities as a fashion photographer. The illustration showed picture 8 with the Margiela jeans and the bottle of Evian. Erwin Wurm told me that he had received the article several times over from "indignant" friends. The consequences? Erwin Wurm toyed with the idea of threatening to sue *Self Service.* But because we all know that the concept of the original is obsolete, they settled out of court—cheerfully. The photographer, who acted on Ridge Forester's behalf, also happens to be the art editor of *Self Service;* he may now be used by Erwin Wurm as sculptural material. The result will be photographically recorded and published in an upcoming issue of *Self Service.*

(Translation: Catherine Schelbert)

CUMULUS

From America

IN EVERY EDITION OF PARKETT, TWO CUMULUS CLOUDS, ONE FROM AMERICA, THE OTHER FROM EUROPE, FLOAT OUT TO AN INTERESTED PUBLIC. THEY CONVEY INDIVIDUAL OPINIONS, ASSESSMENTS, AND MEMORABLE ENCOUNTERS—AS ENTIRELY PERSONAL PRESENTATIONS OF PROFESSIONAL ISSUES.

OUR CONTRIBUTORS TO THIS ISSUE ARE SUELY ROLNIK, A PSYCHOANALYST AND SENIOR PROFESSOR IN CLINICAL PSYCHOLOGY AT THE CATHOLIC UNIVERSITY OF SÃO PAULO, AND MICHELLE NICOL, AN ART CRITIC AND FREELANCE CURATOR, WHO LIVES IN ZURICH.

BEYOND THE IDENTITY PRINCIPLE
THE ANTHROPOPHAGY FORMULA

SUELY ROLNIK

Today's world: an infinite ocean of variable flows with no possibility of the totalization they would have in delineated territories, with no stable frontiers, constantly rearranging. In the opinion of some, a second flood—except that this time the waters will never recede, land will never again be visible, there are many arks, and they will drift forever, captained by myriad Noahs of all shapes and sizes. Never again will we walk the stable landscape of solid land: We must get used to the idea that "it's necessary to sail,"[1] with no fixed direction, no general point of view on this tumultuous and changeable surface. There is no longer a single form for reality with its map of possibilities. Now possibilities reinvent and redistribute themselves constantly, at the mercy of the successive waves that efface the existing forms of reality and generate others, that also end up scattering themselves in the ocean, carried along by the movement of new waves.

Today's subjectivities: Removed from their native soil, they have the gift of ubiquity—they fluctuate at the mercy of the mutable connections of desire in currents from all places and times that all pass simultaneously along the electronic waves. A singular and fluid filter of this immense and also fluid ocean. With no name or permanent address, without identity: metamor-

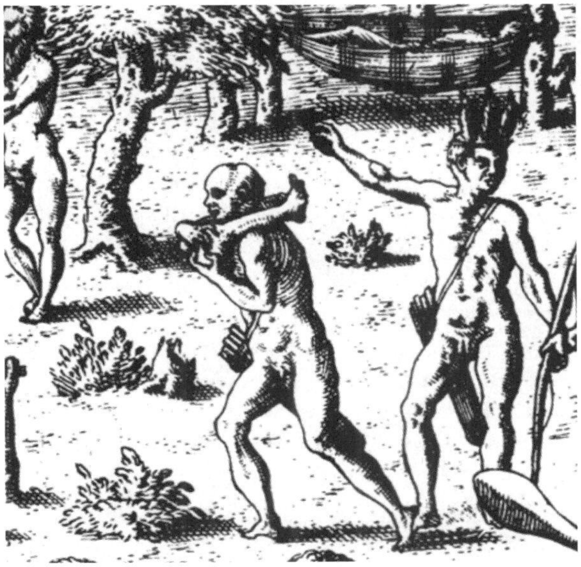

THEODOR DE BRY, detail from a series of engravings in Johannes Stadius, "America tertia pars...," Frankfurt, 1592, Collection Biblioteca Municipal Mario de Andrade, Saõ Paulo / aus der Kupferstichserie zu Johannes Stadius, «America tertia pars... (Warhafftige Historia und beschreibung einer Landtschafft ... in der Newen Welt America gelegen)», Frankfurt 1592.

phosing modulations in an endless process that moves forward tirelessly day after day.

Voices in all languages, from all corners of the earth, the voices of experts and those who are not experts are shuffled together in an infinite conversation, somewhere between afflicted and excited, about the same question: Have we in fact all become homeless? Did the subjective house dissolve, collapse, disappear? Where is identity? How can we construct an identity in this world where national, cultural, ethnic, religious, social, and sexual territories have lost their aura of truth, irreversibly denaturalized themselves, gotten mixed up with everything at hand, fluctuate or cease to exist? How can we reconstruct a territory in this shifting world? Which way do we turn in this disorientation? How can we reorganize some meaning? How do we conquer free zones of serenity? This transnational chorus oscillates between variations on the theme, variations composed by affective positions that run from the infatuated to the apocalyptic. Hope or hopelessness, it's all the same: poles of a moralistic position that adopts a value system and uses it to interpret, judge, and predict what is happening—a happy ending or the end of everything.

Meanwhile, another kind of voice clearly disagrees with this teleological tone. Its timbre expresses neither judgment nor drama, but the vibration of the movements of the world where it is intoned, transmitting the sensation that this world of today is neither better nor worse than others. Like any other, it is unique, with its own problems, its ways of affirming life and also of ruining it, with its territories in the process of disappearing, with other territories beginning to take shape and requiring cartographies of meaning to make them intelligible. In this phase of syntonization, a voice from Brazil can be heard, a voice very old in the tradition of this country, a voice that at a given moment received the name "anthropophagy."

The inspiration for the idea of anthropophagy came from a custom of the Tupi Indians: it consisted of eating their enemies—not just any enemy, only brave warriors. A certain relationship with alterity thus ritualized itself: They chose their others in terms of the vital power imparted by their proximity. They allowed themselves to be affected by their others desired to the point of absorbing them into their bodies, so that elements of their virtues would be integrated into the chemistry of the anthropophagists' souls and promote their refinement.

During the 1930s, anthropophagy acquired a meaning extrapolated from the literal act of devouring practiced by the Indians. The so-called "Anthropophagist Movement" extracted and reaffirmed the ethical formula of the relationship with the other that governs and transfers this ritual to the sphere of culture. In this movement, the active presence of this formula gained visibility in a mode of cultural production practiced in Brazil since its foundation. Brazilian culture is born under the sign of a variable multiplicity of references and their mixture. However, since Brazil's birth, there have also been many strategies of desire with regard to mixture, different degrees of exposure to alterity which this situation intensifies.

Our founding elite, unlike those of other New World nations, is oriented toward Europe and does not invest in the construction of an "at home" in Brazilian territory. The body is "separated from experience," anesthetized to the effects of the cohabiting of heterogeneous groups and, therefore, is deaf to the demands of the cultivation of meaning for the unique problems delineated in this exposition. The tendency that has maintained its hegemony since that time is that of consuming European and, more recently, American, culture which, aside from having constituted itself in its origin as the cartography of an experience of non-mixing, is removed from the context that brought about its production, and is not, moreover, problematized in its consumption in the new context. Mere jokes of erudition and intelligence result in sterile repetitions and an "at home" lacking in elegance and devoid of meaning. It is just this "Dr. side, quotations side, well-known authors side"[2)] with their "speculative tedium,"[3)] that Oswald de Andrade tells us about—a kind of academic superego struggling against thought.

Popular culture and, later, mass culture are traditionally produced starting from the exposition of this varied other, out of the necessity to construct a territory of existence here in Brazil, an "at home" consisting of everyday life—a matter of psychic survival. The result is an exuberant, irreverent, and inventive esthetics. All this production is carried out on the margin of local, official culture, at best disqualifies it or folklorizes it, thereby avoiding any danger of disruptive contamination.

A third tradition, meanwhile, insinuates itself between these two sides, one in which the discriminatory boundary that separates them is erased, promoting a general contamination not only between the erudite and the popular, the national and the international, but also between the archaic and the modern, the rural and the urban, the hand-crafted and the technological. An "at home" takes shape that incarnates all the dynamic heterogeneity of the sensitive substance which constitutes the subjectivity of any Brazilian, a subjectivity that is created and re-created as the effect of an infinite miscegenation—nothing to do with identity. The Anthropophagist Movement makes this position explicit, giving it retrospective visibility, but above all the dignity to affirm it in the present. The creators who take up this position allow themselves to construct their own problems. For this purpose they incorporate the banal in their own way and affirm the exuberance of this irreverent esthetic that impregnates the everyday life of Brazil within the official system of culture, mixing it with the most current and sophisticated erudite repertoires from the so-called hegemonic centers that tend to reign all by themselves in official Brazilian culture, disconnected from any labor of thought.

The anthropophagist strategy allows at least three operations to occur: The first is the bastardization of the culture of the elites and, indirectly, of European culture as a standard. There is neither submissive and sterile repositioning nor opposition maintaining that culture as a reference, but rather a radical dislocation of the idea of "center." The supposed power of the generalization of this or of any other model is overlooked, since all are understood to be provisional coagulations of language, selected in an experimental and unique process of the cultivation of meaning, in the same way, in fact, as that of the indigenous or African universe. Thus the Indians or the Blacks are not presented as "good" humanity, bearers of a truth, to be ingested, in contrast to "bad" European humanity, distant from truth, to be vomited. As Darcy Ribeiro writes, we are "as much dis-Europeans, as we are dis-Indians and dis-Africans."[4)] This is because the selection criteria for the anthropophagist ritual in culture is not the content of a value system in itself but one which functions and allows meaning to be produced. This cannot work for a system as a totality but for some of its elements, which are articulated with elements of other systems thus losing any connotations of identity.

The second operation which the anthropophagy strategy makes viable is the exercise of the creation of culture, which has nothing to do with signifying, explaining, or interpreting to reveal truths. The truth, according to the Anthropophagy Manifesto, "is a lie repeated many times over." To make culture in the style of anthropophagy is related to mapping: to trace a map that participates in the construction of the territory it represents. "Routes. Routes. Routes. Routes. Routes. Routes. Routes." the Manifesto insists seven times in a row. It is from the paradoxical closeness among heterogeneous elements that meaning emanates: route, cartography of real social movements, critical effect. Any pragmatic experimentation, if it is more or less well carried out, is worth more than the sterile imitation of models.

The third operation derives from the first two: the breaking down, already during the 1920s, of the division of the world into "colonized" and "colonizers." At that time the breaking down of the division had barely begun to take shape, but today, in the era of globalized neoliberalism, those figures definitively no longer prevail. The balance of power has shifted; the figures have changed. The pairs that defined political conflict in the modern period have been reshuffled. It is not a matter of a sovereign colonial type any longer: the hegemonic power no longer confronts its Other, there is no more exteriority, because hegemonic power has progressively extended its frontiers until it covers most of the planet.

This strategy of desire defined by the irreverent juxtaposition that creates a tension between worlds that do not touch on the official map of existence, that demystifies every and all value a priori, that decentralizes and renders everything equally bastardized, sets into motion a mode of subjectivization that I will call "anthropophagous." In a first, strictly visible, approximation, anthropophagous subjectivity defines itself as never adhering absolutely to any system of reference, a fluidity to mix any kind of repertory and a freedom of linguistic improvisation that derives from such mixtures. Meanwhile, for an eye attuned to the invisible, anthropophagy is actualized according to different strategies of desire, moved by different vectors of power, that range from a greater or lesser affirmation of life to its virtual negation. They are basically distinguished by the way in which the subjectivity knows and explores the world, by that which motivates its search for meaning and the criterion used to choose what will be absorbed in order to produce that meaning. Actualized in its most active vector, the anthropophagous mode of subjectivization in its invisible facet functions according to some essential characteristics.

Before anything else, this mode depends on the degree of exposure to alterity: to discover and desire the singularity of the other, without feeling shame in discovering and desiring, without feeling shame about expressing that desire, without fear of contaminating oneself, because it is within contamination that our vital powers expand, that the batteries of desire are charged, that the becomings are incarnated—the Tupi formula. This kind of relationship with alterity produces a joy in the body—"the litmus test"[5] as the Manifesto asserts twice, the test of a pulsing vitality.

This capacity depends on a second characteristic actualized in its most active vector: a certain state of the body, in which its nerve fibers vibrate to the music of the universes connected by desire; a certain syntony with affective modulations provoked by this vibration; a tolerance for the pressure that such unfamiliar affects exercise on the subjectivity so it will incarnate them, recreate itself, become another. It is probably what Lygia Clark called the "state of art without art,"[6] and what Oiticica refers to as the "state of invention."[7]

A third trait exercised in its most active vector is that which provides the binding ingredient for an "at home," which is the nomadism of desire that goes its way making its connections, guided predominantly by the point of view of the vibratility of the body and its will to power. An ethical criterion for making choices—again, the Tupi formula.

A fourth characteristic is the kind of subjectivity constituted by an impersonal singularity, a whole dispersed in the multiple connections of desire in the social field and which merges among the assembled worlds. (In contrast the subjectivity determined by an identity-figurative principle consists in the person of an "I," an immured individuality, imprisoned in its psychic living space and commanded by the fear of losing itself.)

A fifth characteristic is the way this kind of subjectivity emerges: Its genesis is carried out by means of alliances and contagion, an infinite rhizome that changes nature and direction at the mercy of the racial mixtures that take place in the great mill of our cultural anthropophagy. (This differs from the development of an identity-figurative subjectivity that is constructed through filiation, promoting the fantasy of a linear evolution and the imprisoning commitment to a system of values assumed as the essence of the revered being.)

The voice of Brazil that is heard in the contemporary debate swirling around the crisis of identity is that of anthropophagous subjectivity in its most active vector. As if we are forever this people of mixed and bastard blood that is now constituting itself all over the Earth (Ribeiro), as if we bring to this globalized conversation a know-how with regard to navigating this infinite, churning ocean of today's world. Basically, what the anthropophagous voice brings to this unique impasse is that it shows not only theoretically but, above all, pragmatically, that the problem being posited is not the reconstitution of an identity, that hallucinated horizon dividing mankind into those with hope and those in despair. The problem is to detach the sensation of subjective consistency from the model of identity; detach oneself from the identity-figurative principle in the construction of an "at home."

If living without a specific house is difficult, there is no human life possible without a mode of being in which one can feel "at home." We are not all becoming homeless: It is not true that the subjective house has disappeared. It is only suffering a radical transformation in the principle of its construction—which is, of course, perturbing. Constructing an "at home" nowadays depends on operations that are rather inactive in modern Western subjectivity, but familiar to the anthropophagous mode at its most active: to be attuned to the transfigurations in the body, to the effects of new connections and flows; catch the wave of events that such currents unleash; to experience concrete arrangements of existence that incarnate these sensitive mutations; to invent new possibilities of life. Such operations depend, of course, on exercising the powers of the body equally inactive in contemporary subjectivity: to expand beyond representation, to conquer an intimacy with the body as a vibratile surface that detects the waves even before they arrive, to learn to catch the wave, establish zones of familiarity within movement itself—that is, "it's necessary to sail," because if we don't, our destiny will probably be shipwreck. An "at home" made of partial, unique, provisional, fluctuating totalities, in a series of constant becomings, that each one (individual or group) constructs using the currents that touch its body and its selective filtration operated by desire.

Freeing ourselves from the concept of the identity-figurative principle is something making itself felt with urgency all over the planet. We are the bearers of a vaccine that allows people to resist this vice: the "anthropophagy vaccine," as one of the Manifestos calls it,[8] is indicated for "the spirit that refuses to conceive the spirit without the body." Oswald de Andrade ultimately defended the thesis that anthropophagy would constitute a "social therapy for the contemporary world."[9] It would seem that it is becoming indispensable for an ecology of the soul (or of desire?) as this millennium ends.

(Translation: Alfred MacAdam)

1) Fernando Pessoa, *Livro do Desassossego (The Book of Disquiet)* n. 495, vol. II (Lisbon: Atica, 1982), p. 24.
2) "Manifesto de Poesia Pau-brasil" (1924), in: *A Utopía Antropofágica: Obras Completas de Oswald de Andrade* (São Paulo: Globo, 1990). [Oswald de Andrade, "Brasil-Wood Poetry Manifesto" (1924), in: *The Anthropophagy Utopia, Complete Works of Oswald de Andrade*]
3) de Andrade, "Manifesto Antropófago" (1928), in: op. cit.
4) Darcy Ribeiro, *O povo brasileiro. A formação e o sentido do Brasil* (São Paulo: Companhia das Letras, 1995).
5) de Andrade, "Manifesto Antropófago."
6) "A propósito da magia do objeto" (1965), in: *Lygia Clark* (Rio de Janeiro: Funarte, 1980).
7) "Eden" (1969), in: *Hélio Oiticica* (Paris: Editions du Jeu de Paume, 1992).
8) de Andrade, "Manifesto Antropófago."
9) de Andrade, "The March of the Utopias"(1953), in: op. cit.

JENSEITS DES IDENTITÄTSPRINZIPS

DIE ANTHROPOPHAGIEFORMEL

SUELY ROLNIK

Die Welt von heute: ein unendlicher Ozean wechselnder Strömungen, die nie das Ganze erfassen können, wie das in klar umrissenen Territorien möglich wäre; ohne feste Grenzen, in immer neuen Zusammensetzungen. Eine zweite Sintflut, wie manche meinen, nur dass das Wasser diesmal nicht zurückgehen, das Land nie wieder sichtbar werden wird, während unzählige Archen für immer dahintreiben werden, gesteuert von Abertausenden von Noahs unterschiedlichster Gestalt und Herkunft. Nie wieder werden wir uns auf festem Boden bewegen können: «Seefahrt tut not, ...»[1] An diesen Gedanken müssen wir uns gewöhnen, dass wir ohne klares Ziel und ohne festen Standpunkt auf stürmischer und wechselhafter Oberfläche unterwegs sind. Es gibt keine einheitliche Gestalt der Realität mehr mit ihren klar umrissenen Möglichkeiten. Nun bilden und verteilen sich die Möglichkeiten von Tag zu Tag neu, Spielbälle der Wellen und Gezeiten, die die Erscheinungsformen der Realität auslöschen und andere erschaffen, die sich erneut im Ozean verteilen, fortgetragen von der Bewegung neuer Wellen.

Die Subjektivitäten von heute: Von ihrer heimischen Erde entfernt, verfügen sie über die Gabe der Allgegenwart – sie fluktuieren, abhängig von den wechselnden Verbindungen des Begehrens der Ströme von allen Orten und Zeiten, die sich alle gleichzeitig den elektronischen Wellen entlang bewegen. Ein einmaliger und fliessender Filter dieses unendlich grossen und ebenso fliessenden Ozeans. Ohne Namen oder feste Adresse und ohne Identität: Modulationen in endloser Abwandlung, in einem Tag für Tag unermüdlich fortschreitenden Prozess.

Stimmen in allen Sprachen, aus allen Ecken der Erde, die Stimmen aller Fachleute und Laien sind in ein unendliches Gespräch verstrickt, das zwischen Trauer und Aufregung schwankt und sich um die eine Frage dreht: Sind wir tatsächlich alle heimatlos geworden? Hat sich das subjektive Zuhause aufgelöst, ist es zusammengebrochen oder verschwunden? Wo ist die Identität? Wie können wir eine Identität finden in einer Welt, in der in nationaler, kultureller, ethnischer, religiöser, gesellschaftlicher und sexueller Hinsicht die Aura der Wahrheit verloren gegangen ist und eine unwiederbringliche Denaturalisierung, Vermischung, schliesslich Fluktuation oder völlige Auflösung stattgefunden hat? Wie können wir uns in dieser wandelbaren Welt wieder ein Territorium errichten? Wohin sollen wir uns in dieser Orientierungslosigkeit wenden? Wie wieder Sinn herstellen? Wie freie Zonen heiterer Gelassenheit erobern? Und dieser transnationale Chor oszilliert in Variationen über das Thema, Variationen, die sich aus

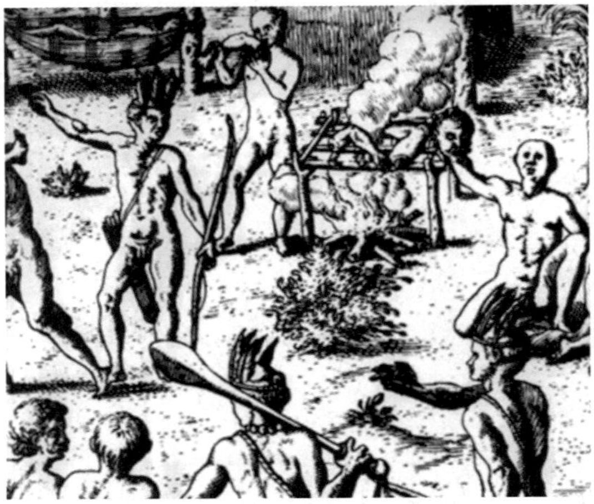

THEODOR DE BRY, detail from a series of engravings in Johannes Stadius, "America tertia pars..." Frankfurt, 1592, Collection Biblioteca Municipal Mario de Andrade, São Paulo / aus der Kupferstichserie zu Johannes Stadius, «America tertia pars... (Warhafftige Historia und beschreibung einer Landtschafft ... in der Newen Welt America gelegen)», Frankfurt 1592.

Gefühlen ergeben, die von Begeisterung bis zur apokalyptischen Endzeitstimmung reichen. Hoffnung oder Hoffnungslosigkeit, es läuft auf dasselbe hinaus: Extreme einer moralistischen Position, die sich eines Wertesystems bedient um zu interpretieren, zu bewerten und vorauszusagen, was geschieht – ein Happy End oder das Ende von allem.

Aber inzwischen widerspricht eine andere Stimme diesem teleologischen Tonfall. Ihre Klangfarbe drückt weder Urteil noch Drama aus, sondern die Schwingung der Bewegungen der Welt, und wo sie sich erhebt, vermittelt sie das Gefühl, dass diese heutige Welt weder besser noch schlechter ist als andere. Wie jede andere Welt ist auch sie einmalig, hat ihre eigenen Probleme und ihre eigene Art das Leben zu bejahen, aber auch zugrunde zu richten; es gibt in ihr Territorien, die im Verschwinden begriffen sind, aber auch solche, die gerade entstehen und nach neuen hermeneutischen Methoden verlangen, die sie verständlich machen und ihre Geburt unterstützen. In dieser Phase der Vielstimmigkeit ist aus Brasilien eine Stimme zu vernehmen, eine in der Tradition dieses Landes sehr alte Stimme, die zu einem bestimmten Zeitpunkt den Namen «Anthropophagie» erhielt.

Der Anthropophagie-Gedanke ist von einem Brauch der Tupi-Indianer inspiriert: Sie pflegten ihre Feinde zu verspeisen – aber nicht jeden Feind, nur tapfere Krieger. Ein bestimmter Umgang mit der Andersartigkeit wurde ritualisiert: Sie suchten ihre Anderen im Hinblick auf die vitale Kraft aus, die durch Nähe intensiviert würde; sie liessen sich von jenen Anderen so hinreissen und begehrten sie derart, dass sie sie ihren eigenen Körpern einverleibten, damit ihre Tugenden auf chemischem Weg in ihre Seelen eingehen und sie vervollkommnen würden.

In den 30er Jahren erhielt der Begriff Anthropophagie eine aus diesem buchstäblichen Akt des Verzehrens abgeleitete Bedeutung. Die sogenannte Anthropophagie-Bewegung extrahierte und verwendete die ethische Formel dieses spezifischen, rituellen Umgangs mit dem Anderen erneut und übertrug sie auf kulturelle Vorgänge. Durch diese Bewegung wurde die unveränderte Wirksamkeit dieser Formel in einem bestimmten kulturellen Schaffen sichtbar, das in Brasilien seit der Gründerzeit betrieben wurde. Die brasilianische Kultur stand schon immer unter dem Zeichen einer lebendigen Vielfalt der Bezugspunkte und ihrer Durchdringung. Seit der Entstehung Brasiliens gab es jedoch auch zahllose andere Ansätze im Umgang mit dem Begehren nach Vermischung und verschiedene Grade der Auseinandersetzung mit dem Anderen, was diese Situation noch verschärfte.

Unsere Gründerelite hat sich im Gegensatz zu der anderer Nationen der Neuen Welt schon immer an Europa orientiert und trug nichts zur Errichtung eines «Zuhause» auf brasilianischem Boden bei. Der Körper blieb von der Erfahrung abgespalten und wurde gegen die Auswirkungen des Zusammenlebens heterogener Gruppen unempfindlich, deshalb ist er taub gegenüber der Forderung nach einer sorgfältigen Klärung der neuartigen Probleme, die hier skizziert werden. Seit jeher herrscht die Tendenz vor, die europäische Kultur zu konsumieren und neuerdings auch die amerikanische, die, abgesehen davon, dass sie von Anfang an ein Musterbeispiel gelebter Nichtvermischung darstellt, aus dem angestammten Kontext ihrer Entstehung gerissen wurde und darüber hinaus auch hinsichtlich ihrer Vereinnahmung im neuen Kontext nicht kritisch betrachtet wird. Eine lächerliche Bildung und ein Denken sind die Folge, was zu sterilen Wiederholungen und einem «Zuhause» ohne jede Eleganz und Bedeutung führt. Es ist nur noch dieses «Doktor sowieso, Zitat sowieso, bekannter Autor sowieso»[2] von jener «spekulativen Langeweile», von der Oswald de Andrade spricht[3] – eine Art akademisches Über-Ich, das sich dem Denken verschliesst.

Auf der anderen Seite entsteht die Volkskultur, später die Massenkultur, traditionell so, dass sie bei diesem variierten Anderen ansetzt, allein schon aus der Notwendigkeit heraus, hier einen Ort der Existenz zu errichten, ein «Zuhause», zu dem ein Alltag gehört – das ist eine Frage des seelischen Überlebens. Das Ergebnis ist eine üppige, respektlose und erfinderische Ästhetik. All dies entsteht an den Rändern der lokalen, offiziellen Kultur, die es ablehnt oder im günstigsten Fall zur Folklore erklärt um jegliche Gefahr der Ansteckung zu vermeiden.

Inzwischen lässt sich eine dritte Tradition zwischen diesen beiden Positionen ausmachen, eine, welche die diskriminierende Grenze, die beide trennt, auslöscht und eine allgemeine gegenseitige Beeinflussung nicht nur zwischen dem Gebildeten und dem Populären, dem Nationalen und dem Internationalen propagiert, sondern auch zwischen dem Archaischen und dem Modernen, dem Land und der Stadt, dem Handwerk und der Technologie. Dabei entsteht wieder ein «Zuhause», das die gesamte dynamische Heterogenität der empfindsamen Substanz, die die Subjektivität des Brasilianers ausmacht, verkörpert, eine Subjektivität, die als Resultat einer unendlichen Rassenvermischung entsteht und wieder ersteht, aber nichts mit Identität zu tun hat. Die Anthropophagie-Bewegung verleiht diesem Sachverhalt Ausdruck, indem sie ihn nachträglich sichtbar macht, ihm aber auch die nötige Würde verleiht um sich in der Gegenwart zu behaupten. Künstler, die diese Position beziehen, nehmen sich das Recht sich ihre Fragen selbst zu stellen. Aus diesem Grund geben sie das Banale auf ihre Weise wieder, bejahen die Üppigkeit der respektlosen Ästhetik, die das brasilianische Alltagsleben innerhalb der offiziellen Kultur prägt, und vermischen sie mit dem gängigsten und raffiniertesten Bildungsrepertoire der sogenannten Herrschaftszentren, die dazu neigen, alles allein zu entscheiden und jeglicher Denkarbeit aus dem Weg zu gehen.

Die anthropophagische Strategie ermöglicht mindestens drei Vorgehensweisen: Die erste ist die Bastardisierung der Elitekultur und damit indirekt auch der europäischen Kultur als Standard. Das heisst weder unterwürfige und sterile Aufarbeitung noch eine Opposition, die jene Kultur als Bezugspunkt beibehält, sondern eine radikale Verlagerung der Zentrumsvorstellung. Die Potenz zur Verallgemeinerung dieses oder jedes anderen Modells wird übersehen, da sie alle als vorübergehende sprachliche Erscheinungen verstanden werden, die in einem experimentellen, einmaligen Prozess der Bedeutungsbildung ausgewählt wurden, wie jenes des eingeborenen oder afrikanischen Universums. Entsprechend werden Indianer und Schwarze nicht etwa als «gute Menschen» dargestellt, die im Besitz einer Wahrheit wären, die man sich einverleiben möchte, im Gegensatz zu den Europäern, den «schlechten» Menschen, fern jeder Wahrheit, die ausgekotzt werden müssen. Wie Darcy Ribeiro schreibt, sind wir «genauso ent-europäisiert wie wir ent-indianisiert und ent-afrikanisiert sind».[4] Das liegt daran, dass die Auswahlkriterien des anthropophagischen Rituals im kulturellen Bereich nicht einem eigentlichen inhaltlichen Wertesystem entsprechen, sondern sich nach dem richten, was funktioniert, was den Fluss von Intensitäten und die Herstellung von Bedeutung ermöglicht. Dies kann zwar für ein System als Ganzes nicht funktionieren, aber für einige seiner Teile in Verbindung mit Teilen anderer Systeme, wobei jedes Anzeichen von Identität verloren geht.

Die zweite Methode, die durch die anthropophagische Strategie am Leben erhalten wird, ist die Praxis einer Kulturerzeugung, die nichts mit Bedeuten, Erklären oder Deuten zur Enthüllung von Wahrheiten am Hut hat. Laut dem *Anthropophagischen Manifest* ist die Wahrheit nichts als «eine oft wiederholte Lüge». Kulturproduktion im anthropophagischen Sinn hat mit Kartographie zu tun: eine Karte erstellen, die an der Entstehung des von ihr dargestellten Territoriums teil hat. «Wege. Wege. Wege. Wege. Wege. Wege. Wege.», wiederholt das Manifest beharrlich, gleich sieben Mal hintereinander. Gerade die paradoxe Nähe unter heterogenen Elementen bringt Bedeutung hervor: Weg, das Aufzeichnen realer gesellschaftlicher Bewegungen, kritische Wirkung. Jedes pragmatische Experiment ist – halbwegs sorgfältig ausgeführt – mehr wert als die sterile Nachahmung von Vorbildern.

Die dritte Methode ergibt sich aus den ersten beiden: das Durchbrechen der Aufteilung der Welt in «Kolonisierte» und «Kolonisatoren», das sich bereits in den 20er Jahren ankündigte. Geriet diese Einteilung damals schon ins Wanken, so ist sie heute, im Zeitalter des globalen Neoliberalismus, endgültig obsolet geworden. Die Achse der Machtverhältnisse hat sich verlagert und ihr Stellenwert hat sich verändert. Die Gegensatzpaare, die für die Konflikte der Moderne bestimmend waren, sind neu gemischt worden. Es geht nicht mehr um die Souveränität in einer kolonialen Welt. Die hegemoniale Macht sieht sich nicht mehr mit ihrem Anderen konfrontiert, es gibt kein Aussen mehr, weil sie ihre Grenzen derart erweitert hat, dass sie fast die ganze Erde bedeckt.

Diese Strategie des Begehrens, die sich durch ein respektloses Aneinanderreihen auszeichnet, das eine Spannung zwischen Welten erzeugt, die auf der offiziellen Karte ihrer Existenz nichts miteinander zu schaffen haben; die jeden Wert a priori entmystifiziert, die alles seines Zentrums beraubt und mit allem anderen vermischt, setzt eine Art Subjektivität in Bewegung, die ich «anthropophagisch» nennen möchte. Bei einer ersten, auf das Sichtbare beschränkten Annäherung definiert sich die anthropophagische Subjektivität als eine, die sich niemals auf ein Bezugssystem festlegt, als eine Fliessende, die nach Belieben verschiedene Repertoires mischt, und als Freiheit der sprachlichen Improvisation, die sich aus diesen Mischungen ergibt. Für ein Auge, das auch für das Unsichtbare empfänglich ist, passt sich die Anthropophagie den jeweiligen Strategien des Begehrens an, die je verschiedenen Machtfaktoren unterliegen, welche von einer mehr oder weniger ausgeprägten Lebensbejahung bis hin zur fast vollständigen Negierung des Lebens reichen. Sie unterscheiden sich vor allem durch die Art, wie die Subjektivität etwas erkennt und die Welt erforscht, durch das Motiv ihrer Bedeutungssuche und das Auswahlkriterium für das zum Erzeugen der Bedeutung Heranzuziehende. In seiner aktivsten Ausprägung folgt der anthropophagische Modus der Subjektivierung im unsichtbaren Bereich einigen wesentlichen Grundzügen.

Vor allen Dingen ist dieser Modus vom Grad des Konfrontiertseins mit dem Anderen abhängig: die Einzigartigkeit des Anderen zu entdecken und zu begehren, ohne dabei Scham zu empfinden, auch keine Scham zu empfinden beim Ausdrücken dieses Begehrens, sich nicht vor Ansteckung zu fürchten, weil durch Ansteckung unsere Lebenskraft wächst, die Batterien des Begehrens aufgeladen werden und das Begehrte sich in uns verkörpert, entsprechend dem Tupi-Prinzip. Diese Art des Umgangs mit dem Anderen erzeugt im Körper eine Freude; das ist «der Litmustest»[5] der pulsierenden Vitalität .

Dass dies möglich ist, hängt von einem zweiten Faktor ab: einer bestimmten Körperverfassung, bei der die Nervenstränge zur Musik der Sphären pulsieren, die sich im Begehren vereinen; eine gewisse Übereinstimmung mit affektiven Modulationen, die durch diese Schwingungen erzeugt werden; eine Empfänglichkeit für den Druck, den derart ungewohnte Affekte auf die Subjektivität ausüben, bis sie diese aufnimmt und verkörpert, sich selbst neu kreiert, eine andere wird. Das ist es wahrscheinlich, was Lygia Clark den «Kunstzustand ohne Kunst»[6] nennt, und das, worauf sich Oiticica als den «Zustand der Erfindung» bezieht.[7]

Ein dritter Grundzug dieses Modus der Subjektivierung ist derjenige, der das Bindemittel für ein «Zuhause» liefert, das Nomadentum des Begehrens, das auf seinem eigenen Weg seine Beziehungen herstellt und sich dabei vorwiegend von der Vibrationsfähigkeit des Körpers und seinem Willen zur Macht leiten lässt: ein ethisches Auswahlkriterium – auch hier wieder das Tupi-Prinzip.

Ein viertes Charakteristikum ist die Art Subjektivität, die eine unpersönliche Einheit darstellen kann, ein Ganzes, das in die vielfältigen Verbindungen des Begehrens im gesellschaftlichen Bereich verstreut ist und sich in den versammelten Welten auflöst, während die Subjektivität, die sich vom Identität-Gestalt-Prinzip her bestimmt, aus der Person eines «Ich» besteht, einer abgeschlossenen Individualität, die in ihrem psychischen Lebensraum gefangen ist und von der Angst beherrscht wird sich selbst zu verlieren.

Ein fünftes Charakteristikum ist die Art und Weise, wie diese Subjektivität in Erscheinung tritt. Ihre Genese ereignet sich aufgrund von Bündnissen und Ansteckung, ein unendliches Rhizom, das seine Natur und Richtung nach dem Zufall der Rassenmischungen ändert, die in der grossen Mühle der kulturellen Anthropophagie stattfinden. (Anders als die Entwicklung der Identität-Gestalt-Subjektivität, die aus Verwandtschaftsverhältnissen heraus entsteht und so die Phantasie einer linearen Evolution fördert und die einengende Bindung an ein Wertesystem, das als Essenz des höchsten Wesens verstanden wird.)

Die Stimme Brasiliens, die in der derzeitigen Diskussion über die Krise der Identität zu vernehmen ist, ist die einer solchen hochaktiven, anthropophagischen Subjektivität. Als wären wir für immer dieses Volk mit dem gemischten und unreinen Blut, das sich jetzt über die ganze Erde verbreitet (Ribeiro), als hätten wir in diesem globalen Diskurs ein Know-how beizusteuern, was die Navigation auf dem unendlichen bewegten Ozean der Welt von heute angeht. Die einmalige Leistung dieser anthropophagischen Stimme in dieser verfahrenen Situation ist, dass sie nicht nur theoretisch, sondern auch pragmatisch zeigt, dass es nicht um die Wiederherstellung einer Identität geht, diesen halluzinierten Horizont, der die Menschheit in die Hoffnungsvollen und die Verzweifelten unterteilt. Das Problem besteht darin, das Gefühl der subjektiven Beständigkeit vom Modell der Identität zu lösen; sich selbst vom Identitäts-Gestalt-Prinzip bei der Schaffung eines «Zuhause» zu befreien.

Ist es schon schwierig, ohne konkretes Dach über dem Kopf zu leben, so ist kein menschliches Leben möglich ohne eine Lebensweise, die ein Gefühl des «Zuhause» erlaubt. Wir werden nicht alle obdachlos: Es trifft nicht zu, dass das subjektive Haus verschwunden ist. Es unterliegt nur einer radikalen Transformation seines Konstruktionsprinzips, was natürlich beunruhigend ist. In der heutigen Zeit ein «Zuhause» zu bauen, macht Methoden erforderlich, die in der modernen westlichen Subjektivität eher ungenutzt bleiben, aber der anthropophagischen Lebensweise in ihren aktivsten Formen durchaus vertraut sind: sich auf Umwandlungen im Körper einzustellen, aber auch auf Wirkungen von Informationen, Verknüpfungen von Strömen; die Welle der von solchen Strömen ausgelösten Ereignisse zu reiten; das Erproben von Existenzformen, die diese empfindlichen Veränderungen widerspiegeln; die Erfindung neuer Lebensmöglichkeiten. Solch ein Vorgehen erfordert natürlich den Einsatz von Körperkräften, die in der zeitgenössischen Subjektivität ebenfalls brachliegen. Es gilt über die blosse Repräsentation hinauszugehen und eine Intimität mit dem Körper als schwingender Oberfläche herzustellen, welche die Wellen spürt, bevor sie anrollen; die Welle reiten zu lernen; eine Vertrautheit innerhalb der Bewegung selbst herzustellen, denn: «Seefahrt tut not.» Tun wir dies nicht, werden wir Schiffbruch erleiden. Ein «Zuhause», das sich aus unvollständigen, einmaligen, provisorischen, fluktuierenden Entitäten in einem Prozess ständigen Werdens zusammensetzt, ein «Zuhause», das jeder (Individuum oder Gruppe) konstruiert, indem er die Strömungen benutzt, die den Körper berühren, aber auch die selektive Filterung, die vom Begehren gesteuert wird.

Dass wir uns dringend vom Konzept des Identisch-Gestalthaften befreien müssen, macht sich überall auf der Welt bemerkbar. Wir Brasilianer sind die Träger eines Impfstoffes, der es möglich macht, diesem Übel zu widerstehen. Der «Impfstoff der Anthropophagie»[8] ist angesagt bei einem «Geist, der den Geist nicht ohne Körper denken will». Oswald de Andrade vertrat letztlich die These, dass die Anthropophagie eine «gesellschaftliche Therapie für die moderne Welt» darstelle.[9] Es macht ganz den Anschein, dass sie unentbehrlich sein wird für die Ökologie der Seele (oder des Begehrens?) am Ende dieses Jahrtausends.

(Übersetzung: Egbert Hörmann)

1) Fernando Pessoa, *Das Buch der Unruhe*, Ammann Verlag, Zürich 1985, S. 15.
2) Oswald de Andrade, «Manifesto de Poesia Pau-brasil» (1924), in: *A Utopia Antropofágica: Obras Completas de Oswald de Andrade*, São Paulo 1990.
3) Oswald de Andrade, «Manifesto Antropófago» (1928), in: op. cit.
4) Darcy Ribeiro, *O povo brasileiro. A formação e o sentido do Brasil*, Companhia das Letras, São Paulo 1995.
5) de Andrade, «Manifesto Antropófago».
6) «A proposito da magia do objeto» (1965), in: *Lygia Clark*, Col. Arte Brasilera Contemporánea, Rio de Janeiro 1980.
7) «Eden» (1969), in: *Hélio Oiticica*, Galerie Nationale du Jeu de Paume, Paris 1992.
8) Oswald de Andrade, «Manifesto Antropófago».
9) Oswald de Andrade, «The March of the Utopias» (1953), in: *A Utopia Antropofágica. Obras Completas de Oswald de Andrade.*

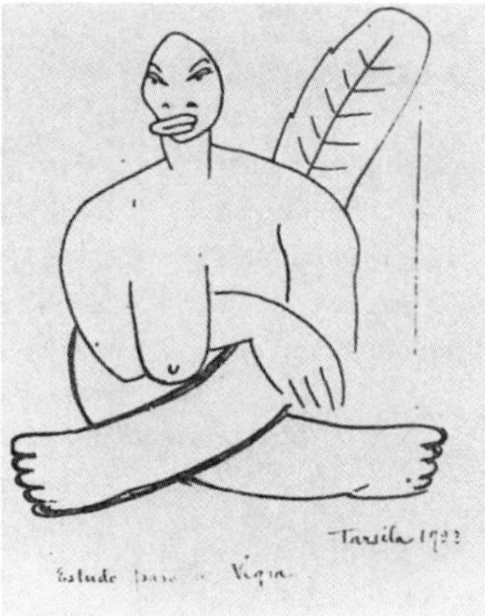

TARSILA DO AMARAL, ESTUDO PARA "A NEGRA," 1923, Tusche und Bleistift auf Papier, 25,4 x 19 cm / ink and pencil on paper, 10 x 7 1/2".

Kleinbörse für Waren, Fragen und Ideen / Exchange of commodities: real and idea

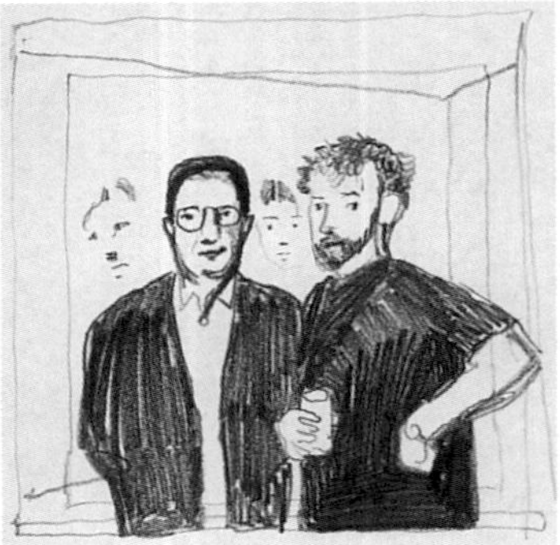

Boris Groys und Pawel Pepperstein im RAUM DER GESICHTER, Kunsthaus Zug, 1998. Skizze von Pepperstein nach einem Vernissage-Photo von Guido Baselgia. / Boris Groys and Pavel Pepperstein in the ROOM OF FACES at the Kunsthaus Zug, 1998. Draft by Pavel Pepperstein after a photograph taken by Guido Baselgia at the opening.

Akademie Schloss Solitude

July 31, 1999 is the deadline to apply for a grant to participate in the Academy's program 2000–2001. The selected participants will be informed by mail in October 1999. The earliest start for the grant is March 2000. For information and application forms contact the Akademie Schloss Solitude. See address below.

Der 31. Juli 1999 ist Schlusstermin für Bewerbungen um ein Stipendium zur Teilnahme am Programm der Akademie für die Jahre 2000-2001. Im Oktober werden ausgewählte Bewerber per Post kontaktiert. Das Solitude-Stipendium beginnt frühestens im März 2000. Information und Bewerbungsformulare verlangen Sie bitte direkt bei:

Akademie Schloss Solitude, Stiftung des Öffentlichen Rechts, Solitude 3, D-70197 Stuttgart
Tel. +49 711 9 96 19 0, Fax: +49 711 9 96 19 50
Internet: www.akademie-solitude.de
E-mail: mail@akademie-solitude.de

For Easy Rider or Ed Ruscha fans and addicts of the sixties in general:
Tony Shafrazi Gallery, New York, will soon publish 400 pages of photographs by Dennis Hopper: a fascinating book portraying Los Angeles in the sixties with pictures of Hopper's friends, contemporaries, artists and fellow actors as well as their comments and reminiscences.

Für Fans von Easy Rider, Ed Ruscha und den Sixties:
Demnächst gibt die Tony Shafrazi Galerie in New York ein 400 Seiten starkes Buch mit Photos von Easy-Rider-Darsteller Dennis Hopper heraus: ein faszinierendes Buch, ein Porträt von Los Angeles in den 60er Jahren, mit Photos von Hoppers Freunden und Zeitgenossen, von Künstlern und Schauspielern mit deren Erinnerungen und Kommentaren.

Tony Shafrazi Gallery
119 Wooster Street, New York, NY 10012
Fax 212 334-9499

SUSRET-ART Ein humanitäres Kunstprojekt

Susret ist das serbokroatische Wort für Begegnung und der Name einer aussergewöhnlichen Kunstmanufaktur aus Frastanz in Vorarlberg. Das Atelier geht auf ein einzigartiges Kunsttherapie- und Sozialprojekt für kriegstraumatisierte bosnische Frauen zurück. Talentierte Hände weben hier in Museumsqualität Teppiche, Tapisserien und textile Objekte nach Entwürfen renommierter internationaler Künstler und knüpfen damit an die Tradition der Webwerkstätten der Bauhaus-Gruppe und der Wiener Werkstätte an. Die Auflagen der zeitgenössischen Werke sind streng limitiert und werden vom Künstler zertifiziert. Ausstellungen in Europa, New York, Los Angeles. Sammlerobjekte. Ankäufe durch diverse Museen und Galerien.

DESIGN: GARY HUME, TAPISSERIE, OHNE TITEL, 1998; Schuss: Kammgarne, Gobelingarne; Kette: Baumwolle, 258 Arbeitsstunden, 194 x 135 cm / TAPESTRY, UNTITLED, weft: yarn, gobelin yarn; warp: cotton; 258 hours of work, 76 3/8 x 53 7/8".

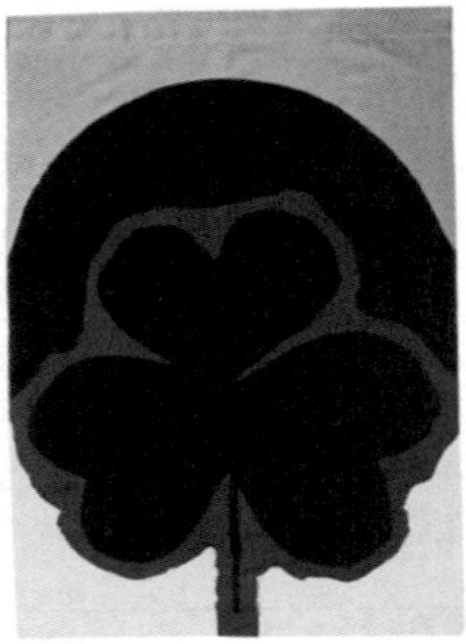

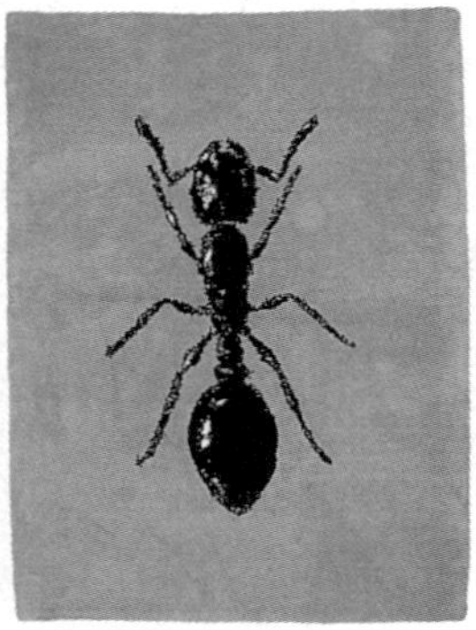

DESIGN: PETER KOGLER, KNÜPFTEPPICH, OHNE TITEL, 1997, Schuss und Flor: Schurwolle; Kette: Baumwolle, 350 Arbeitsstunden, 280 x 200 cm / CARPET, UNTITLED, weft and pile: virgin wool; warp: cotton, 350 hours of work, 110 1/4 x 78 3/4".

Garderobe

'gär-,drōb

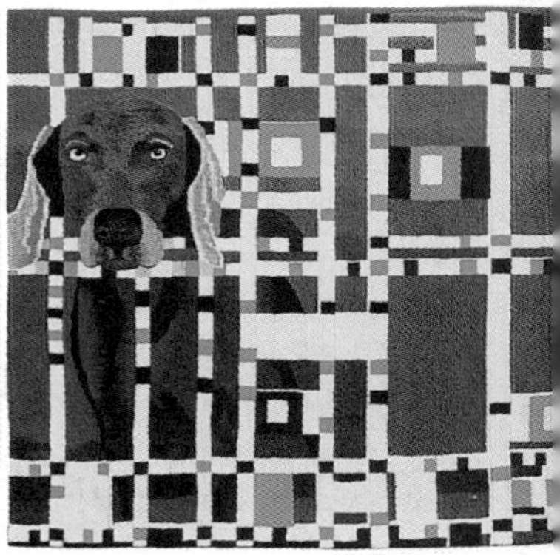

DESIGN: WILLIAM WEGMAN, TAPISSERIE, «FAYDRIAN», 1998, Schuss: Kammgarne, Gobelingarne; Kette: Baumwolle; 200 Arbeitsstunden, 90 x 90 cm / TAPESTRY, "FAYDRIAN," weft: yarn, gobelin yarn; warp: cotton; 200 hours of work, 35 3/8 x 35 3/8".

A humanitarian art project

SUSRET is the Serbo-Croatian word fo "encounter" and the name of an unusua art workshop in Frastanz, Austria. Th workshop has grown out of a unique socia and art therapy project for women trau matized by the war in Bosnia. Talente hands weave museum-quality carpets, tap estries, and textile objects after the de signs of renowned international artists thus continuing the tradition of the weav ing manufactories of the Bauhaus and th Wiener Werkstätte. The editions of thes contemporary works are strictly limite and certified by the artists. Exhibitions i Europe, New York, Los Angeles. Collec tor's items. Purchased by diverse museum and galleries.

Susret-ART, Project "Artists & Refugees"
Fellengattnerstrasse 8
A-6820 Frastanz-Felsenau
Tel./Fax: 0043-5522-81241

Carpets & War / Teppiche und Krieg

For a variation on the making of carpets as a means of dealing with the trauma of war (in Afghanistan), see "War—Sign—War," in: *Parkett* no. 24, 1990, pp. 107 ff. / Über das Teppichknüpfen im Zusammenhang mit traumatischen Kriegserfahrungen (damals in Afghanistan) vgl. auch «Krieg – Zeichen – Krieg», *Parkett* Nr. 24, 1990, S. 107 ff.

Anzeigenbedingungen: Kauf eines Abonnements bzw. eines Geschenkabonnements be Platzierung eines Inserates. / Advertising rates: Order of one (gift) subscription per ad.

PARKETT

ARTISTS' EDITIONS FOR PARKETT SUBSCRIBERS

55

The PARKETT Series is created in collaboration with artists, who contribute an original work available exclusively to the subscribers in the form of a signed limited SPECIAL EDITION. The available works are also reproduced in each PARKETT issue.

Each SPECIAL EDITION is available by order from any one of our offices in New York or Zurich. Just fill in the details below and send this card to the office nearest you. Once your order has been processed, you will be issued with an invoice and your personal edition number. Upon receipt of payment, you will receive the SPECIAL EDITION. (Please note that supply is subject to availability. PARKETT does not assume responsibility for any delays in production of SPECIAL EDITIONS. Postage is not included.)

☐ As a subscriber to PARKETT, I would like to order the following Special Edition(s), signed and numbered by the artist.

PARKETT No.	ARTIST	
PARKETT No.	ARTIST	NAME:
PARKETT No.	ARTIST	ADDRESS:
PARKETT No.	ARTIST	CITY:
PARKETT No.	ARTIST	STATE/ZIP:
PARKETT No.	ARTIST	COUNTRY:
PARKETT No.	ARTIST	PHONE:

☐ I have indicated my way of payment on the reverse side of this form.

Send this form to the PARKETT office nearest you:
PARKETT PUBLISHERS 155 AV. OF THE AMERICAS NEW YORK, NY 10013 PHONE (212) 673-2660 FAX (212) 271-0704
PARKETT VERLAG QUELLENSTRASSE 27 CH-8031 ZÜRICH TELEFON +41-1-271 81 40 FAX +41-1-272 43 01
PARKETT VERLAG TANNENWALDALLEE 17 D-61348 BAD HOMBURG FAX 06172-937 444 www.parkettart.com

PARKETT

KÜNSTLEREDITIONEN FÜR PARKETT-ABONNENTEN

55

Die PARKETT-Buchreihe entsteht in Zusammenarbeit mit Künstlern, die eigens für die Abonnenten einen Originalbeitrag in Form einer limitierten und signierten EDITION gestalten. Diese Editionen sind auch in der Zeitschrift abgebildet und können mit dieser Bestellkarte in jedem unserer Büros in Zürich, Frankfurt oder New York bestellt werden. Sie erhalten dann Ihre persönliche Editionsnummer und eine Rechnung. Sobald wir Ihre Zahlung erhalten haben, schicken wir Ihnen Ihre Edition(en). (Lieferung nur solange vorrätig. PARKETT übernimmt keine Verantwortung für allfällige Verzögerungen bei der Herstellung der Vorzugsausgaben. Versandkosten zuzüglich.)

☐ Ich bin PARKETT-Abonnent(in) und bestelle folgende EDITION(EN), numeriert und vom Künstler signiert:

PARKETT Nr.	KÜNSTLER/IN	
PARKETT Nr.	KÜNSTLER/IN	NAME:
PARKETT Nr.	KÜNSTLER/IN	STRASSE:
PARKETT Nr.	KÜNSTLER/IN	PLZ/STADT:
PARKETT Nr.	KÜNSTLER/IN	LAND:
PARKETT Nr.	KÜNSTLER/IN	TEL.:

☐ Meine Zahlungsweise habe ich auf der Rückseite angegeben.

Senden Sie die Bestellkarte an das PARKETT-Büro in Ihrer Nähe:
PARKETT VERLAG QUELLENSTRASSE 27 CH-8031 ZÜRICH TELEFON +41-1-271 81 40 FAX +41-1-272 43 01
PARKETT VERLAG TANNENWALDALLEE 17 D-61348 BAD HOMBURG FAX 06172-937 444 www.parkettart.com
PARKETT PUBLISHERS 155 AV. OF THE AMERICAS NEW YORK, NY 10013 PHONE (212) 673-2660 FAX (212) 271-0704

PARKETT

SUBSCRIBE, COMPLETE OR SEND A GIFT SUBSCRIPTION TO THE BEST BOOK SERIES ON CONTEMPORARY ARTISTS

55

I subscribe to the PARKETT series, starting with issue no. ______

☐ for 1 year (3 issues) at US$ 80 (USA/Canada), SFr. 118.– (Europe), SFr. 140.– (Rest of the world).

☐ for 2 years (6 issues) at US$ 145 (USA/Canada), SFr. 215.– (Europe), SFr. 265.– (Rest of the world).

☐ for 1 year (3 issues) at a 20% student discount (US$ 65 for USA/ Canada, SFr. 95.– for Europe). A copy of my student ID is enclosed.

Send a gift subscription in my name, starting with issue no. ______

☐ for 1 year (3 issues) at US$ 80 (USA/Canada), SFr. 118.– (Europe), SFr. 140.– (Rest of the world).

☐ for 2 years (6 issues) at US$ 145 (USA/Canada), SFr. 215.– (Europe), SFr. 265.– (Rest of the world).

A gift card in my name will be sent to the recipient.

Postage included. All prices subject to change.

☐ I wish to complete my PARKETT collection and order the following issue no(s):

______

at SFr. 43.– each (up to no 43: SFr. 30.–; no. 44–48: SFr. 39.–), postage not included. Within the USA & Canada $ 32 (up to no. 43: $ 19.50; no. 44–48: $ 29), add postage: $ 5 (USA), $ 10 (Canada). (Sold out: No. 1–10, 13, 16, 19, 27, 29–31, 35)

☐ I wish to order the catalog raisonné of all PARKETT Artists' Editions from 1984–95 (SILENT & VIOLENT, 183 pages of which 144 in color, text by Susan Tallman, short artists' biographies) for Sfr. 49.– (USA: $ 39), excl. postage.

☐ I wish to order ______ copies of the new set of 105 postcards featuring PARKETT Artists' Editions for Sfr. 48.– (USA: $ 32) per set, excl. postage.

NAME: ______

ADDRESS: ______

CITY: ______

STATE/ZIP: ______

COUNTRY: ______

TEL.: ______ FAX: ______

GIFT RECIPIENT: ______

ADDRESS: ______

CITY: ______

STATE/ZIP: ______

COUNTRY: ______

☐ Charge my Visa Card ☐ Mastercard ☐ AMEX

Card No. ______ Expiration date ______

☐ Payment enclosed (US check or money order) ☐ Bill me

DATE ______

SIGNATURE ______

Send this form to the PARKETT office nearest you:

PARKETT PUBLISHERS 155 AV. OF THE AMERICAS NEW YORK, NY 10013 PHONE (212) 673-2660 FAX (212) 271-0704

PARKETT VERLAG QUELLENSTRASSE 27 CH-8031 ZÜRICH TELEFON +41-1-271 81 40 FAX +41-1-272 43 01

PARKETT VERLAG TANNENWALDALLEE 17 D-61348 BAD HOMBURG FAX 06172-937 444 www.parkettart.com

PARKETT

ABONNIEREN, VERVOLLSTÄNDIGEN ODER VERSCHENKEN SIE DIE UMFASSENDSTE BUCHREIHE ÜBER GEGENWARTSKÜNSTLER

55

Ich abonniere die PARKETT-Reihe ab Nr. ______

☐ für 1 Jahr (3 Ausgaben) zu: DM 130.– (BRD), SFr. 108.– (Schweiz), SFr. 118.– (übriges Europa).

☐ für 2 Jahre (6 Ausgaben) zu: DM 238.– (BRD), SFr. 190.– (Schweiz), SFr. 215.– (übriges Europa).

☐ für 1 Jahr (3 Ausgaben) mit 20% Studentenermässigung (BRD: DM 104.–/Schweiz: SFr. 87.–/Europa: SFr. 95.–). Eine Kopie meines Studentenausweises lege ich bei.

Ich verschenke ein PARKETT-Abonnement ab Nr. ______

☐ für 1 Jahr (3 Ausgaben) zu: DM 130.– (BRD), SFr. 108.– (Schweiz), SFr. 118.– (übriges Europa).

☐ für 2 Jahre (6 Ausgaben) zu: DM 238.– (BRD), SFr. 190.– (Schweiz), SFr. 215.– (übriges Europa).

Das Geschenk-Abo mit einer Geschenkkarte wird in meinem Namen versandt.

Preise einschliesslich Versandkosten. Preisänderungen vorbehalten.

☐ Ich möchte meine PARKETT-Sammlung vervollständigen und bestelle die folgende(n) noch erhältliche(n) Ausgabe(n) Nr. ______ zu je DM 49.–/SFr. 43.– (bis Nr. 43: DM 35.–/SFr. 30.–; Nr. 44–48: DM 45.–/ SFr. 39.–, zzgl. Versandkosten (vergriffen: Nr. 1–10, 13, 16, 19, 27, 29–31, 35)

☐ Ich bestelle das Werkverzeichnis der PARKETT-Künstlereditionen von 1984–95 (SILENT & VIOLENT, 183 S., davon 144 farbig, Text von Susan Tallman, Kurzbiographien der Künstler) für DM 60.–/SFr. 49.– zzgl. Versandkosten.

☐ Ich bestelle ______ Ex. des neuen Postkarten-Sets mit 105 PARKETT-Künstlereditionen zum Preis von DM 55.–/SFr. 48.– pro Set, zzgl. Versandkosten.

NAME: ______

STRASSE: ______

PLZ/STADT: ______

LAND: ______

TEL.: ______ FAX: ______

BESCHENKTE(R): ______

STRASSE: ______

PLZ/STADT: ______

LAND: ______

☐ Ich zahle mit Visa ☐ Eurocard/Mastercard ☐ AMEX

Karten Nr. ______ Gültig bis ______

☐ Mein Scheck über SFr./DM ______ liegt bei.

☐ Bitte senden Sie mir eine Rechnung.

DATUM ______

UNTERSCHRIFT ______

Senden Sie die Bestellkarte an das PARKETT-Büro in Ihrer Nähe:

PARKETT VERLAG QUELLENSTRASSE 27 CH-8031 ZÜRICH TELEFON +41-1-271 81 40 FAX +41-1-272 43 01

PARKETT VERLAG TANNENWALDALLEE 17 D-61348 BAD HOMBURG FAX 06172-937 444 www.parkettart.com

PARKETT PUBLISHERS 155 AV. OF THE AMERICAS NEW YORK, NY 10013 PHONE (212) 673-2660 FAX (212) 271-0704

COMPLETE YOUR PARKETT LIBRARY
VERVOLLSTÄNDIGEN SIE IHRE PARKETT-BIBLIOTHEK

OUT OF PRINT / VERGRIFFEN: **NO. 1** ENZO CUCCHI, **2** SIGMAR POLKE, **3** MARTIN DISLER, **4** MERET OPPENHEIM, **5** ERIC FISCHL, **6** JANNIS KOUNELLIS, **7** BRICE MARDEN, **8** MARKUS RAETZ, **9** FRANCESCO CLEMENTE, **10** BRUCE NAUMAN, **12** ANDY WARHOL, **13** REBECCA HORN, **16** ROBERT WILSON, **17** FISCHLI/WEISS, **19** JEFF KOONS, MARTIN KIPPENBERGER, **22** CHRISTIAN BOLTANSKI, JEFF WALL, **25** KATHARINA FRITSCH, JAMES TURRELL, **27** LOUISE BOURGEOIS, ROBERT GOBER, **29** CINDY SHERMAN, JOHN BALDESSARI, **30** SIGMAR POLKE, **31** DAVID HAMMONS, MIKE KELLEY, **35** GERHARD RICHTER

For out-of-print issues you can register your name and address with Parkett and you will be notified, if your issue(s) become(s) available on the secondary market / Für vergriffene Bände nimmt der Verlag gerne Ihren Suchauftrag entgegen und macht Ihnen bei allfälliger Verfügbarkeit im Handel ein Angebot.

COLLABORATIONS

RONI HORN
MARIKO MORI
BEAT STREULI
SCHORR, GUNNARSSON, GOROVOY, LEWIS
SPECTOR, BRYSON, NAKAZAWA, NICHOLS
GOODEVE, STALS, DANTO, AMANO, SMITH
INSERT: **MATTHEW RITCHIE**
VINCENT KATZ: **ALEX KATZ**
HORST BREDEKAMP: **STEPHAN VON HUENE**
PAUL D. MILLER: **SHIRIN NESHAT**
LES INFOS:
OKWUI ENWEZOR & WILLIAM KENTRIDGE
CUMULUS: VALÉRIA PICCOLI, MARIA LIND

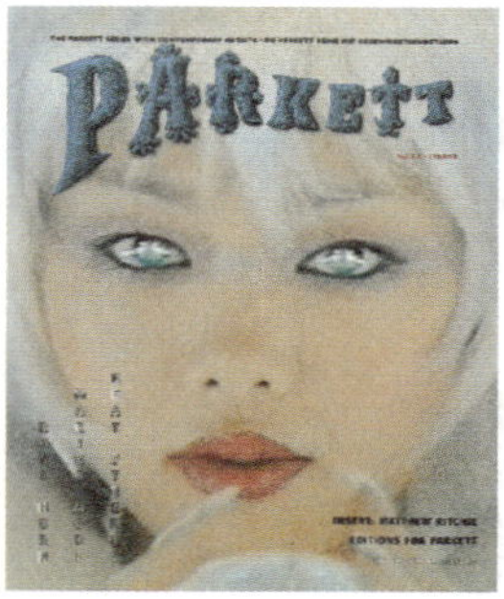

No. 54 - **ISBN 3-907582-04-7**

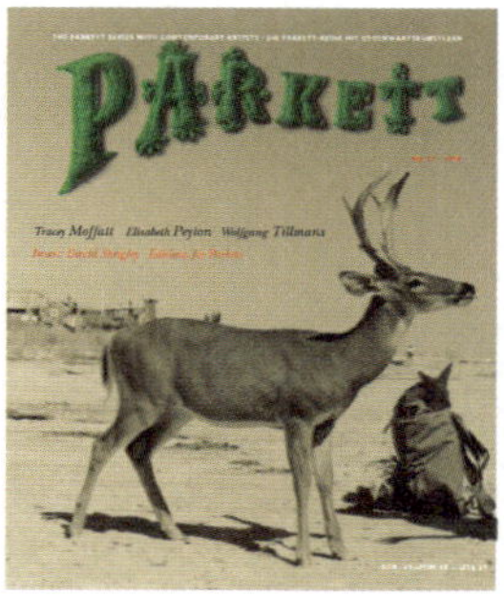

53 - **ISBN 3-907582-03-9**

TRACEY MOFFATT
ELIZABETH PEYTON
WOLFGANG TILLMANS
MARTIN, LAJER-BURCHARTH, RIMANELLI
PILGRIM, URSPRUNG, LIEBMANN, MATSUI
WAKEFIELD, BUDNEY, NESBITT, ZIEGLER
INSERT: **DAVID SHRIGLEY**
CATHERINE BERNARD: **JOHAN GRIMONPREZ**
BERNARD MARCADÉ: **ROBERT GOBER**
LES INFOS DE L'ENFER: VALERIA LIEBERMANN
CUMULUS: BLESSING, AUPETITALLOT
BALKON: STEINER/MAGNAGUAGNO

KAREN KILIMNIK
MALCOLM MORLEY
UGO RONDINONE
SCHORR, BÜRGI, JUNCOSA, MORLEY,
BENSZTEJN, BONAMI, VERWOERT, HOPTMAN,
INSERT: **THOMAS BAYRLE**
ED WHITE: **JEAN MICHEL OTHONIEL**
NEVILLE WAKEFIELD: **RICHARD SERRA**
GILDA WILLIAMS: **GILLIAN WEARING**
ROBERT GRESKOVIC: **MERCE CUNNINGHAM**
CUMULUS: WALKER, KURZMEYER
BALKON: CECILIA VICUÑA

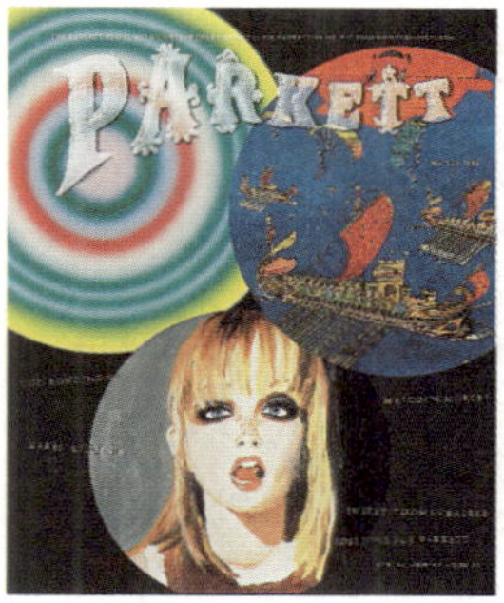

No. 52 - **ISBN 3-907582-02-0**

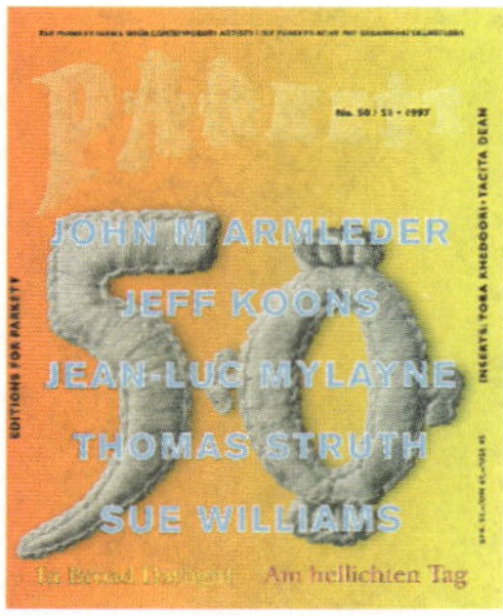

50/51 - **ISBN 3-907582-00-4**

JOHN M ARMLEDER, JEFF KOONS
JEAN-LUC MYLAYNE
THOMAS STRUTH, SUE WILLIAMS
DI PIETRANTONIO, BOVIER, MUNIZ,
SEWARD, LOERS, NICHOLS GOODEVE,
COOKE, DION, ARNAUDET, MYLAYNE,
CURIGER, LINGWOOD, OKUTSU, BRYSON,
SCHJELDAHL, NESBIT, DANNATT, CAMHI
INSERTS: **TOBA KHEDOORI, TACITA DEAN**
ONFRAY: **HYACINTHE RIGAUD,** NICOL: **SAM SAMORE**
MURPHY, VAN DER WALLE, STEINER,
KURT W. FORSTER: **FRANK GEHRY**
CUMULUS: COLEMAN, BIRNBAUM

LAURIE ANDERSON
DOUGLAS GORDON
JEFF WALL
FLOOD, BEZZOLA, FERGUSON
GILLICK/GORDON, BRYSON, PONTBRIAND
SCHORR, ANDERSON, BURCKHARDT, BUDNEY
INSERT: **SILVIA BÄCHLI**
COLIN DE LAND: **JOHN WATERS**
ROBERT STORR: **SEYDOU KEITA**
DANIELA SALVIONI: **CLEGG & GUTTMANN**
CUMULUS: KITTELMANN, MEYER

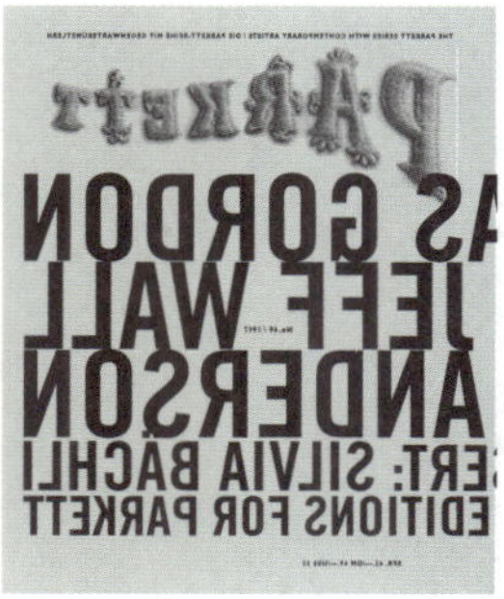

No. 49 - **ISBN 3-907509-99-4**

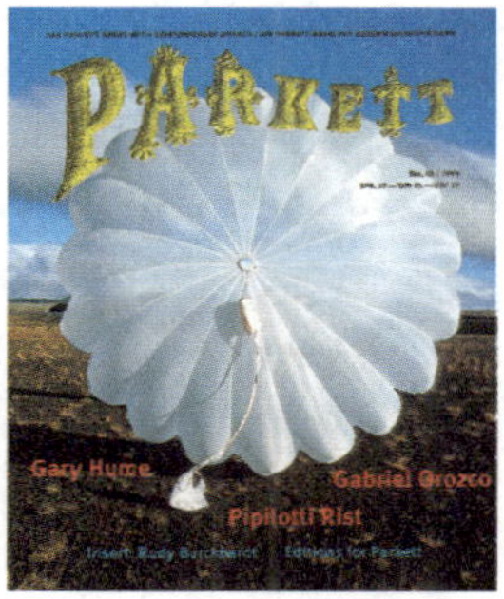

No. 48 - **ISBN 3-907509-98-6**

GARY HUME
GABRIEL OROZCO
PIPILOTTI RIST
BOVIER, MUIR, FOGLE, BONAMI
DE ZEGHER, SPECTOR, URSPRUNG
BABIAS, COLOMBO, ANDERSON
INSERT: **RUDY BURCKHARDT**
VINCENT KATZ: **RUDY BURCKHARDT**
VAN DER WALLE: **CHARLES LONG**
& STEREOLAB
FAYE HIRSCH: **BRUCE CONNER**
CHRISTOPH DOSWALD: **IAN ANÜLL**
CUMULUS: LEGGAT, SCHNEIDER

TONY OURSLER
RAYMOND PETTIBON
THOMAS SCHÜTTE
COOKE, RICHARD, NERI,
LEWIS, GROYS, ALS, RUGOFF,
GOODEVE, SEARLE, MARI, REUST,
WAKEFIELD, LOOCK, JANUS
INSERT: **ZOE LEONARD & CHERYL DUNYE**
JURI STEINER: **EMMA KUNZ**
MAX WECHSLER: **CHRISTOPH RÜTIMANN**
SUSAN MORGAN: **DIANE ARBUS**
CUMULUS: PRINCENTHAL, BOVIER/CHERIX

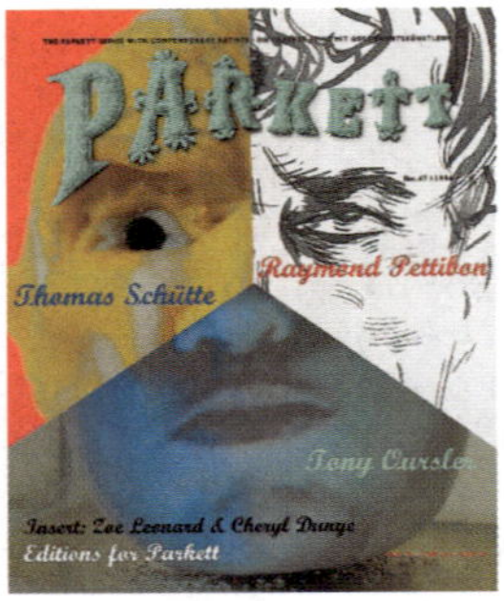

No. 47 - ISBN 3-907509-97-8

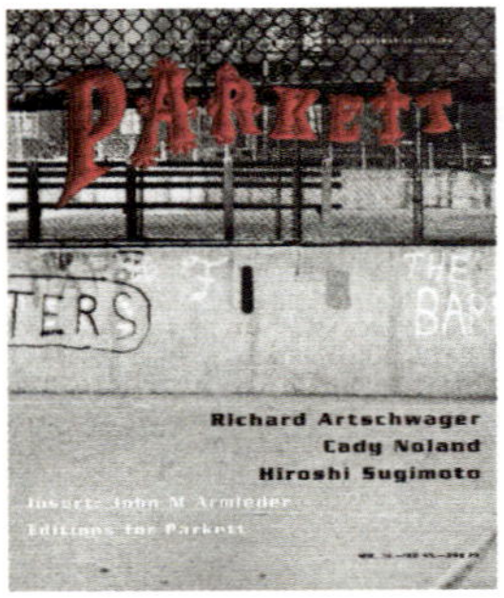

No. 46 - ISBN 3-907509-96-X

RICHARD ARTSCHWAGER
CADY NOLAND
HIROSHI SUGIMOTO
DEITCHER, SCHAFFNER, FORSTER, MUNIZ
ARMSTRONG, RELYEA, BOGDAN, GOODEVE
NICKAS, BRYSON, RUGOFF, DENSON
INSERT: **JOHN M ARMLEDER**
ROLAND WÄSPE: **ERWIN WURM**
DANIEL BIRNBAUM: **ÖYVIND FAHLSTRÖM**
LES INFOS DU PARADIS: ROBERT FLECK
CUMULUS: MILLER, VETTESE
BALKON: MARTIN HELLER

MATTHEW BARNEY
SARAH LUCAS
ROMAN SIGNER
BRYSON, ONFRAY, SEWARD, GOODEVE,
SALTZ, VAN ADRICHEM, SCHORR, FREEDMAN,
JOUANNAIS, BITTERLI, DOSWALD,
VIEWING, WECHSLER, DELAND
INSERT: **ELLIOTT PUCKETTE**
HEIDI GILPIN: **WILLIAM FORSYTHE**
ROBYN McKENZIE: **GEOFF LOWE**
MICHAEL TARANTINO: **CHANTAL AKERMAN**
CUMULUS: McEVILLEY, WAKEFIELD

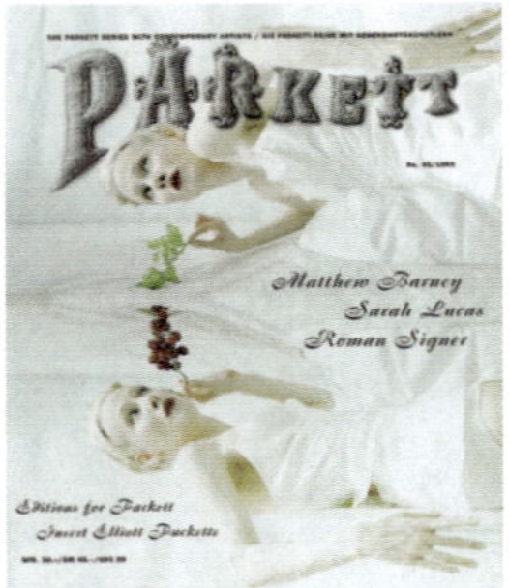

No. 45 - ISBN 3-907509-95-1

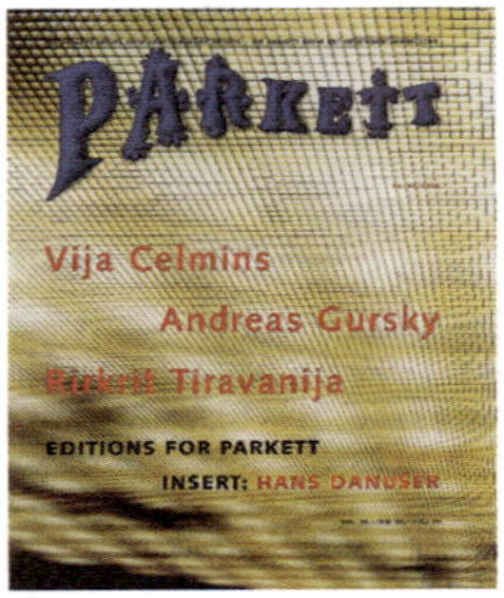

No. 44 - ISBN 3-907509-94-3

VIJA CELMINS
ANDREAS GURSKY
RIRKRIT TIRAVANIJA
PRINCENTHAL, LEWIS, SILVERTHORNE
SHIFF, CRIQUI, BURCKHARDT, WAKEFIELD
SCHORR, MELO, GILLICK, FLOOD, STEINER
INSERT: **HANS DANUSER**
LES INFOS: LIAM GILLICK & DOUGLAS GORDON
LYNNE COOKE, DAVID DEITCHER
DANIEL KURJAKOVIC: **MARIE JOSÉ BURKI**
NAN GOLDIN: **PETER HUJAR**
NOEMI SMOLIK: **ANDREAS SLOMINSKI**
JASON SIMON: **MARK DION**
LUK LAMBRECHT: **MARK LUYTEN**

JUAN MUÑOZ
SUSAN ROTHENBERG
LYNNE COOKE, ALEXANDRE MELO
JAMES LINGWOOD, GAVIN BRYARS
ROBERT CREELEY, INGRID SCHAFFNER
JEAN-CHRISTOPHE AMMANN
MARK STEVENS, JOAN SIMON
INSERT: **ROBERT SMITHSON**
NEVILLE WAKEFIELD
MICHELLE NICOL: **CARSTEN HÖLLER**
HANS-ULRICH OBRIST: **FABRICE HYBERT**

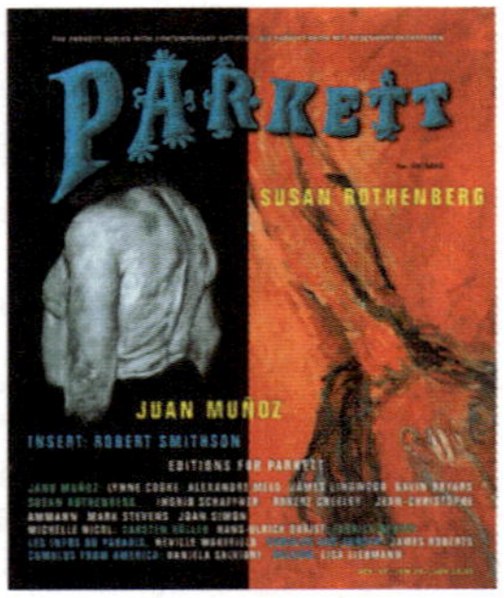

No. 43 - ISBN 3-907509-93-5

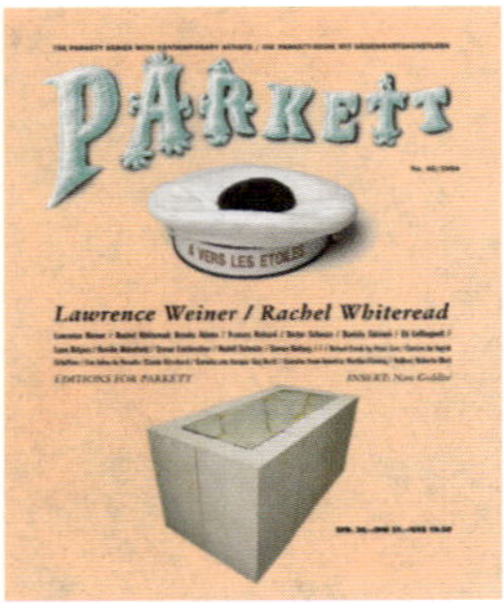

No. 42 - ISBN 3-907509-92-7

LAWRENCE WEINER
RACHEL WHITEREAD
BROOKS ADAMS, FRANCES RICHARD
DIETER SCHWARZ, DANIELA SALVIONI
ED LEFFINGWELL, LANE RELYEA
NEVILLE WAKEFIELD, RUDOLF SCHMITZ
TREVOR FAIRBROTHER, SIMON WATNEY
INSERT: **NAN GOLDIN**
VINCE LEO: **ROBERT FRANK**
CLAUDE RITSCHARD: **MARKUS RAETZ**

FRANCESCO CLEMENTE
GÜNTHER FÖRG
PETER FISCHLI/DAVID WEISS
DAMIEN HIRST
JENNY HOLZER
REBECCA HORN
SIGMAR POLKE
HOLLAND COTTER, BORIS GROYS
MAX WECHSLER, DAVID RIMANELLI
JOAN SIMON, GORDON BURN
GILBERT LASCAULT, WERNER SPIES
BICE CURIGER, JEFF PERRONE
G. ROGER DENSON, VIK MUNIZ
DAVE HICKEY

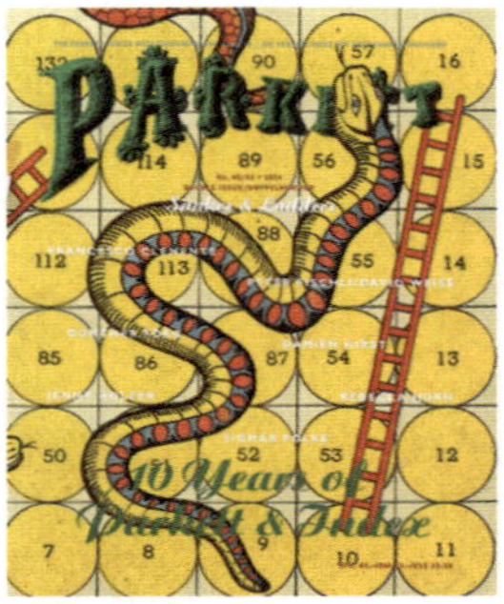

40/41 - ISBN 3-907509-90-0

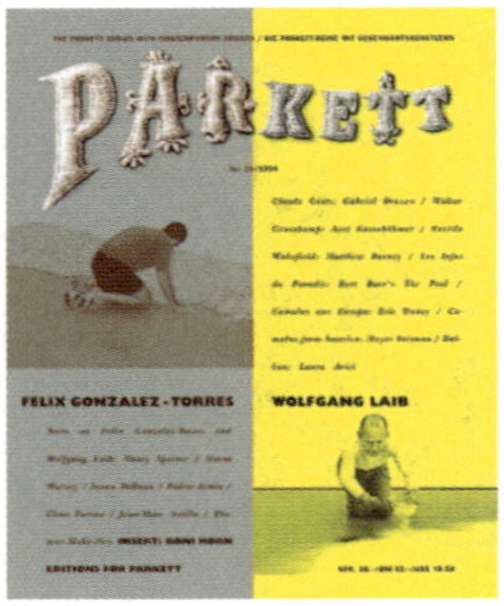

No. 39 - ISBN 3-907509-89-7

FELIX GONZALEZ-TORRES
WOLFGANG LAIB
NANCY SPECTOR, SIMON WATNEY,
SUSAN TALLMAN, DIDIER SEMIN,
CLARE FARROW, JEAN-MARC AVRILLA,
THOMAS McEVILLEY
CLAUDE GINTZ: **GABRIEL OROZCO**
WALTER GRASSKAMP: **AXEL KASSEBÖHMER**
NEVILLE WAKEFIELD: **MATTHEW BARNEY**
INSERT: **RONI HORN**
LES INFOS DU PARADIS: **BURT BARR**
CUMULUS: **MEYER VAISMAN**

ROSS BLECKNER
MARLENE DUMAS
EDMUND WHITE, SIMON WATNEY
JOSE LUIS BREA, MARINA WARNER
ANNA TILROE, INGRID SCHAFFNER
ULRICH LOOCK
INSERT: **RUDI MOLACEK**
HARTMUT BÖHME
MAX WECHSLER: **ADRIAN SCHIESS**
DORIS VON DRATHEN:
RACHEL WHITEREAD

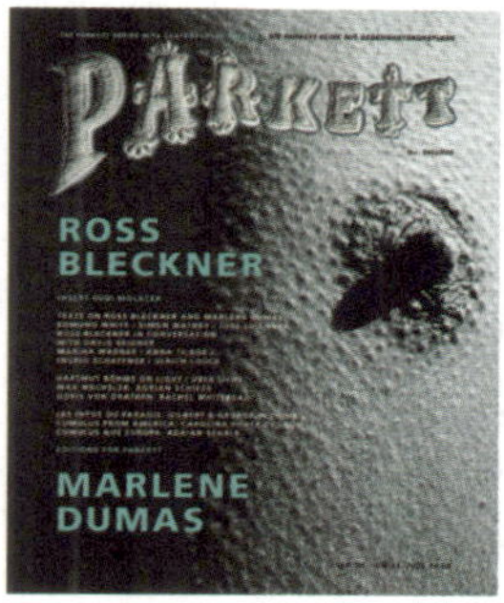

No. 38 - ISBN 3-907509-88-9

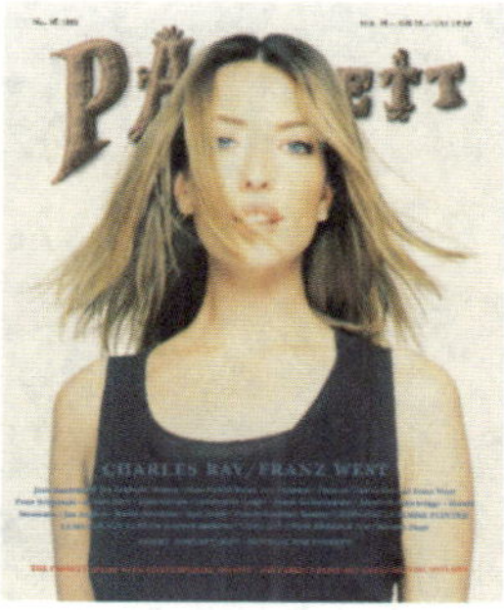

No. 37 - ISBN 3-907509-87-0

CHARLES RAY
FRANZ WEST
KLAUS KERTESS, CHRISTOPHER KNIGHT
PETER SCHJELDAHL, ROBERT STORR
JAN AVGIKOS, AXEL HUBER
MARTIN PRINZHORN, ELISABETH
SCHLEBRÜGGE, HARALD SZEEMANN,
DENYS ZACHAROPOULOS
INSERT: **PIPILOTTI RIST**
JEAN BAUDRILLARD
HANS RUDOLF REUST: **LUC TUYMANS**
PARKETT INQUIRY:
CHERCHEZ LA FEMME PEINTRE!

STEPHAN BALKENHOL
SOPHIE CALLE
NEAL BENEZRA, VIK MUNIZ, MAX KATZ
JEAN-CHRISTOPHE AMMANN
LUC SANTE, JOSEPH GRIGELY
PATRICK FREY, ROBERT BECK
INSERT: **RICHMOND BURTON**
URSULA PANHANS-BÜHLER: **EVA HESSE**
DOUGLAS BLAU: **JON KESSLER**
KIRBY GOOKIN: **LIZ LARNER**
LÁSZLÓ FÖLDÉNYI:
RUDOLF SCHWARZKOGLER

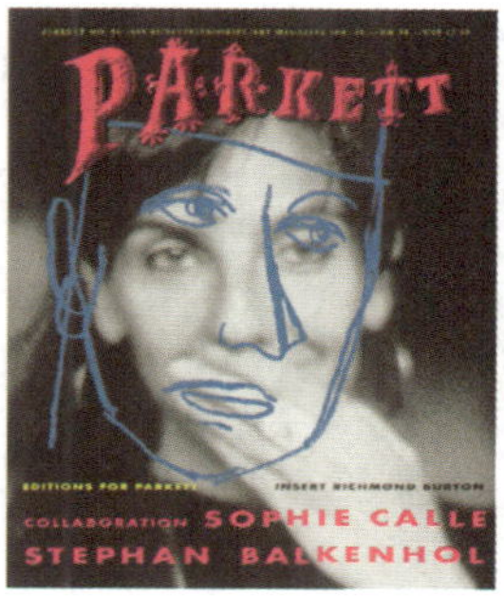

No. 36 - ISBN 3-907509-86-2

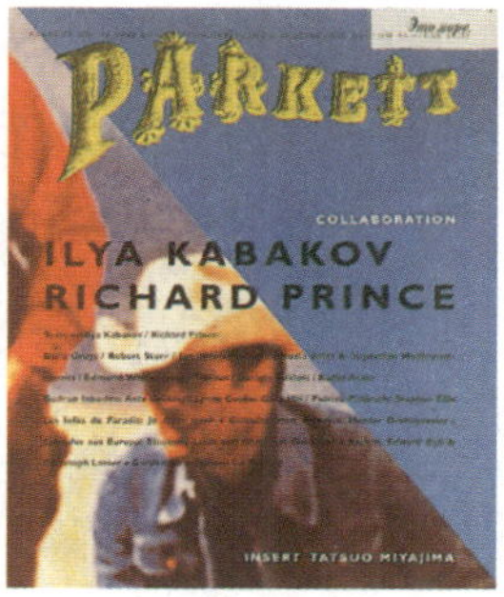

No. 34 - ISBN 3-907509-84-6

ILYA KABAKOV
RICHARD PRINCE
BORIS GROYS, ROBERT STORR
JAN THORN-PRIKKER
CLAUDIA JOLLES, EDMUND WHITE
SUSAN TALLMAN, DANIELA
SALVIONI, KATHY ACKER
INSERT: **TATSUO MIYAJIMA**
GUDRUN INBODEN: **ASTA GRÖTING**
LYNNE COOKE: **GARY HILL**
PATRICK McGRATH: **STEPHEN ELLIS**

ROSEMARIE TROCKEL
CHRISTOPHER WOOL
VERONIQUE BACCHETTA,
BARRETT WATTEN,
ANNE WAGNER, JIM LEWIS,
GREIL MARCUS, JEFF PERRONE,
DIEDRICH DIEDERICHSEN
INSERT: **ADRIAN SCHIESS**
MARINA WARNER: **PENIS PLENTY**
G. ROGER DENSON:
DENNIS OPPENHEIM
CAMIEL VAN WINKEL

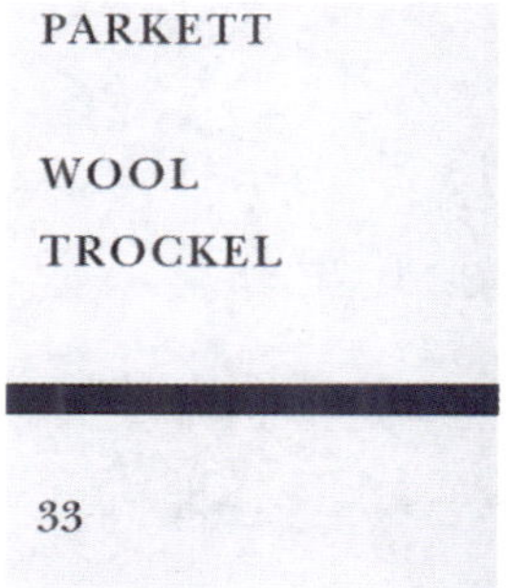

No. 33 - ISBN 3-907509-83-3

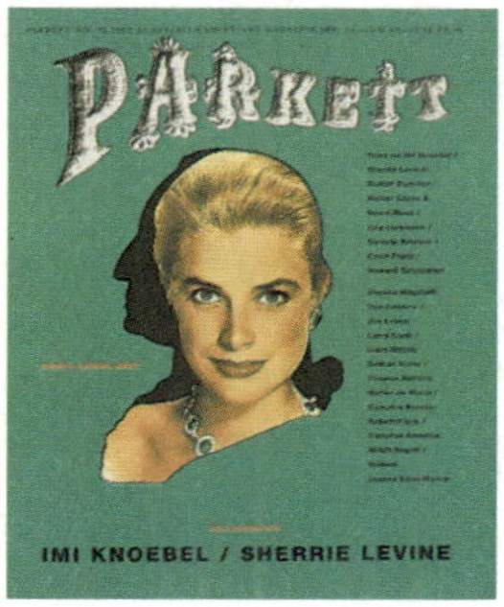

No. 32 - ISBN 3-907509-82-X

IMI KNOEBEL
SHERRIE LEVINE
RUDOLF BUMILLER
RAINER CRONE/DAVID MOOS
LISA LIEBMANN, DANIELA SALVIONI
ERICH FRANZ, HOWARD SINGERMANN
INSERT: **DAMIEN HIRST**
SHEENA WAGSTAFF: **VIJA CELMINS**
JIM LEWIS: **LARRY CLARK**
LIAM GILLICK: **BETHAN HUWS**
THOMAS KELLEIN: **WALTER DE MARIA**

FRANZ GERTSCH
THOMAS RUFF
HELMUT FRIEDEL, ULRICH LOOCK
I. MICHAEL DANOFF, AMEI WALLACH
RAINER MICHAEL MASON
MARC FREIDUS, JÖRG JOHNEN
TREVOR FAIRBROTHER/NORMAN BRYSON
INSERT: **LIZ LARNER**
JAMES LEWIS: **RICHARD PRINCE**
DAVID HICKEY:
THE INVISIBLE DRAGON/
DER UNSICHTBARE DRACHEN
PAUL TAYLOR: **JAMES ROSENQUIST**

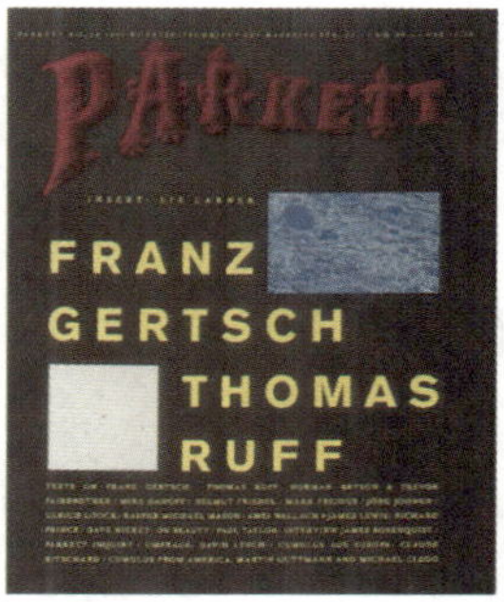

No. 28 - ISBN 3-907509-78-1

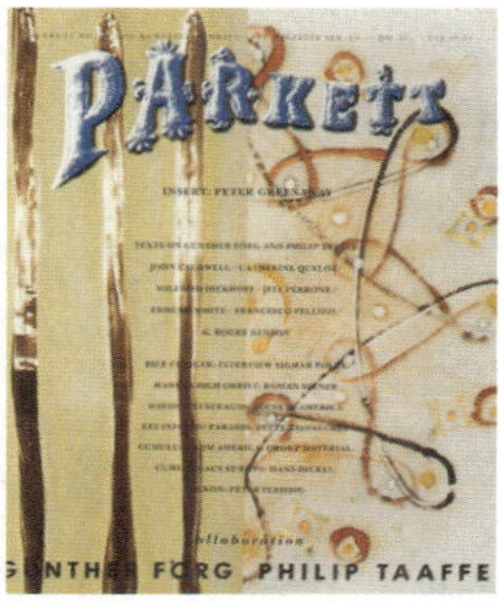

No. 26 - ISBN 3-907509-76-5

GÜNTHER FÖRG
PHILIP TAAFFE
JOHN CALDWELL, CATHERINE QUELOZ
WILFRIED DICKHOFF
JEFF PERRONE, EDMUND WHITE
FRANCESCO PELLIZZI
G. ROGER DENSON
INSERT: **PETER GREENAWAY**
BICE CURIGER: **SIGMAR POLKE**
HANS-ULRICH OBRIST:
ROMAN SIGNER
DAVID LEVI STRAUSS:
JOSEPH BEUYS

ALIGHIERO E BOETTI
JEAN-CHRISTOPHE AMMANN
GIOVAN BATTISTA SALERNO
RAINER CRONE & DAVID MOOS
FRIEDEMANN MALSCH
JEAN-PIERRE BORDAZ
ALAIN CUEFF
INSERT: **CINDY SHERMAN**
SHEENA WAGSTAFF:
SOPHIE CALLE
HERBERT LACHMEYER/
BRIGITTE FELDERER: **FRANZ WEST**
JUTTA KOETHER: **MIKE KELLEY**

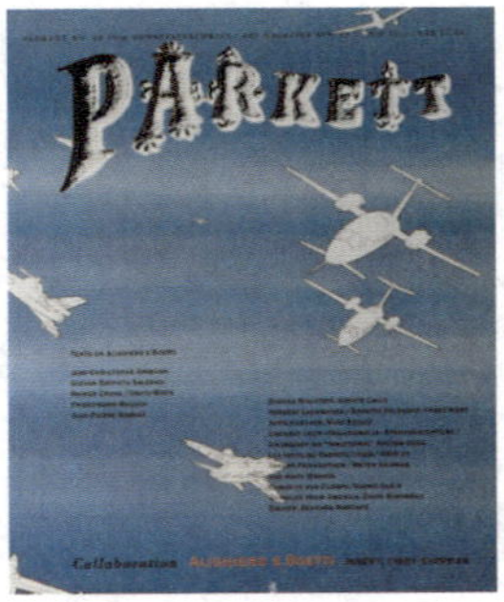

No. 24 - ISBN 3-907509-74-9

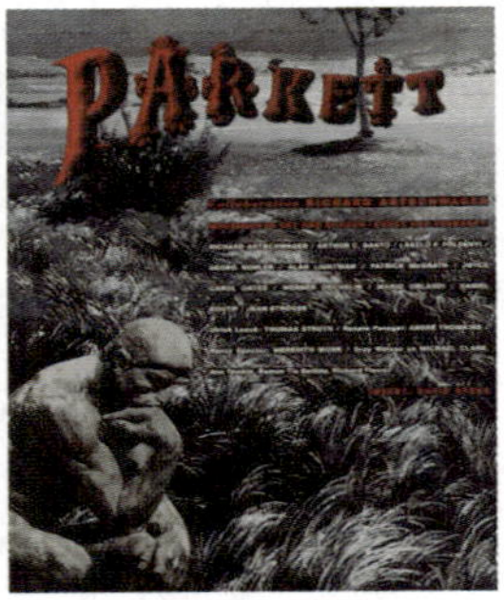

No. 23 - ISBN 3-907509-73-0

RICHARD ARTSCHWAGER
ARTHUR C. DANTO, GEORG KOHLER,
MARIO A. ORLANDO, JOYCE
CAROL OATES, WERNER OECHSLIN,
ALAN LIGHTMAN, PATRICK
McGRATH, DANIEL SOUTIF,
LASZLO F. FÖLDENYI, JEAN STROUSE
INSERT: **DAVID BYRNE**
RENATE PUVOGEL: **ANDRÉ THOMKINS**
ULRICH LOOCK: **THOMAS STRUTH**
NANCY SPECTOR: **MEREDITH MONK**

ALEX KATZ
JOHN RUSSELL, BROOKS ADAMS,
DAVID RIMANELLI, FRANCESCO
CLEMENTE, MICHAEL KRÜGER,
RICHARD FLOOD, PATRICK FREY,
CARL STIGLIANO, BICE CURIGER,
GLENN O'BRIEN
INSERT: **WILLIAM WEGMAN**
LISA LIEBMAN: **ROBERT GOBER**
JACQUELINE BURCKHARDT:
GIULIO ROMANO

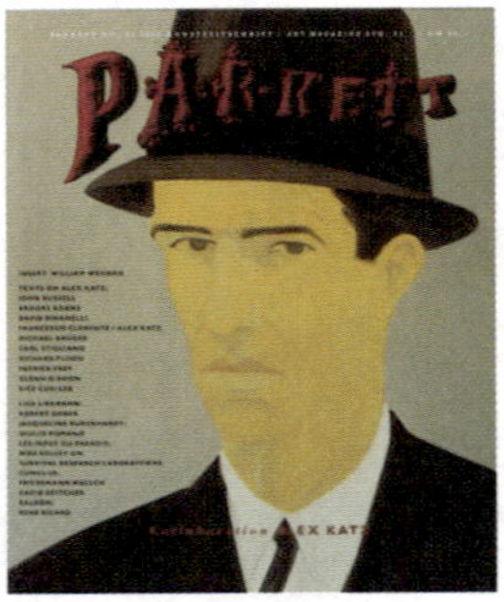

No. 21 - ISBN 3-907509-71-4

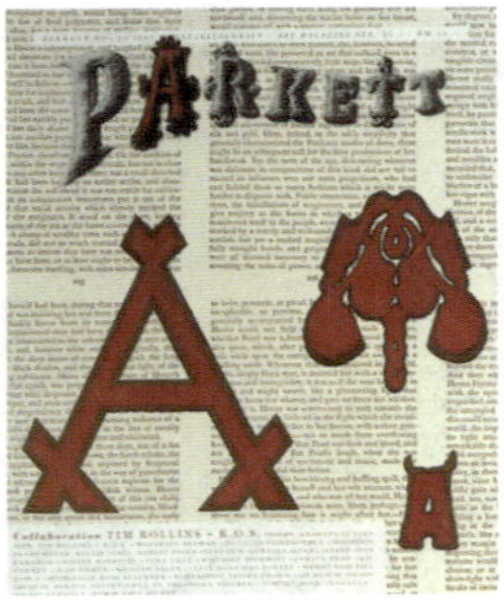

No. 20 - ISBN 3-907509-70-6

TIM ROLLINS + K.O.S.
MARSHALL BERMAN
TREVOR FAIRBROTHER
STATEMENTS, DIALOGUE 5
INSERT: **ANDREAS GURSKY**
MICHAEL NASH: **BILL VIOLA**
STEPHEN ELLIS: **ROSS BLECKNER**
KLAUS KERTESS: **TRISHA BROWN**

EDWARD RUSCHA
DAVE HICKEY, DENNIS HOPPER
ALAIN CUEFF, JOHN MILLER
CHRISTOPHER KNIGHT
INSERT: **BOYD WEBB**
JAN THORN-PRIKKER: **WOLS**
LYNNE COOKE: **TONY CRAGG**
BROOKE ADAMS: **JULIAN SCHNABEL**
DER KÜNSTLER ALS EXEM-
PLARISCH LEIDENDER?
EINE UMFRAGE / THE ARTIST AS A
MODEL SUFFERER? AN INQUIRY

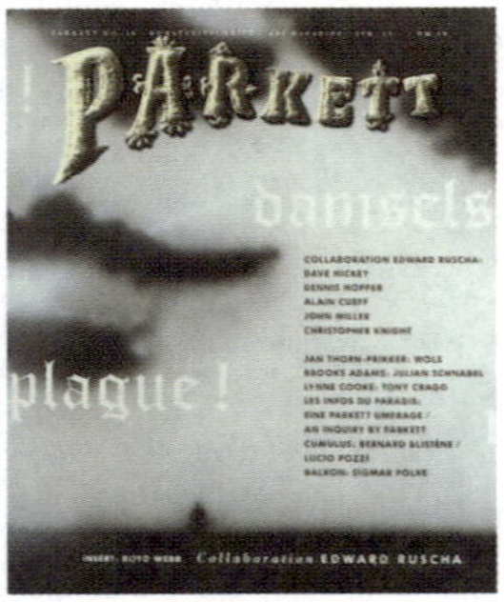

No. 18 - ISBN 3-907509-68-4

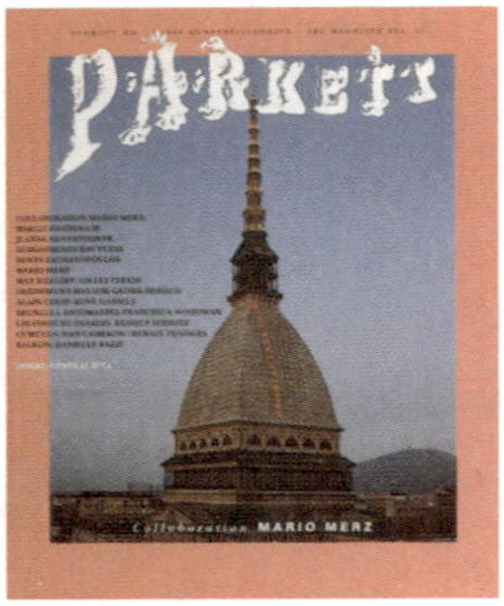

No. 15 - ISBN 3-907509-65-X

MARIO MERZ
MARLIS GRÜTERICH, JEANNE
SILVERTHORNE, DEMOSTHENES
DAVVETAS, HARALD SZEEMANN,
DENYS ZACHAROPOULOS
INSERT: **GENERAL IDEA**
MAX KOZLOFF: **GILLES PERESS**
FRIEDEMANN MALSCH:
GEORG HEROLD
BRUNELLA ANTOMARINI:
FRANCESCA WOODMAN

GILBERT & GEORGE
DUNCAN FALLOWELL, MARIO
CODOGNATO, JEREMY COOPER,
DEMOSTHENES DAVVETAS,
WOLF JAHN
INSERT: **ROSEMARIE TROCKEL**
ROBERT STORR: **NANCY SPERO**
HAIM STEINBACH: **MANIFESTO**
JÖRG ZUTTER: **THOMAS HUBER**

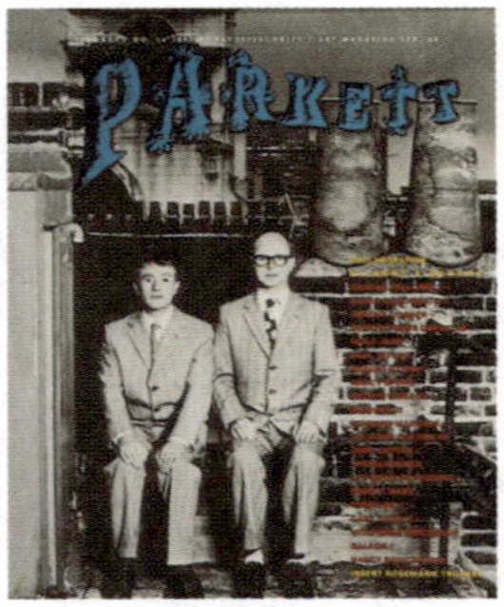

No. 14 - ISBN 3-907509-64-1

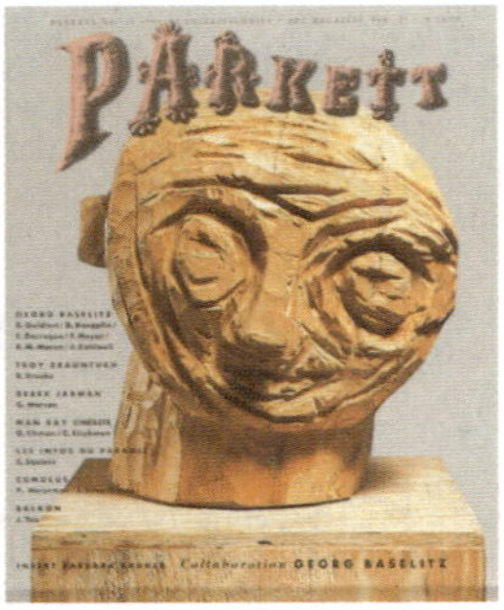

No. 11 - ISBN 3-907509-61-7

GEORG BASELITZ
REMO GUIDIERI, DIETER
KOEPPLIN, ERIC DARRAGON,
RAINER MICHAEL MASON, FRANZ
MEYER, JOHN CALDWELL
INSERT: **BARBARA KRUGER**
GRAY WATSON: **DEREK JARMAN**
CAROL SQUIERS:
PHOTO OPPORTUNITY
ROSETTA BROOKS:
TROY BRAUNTUCH

PARKETT

ARTISTS' MONOGRAPHS & EDITIONS / KÜNSTLERMONOGRAPHIEN & EDITIONEN,

FOR AVAILABILITY SEE NEXT PAGE / LIEFERBARKEIT SIEHE FOLGENDE SEITE

Laurie Anderson, vol. 49
John Armleder, vol. 50/51
Richard Artschwager, vol. 23, vol. 46
John Baldessari, vol. 29
Stephan Balkenhol, vol. 36
Matthew Barney, vol. 45
Georg Baselitz, vol. 11
Ross Bleckner, vol. 38
Alighiero e Boetti, vol. 24
Christian Boltanski, vol. 22
Louise Bourgeois, vol. 27
Sophie Calle, vol. 36
Vija Celmins, vol. 44
Francesco Clemente, vol. 9 & 40/41
Enzo Cucchi, vol. 1
Martin Disler, vol. 3
Marlene Dumas, vol. 38
Eric Fischl, vol. 5
Peter Fischli/David Weiss, vol.17, 40/41
Günther Förg, vol. 26 & 40/41
Katharina Fritsch, vol. 25
Franz Gertsch, vol. 28
Gilbert & George, vol. 14
Robert Gober, vol. 27
Felix Gonzalez-Torres, vol. 39
Douglas Gordon, vol. 49
Andreas Gursky, vol. 44
David Hammons, vol. 31
Damien Hirst, vol. 40/41
Jenny Holzer, vol. 40/41
Rebecca Horn, vol. 13 & 40/41
Roni Horn, vol. 54
Gary Hume, vol. 48
Ilya Kabakov, vol. 34
Alex Katz, vol. 21
Mike Kelley, vol. 31
Karen Kilimnik, vol 52
Martin Kippenberger, vol. 19
Imi Knoebel, vol. 32
Jeff Koons, vol. 19, 50/51
Jannis Kounellis, vol. 6
Wolfgang Laib, vol. 39
Sherrie Levine, vol. 32
Sarah Lucas, vol. 45
Brice Marden, vol. 7
Mario Merz, vol. 15
Tracey Moffatt, vol. 53
Mariko Mori, vol. 54
Malcolm Morley, vol. 52
Juan Muñoz, vol. 43
Jean-Luc Mylayne, vol. 50/51
Cady Noland, vol. 46
Bruce Nauman, vol. 10
Meret Oppenheim, vol. 4
Gabriel Orozco, vol. 48
Tony Oursler, vol. 47
Raymond Pettibon, vol. 47
Elizabeth Peyton, vol. 53
Sigmar Polke, vol. 2, 30 & 40/41
Richard Prince, vol. 34
Markus Raetz, vol. 8
Charles Ray, vol. 37
Gerhard Richter, vol. 35
Pipilotti Rist, vol. 48
Tim Rollins & K.O.S., vol. 20
Ugo Rondinone, vol. 52
Susan Rothenberg, vol. 43
Thomas Ruff, vol. 28
Edward Ruscha, vol. 18 & 55
Thomas Schütte, vol. 47
Cindy Sherman, vol. 29
Roman Signer, vol. 45
Andreas Slominski, vol. 55
Beat Streuli, vol. 54
Thomas Struth, vol. 50/51
Hiroshi Sugimoto, vol. 46
Philip Taaffe, vol. 26
Sam Taylor-Wood, vol. 55
Wolfgang Tillmans, vol. 53
Rirkrit Tiravanija, vol. 44
Rosemarie Trockel, vol. 33
James Turrell, vol. 25
Jeff Wall, vol. 22 & 49
Andy Warhol, vol. 12
Lawrence Weiner, vol. 42
Franz West, vol. 37
Rachel Whiteread, vol. 42
Sue Williams, vol 50/51
Robert Wilson, vol. 16
Christopher Wool, vol. 33

vol.	Collaboration		
55	Edward Ruscha	m	e
	Andreas Slominski	m	e
	Sam Taylor-Wood	m	e
54	Roni Horn	m	e
	Mariko Mori	m	e
	Beat Streuli	m	e
53	Tracey Moffatt	m	e
	Elizabeth Peyton	m	
	Wolfgang Tillmans	m	e
52	Karen Kilimnik	m	e
	Malcolm Morley	m	e
	Ugo Rondinone	m	e
50/51	John Armleder	m	e
	Jeff Koons	m	e
	Jean-Luc Mylayne	m	e
	Thomas Struth	m	
	Sue Williams	m	e
49	Laurie Anderson	m	e
	Douglas Gordon	m	e
	Jeff Wall	m	
48	Gary Hume	m	
	Gabriel Orozco	m	
	Pipilotti Rist	m	
47	Tony Oursler	m	
	Raymond Pettibon	m	e
	Thomas Schütte	m	e
46	Richard Artschwager	m	
	Cady Noland	m	e
	Hiroshi Sugimoto	m	
45	Matthew Barney	m	
	Sarah Lucas	m	e
	Roman Signer	m	e
44	Vija Celmins	m	
	Andreas Gursky	m	
	Rirkrit Tiravanija	m	e
43	Juan Muñoz	m	e
	Susan Rothenberg	m	e
42	Lawrence Weiner	m	e
	Rachel Whiteread	m	
40/41	Francesco Clemente	m	e
	Peter Fischli/David Weiss	m	
	Günther Förg	m	
	Damien Hirst	m	
	Jenny Holzer	m	
	Rebecca Horn	m	
	Sigmar Polke	m	e
39	Felix Gonzalez-Torres	m	
	Wolfgang Laib	m	e
38	Ross Bleckner	m	
	Marlene Dumas	m	

vol.	Collaboration		
37	Charles Ray	m	
	Franz West	m	e
36	Stephan Balkenhol	m	e
36	Sophie Calle	m	e
35	Gerhard Richter		
34	Ilya Kabakov	m	
	Richard Prince	m	e
33	Rosemarie Trockel	m	e
	Christopher Wool	m	
32	Imi Knoebel		
	Sherrie Levine		
31	David Hammons		e
	Mike Kelley		
30	Sigmar Polke		
29	John Baldessari		
	Cindy Sherman		e
28	Franz Gertsch	m	e
	Thomas Ruff	m	e
27	Louise Bourgeois		
	Robert Gober		
26	Günther Förg	m	
	Philip Taaffe	m	
25	Katharina Fritsch	m	e
	James Turrell	m	e
24	Alighiero e Boetti	m	e
23	Richard Artschwager	m	
22	Christian Boltanski	m	
	Jeff Wall	m	
21	Alex Katz	m	e
20	Tim Rollins + K.O.S.	m	
19	Martin Kippenberger		
	Jeff Koons		
18	Ed Ruscha	m	
17	Peter Fischli/David Weiss		
16	Robert Wilson		
15	Mario Merz	m	
14	Gilbert & George	m	
13	Rebecca Horn		
12	Andy Warhol		
11	Georg Baselitz	m	
10	Bruce Nauman		
9	Francesco Clemente		
8	Markus Raetz		
7	Brice Marden		
6	Jannis Kounellis		
5	Eric Fischl		
4	Meret Oppenheim		
3	Martin Disler		
2	Sigmar Polke		
1	Enzo Cucchi		

m = available monograph / erhältliche Monographie, e = available edition / erhältliche Edition
Delivery subject to availability at time of order / Lieferung solange Vorrat

Each volume of PARKETT is created in collaboration with artists, who contribute an original work specially made for the readers of PARKETT. The works are available in a signed and numbered Special Edition. Prices are subject to change. Postage is not included.

EDITIONS FOR PARKETT

Jeder PARKETT-Band entsteht in Collaboration mit Künstlern, die eigens für die Leser von PARKETT Originalbeiträge gestalten. Diese Vorzugsausgaben sind als nummerierte und signierte Editionen erhältlich. Preisänderungen vorbehalten. Versandkosten und MwSt. (Schweiz) nicht inbegriffen.

Los Angeles: an intersection where angels do not fear to tread.

Eine Kreuzung in L.A. und im Raum zwischen Leben und Kunst: Folge der Abzweigung!

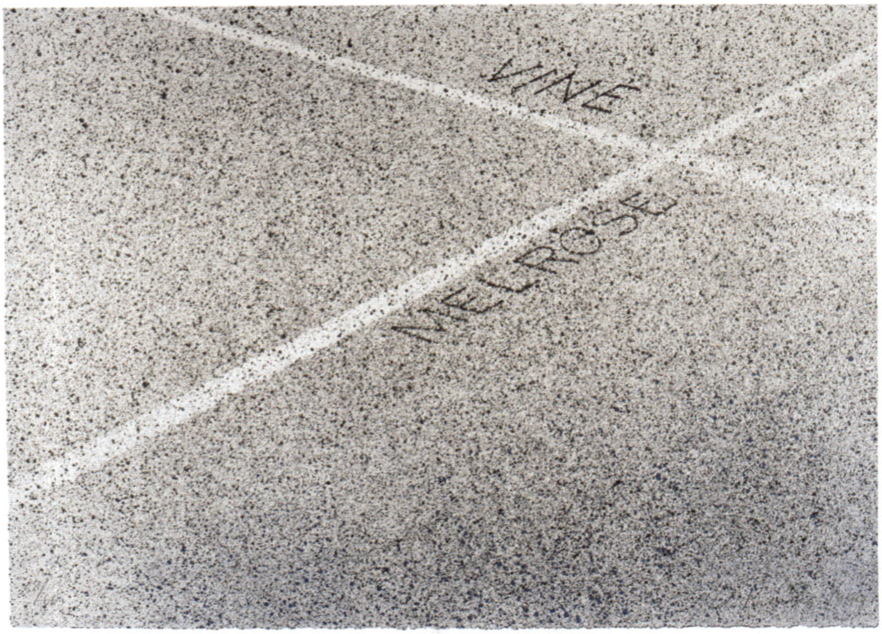

PARKETT 55

EDWARD RUSCHA

VINE / MELROSE, 1999

Two-color lithograph on Rives,
22¼ x 30⅛"
Printed by Hamilton Press, Venice, California
Edition of 60, signed and numbered,
$ 1100 / € 1000

VINE / MELROSE, 1999

Zweifarbige Lithographie auf Rives,
56,5 x 76,5 cm
Druck: Hamilton Press, Venice, California
Auflage: 60, signiert und nummeriert,
sFr. 1600.–

Measure for Measure – every inch a hyper-reality that begs authenticity and gauges only imponderables.

Zentimeter um Zentimeter und Zoll für Zoll: Slominski in Lebensgrösse.

PARKETT 55

ANDREAS SLOMINSKI

ZOLLSTOCK, 1999

Der Zollstock wird aufgeklappt verschickt.
Länge: 2 m
Auflage: 55, mit signiertem und nummeriertem Zertifikat, **sFr. 400.–**

FOLDING RULE, 1999

The rule will be delivered extended.
Length: 78¹¹⁄₁₆"
Edition of 55, with a signed and numbered certificate, **$ 270 / € 250**

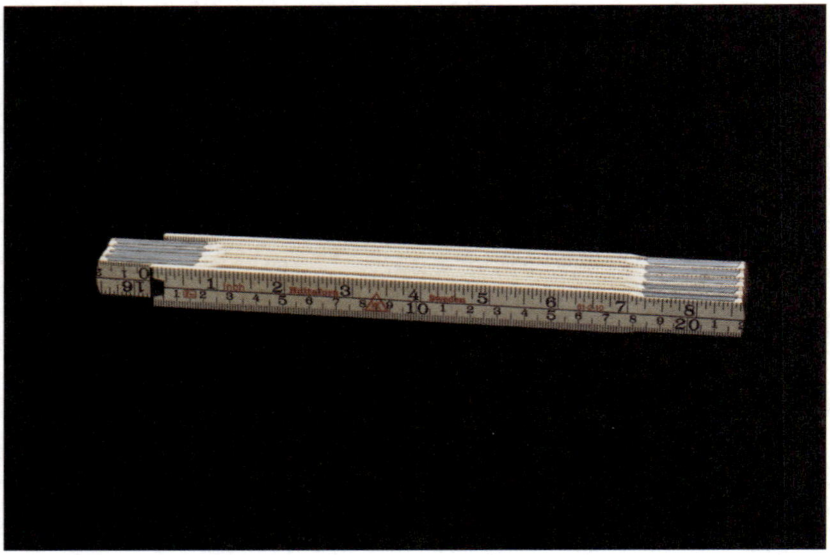

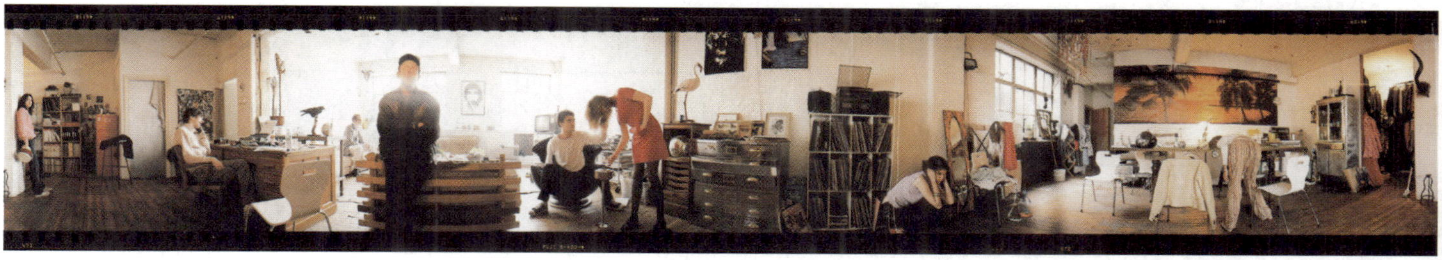

A loop in space and time: The revolution has been arrested, each figure suspended in the moment of "taking a giant step."

Erlebte Raumschleife als Innenraumrevolte

PARKETT 55

SAM TAYLOR-WOOD

FIVE REVOLUTIONARY SECONDS XIV (SKETCH), 1999

C-print, 360-degree panorama shot, 2¾ x 16½"

Edition of 50, signed and numbered, **$ 650 / € 560**

FÜNF REVOLUTIONÄRE SEKUNDEN XIV (ENTWURF), 1999

C-Print, 360-Grad-Panorama-Aufnahme, 7 x 42 cm

Auflage: 50, signiert und nummeriert, **sFr. 900.–**

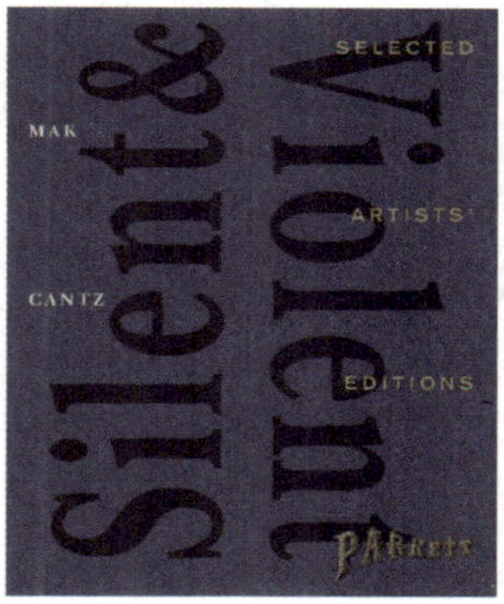

SILENT & VIOLENT

CATALOG RAISONNÉ OF ALL PARKETT ARTISTS' EDITIONS
from No. 1–44, 183 pages, 144 in color
text by Susan Tallmann, short biographies of all artists

WERKVERZEICHNIS ALLER PARKETT-KÜNSTLER-EDITIONEN
von Nr. 1–44, 183 Seiten, davon 144 in Farbe
Text von Susan Tallmann, Kurzbiographien der Künstler

sFr. 49.– / $ 39 / € 30

ISBN 3-89322-796-3 (engl.), ISBN 3-89322-787-3 (dt.)

NEW PARKETT-POSTCARD SET
featuring 105 artists' editions made for Parkett

DAS NEUE PARKETT-POSTKARTEN-SET
mit 105 Editionen, die von Künstlern für Parkett geschaffen wurden.

sFr. 48.– / $ 32 / € 30

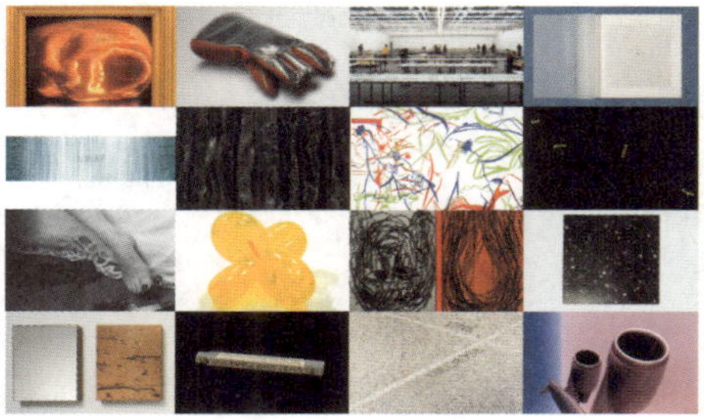

EXHIBITIONS

ZÜRICH

ACP VIVIANE EHRLI	Austrasse 38, 8045 Zürich, Tel. 01 463 63 53	ISTVÁN HAÁSZ – PASTELLE UND RELIEFS	**27.5.–24.7.99**
		LYNN MCCARTY – MALEREI AUS NEW YORK	**27.5.–24.7.99**
THOMAS AMMANN FINE ART	Restelbergstrasse 97, P.O. Box 922, 8044 Zürich, Tel. 01 360 51 60	IMPRESSIONISTS & 20TH CENTURY MASTERS	
		WILLEM DE KOONING	**15.6.–30.9.99**
ARS FUTURA	Bleicherweg 45, 8002 Zürich, Tel. 01 201 88 10	STEFAN BANZ	**21.5.–10.7.99**
		ART 30'99 BASEL, H212/ST04 ART STATEMENT MIT OLAF BREUNING	**16.6.–21.6.99**
BOB VAN ORSOUW	Limmatstrasse 270, 8005 Zürich, Tel. 01 273 11 00	PAUL MORRISON, CARL OSTENDARP, ALAN UGLOW	**13.3.–24.4.99**
		T. HUBBARD / A. BIRCHLER	**8.5.–10.7.99**
		ART 30'99 BASEL	**16.6.–21.6.99**
		JULIAN OPIE	**28.8.–2.10.99**
MAI 36 GALERIE	Rämistrasse 37, 8001 Zürich, Tel. 01 261 68 80	TWO DOORS – TRUE VALUE	**1.6.–17.7.99**
		ART 30'99 BASEL, H214/F04 ART SCULPTURE, H301/S30	**16.6.–21.6.99**
MARK MÜLLER	Gessnerallee 36, 8001 Zürich, Tel. 01 211 81 55	JEAN PFAFF, WERKE 1997–1999	**5.6.–17.7.99**
		ART 30'99 BASEL, H214/G5 ART SCULPTURE, STEFAN GRITSCH	**16.6.–21.6.99**
		PATRICK ROHNER, MALEREI JÜRG STÄUBLE, INSTALLATION	**26.8.–16.10.99**
SEMINA RERUM IRÈNE PREISWERK	Cäcilienstrasse 3, 8032 Zürich, Tel. 01 251 26 39	ERIK STEFFENSEN LANDSCHAFTEN IM NICHTS	**BIS 10.7.99**
		SOMMERPAUSE	**17.7.–17.8.99**
		WOLKEN – WASSER – STEIN THEMATISCHE GRUPPENAUSSTELLUNG	**28.8.–9.10.99**

E X H I B I T I O N S

ANNEMARIE VERNA	Neptunstrasse 42 8032 Zürich Tel. 01 262 38 20	TWO DOORS – TRUE VALUE MAI 36 / ANNEMARIE VERNA GALERIE NEUE STANDPUNKTE	**1.6.–17.7.99**
		ART 30'99 BASEL, H202/H01	**16.6.–21.6.99**
JAMILEH WEBER	Waldmannstrasse 6 8001 Zürich Tel. 01 252 10 66	DARRYL POTTORF IN COLORS – NEW PAINTINGS	**30.5.–26.6.99**
		ART 30'99 BASEL, H202/E5	**16.6.–21.6.99**
GALERIE SCHEDLER	Josefstrasse 53 8005 Zürich Tel. 01 440 61 20	RICHARD MÜLLER, «FAUX-TERRAIN»	**4.6.–3.7.99**
		JAN CZERWINSKI	**26.8.–25.9.99**
		GALERIE SCHEDLER WARTH: PIERRE SUTTER, NEW WORKS	**30.5.–4.7.99**
		BERN	
GALERIE ERIKA + OTTO FRIEDRICH	Lorrainestrasse 19 Postfach 323 3013 Bern Tel. 031 331 33 30	LISA HOEVER, MALEREI	**7.5.–4.7.99**
		ART 30'99 BASEL, H214/H02	**16.6.–21.6.99**
		MARK MANDERS	**10.9.–16.10.99**
		FRIBOURG	
MUSÉE D'ART ET D'HISTOIRE	12, rue de Morat 1700 Fribourg Tel. 026 322 85 71	MIOTTE ARBEITEN AUS DEN JAHREN 1945 BIS 1999	**9.4.–23.5.99**
		GENÈVE	
DANIEL VARENNE	8, rue Toepffer 1206 Genève Tel. 022 789 16 75	PAINTINGS AND DRAWINGS 19TH AND 20TH CENTURY	
		ST. GALLEN	
WILMA LOCK	Schmiedgasse 15 9000 St. Gallen Tel. 071 222 62 52	STEPHEN WESTFALL	**29.5.–7.7.99**
		NACH VEREINBARUNG	**8.7.–31.8.99**
		DANIEL ZIMMERMANN	**4.9.–30.10.99**
SAMMLUNG HAUSER UND WIRTH (Lokremise St. Gallen)	Grünbergstrasse 7 9000 St. Gallen Tel. 071 228 55 55	«DIMENSIONS OF THE MIND» BY PAUL MCCARTHY	**13.6.–10.10.99**

A SUMMER SHOW

MAY 28 – AUGUST

RICHARD ARTSCHWAGER
JOHN BALDESSARI
CHRISTIAN BOLTANSKI
MAURIZIO CATTELAN
TONY CRAGG
RICHARD DEACON
DAN GRAHAM
WILLIAM KENTRIDGE
ANSELM KIEFER
SOL LEWITT
STEVE MCQUEEN
JUAN MUÑOZ
CLAES OLDENBURG
GABRIEL OROZCO
GIUSEPPE PENONE
GERHARD RICHTER
THOMAS SCHÜTTE
THOMAS STRUTH
FRANCESCA WOODMAN

MARIAN GOODMAN GALLERY

24 WEST 57TH STREET NEW YORK, NY 10019 TEL 212 977-7160
FAX 212 581-5187 GOODMAN@MARIANGOODMAN.COM

Summer 1999

Terry Winters Graphic Primitives

Pure Products of America:
Photographs 1968 to 1978
by Robert Adams, Bill Owens
& Henry Wessel

Anni Albers, Robert Beck,
Cady Noland, Joan Semmel
curated by Robert Gober

November 1999

Sam Taylor-Wood

Matthew Marks Gallery
New York

ANDREAS
SLOMINSKI
IS
REPRESENTED
BY
JABLONKA
GALERIE
KÖLN

ED RUSCHA

IS REPRESENTED BY

GAGOSIAN GALLERY

29. MAI BIS 17. JULI 1999

ON KAWARA

GALERIE HAUSER & WIRTH

Limmatstrasse 270, 8005 Zürich / Tel: +41 1 446 80 50, Fax: +41 1 446 80 55 / e-mail: info@ghw.ch
Öffnungszeiten: Di bis Fr 12 bis 18 Uhr, Sa 11 bis 16 Uhr

29. MAI BIS 17. JULI 1999

J.F. SCHNYDER

GALERIE HAUSER & WIRTH & PRESENHUBER

Limmatstrasse 270, 8005 Zürich / Tel: +41 1 446 80 60, Fax: +41 1 446 80 65 / e-mail: info@ghwp.ch
Öffnungszeiten: Di bis Fr 12 bis 18 Uhr, Sa 11 bis 16 Uhr

29. MAI BIS 17. JULI 1999

ON KAWARA

GALERIE HAUSER & WIRTH

Limmatstrasse 270, 8005 Zürich / Tel: +41 1 446 80 50, Fax: +41 1 446 80 55 / e-mail: info@ghw.ch
Öffnungszeiten: Di bis Fr 12 bis 18 Uhr, Sa 11 bis 16 Uhr

29. MAI BIS 17. JULI 1999

J.F. SCHNYDER

GALERIE HAUSER & WIRTH & PRESENHUBER

Limmatstrasse 270, 8005 Zürich / Tel: +41 1 446 80 60, Fax: +41 1 446 80 65 / e-mail: info@ghwp.ch
Öffnungszeiten: Di bis Fr 12 bis 18 Uhr, Sa 11 bis 16 Uhr

Barry Flanagan

3 JUNE – 4 SEPTEMBER 1999

ART/30/Basel

16 JUNE – 21 JUNE 1999

Josef Albers

9 SEPTEMBER – 30 OCTOBER 1999

---

karyn lovegrove gallery

Howard Arkley

26 June–7 August 1999

The official Australian representative
of the 48th Venice Biennale

Karyn Lovegrove Gallery
6150 Wilshire Boulevard #8
Los Angeles CA 90048 USA
Telephone: (323) 525 1755
Facsimile: (323) 525 1245
Email: lovegrovek@aol.com

UMEDALEN SKULPTUR 99

5/6 - 5/9 1999

BONK BUSINESS INC.
ANTHONY CRAGG
CECILIA EDEFALK
PETER FISCHLI AND DAVID WEISS
TINA ERIKSSON FREDRIKSSON/
CHRISTOFER FREDRIKSSON
GARY HILL
FINNBOGI PETURSSON
RAGNA ROBERTSDOTTIR
ULF ROLLOF
ANU TUOMINEN

JUNE

3 June – 15 August **Moderna Museet Projekt: Ann Lislegaard**

19 June – 12 September **Robert Smithson**

Box 16382 SE - Stockholm, Sweden
t: 46 8 5195 5249 f: 46 8 5195 5250
www.modernamuseet.se
Address: Skeppsholmen

MODERNA MUSEET
MODERN MUSEUM

Sponsors: NCC, SAS and Pharmacia and Upjohn
Moderna Museet collaborates with Mix Megapol and BMW

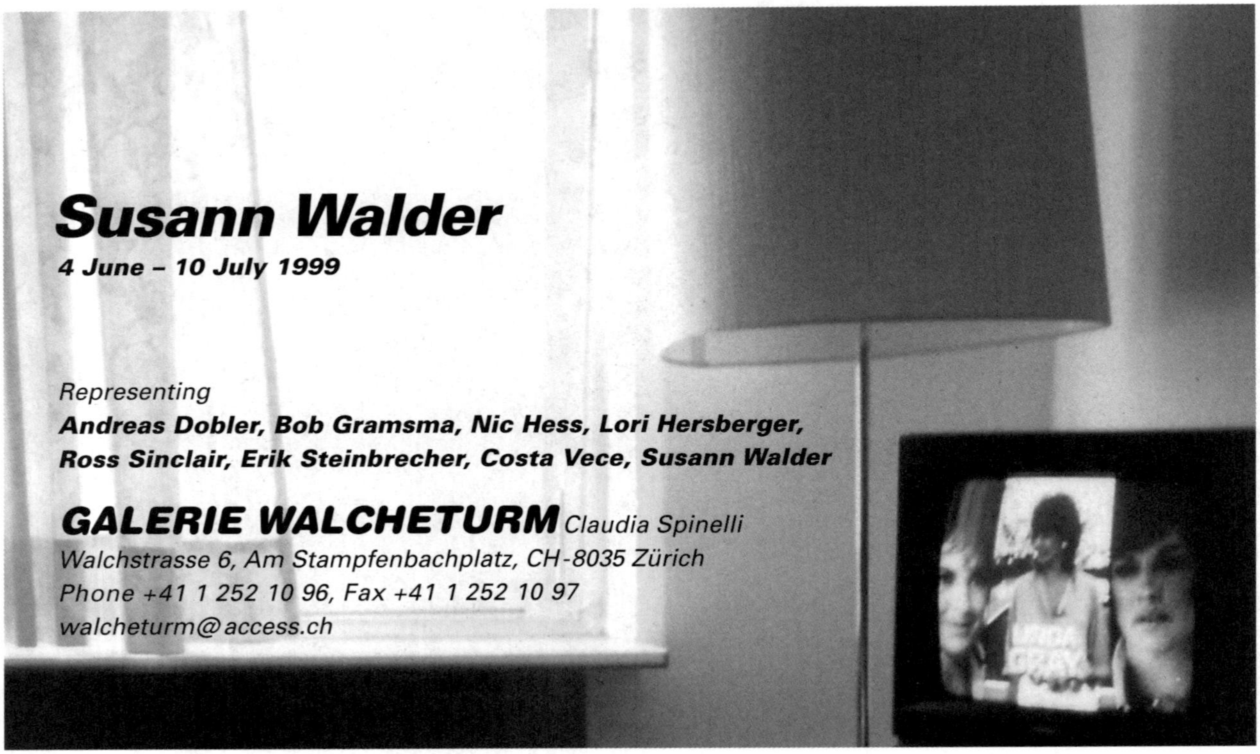

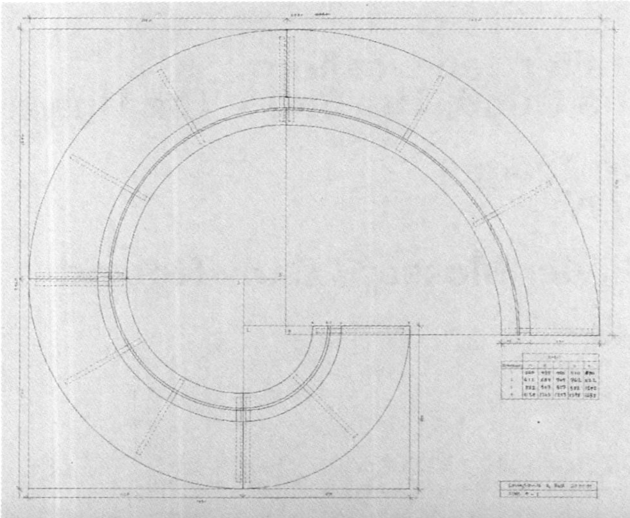

Langlands & Bell
Untitled 1999

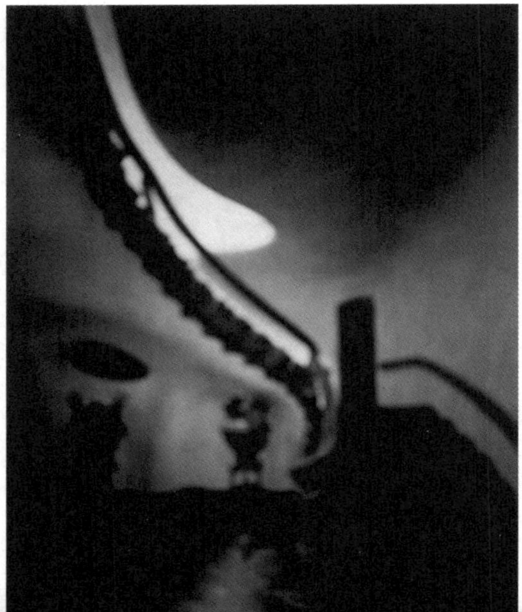

Hiroshi Sugimoto
Casa Battló – Gaudí 1998

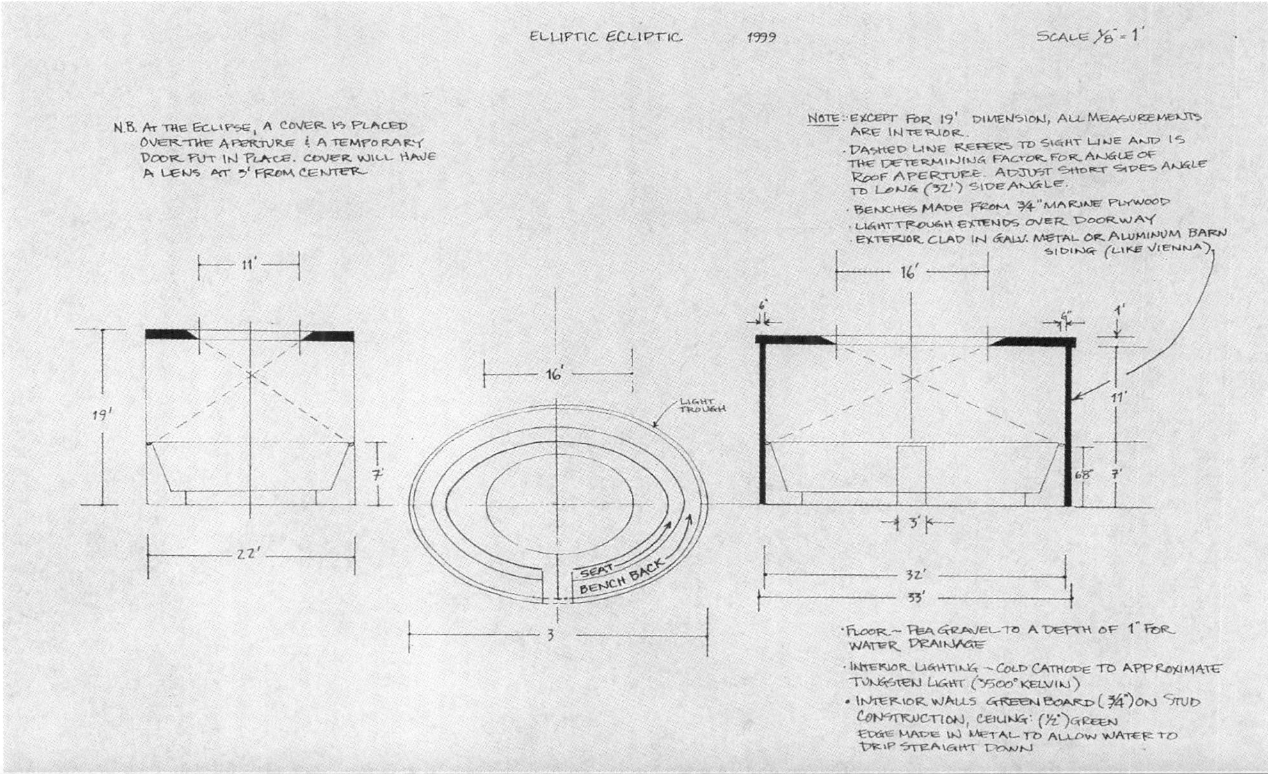

JAMES TURRELL

ann hamilton

United States Pavilion
48th Venice Biennale
Venice, Italy

June 12–
November 7, 1999

Helaine Posner and Katy Kline, Commissioners

For information contact
Fitz & Co
Tel 212 627 1455
artpr@fitzandco.com

ann hamilton is represented by Sean Kelly Gallery, New York

Official U.S. participation in the 48th Venice Biennale is made possible by major support from the Fund for U.S. Artists at International Festivals and Exhibitions, a public/private partnership of the United States Information Agency, the National Endowment for the Arts, the Rockefeller Foundation, and The Pew Charitable Trusts.

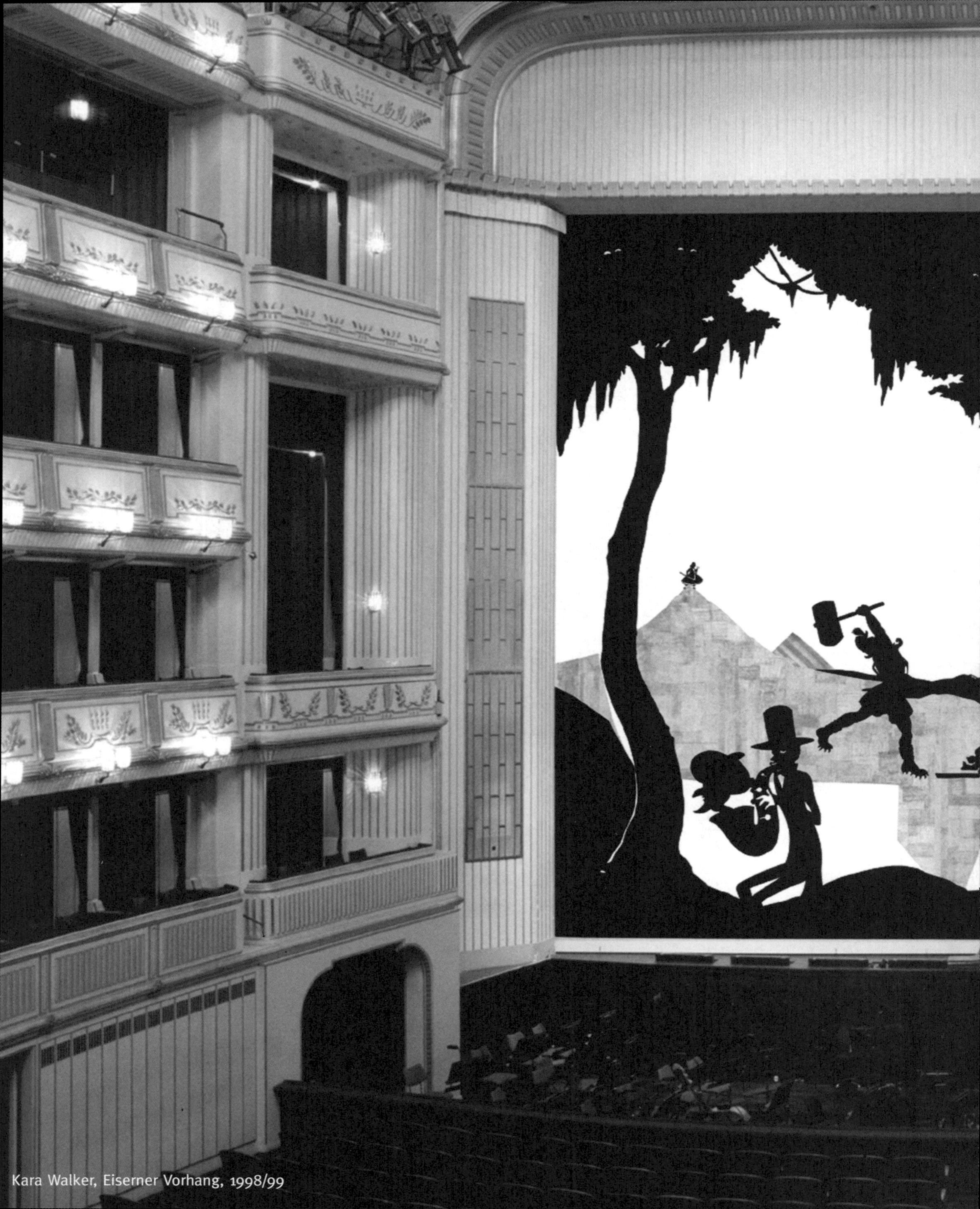

Kara Walker, Eiserner Vorhang, 1998/99

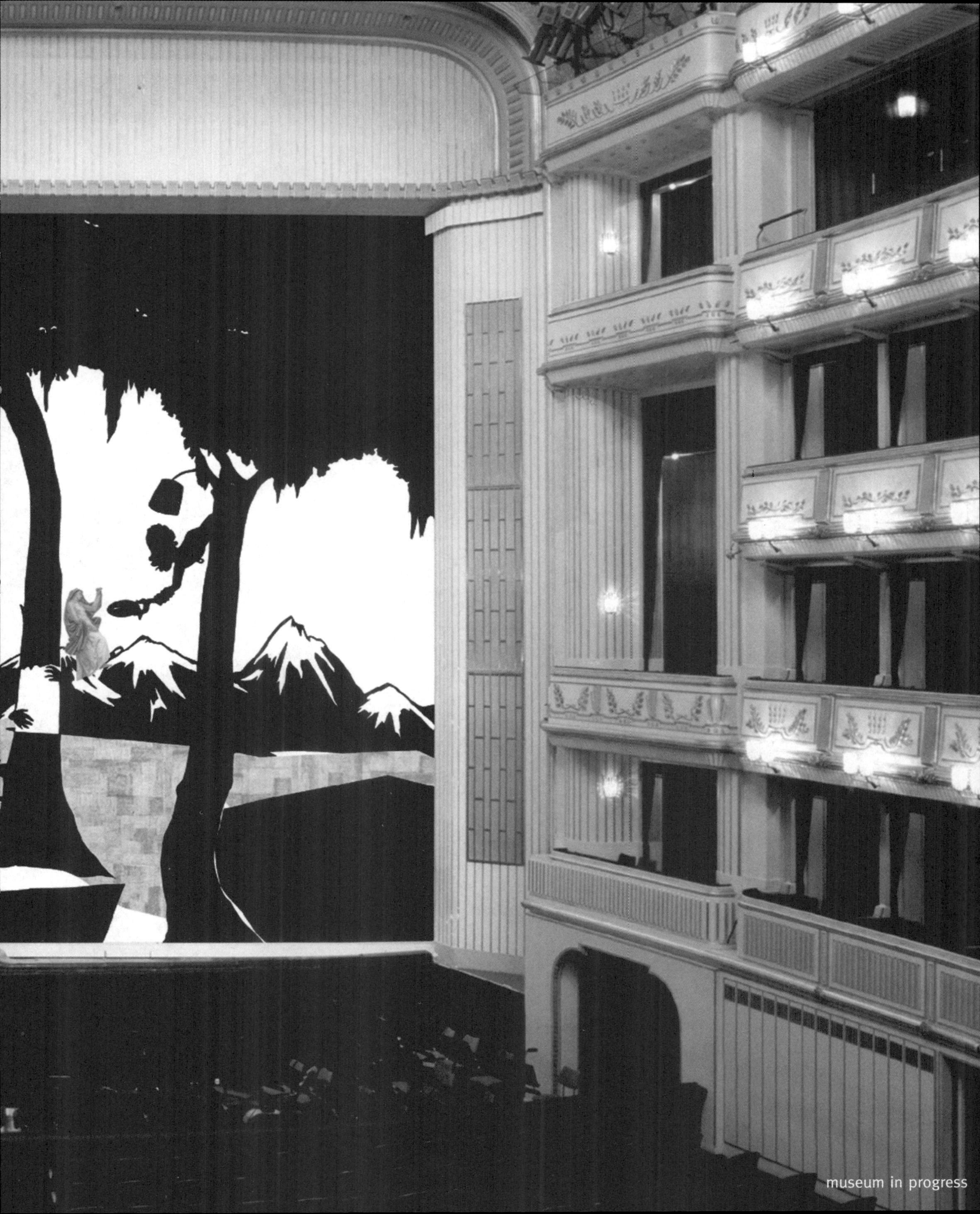

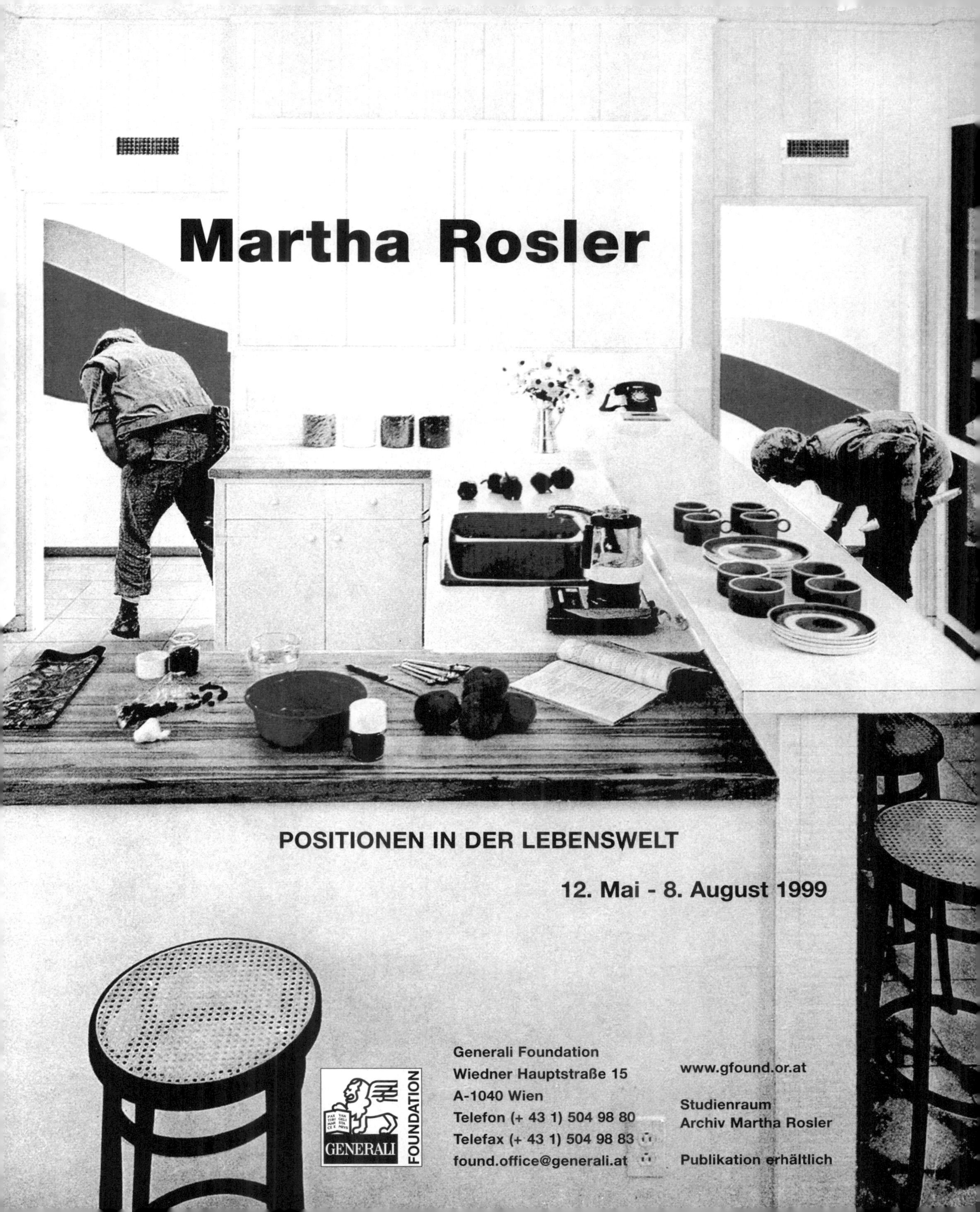
Martha Rosler
POSITIONEN IN DER LEBENSWELT
12. Mai - 8. August 1999
GENERALI FOUNDATION
Generali Foundation
Wiedner Hauptstraße 15
A-1040 Wien
Telefon (+ 43 1) 504 98 80
Telefax (+ 43 1) 504 98 83
found.office@generali.at
www.gfound.or.at
Studienraum
Archiv Martha Rosler
Publikation erhältlich

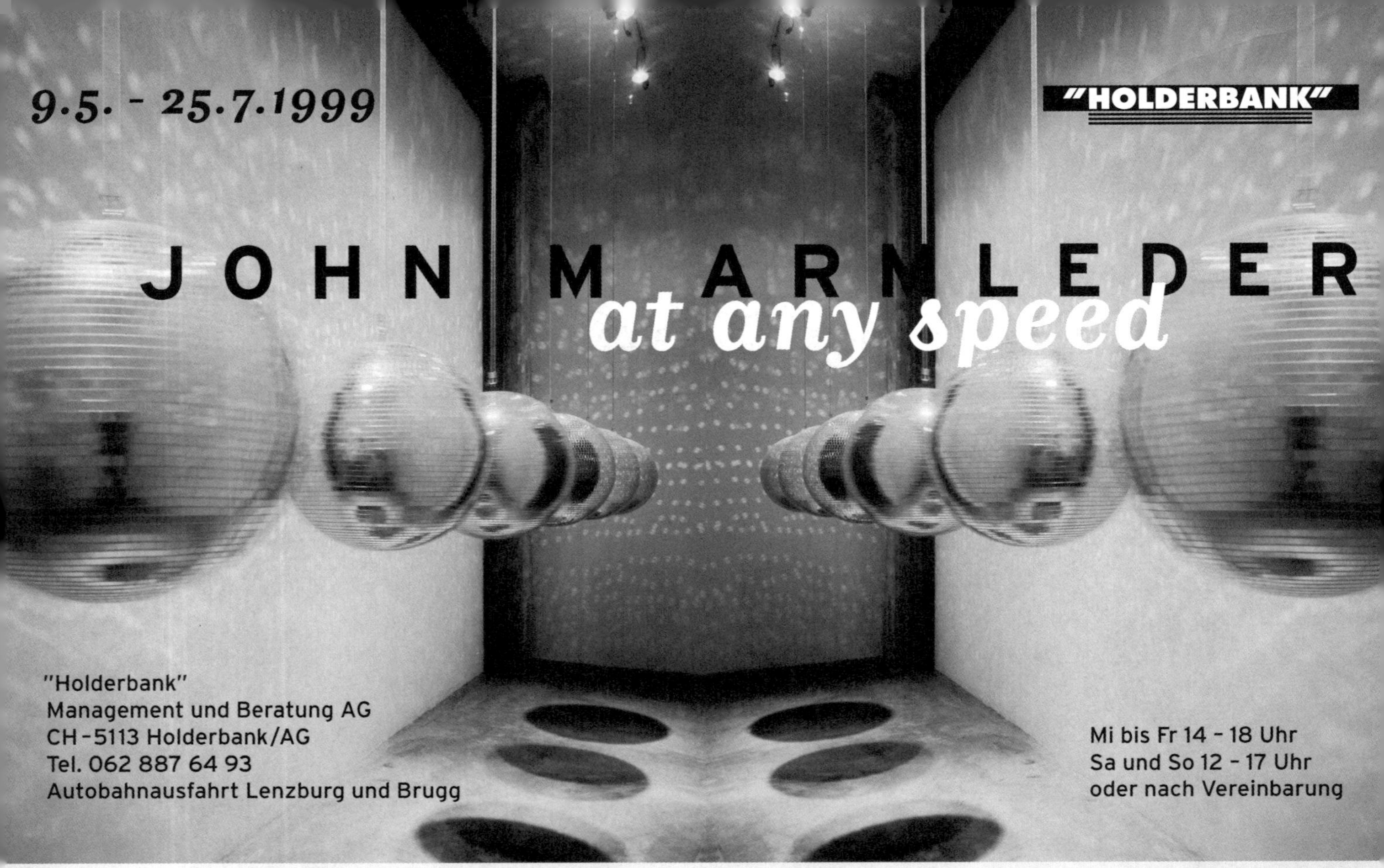
9.5. - 25.7.1999
"HOLDERBANK"
JOHN M ARMLEDER
at any speed
"Holderbank"
Management und Beratung AG
CH-5113 Holderbank/AG
Tel. 062 887 64 93
Autobahnausfahrt Lenzburg und Brugg
Mi bis Fr 14 - 18 Uhr
Sa und So 12 - 17 Uhr
oder nach Vereinbarung

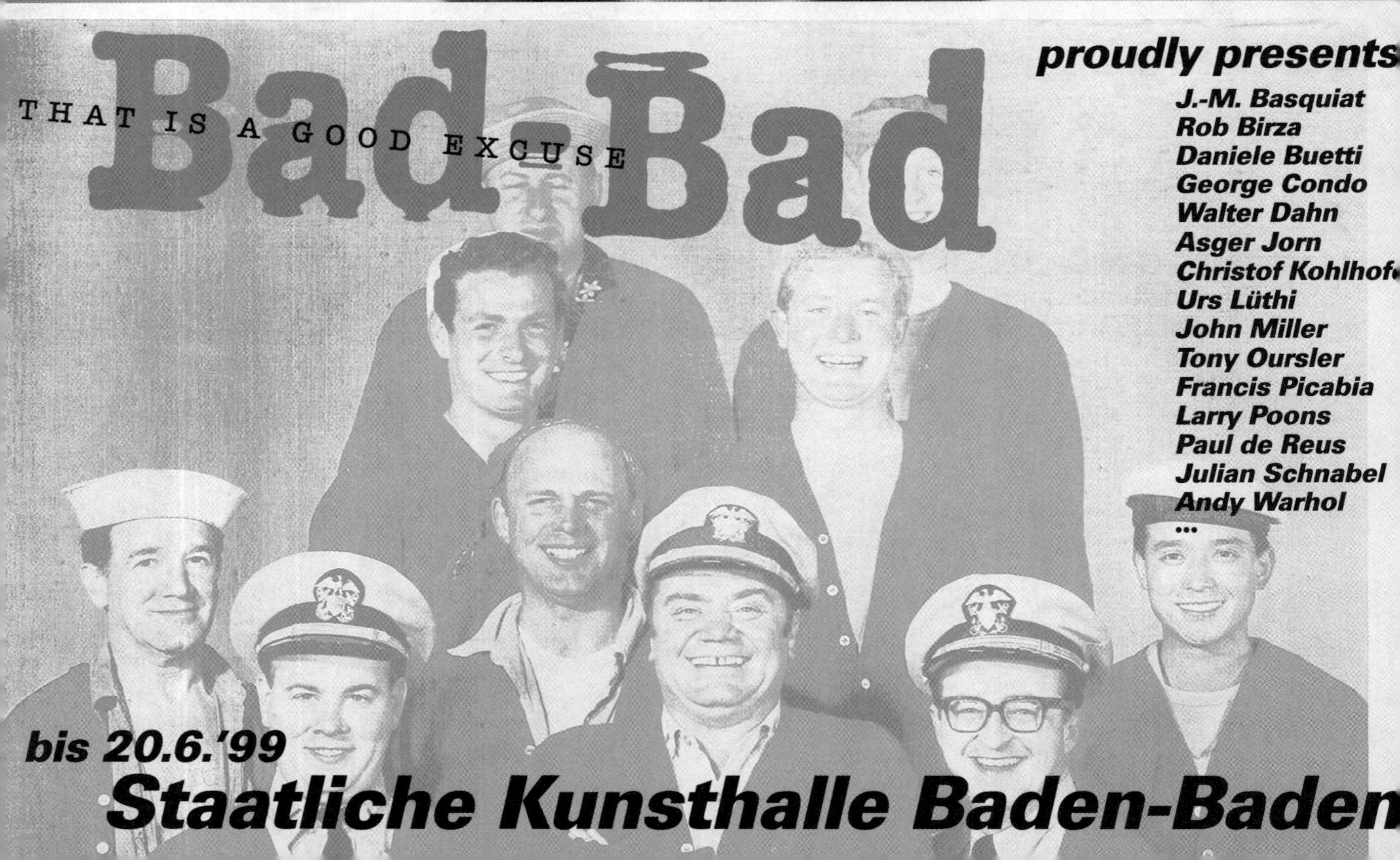
Bad-Bad
THAT IS A GOOD EXCUSE
proudly presents
J.-M. Basquiat
Rob Birza
Daniele Buetti
George Condo
Walter Dahn
Asger Jorn
Christof Kohlhof
Urs Lüthi
John Miller
Tony Oursler
Francis Picabia
Larry Poons
Paul de Reus
Julian Schnabel
Andy Warhol
...
bis 20.6.'99
Staatliche Kunsthalle Baden-Baden

Kunsthalle
Basel

Nach-Bild
Beispiele zur zeitgenössischen Malerei
12. Juni - 22. August 1999

Qui Shi-hua
3. Juli - 3. Oktober 1999

Kunsthalle Basel, Steinenberg 7, CH-4051 Basel, Telefon 061 / 206 99 00, Fax 061 / 206 9919
Öffnungszeiten: Dienstag - Sonntag 11 - 17 Uhr, Mittwoch 11 - 20.30 Uhr, Montag geschlossen. Führungen: Sonntag 11 Uhr

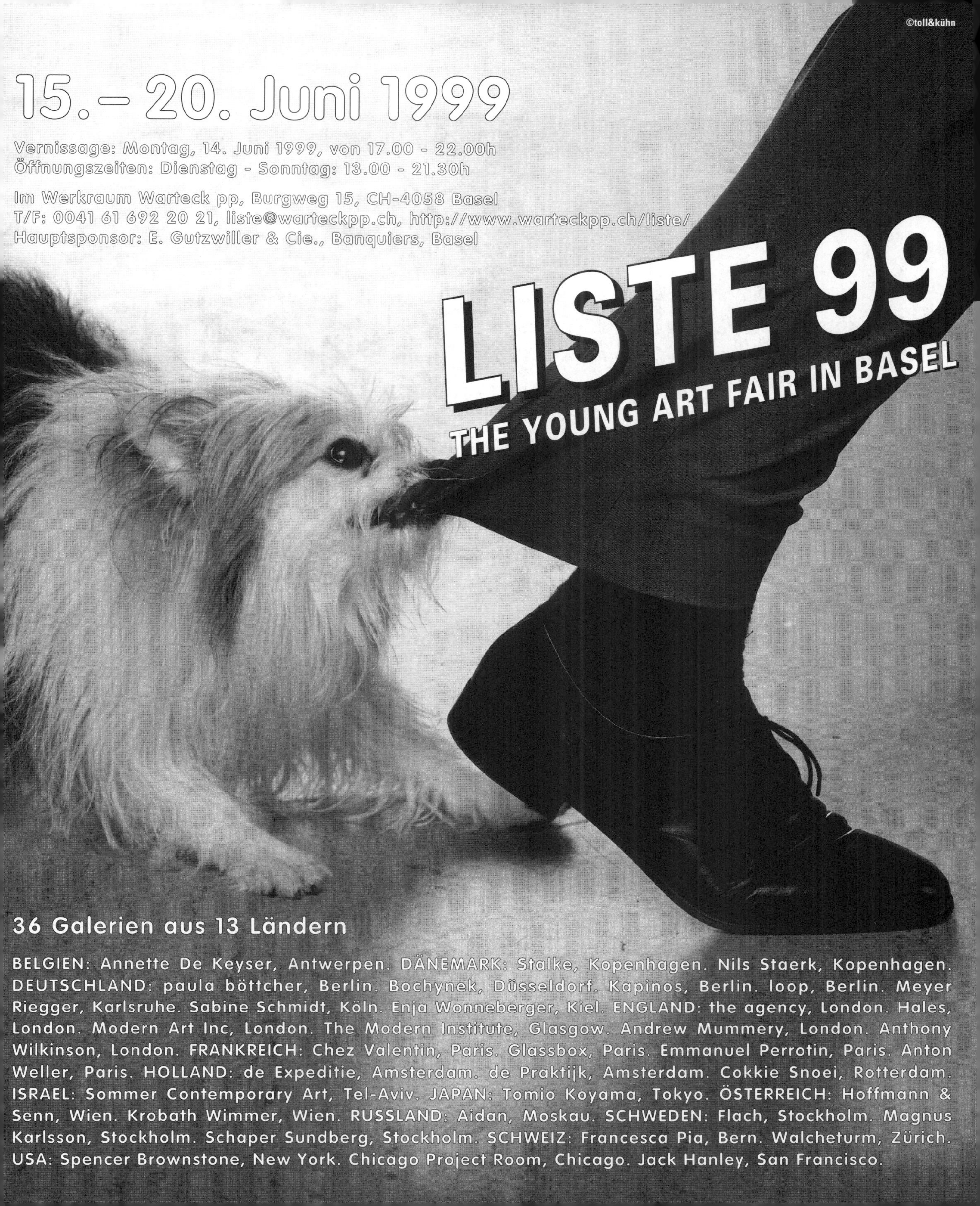
©toll&kühn
15. – 20. Juni 1999
Vernissage: Montag, 14. Juni 1999, von 17.00 - 22.00h
Öffnungszeiten: Dienstag - Sonntag: 13.00 - 21.30h
Im Werkraum Warteck pp, Burgweg 15, CH-4058 Basel
T/F: 0041 61 692 20 21, liste@warteckpp.ch, http://www.warteckpp.ch/liste/
Hauptsponsor: E. Gutzwiller & Cie., Banquiers, Basel
LISTE 99
THE YOUNG ART FAIR IN BASEL
36 Galerien aus 13 Ländern
BELGIEN: Annette De Keyser, Antwerpen. DÄNEMARK: Stalke, Kopenhagen. Nils Staerk, Kopenhagen. DEUTSCHLAND: paula böttcher, Berlin. Bochynek, Düsseldorf. Kapinos, Berlin. loop, Berlin. Meyer Riegger, Karlsruhe. Sabine Schmidt, Köln. Enja Wonneberger, Kiel. ENGLAND: the agency, London. Hales, London. Modern Art Inc, London. The Modern Institute, Glasgow. Andrew Mummery, London. Anthony Wilkinson, London. FRANKREICH: Chez Valentin, Paris. Glassbox, Paris. Emmanuel Perrotin, Paris. Anton Weller, Paris. HOLLAND: de Expeditie, Amsterdam. de Praktijk, Amsterdam. Cokkie Snoei, Rotterdam. ISRAEL: Sommer Contemporary Art, Tel-Aviv. JAPAN: Tomio Koyama, Tokyo. ÖSTERREICH: Hoffmann & Senn, Wien. Krobath Wimmer, Wien. RUSSLAND: Aidan, Moskau. SCHWEDEN: Flach, Stockholm. Magnus Karlsson, Stockholm. Schaper Sundberg, Stockholm. SCHWEIZ: Francesca Pia, Bern. Walcheturm, Zürich. USA: Spencer Brownstone, New York. Chicago Project Room, Chicago. Jack Hanley, San Francisco.

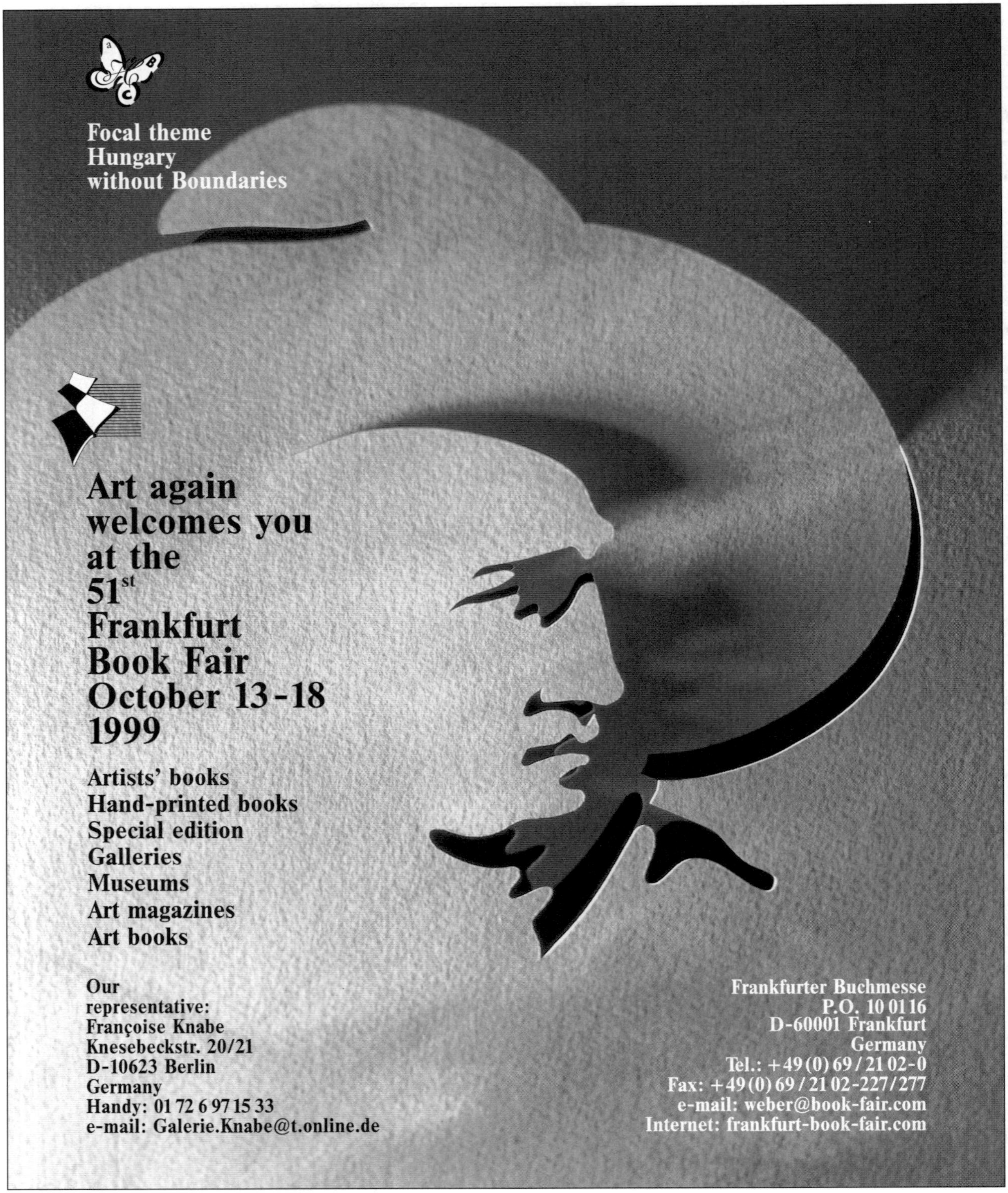
Focal theme
Hungary
without Boundaries
Art again
welcomes you
at the
51st
Frankfurt
Book Fair
October 13-18
1999
Artists' books
Hand-printed books
Special edition
Galleries
Museums
Art magazines
Art books
Our
representative:
Françoise Knabe
Knesebeckstr. 20/21
D-10623 Berlin
Germany
Handy: 01 72 6 97 15 33
e-mail: Galerie.Knabe@t.online.de
Frankfurter Buchmesse
P.O. 10 01 16
D-60001 Frankfurt
Germany
Tel.: +49 (0) 69 / 21 02-0
Fax: +49 (0) 69 / 21 02-227/277
e-mail: weber@book-fair.com
Internet: frankfurt-book-fair.com

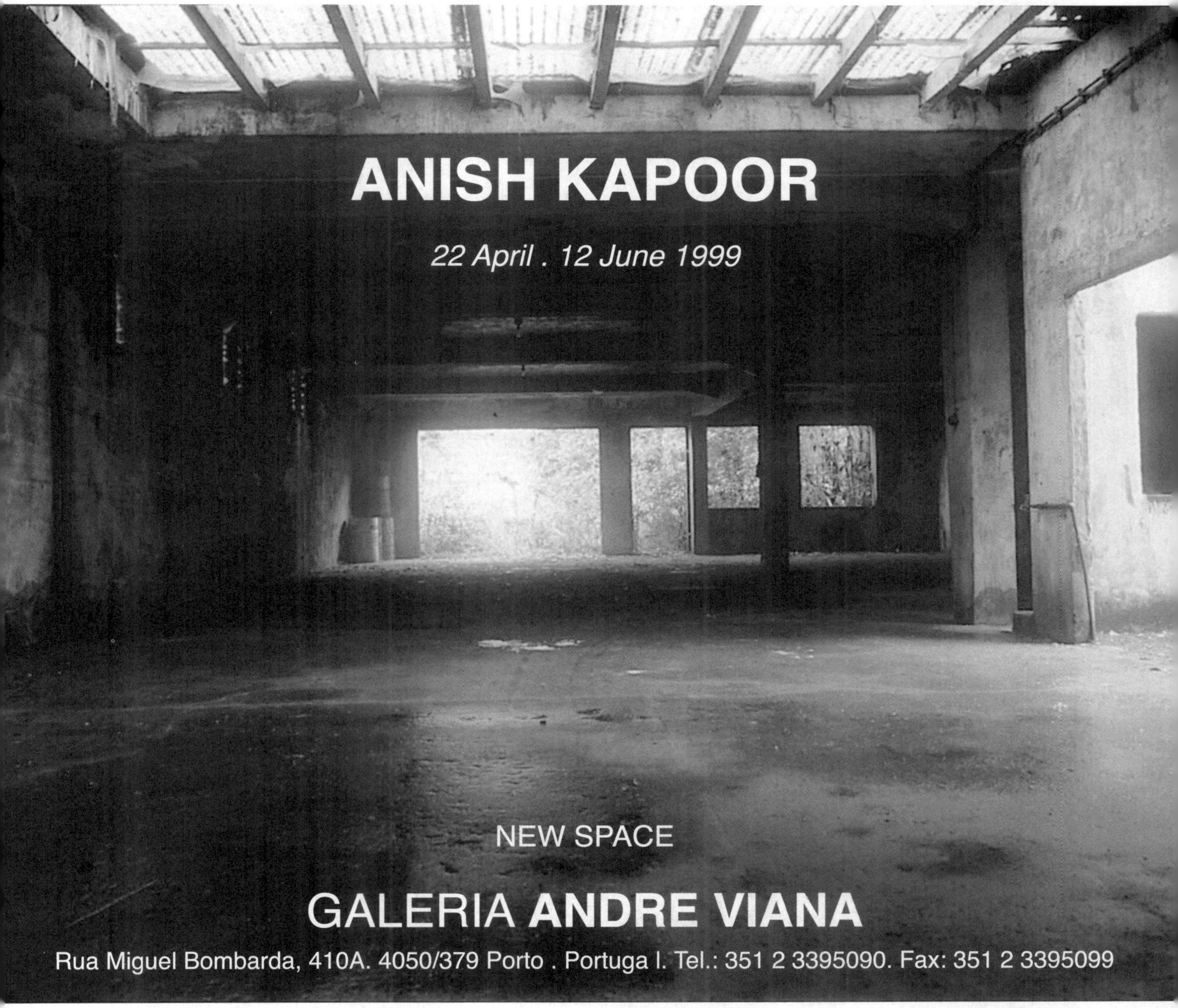
ANISH KAPOOR
22 April . 12 June 1999
NEW SPACE
GALERIA ANDRE VIANA
Rua Miguel Bombarda, 410A. 4050/379 Porto . Portuga l. Tel.: 351 2 3395090. Fax: 351 2 3395099

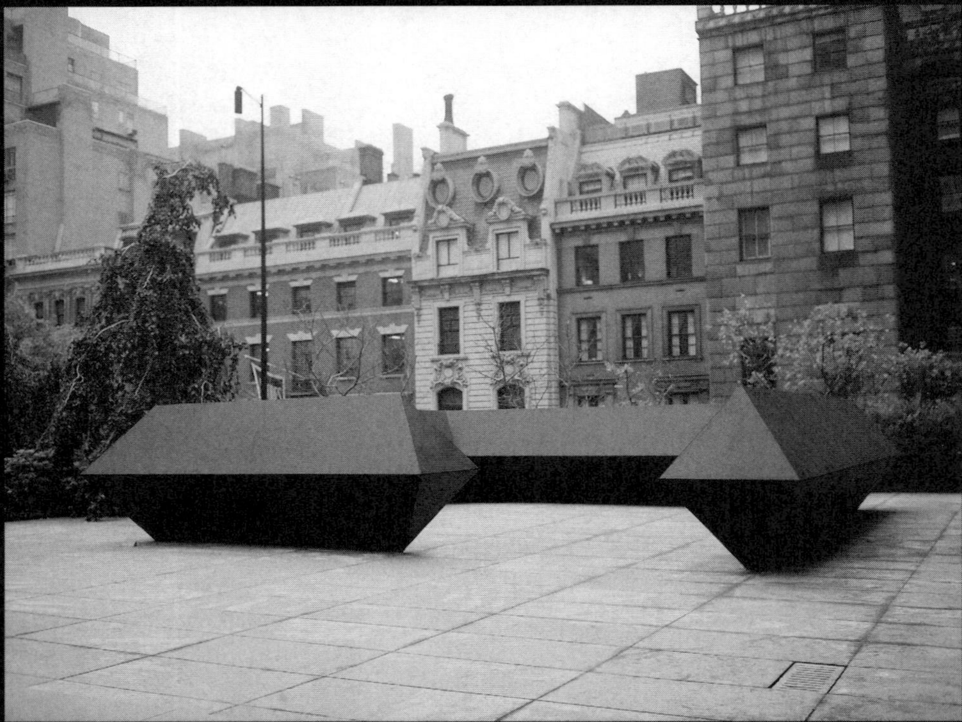

Stinger, 1968, plywood mock-up at *Art of the Real USA 1948-1968*, The Museum of Modern Art, New York

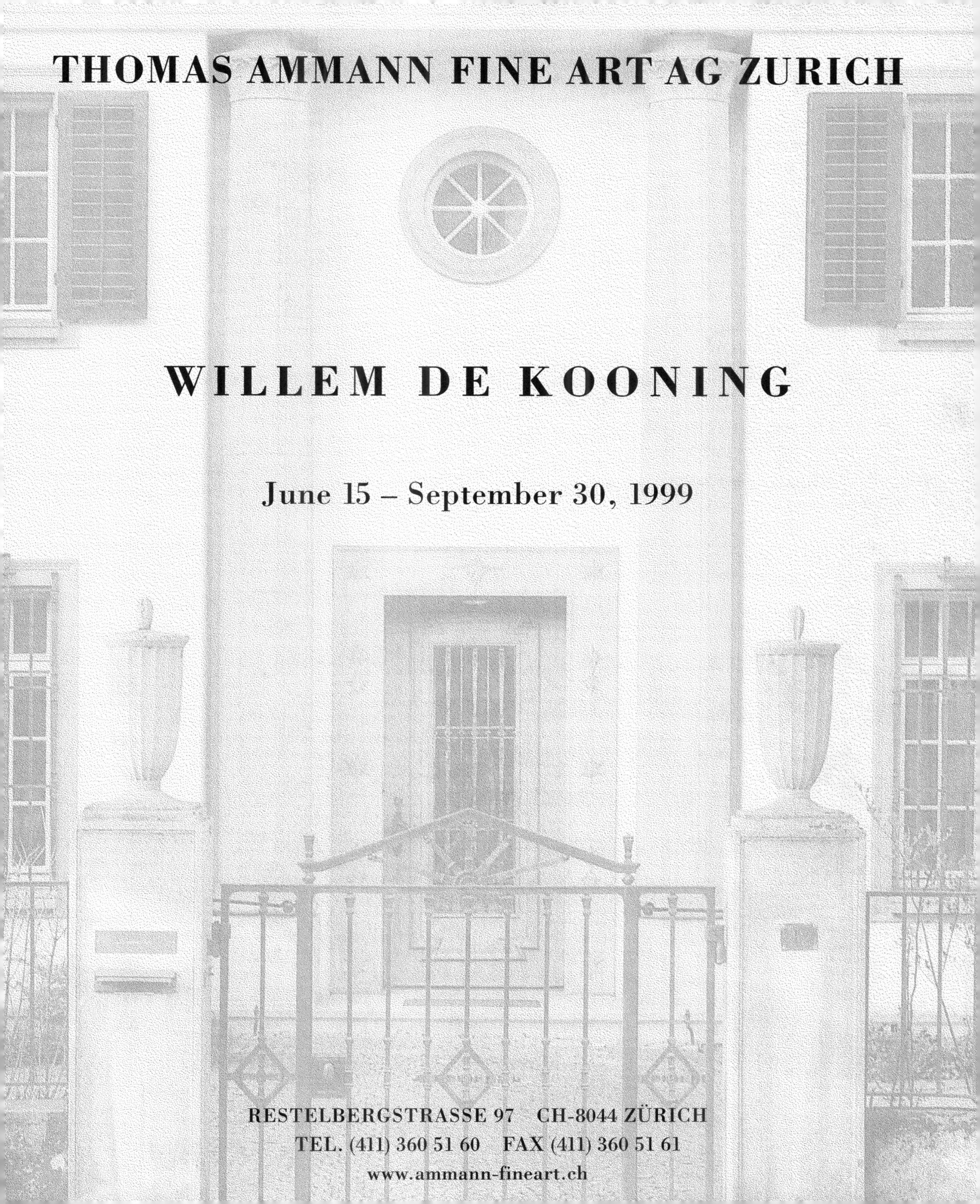
THOMAS AMMANN FINE ART AG ZURICH
WILLEM DE KOONING
June 15 – September 30, 1999
RESTELBERGSTRASSE 97 CH-8044 ZÜRICH
TEL. (411) 360 51 60 FAX (411) 360 51 61
www.ammann-fineart.ch